DUMB HEART

a **GET FUZZY** collection by darby conley

Andrews McMeel
Publishing, LLC

Kansas City • Sydney • London

Get Fuzzy is distributed internationally by United Feature Syndicate, Inc.

09 10 11 12 13 RR2 10 9 8 7 6 5 4 3 2 1

ISBN-13: 978-0-7407-9189-5
ISBN-10: 0-7407-9189-3

Library of Congress Control Number: 2009931845
www.andrewsmcmeel.com

Get Fuzzy can be viewed on the Internet at
www.comics.com/get_fuzzy.

For Dylan
here, eat this book and stop kicking me.

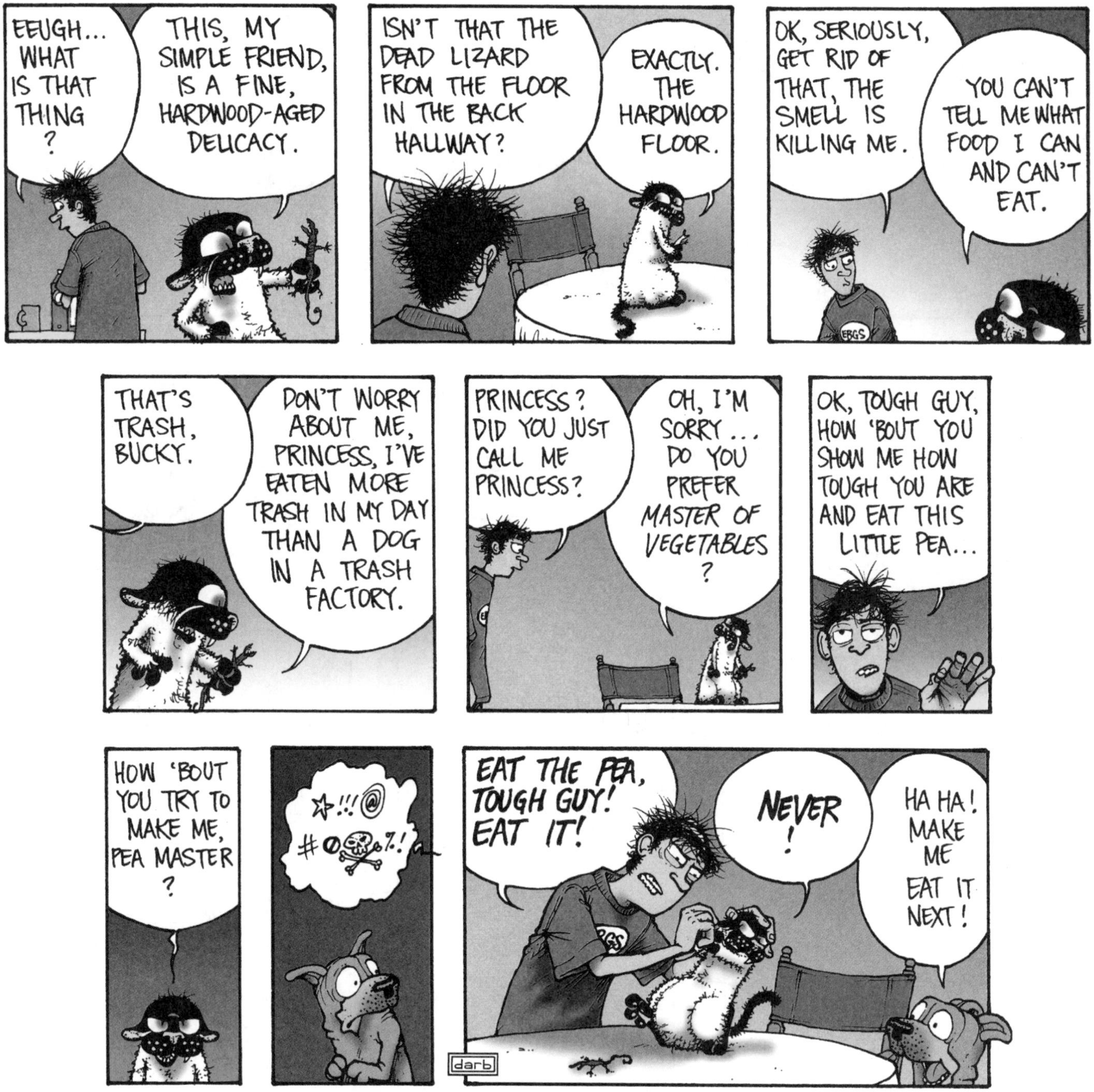
EEUGH... WHAT IS THAT THING?
THIS, MY SIMPLE FRIEND, IS A FINE, HARDWOOD-AGED DELICACY.
ISN'T THAT THE DEAD LIZARD FROM THE FLOOR IN THE BACK HALLWAY?
EXACTLY. THE HARDWOOD FLOOR.
OK, SERIOUSLY, GET RID OF THAT, THE SMELL IS KILLING ME.
YOU CAN'T TELL ME WHAT FOOD I CAN AND CAN'T EAT.
EBGS
THAT'S TRASH, BUCKY.
DON'T WORRY ABOUT ME, PRINCESS, I'VE EATEN MORE TRASH IN MY DAY THAN A DOG IN A TRASH FACTORY.
PRINCESS? DID YOU JUST CALL ME PRINCESS?
OH, I'M SORRY... DO YOU PREFER *MASTER OF VEGETABLES*?
OK, TOUGH GUY, HOW 'BOUT YOU SHOW ME HOW TOUGH YOU ARE AND EAT THIS LITTLE PEA...
HOW 'BOUT YOU TRY TO MAKE ME, PEA MASTER?
☆!!!@ # %!
EAT THE PEA, TOUGH GUY! EAT IT!
NEVER!
HA HA! MAKE ME EAT IT NEXT!
EBGS
darb

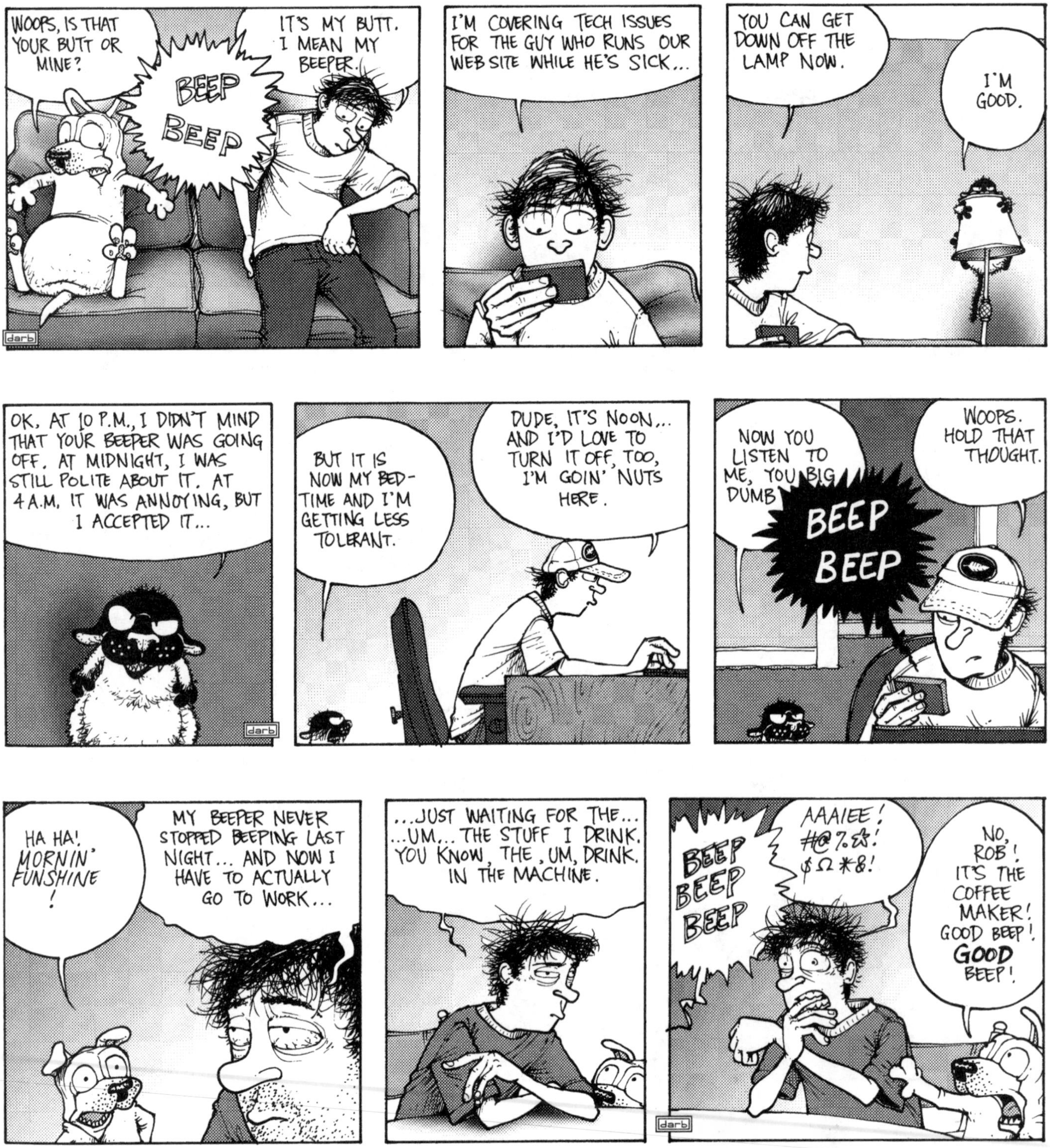
WOOPS, IS THAT YOUR BUTT OR MINE?
IT'S MY BUTT. I MEAN MY BEEPER.
BEEP BEEP
darb
I'M COVERING TECH ISSUES FOR THE GUY WHO RUNS OUR WEB SITE WHILE HE'S SICK...
YOU CAN GET DOWN OFF THE LAMP NOW.
I'M GOOD.
OK, AT 10 P.M., I DIDN'T MIND THAT YOUR BEEPER WAS GOING OFF. AT MIDNIGHT, I WAS STILL POLITE ABOUT IT. AT 4 A.M. IT WAS ANNOYING, BUT I ACCEPTED IT...
darb
BUT IT IS NOW MY BEDTIME AND I'M GETTING LESS TOLERANT.
DUDE, IT'S NOON... AND I'D LOVE TO TURN IT OFF, TOO, I'M GOIN' NUTS HERE.
NOW YOU LISTEN TO ME, YOU BIG DUMB
BEEP BEEP
WOOPS. HOLD THAT THOUGHT.
HA HA! MORNIN' FUNSHINE!
MY BEEPER NEVER STOPPED BEEPING LAST NIGHT... AND NOW I HAVE TO ACTUALLY GO TO WORK...
...JUST WAITING FOR THE... ...UM... THE STUFF I DRINK. YOU KNOW, THE, UM, DRINK. IN THE MACHINE.
BEEP BEEP BEEP
AAAIEE! #@%✩! $Ω*&!
NO, ROB! IT'S THE COFFEE MAKER! GOOD BEEP! GOOD BEEP!
darb

WHAT'S THIS?

MY NEW CONVENIENCE STORE.

WHY IS IT CALLED 3½-2?

BECAUSE I'M ONLY OPEN MONDAY, TUESDAY, AND EVERY OTHER WEDNESDAY FROM 9:30 TO 11:30.

WELL, THAT'S NOT PARTICULARLY CONVENIENT.

WE'RE 15 FEET CLOSER TO THE KITCHEN THAN THE LIVING ROOM IS. THAT'S THE CONVENIENT BIT.

FIVE DOLLARS FOR A PEANUT? WELL, THAT'S CERTAINLY NOT CONVENIENT.

REALLY? IT IS FOR ME... I GUESS IT'S ALL RELATIVE.

MAY I TAKE YOUR ORDER, MA'AM?

I'M GETTING COMPLAINTS ABOUT YOUR CONVENIENCE STORE.

REALLY? HERE, HAVE A COMPLIMENTARY CORNRAT.

THAT'S YOUR IDEA OF A BRIBE? RAT ON A STICK? LOOK, SATCHEL TOLD ME YOU SOLD HIM A BAG FULL OF DEAD GRASS WITH A DEAD RAT SPRAY-PAINTED BLUE IN IT.

THE NUMBER FIVE, YES.

HE SAYS HE ORDERED THE SURF 'N' TURF.

YOU WILL FIND THAT THE MENU CLEARLY STATES SMURF 'N' TURF, MA'AM.

SATCHEL SAYS YOU SOLD HIM A BOX OF FIG NELSONS BUT IT WAS EMPTY.

TECHNICALLY I SOLD IT AS A FIG NELSONS BOX. NOT A BOX OF FIG NELSONS. CAVEAT EMPTY-HEADED, I GUESS.

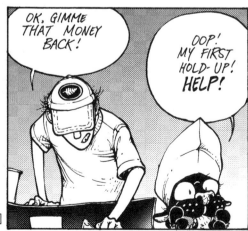

OK, GIMME THAT MONEY BACK!

OOP! MY FIRST HOLD-UP! HELP!

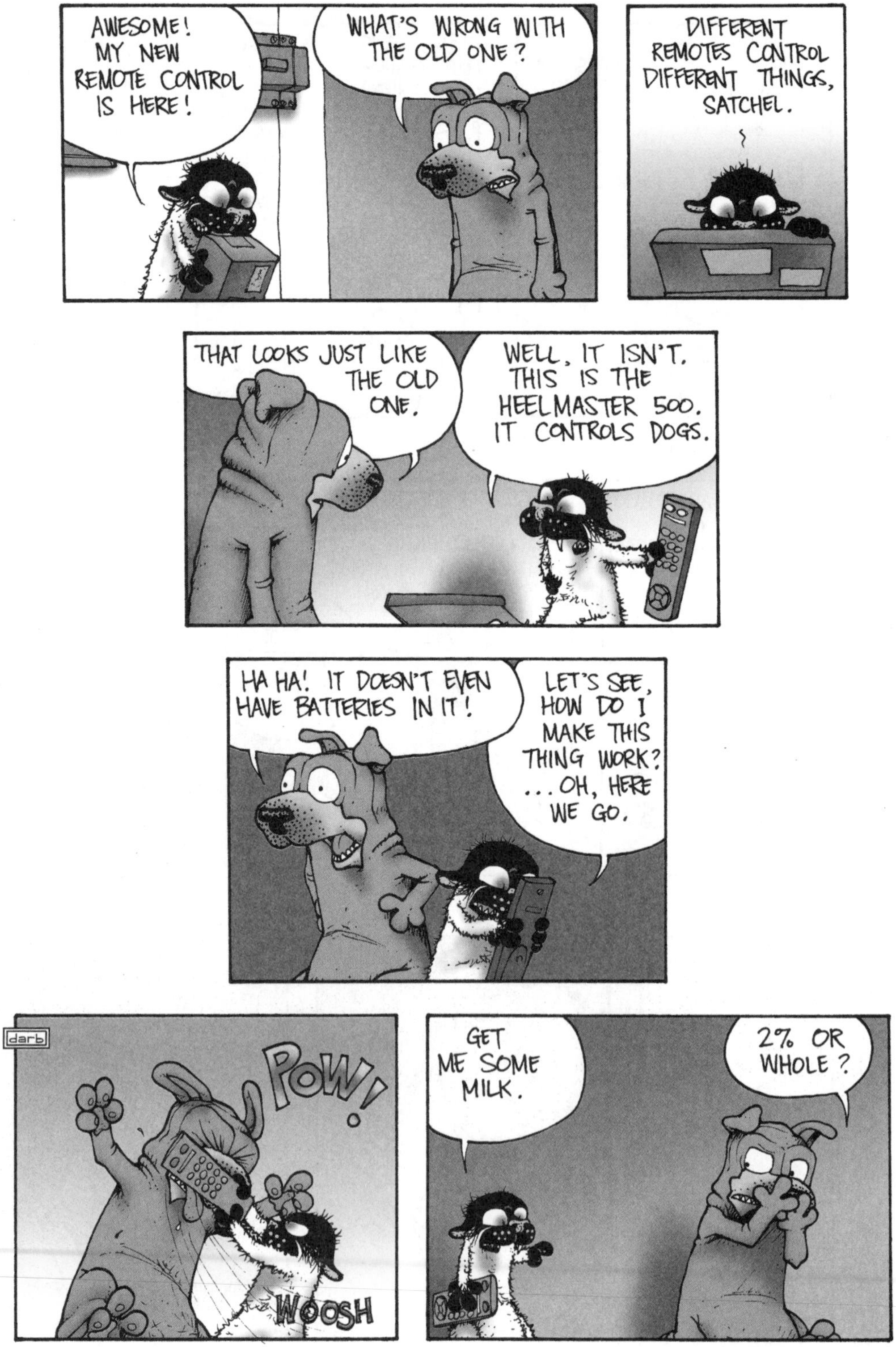
AWESOME! MY NEW REMOTE CONTROL IS HERE!
WHAT'S WRONG WITH THE OLD ONE?
DIFFERENT REMOTES CONTROL DIFFERENT THINGS, SATCHEL.
THAT LOOKS JUST LIKE THE OLD ONE.
WELL, IT ISN'T. THIS IS THE HEELMASTER 500. IT CONTROLS DOGS.
HA HA! IT DOESN'T EVEN HAVE BATTERIES IN IT!
LET'S SEE, HOW DO I MAKE THIS THING WORK? ...OH, HERE WE GO.
darb
POW!
WOOSH
GET ME SOME MILK.
2% OR WHOLE?

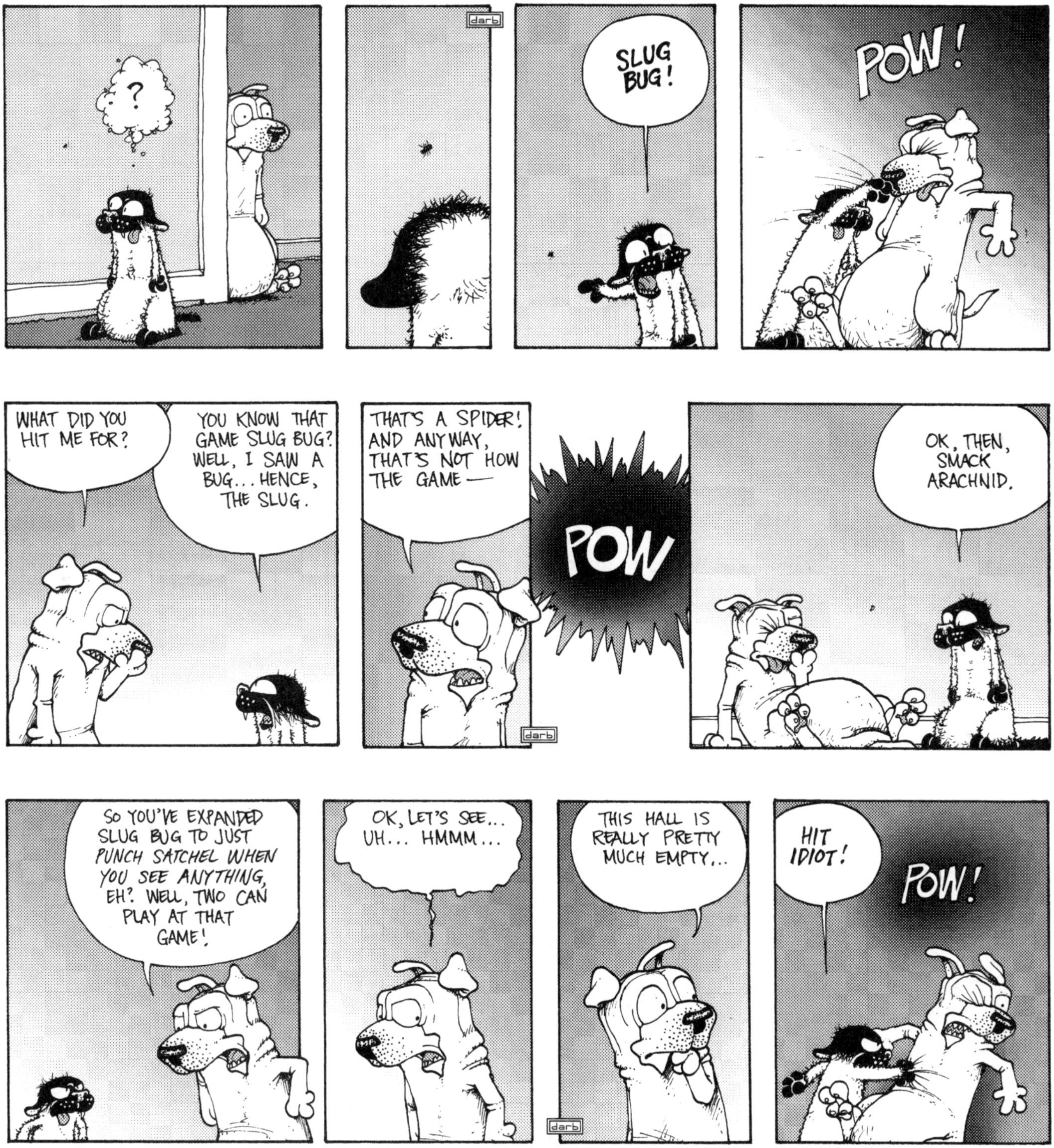
?
darb
SLUG BUG!
POW!
WHAT DID YOU HIT ME FOR?
YOU KNOW THAT GAME SLUG BUG? WELL, I SAW A BUG... HENCE, THE SLUG.
THAT'S A SPIDER! AND ANYWAY, THAT'S NOT HOW THE GAME—
POW
darb
OK, THEN, SMACK ARACHNID.
SO YOU'VE EXPANDED SLUG BUG TO JUST PUNCH SATCHEL WHEN YOU SEE ANYTHING, EH? WELL, TWO CAN PLAY AT THAT GAME!
OK, LET'S SEE... UH... HMMM...
THIS HALL IS REALLY PRETTY MUCH EMPTY...
darb
HIT IDIOT!
POW!

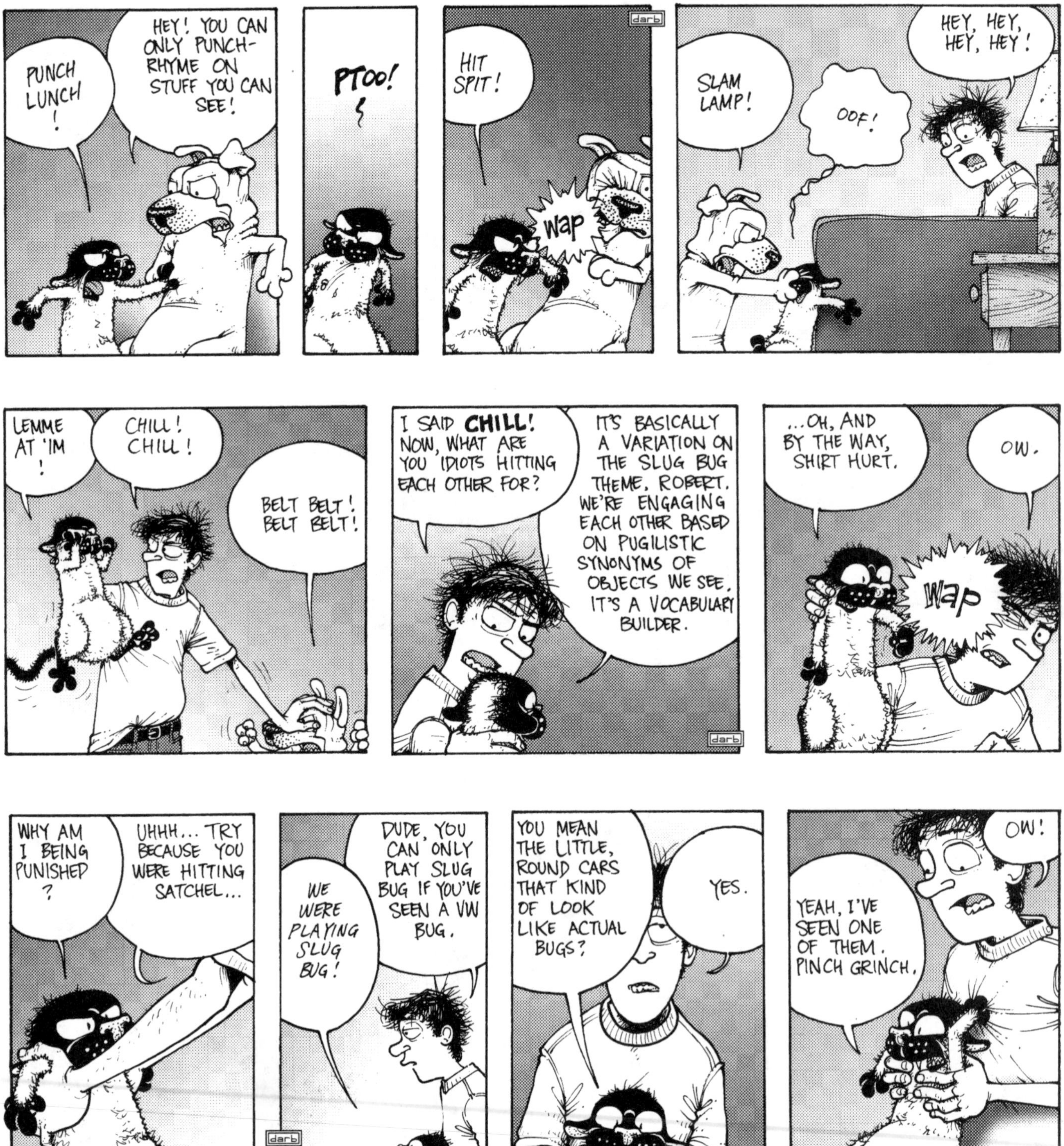

PUNCH LUNCH !
HEY! YOU CAN ONLY PUNCH-RHYME ON STUFF YOU CAN SEE!
PTOO!
HIT SPIT!
WAP
SLAM LAMP!
OOF!
HEY, HEY, HEY, HEY!
LEMME AT 'IM !
CHILL! CHILL!
BELT BELT! BELT BELT!
I SAID **CHILL!** NOW, WHAT ARE YOU IDIOTS HITTING EACH OTHER FOR?
IT'S BASICALLY A VARIATION ON THE SLUG BUG THEME, ROBERT. WE'RE ENGAGING EACH OTHER BASED ON PUGILISTIC SYNONYMS OF OBJECTS WE SEE. IT'S A VOCABULARY BUILDER.
...OH, AND BY THE WAY, SHIRT HURT.
OW.
WAP
WHY AM I BEING PUNISHED ?
UHHH... TRY BECAUSE YOU WERE HITTING SATCHEL...
WE WERE PLAYING SLUG BUG!
DUDE, YOU CAN ONLY PLAY SLUG BUG IF YOU'VE SEEN A VW BUG.
YOU MEAN THE LITTLE, ROUND CARS THAT KIND OF LOOK LIKE ACTUAL BUGS?
YES.
OW!
YEAH, I'VE SEEN ONE OF THEM. PINCH GRINCH.

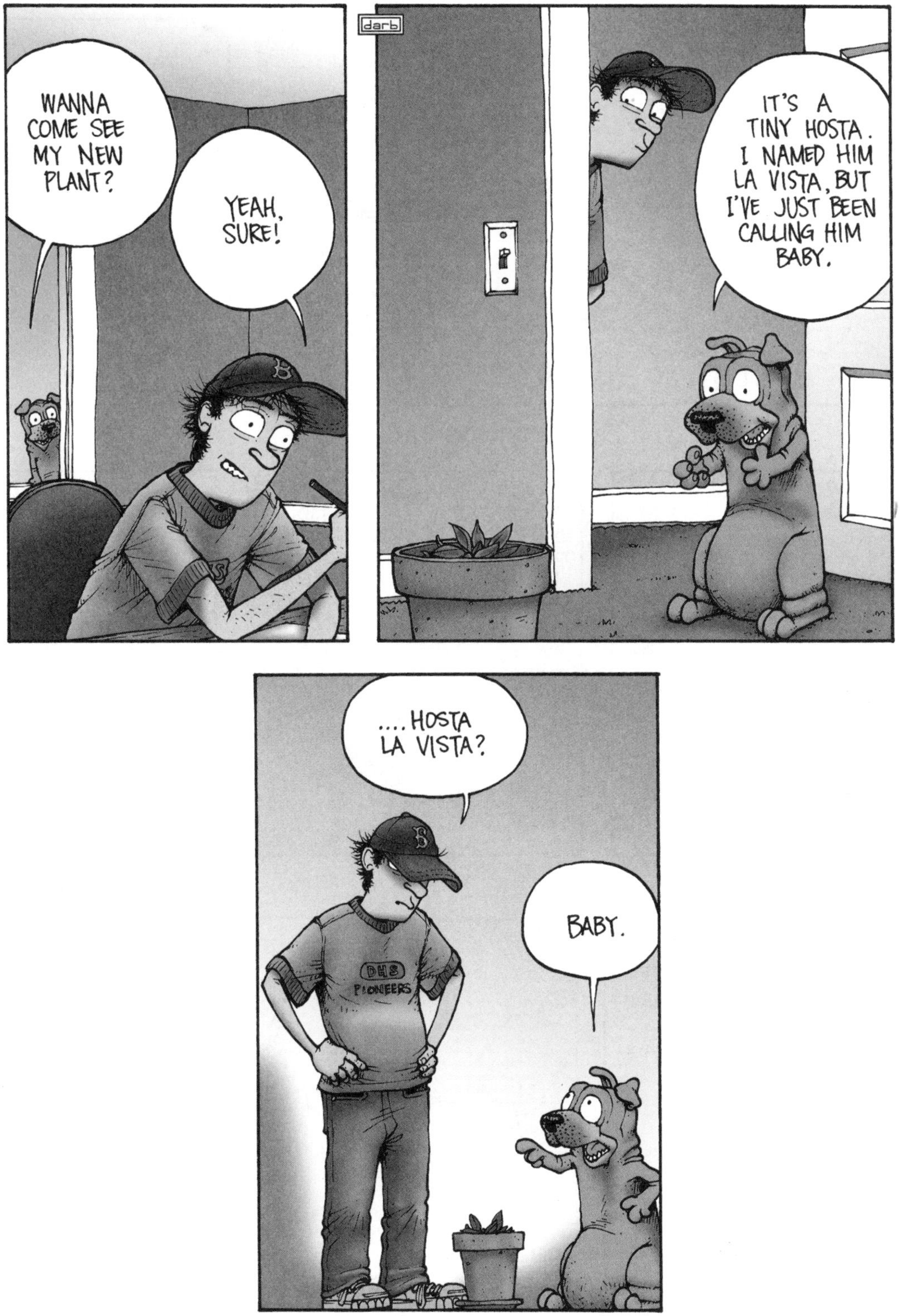
darb
WANNA COME SEE MY NEW PLANT?
YEAH, SURE!
IT'S A TINY HOSTA. I NAMED HIM LA VISTA, BUT I'VE JUST BEEN CALLING HIM BABY.
....HOSTA LA VISTA?
BABY.
DHS PIONEERS

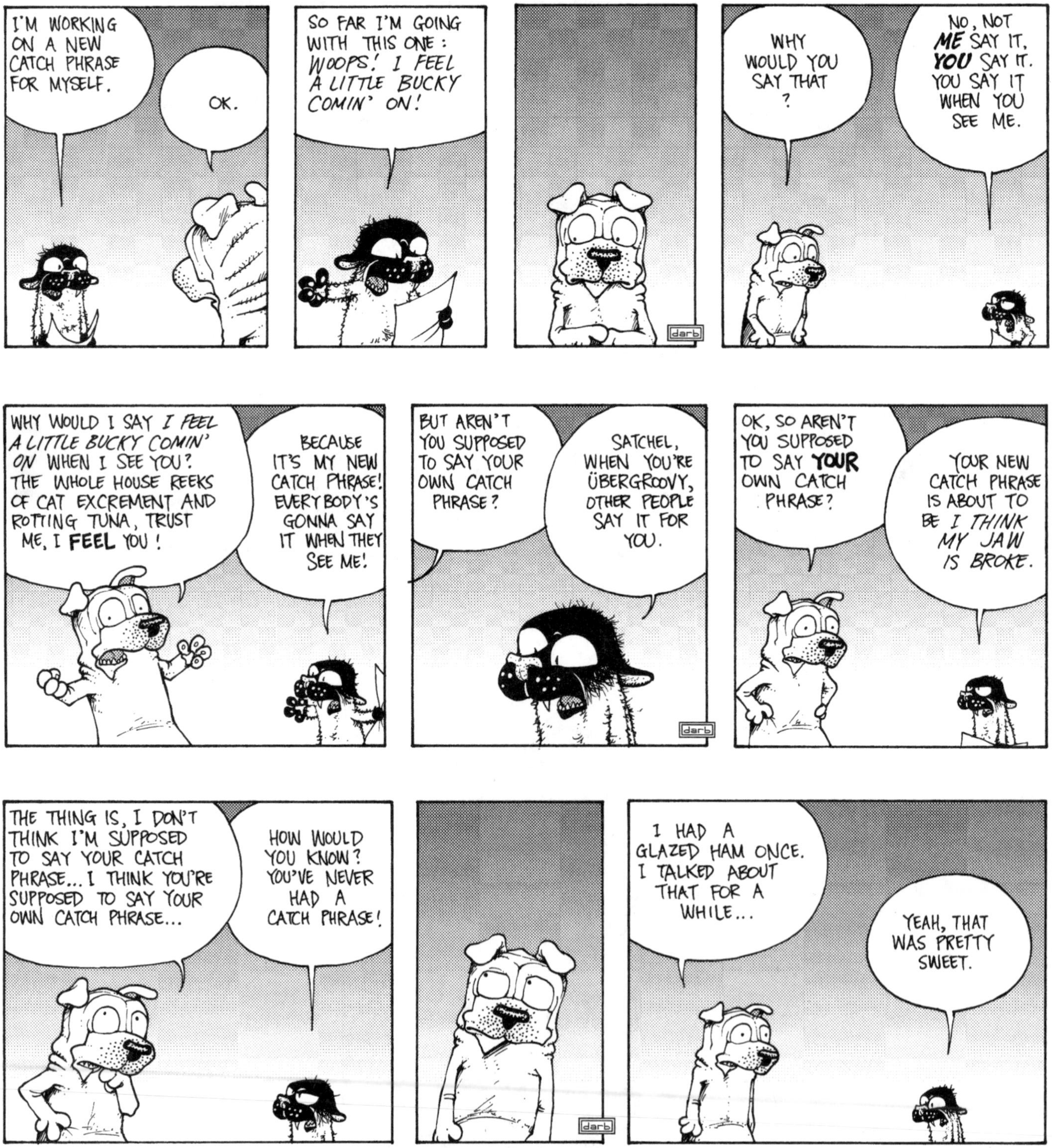
I'M WORKING ON A NEW CATCH PHRASE FOR MYSELF.
OK.
SO FAR I'M GOING WITH THIS ONE: *WOOPS! I FEEL A LITTLE BUCKY COMIN' ON!*
WHY WOULD YOU SAY THAT?
NO, NOT **ME** SAY IT. **YOU** SAY IT. YOU SAY IT WHEN YOU SEE ME.
darb
WHY WOULD I SAY *I FEEL A LITTLE BUCKY COMIN' ON* WHEN I SEE YOU? THE WHOLE HOUSE REEKS OF CAT EXCREMENT AND ROTTING TUNA, TRUST ME, I **FEEL** YOU!
BECAUSE IT'S MY NEW CATCH PHRASE! EVERYBODY'S GONNA SAY IT WHEN THEY SEE ME!
BUT AREN'T YOU SUPPOSED TO SAY YOUR OWN CATCH PHRASE?
SATCHEL, WHEN YOU'RE ÜBERGROOVY, OTHER PEOPLE SAY IT FOR YOU.
OK, SO AREN'T YOU SUPPOSED TO SAY **YOUR** OWN CATCH PHRASE?
YOUR NEW CATCH PHRASE IS ABOUT TO BE *I THINK MY JAW IS BROKE.*
darb
THE THING IS, I DON'T THINK I'M SUPPOSED TO SAY YOUR CATCH PHRASE... I THINK YOU'RE SUPPOSED TO SAY YOUR OWN CATCH PHRASE...
HOW WOULD YOU KNOW? YOU'VE NEVER HAD A CATCH PHRASE!
I HAD A GLAZED HAM ONCE. I TALKED ABOUT THAT FOR A WHILE...
YEAH, THAT WAS PRETTY SWEET.
darb

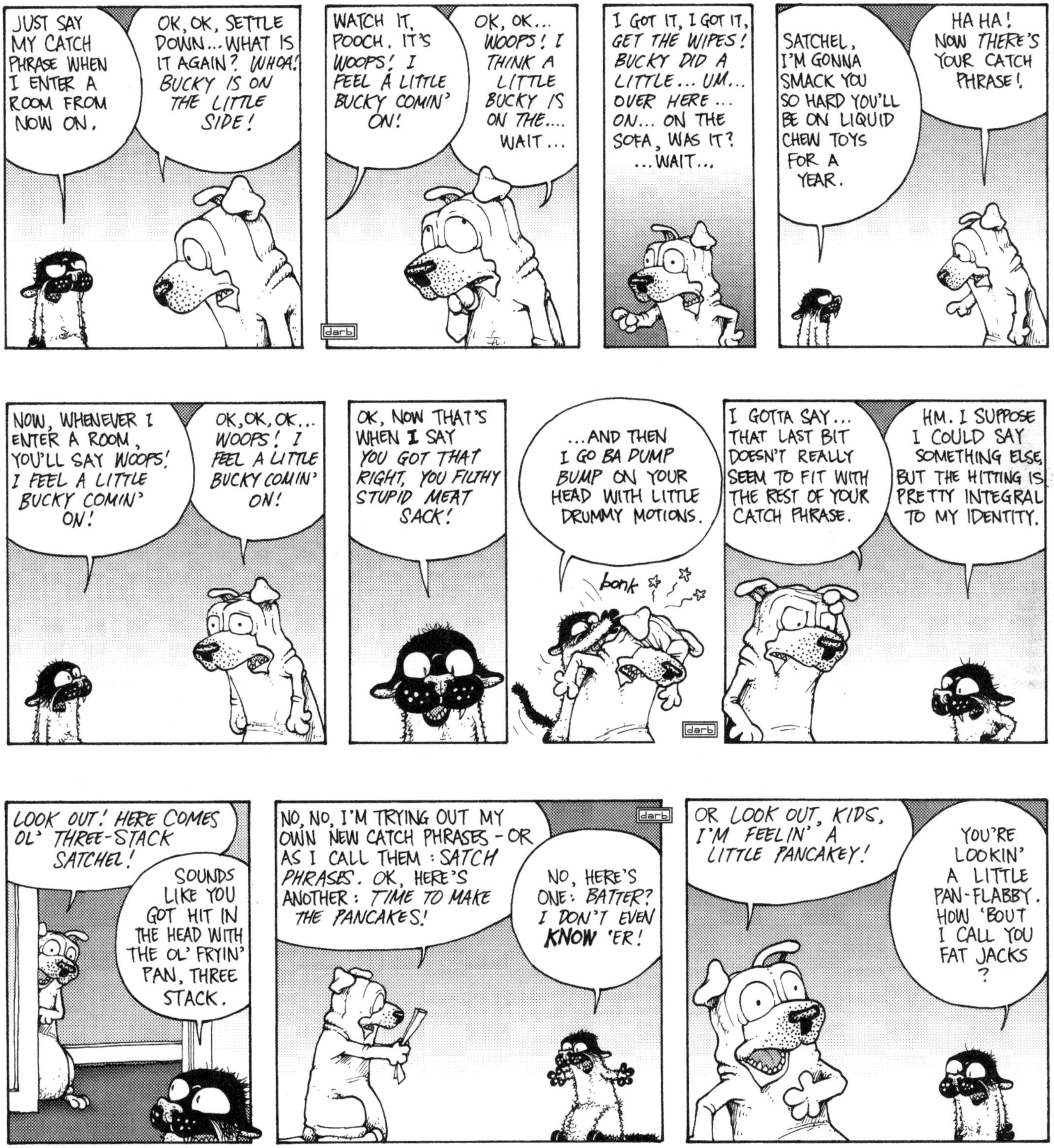
JUST SAY MY CATCH PHRASE WHEN I ENTER A ROOM FROM NOW ON.
OK, OK, SETTLE DOWN... WHAT IS IT AGAIN? WHOA! BUCKY IS ON THE LITTLE SIDE!
WATCH IT, POOCH. IT'S WOOPS! I FEEL A LITTLE BUCKY COMIN' ON!
OK, OK... WOOPS! I THINK A LITTLE BUCKY IS ON THE.... WAIT...
I GOT IT, I GOT IT, GET THE WIPES! BUCKY DID A LITTLE... UM... OVER HERE... ON... ON THE SOFA, WAS IT? ...WAIT...
SATCHEL, I'M GONNA SMACK YOU SO HARD YOU'LL BE ON LIQUID CHEW TOYS FOR A YEAR.
HA HA! NOW THERE'S YOUR CATCH PHRASE!
darb
NOW, WHENEVER I ENTER A ROOM, YOU'LL SAY WOOPS! I FEEL A LITTLE BUCKY COMIN' ON!
OK, OK, OK... WOOPS! I FEEL A LITTLE BUCKY COMIN' ON!
OK, NOW THAT'S WHEN I SAY YOU GOT THAT RIGHT, YOU FILTHY STUPID MEAT SACK!
...AND THEN I GO BA DUMP BUMP ON YOUR HEAD WITH LITTLE DRUMMY MOTIONS.
bonk
I GOTTA SAY... THAT LAST BIT DOESN'T REALLY SEEM TO FIT WITH THE REST OF YOUR CATCH PHRASE.
HM. I SUPPOSE I COULD SAY SOMETHING ELSE, BUT THE HITTING IS PRETTY INTEGRAL TO MY IDENTITY.
darb
LOOK OUT! HERE COMES OL' THREE-STACK SATCHEL!
SOUNDS LIKE YOU GOT HIT IN THE HEAD WITH THE OL' FRYIN' PAN, THREE STACK.
NO, NO, I'M TRYING OUT MY OWN NEW CATCH PHRASES - OR AS I CALL THEM: SATCH PHRASES. OK, HERE'S ANOTHER: TIME TO MAKE THE PANCAKES!
NO, HERE'S ONE: BATTER? I DON'T EVEN KNOW 'ER!
OR LOOK OUT, KIDS, I'M FEELIN' A LITTLE PANCAKEY!
YOU'RE LOOKIN' A LITTLE PAN-FLABBY. HOW 'BOUT I CALL YOU FAT JACKS?
darb

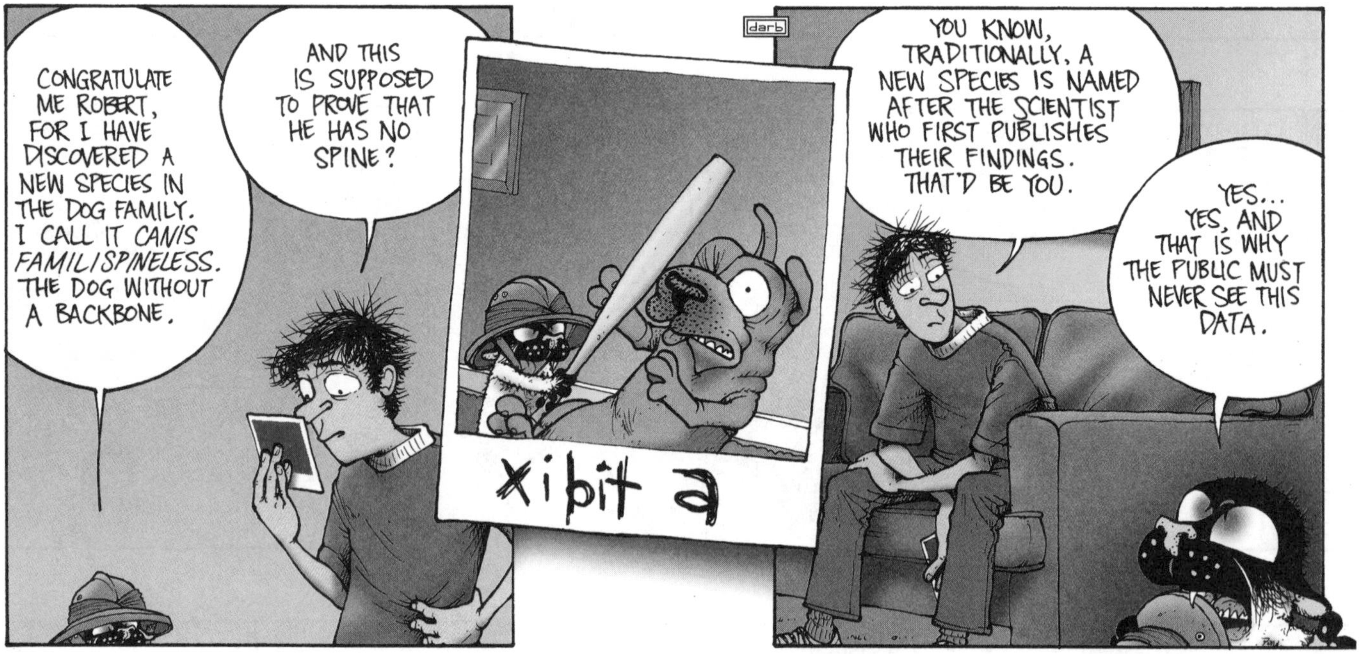
CONGRATULATE ME ROBERT, FOR I HAVE DISCOVERED A NEW SPECIES IN THE DOG FAMILY. I CALL IT *CANIS FAMILISPINELESS*. THE DOG WITHOUT A BACKBONE.
AND THIS IS SUPPOSED TO PROVE THAT HE HAS NO SPINE?
xibit a
darb
YOU KNOW, TRADITIONALLY, A NEW SPECIES IS NAMED AFTER THE SCIENTIST WHO FIRST PUBLISHES THEIR FINDINGS. THAT'D BE YOU.
YES... YES, AND THAT IS WHY THE PUBLIC MUST NEVER SEE THIS DATA.

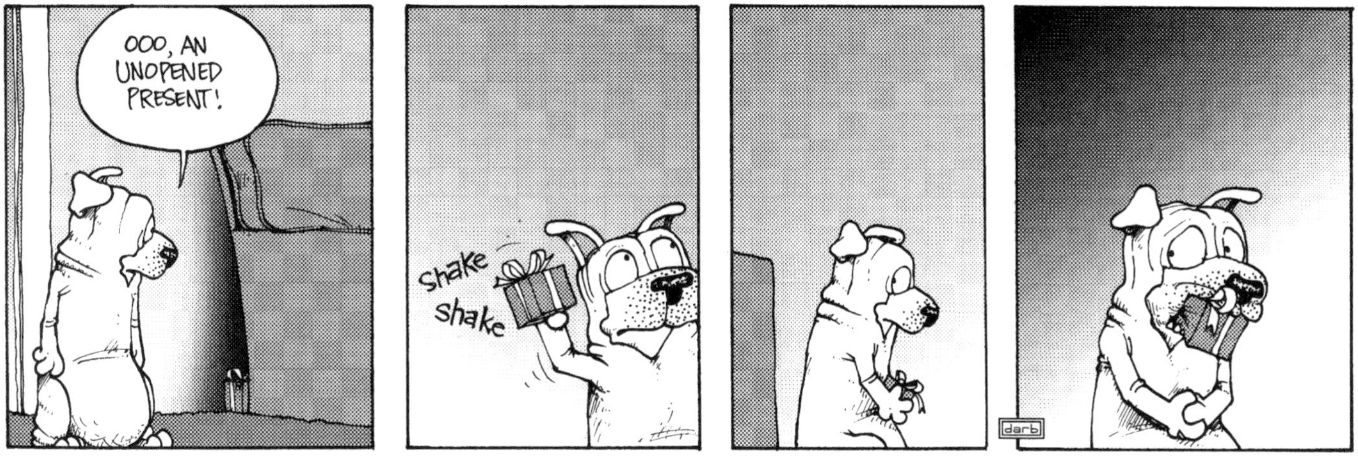
OOO, AN UNOPENED PRESENT!
shake shake
darb

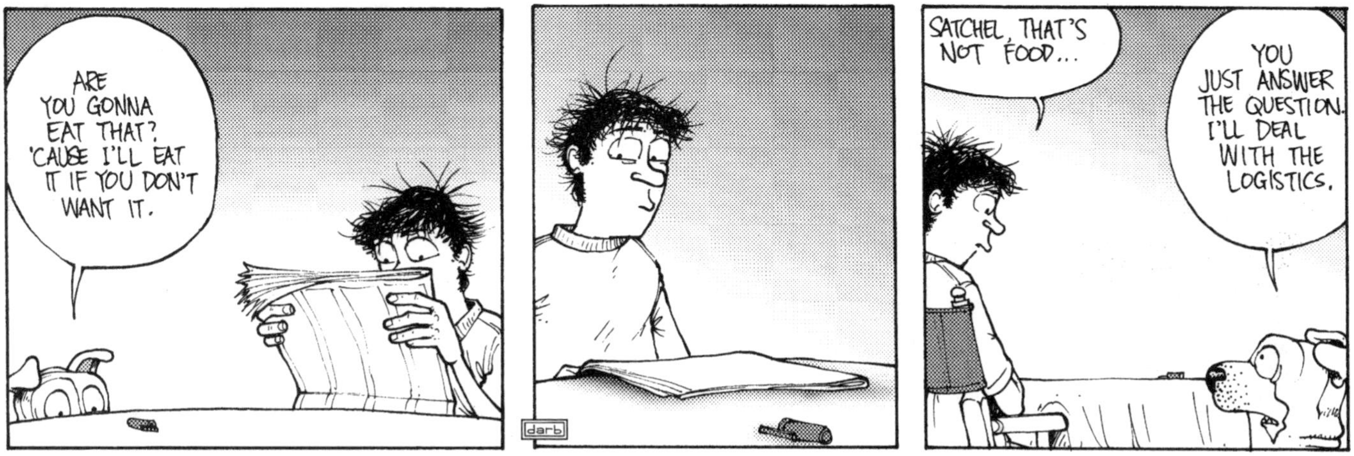
ARE YOU GONNA EAT THAT? 'CAUSE I'LL EAT IT IF YOU DON'T WANT IT.
darb
SATCHEL, THAT'S NOT FOOD...
YOU JUST ANSWER THE QUESTION. I'LL DEAL WITH THE LOGISTICS.

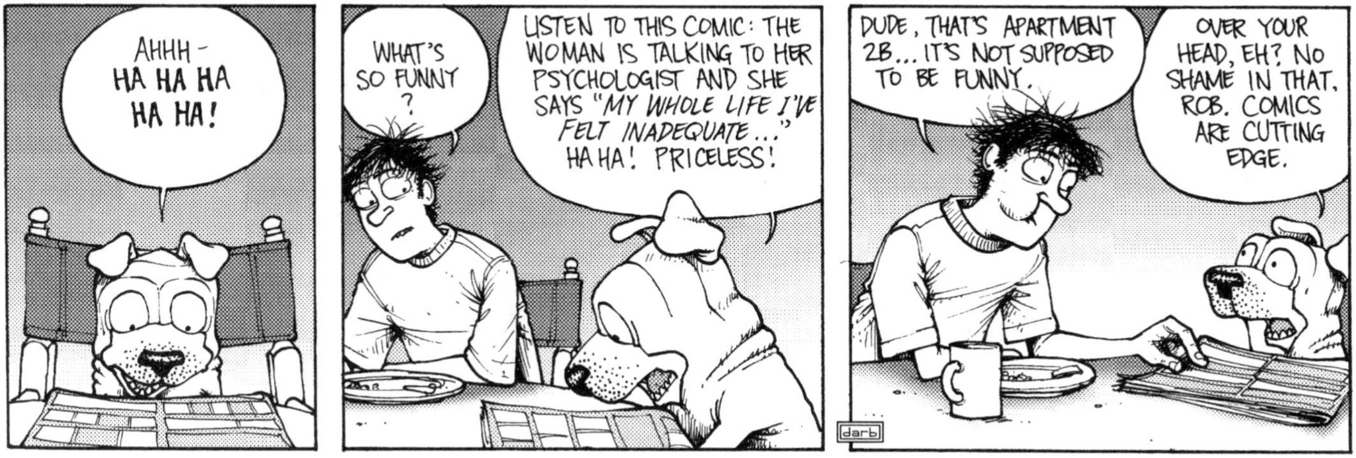
AHHH- HA HA HA HA HA!
WHAT'S SO FUNNY?
LISTEN TO THIS COMIC: THE WOMAN IS TALKING TO HER PSYCHOLOGIST AND SHE SAYS "MY WHOLE LIFE I'VE FELT INADEQUATE..." HA HA! PRICELESS!
DUDE, THAT'S APARTMENT 2B... IT'S NOT SUPPOSED TO BE FUNNY.
OVER YOUR HEAD, EH? NO SHAME IN THAT, ROB. COMICS ARE CUTTING EDGE.
darb

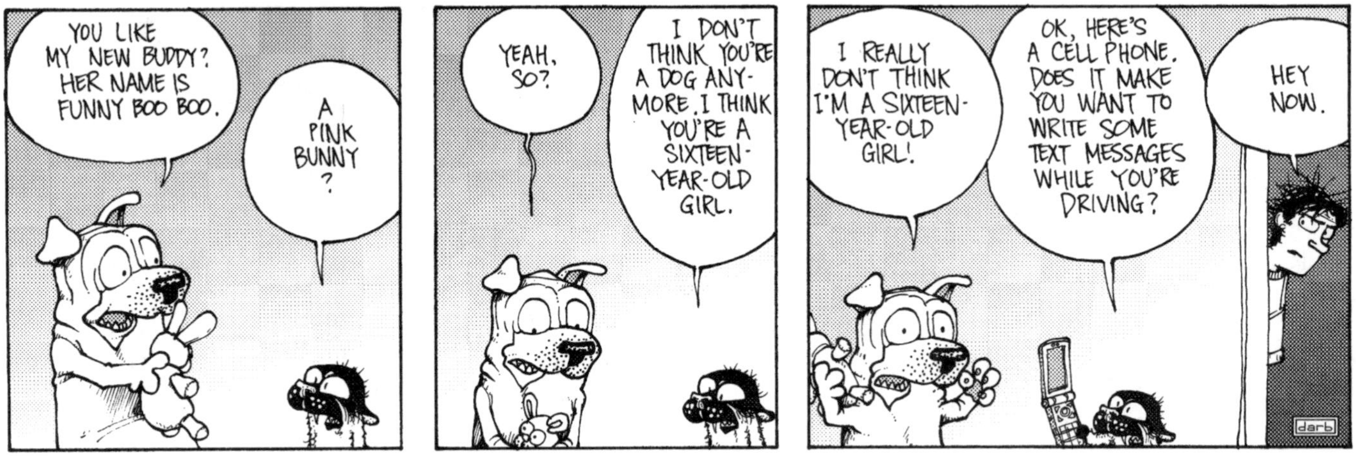
YOU LIKE MY NEW BUDDY? HER NAME IS FUNNY BOO BOO.
A PINK BUNNY?
YEAH, SO?
I DON'T THINK YOU'RE A DOG ANYMORE. I THINK YOU'RE A SIXTEEN-YEAR-OLD GIRL.
I REALLY DON'T THINK I'M A SIXTEEN-YEAR-OLD GIRL!
OK, HERE'S A CELL PHONE. DOES IT MAKE YOU WANT TO WRITE SOME TEXT MESSAGES WHILE YOU'RE DRIVING?
HEY NOW.
darb

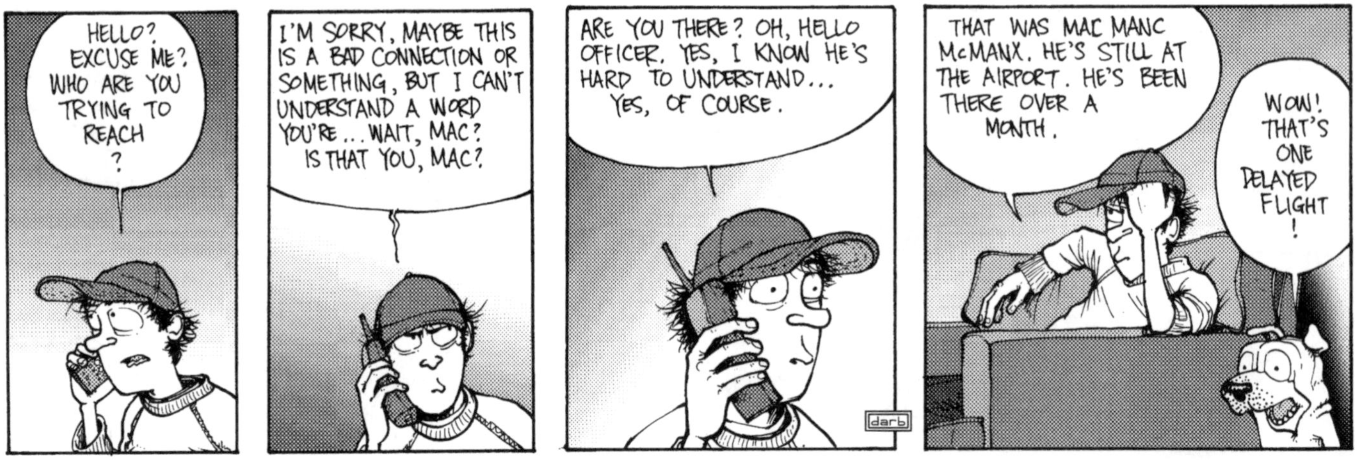
HELLO? EXCUSE ME? WHO ARE YOU TRYING TO REACH?
I'M SORRY, MAYBE THIS IS A BAD CONNECTION OR SOMETHING, BUT I CAN'T UNDERSTAND A WORD YOU'RE... WAIT, MAC? IS THAT YOU, MAC?
ARE YOU THERE? OH, HELLO OFFICER. YES, I KNOW HE'S HARD TO UNDERSTAND... YES, OF COURSE.
darb
THAT WAS MAC MANC McMANX. HE'S STILL AT THE AIRPORT. HE'S BEEN THERE OVER A MONTH.
WOW! THAT'S ONE DELAYED FLIGHT!

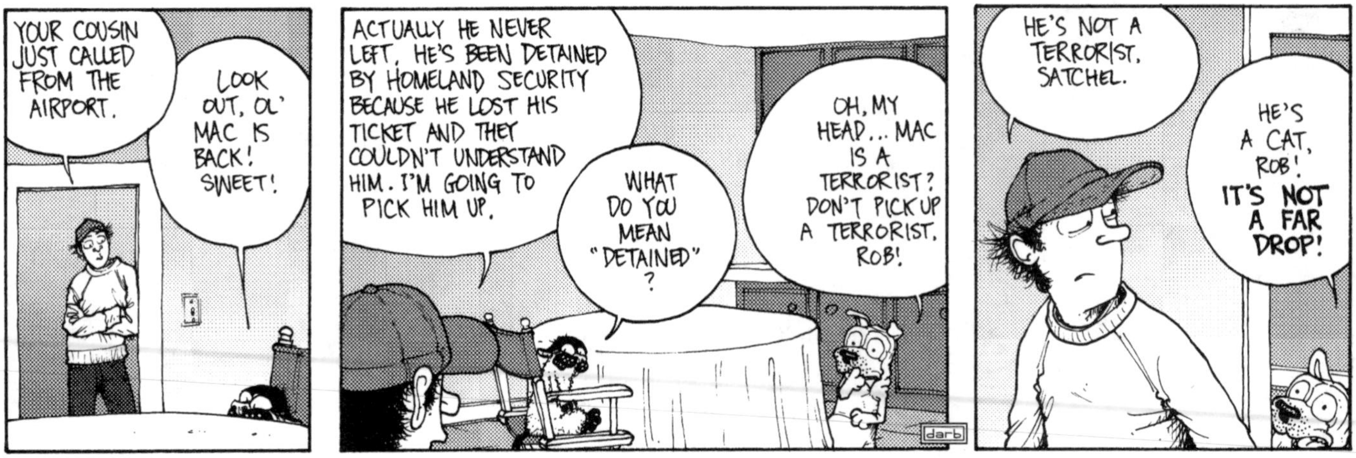
YOUR COUSIN JUST CALLED FROM THE AIRPORT.
LOOK OUT, OL' MAC IS BACK! SWEET!
ACTUALLY HE NEVER LEFT. HE'S BEEN DETAINED BY HOMELAND SECURITY BECAUSE HE LOST HIS TICKET AND THEY COULDN'T UNDERSTAND HIM. I'M GOING TO PICK HIM UP.
WHAT DO YOU MEAN "DETAINED"?
OH, MY HEAD... MAC IS A TERRORIST? DON'T PICK UP A TERRORIST, ROB!
darb
HE'S NOT A TERRORIST, SATCHEL.
HE'S A CAT, ROB! IT'S NOT A FAR DROP!

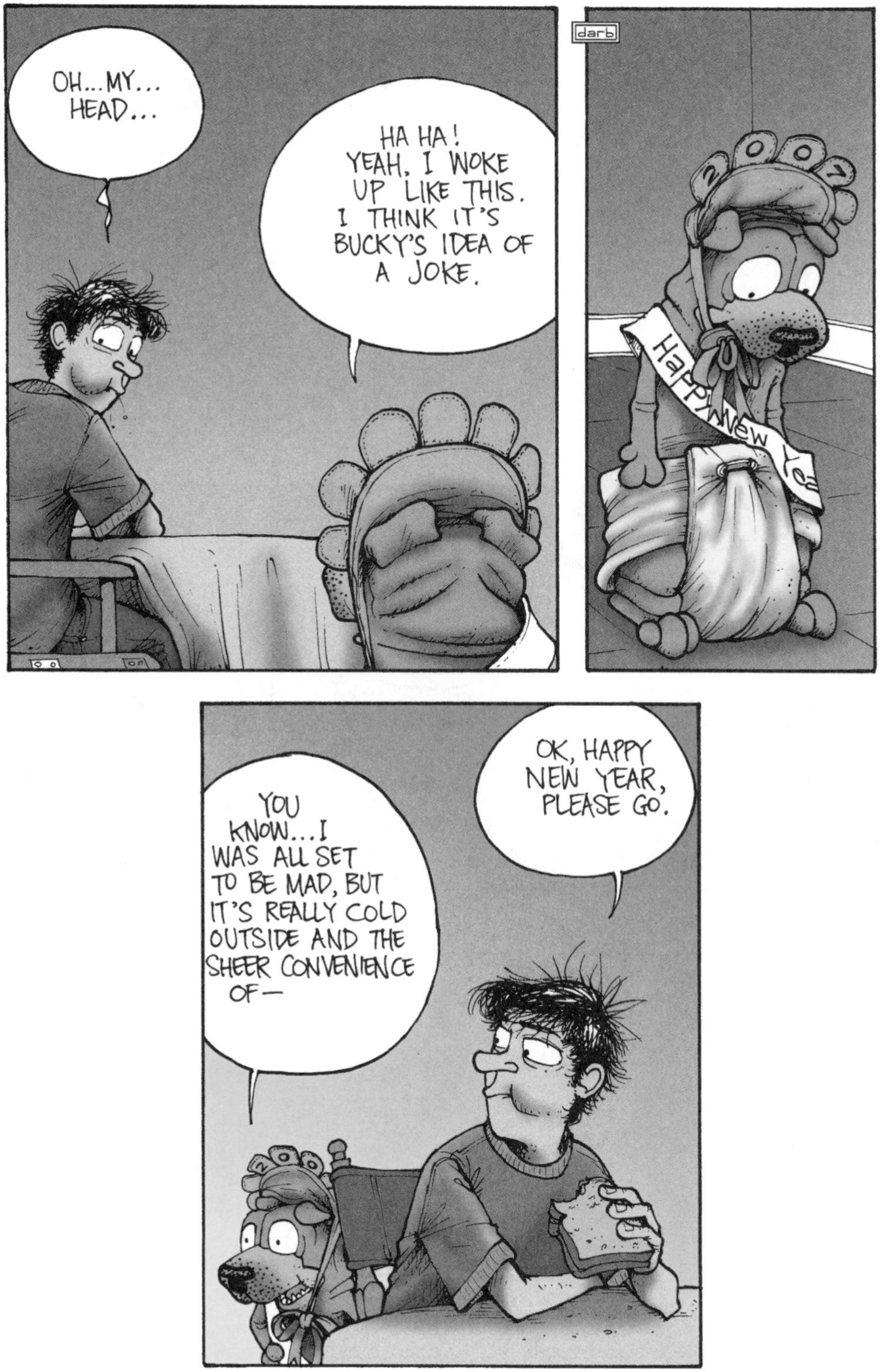
OH...MY... HEAD...
HA HA! YEAH, I WOKE UP LIKE THIS. I THINK IT'S BUCKY'S IDEA OF A JOKE.
darb
2007
Happy New Year
YOU KNOW...I WAS ALL SET TO BE MAD, BUT IT'S REALLY COLD OUTSIDE AND THE SHEER CONVENIENCE OF—
OK, HAPPY NEW YEAR, PLEASE GO.

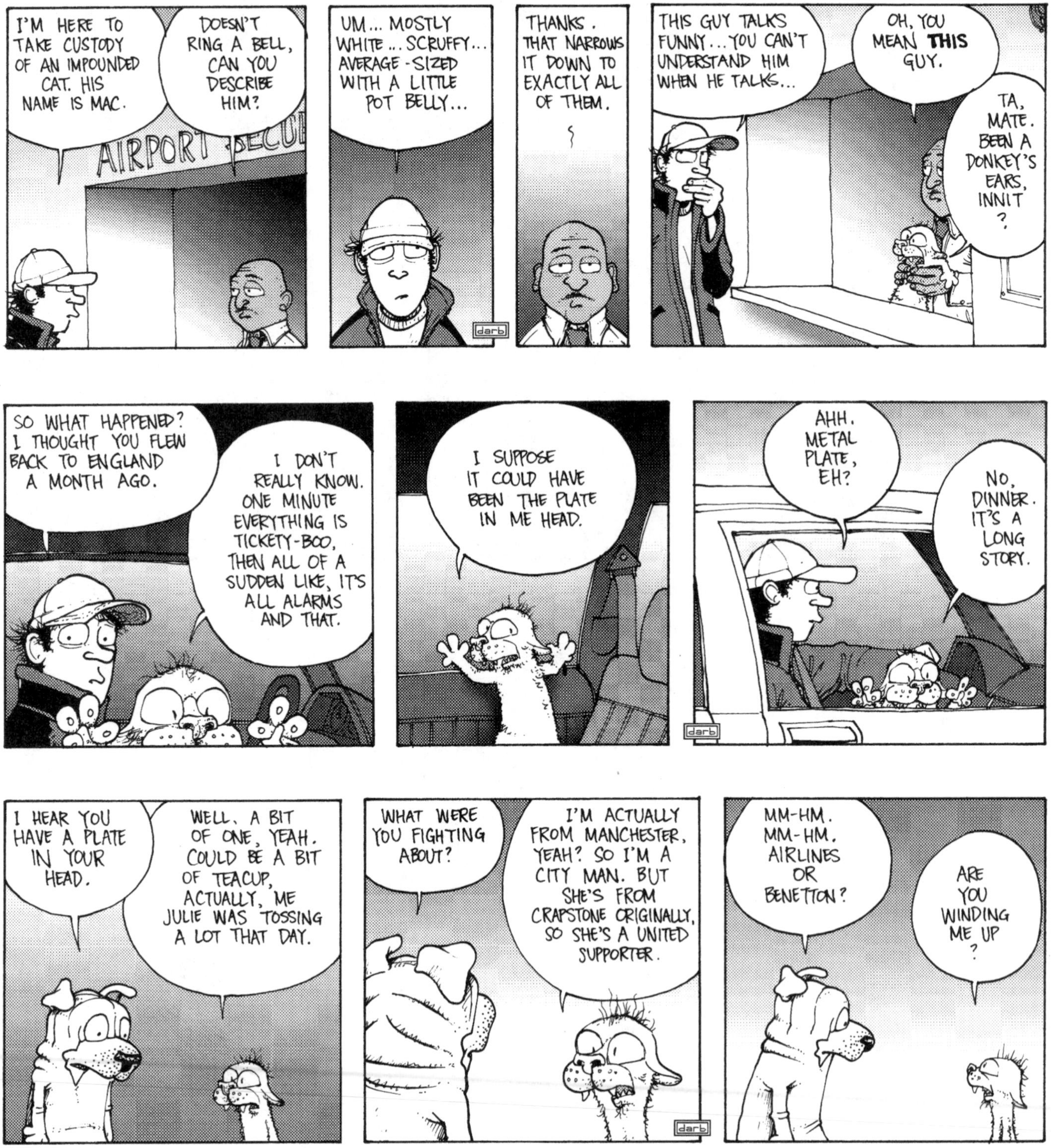
I'M HERE TO TAKE CUSTODY OF AN IMPOUNDED CAT. HIS NAME IS MAC.
DOESN'T RING A BELL, CAN YOU DESCRIBE HIM?
AIRPORT SECU
UM... MOSTLY WHITE... SCRUFFY... AVERAGE-SIZED WITH A LITTLE POT BELLY...
THANKS. THAT NARROWS IT DOWN TO EXACTLY ALL OF THEM.
THIS GUY TALKS FUNNY... YOU CAN'T UNDERSTAND HIM WHEN HE TALKS...
OH, YOU MEAN **THIS** GUY.
TA, MATE. BEEN A DONKEY'S EARS, INNIT?
SO WHAT HAPPENED? I THOUGHT YOU FLEW BACK TO ENGLAND A MONTH AGO.
I DON'T REALLY KNOW. ONE MINUTE EVERYTHING IS TICKETY-BOO, THEN ALL OF A SUDDEN LIKE, IT'S ALL ALARMS AND THAT.
I SUPPOSE IT COULD HAVE BEEN THE PLATE IN ME HEAD.
AHH. METAL PLATE, EH?
NO, DINNER. IT'S A LONG STORY.
I HEAR YOU HAVE A PLATE IN YOUR HEAD.
WELL, A BIT OF ONE, YEAH. COULD BE A BIT OF TEACUP, ACTUALLY, ME JULIE WAS TOSSING A LOT THAT DAY.
WHAT WERE YOU FIGHTING ABOUT?
I'M ACTUALLY FROM MANCHESTER, YEAH? SO I'M A CITY MAN. BUT SHE'S FROM CRAPSTONE ORIGINALLY, SO SHE'S A UNITED SUPPORTER.
MM-HM. MM-HM. AIRLINES OR BENETTON?
ARE YOU WINDING ME UP?

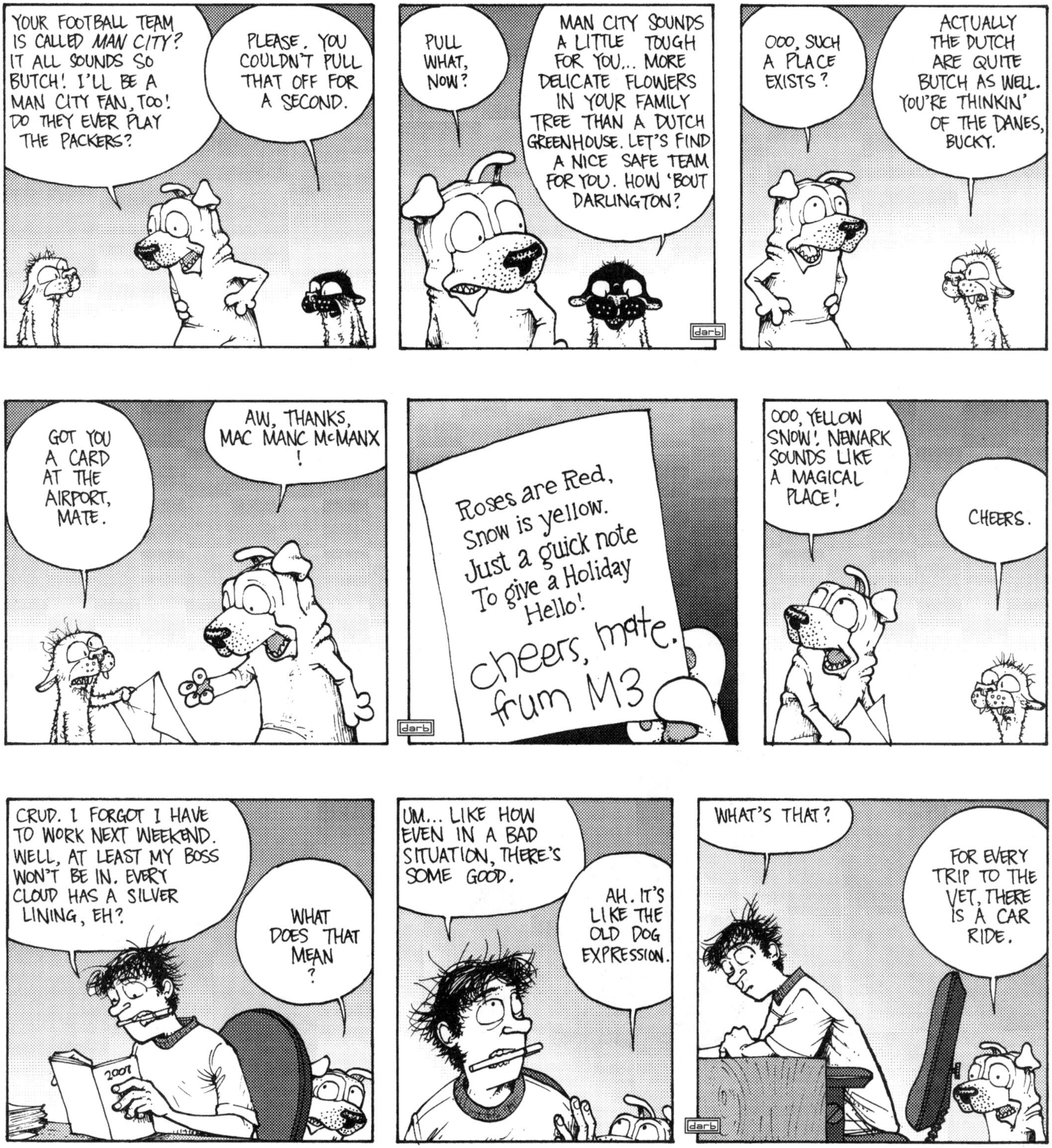
YOUR FOOTBALL TEAM IS CALLED *MAN CITY*? IT ALL SOUNDS SO BUTCH! I'LL BE A MAN CITY FAN, TOO! DO THEY EVER PLAY THE PACKERS?
PLEASE. YOU COULDN'T PULL THAT OFF FOR A SECOND.
PULL WHAT, NOW?
MAN CITY SOUNDS A LITTLE TOUGH FOR YOU... MORE DELICATE FLOWERS IN YOUR FAMILY TREE THAN A DUTCH GREENHOUSE. LET'S FIND A NICE SAFE TEAM FOR YOU. HOW 'BOUT DARLINGTON?
OOO, SUCH A PLACE EXISTS?
ACTUALLY THE DUTCH ARE QUITE BUTCH AS WELL. YOU'RE THINKIN' OF THE DANES, BUCKY.
darb
GOT YOU A CARD AT THE AIRPORT, MATE.
AW, THANKS, MAC MANC McMANX!
Roses are Red, Snow is yellow. Just a quick note To give a Holiday Hello!
cheers, mate. frum M3
OOO, YELLOW SNOW! NEWARK SOUNDS LIKE A MAGICAL PLACE!
CHEERS.
darb
CRUD. I FORGOT I HAVE TO WORK NEXT WEEKEND. WELL, AT LEAST MY BOSS WON'T BE IN. EVERY CLOUD HAS A SILVER LINING, EH?
WHAT DOES THAT MEAN?
2007
UM... LIKE HOW EVEN IN A BAD SITUATION, THERE'S SOME GOOD.
AH. IT'S LIKE THE OLD DOG EXPRESSION.
WHAT'S THAT?
FOR EVERY TRIP TO THE VET, THERE IS A CAR RIDE.
darb

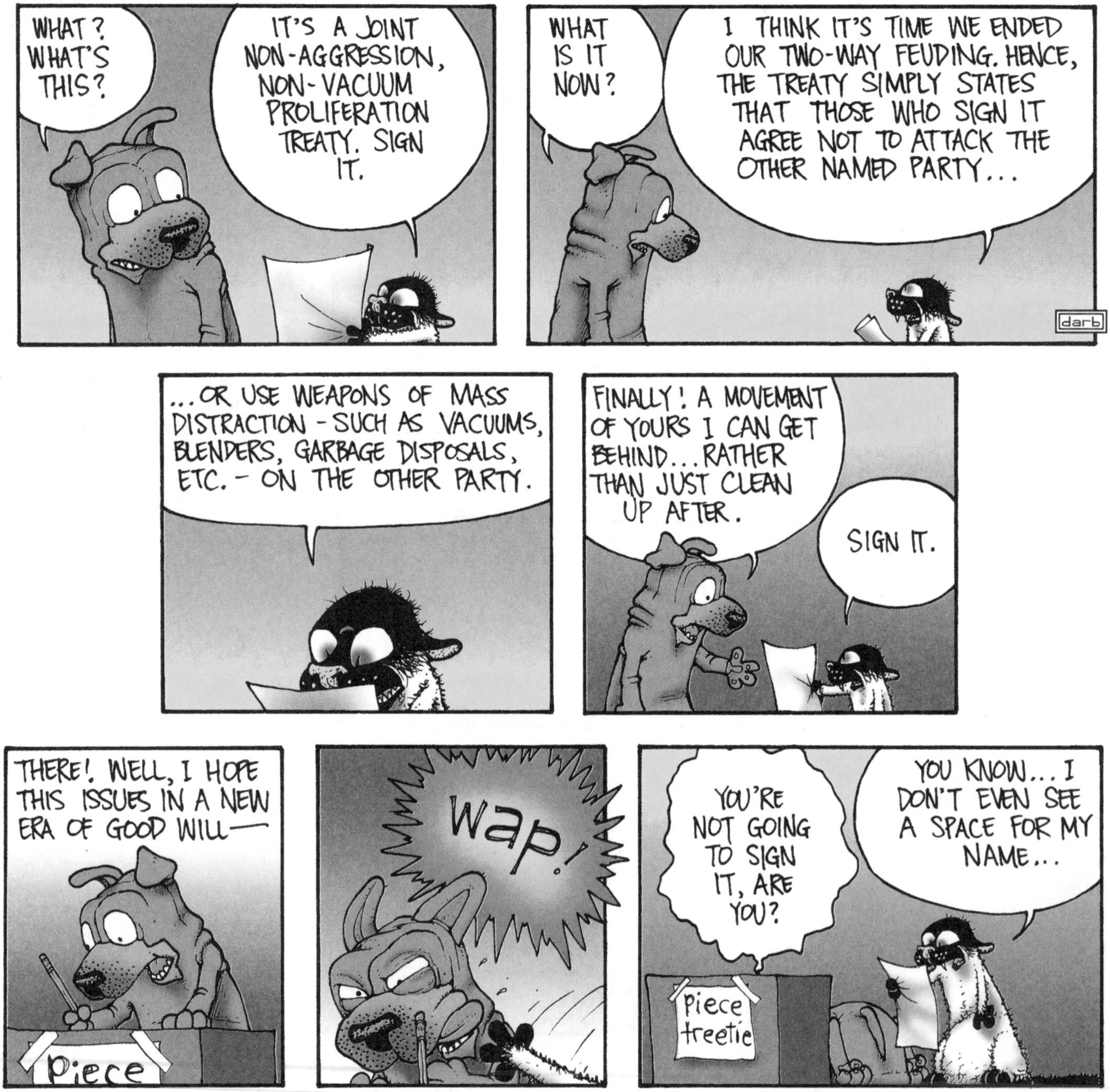
WHAT? WHAT'S THIS?
IT'S A JOINT NON-AGGRESSION, NON-VACUUM PROLIFERATION TREATY. SIGN IT.
WHAT IS IT NOW?
I THINK IT'S TIME WE ENDED OUR TWO-WAY FEUDING. HENCE, THE TREATY SIMPLY STATES THAT THOSE WHO SIGN IT AGREE NOT TO ATTACK THE OTHER NAMED PARTY...
darb
...OR USE WEAPONS OF MASS DISTRACTION - SUCH AS VACUUMS, BLENDERS, GARBAGE DISPOSALS, ETC. - ON THE OTHER PARTY.
FINALLY! A MOVEMENT OF YOURS I CAN GET BEHIND... RATHER THAN JUST CLEAN UP AFTER.
SIGN IT.
THERE! WELL, I HOPE THIS ISSUES IN A NEW ERA OF GOOD WILL—
Piece
wap!
YOU'RE NOT GOING TO SIGN IT, ARE YOU?
YOU KNOW... I DON'T EVEN SEE A SPACE FOR MY NAME...
Piece treetie

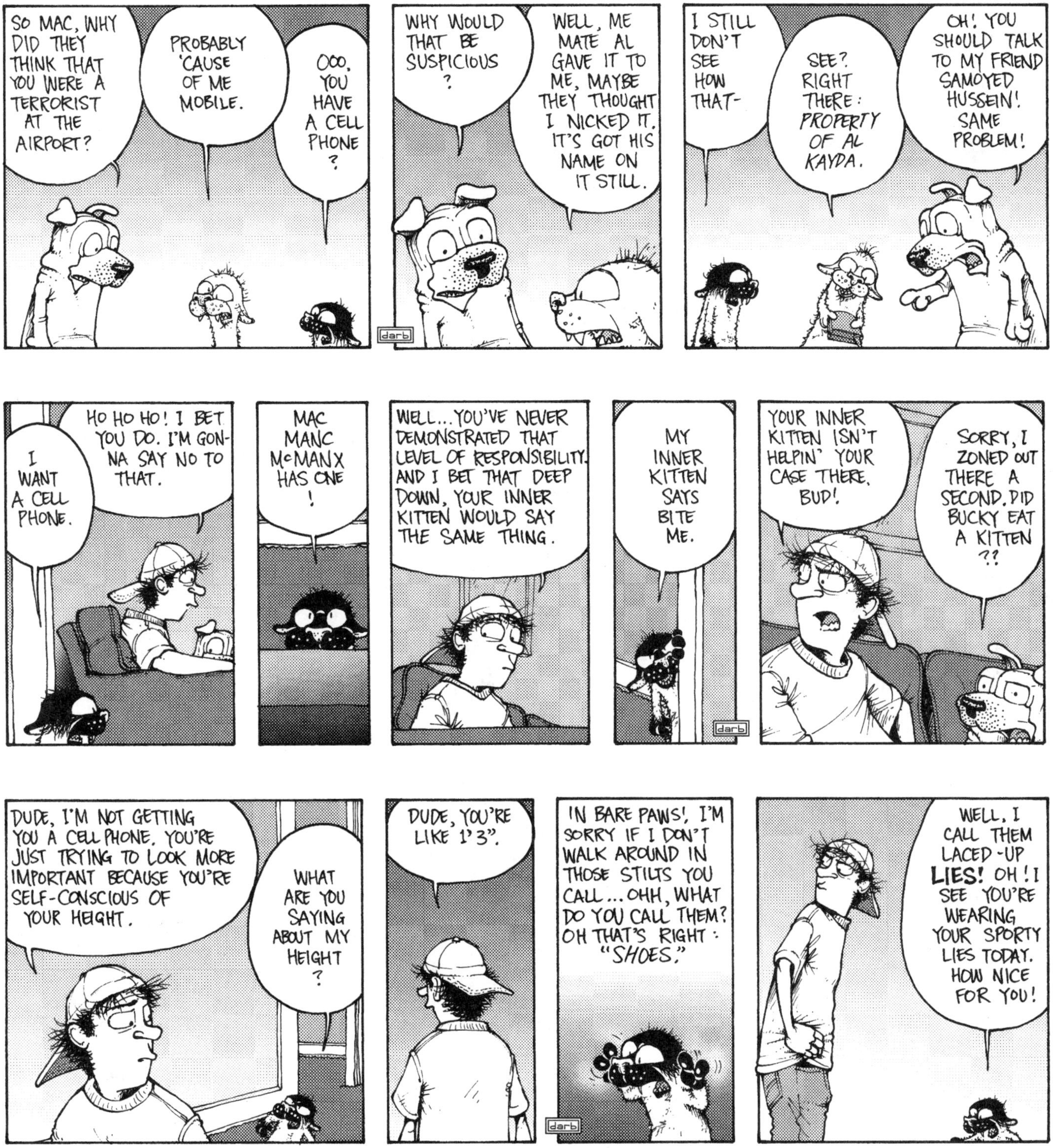

SO MAC, WHY DID THEY THINK THAT YOU WERE A TERRORIST AT THE AIRPORT?
PROBABLY 'CAUSE OF ME MOBILE.
OOO. YOU HAVE A CELL PHONE?
WHY WOULD THAT BE SUSPICIOUS?
WELL, ME MATE AL GAVE IT TO ME, MAYBE THEY THOUGHT I NICKED IT. IT'S GOT HIS NAME ON IT STILL.
I STILL DON'T SEE HOW THAT-
SEE? RIGHT THERE: *PROPERTY OF AL KAYDA.*
OH! YOU SHOULD TALK TO MY FRIEND SAMOYED HUSSEIN! SAME PROBLEM!
darb
I WANT A CELL PHONE.
HO HO HO! I BET YOU DO. I'M GON-NA SAY NO TO THAT.
MAC MANC McMANX HAS ONE!
WELL... YOU'VE NEVER DEMONSTRATED THAT LEVEL OF RESPONSIBILITY. AND I BET THAT DEEP DOWN, YOUR INNER KITTEN WOULD SAY THE SAME THING.
MY INNER KITTEN SAYS BITE ME.
YOUR INNER KITTEN ISN'T HELPIN' YOUR CASE THERE, BUD!
SORRY, I ZONED OUT THERE A SECOND. DID BUCKY EAT A KITTEN??
darb
DUDE, I'M NOT GETTING YOU A CELL PHONE. YOU'RE JUST TRYING TO LOOK MORE IMPORTANT BECAUSE YOU'RE SELF-CONSCIOUS OF YOUR HEIGHT.
WHAT ARE YOU SAYING ABOUT MY HEIGHT?
DUDE, YOU'RE LIKE 1'3".
IN BARE PAWS! I'M SORRY IF I DON'T WALK AROUND IN THOSE STILTS YOU CALL... OHH, WHAT DO YOU CALL THEM? OH THAT'S RIGHT: "*SHOES.*"
WELL, I CALL THEM LACED-UP **LIES!** OH! I SEE YOU'RE WEARING YOUR SPORTY LIES TODAY. HOW NICE FOR YOU!
darb

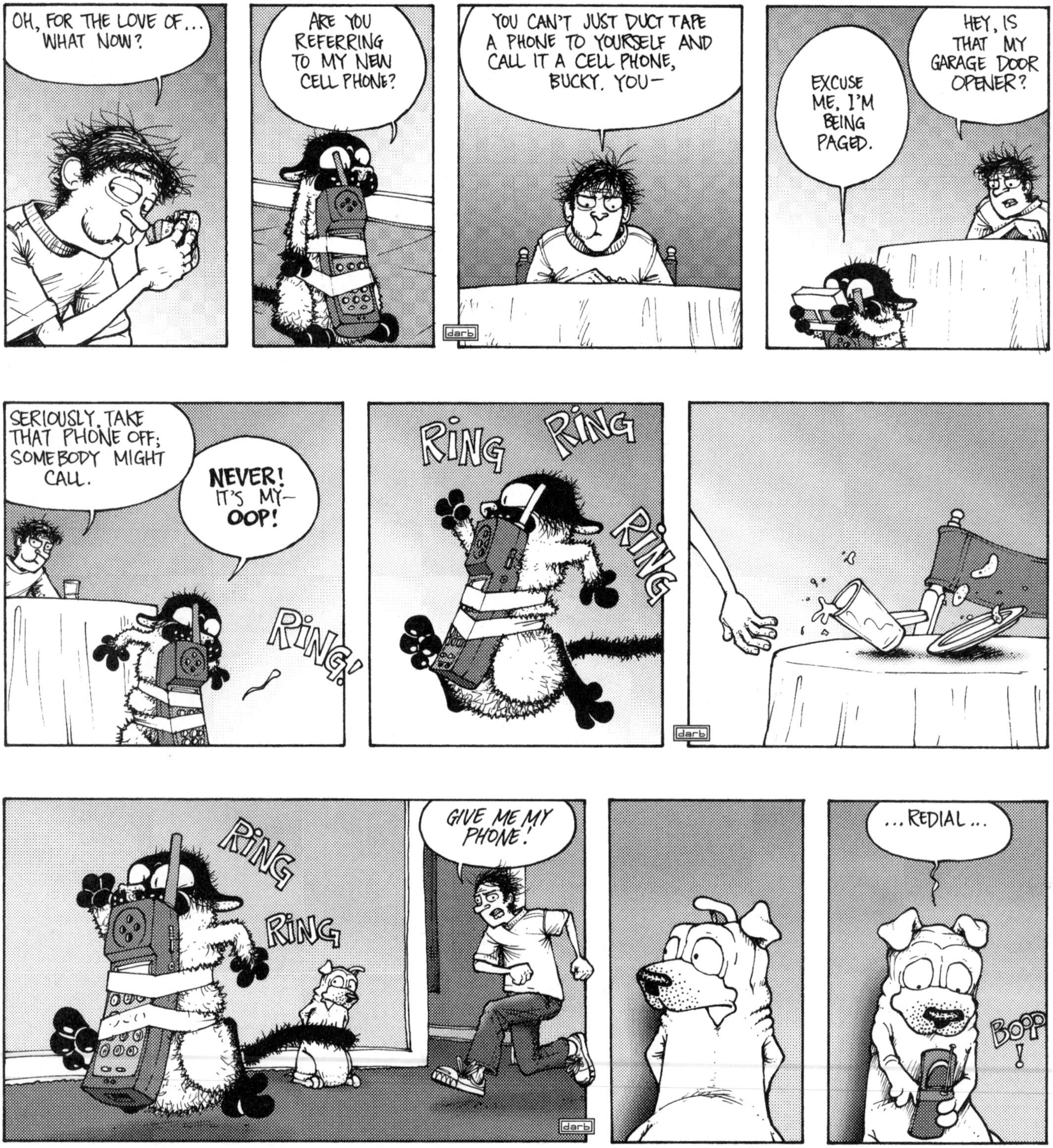
OH, FOR THE LOVE OF... WHAT NOW?
ARE YOU REFERRING TO MY NEW CELL PHONE?
YOU CAN'T JUST DUCT TAPE A PHONE TO YOURSELF AND CALL IT A CELL PHONE, BUCKY. YOU—
darb
HEY, IS THAT MY GARAGE DOOR OPENER?
EXCUSE ME, I'M BEING PAGED.
SERIOUSLY, TAKE THAT PHONE OFF; SOMEBODY MIGHT CALL.
NEVER! IT'S MY— OOP!
RING!
RING RING RING
darb
RING RING
GIVE ME MY PHONE!
darb
...REDIAL...
BOOP!

Say NO to DRUGS!
Say NO to DRUGS!
Say NO to DRUGS!
darb
Say NO to D GS!

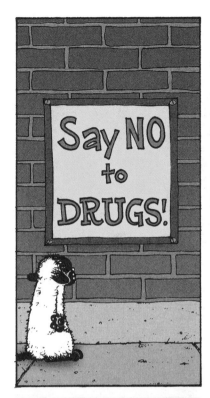

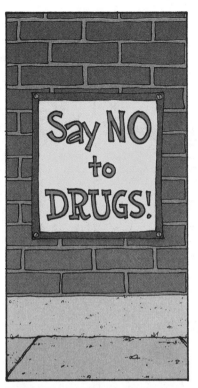

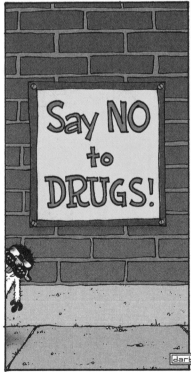

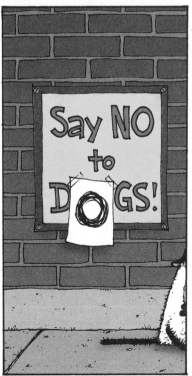

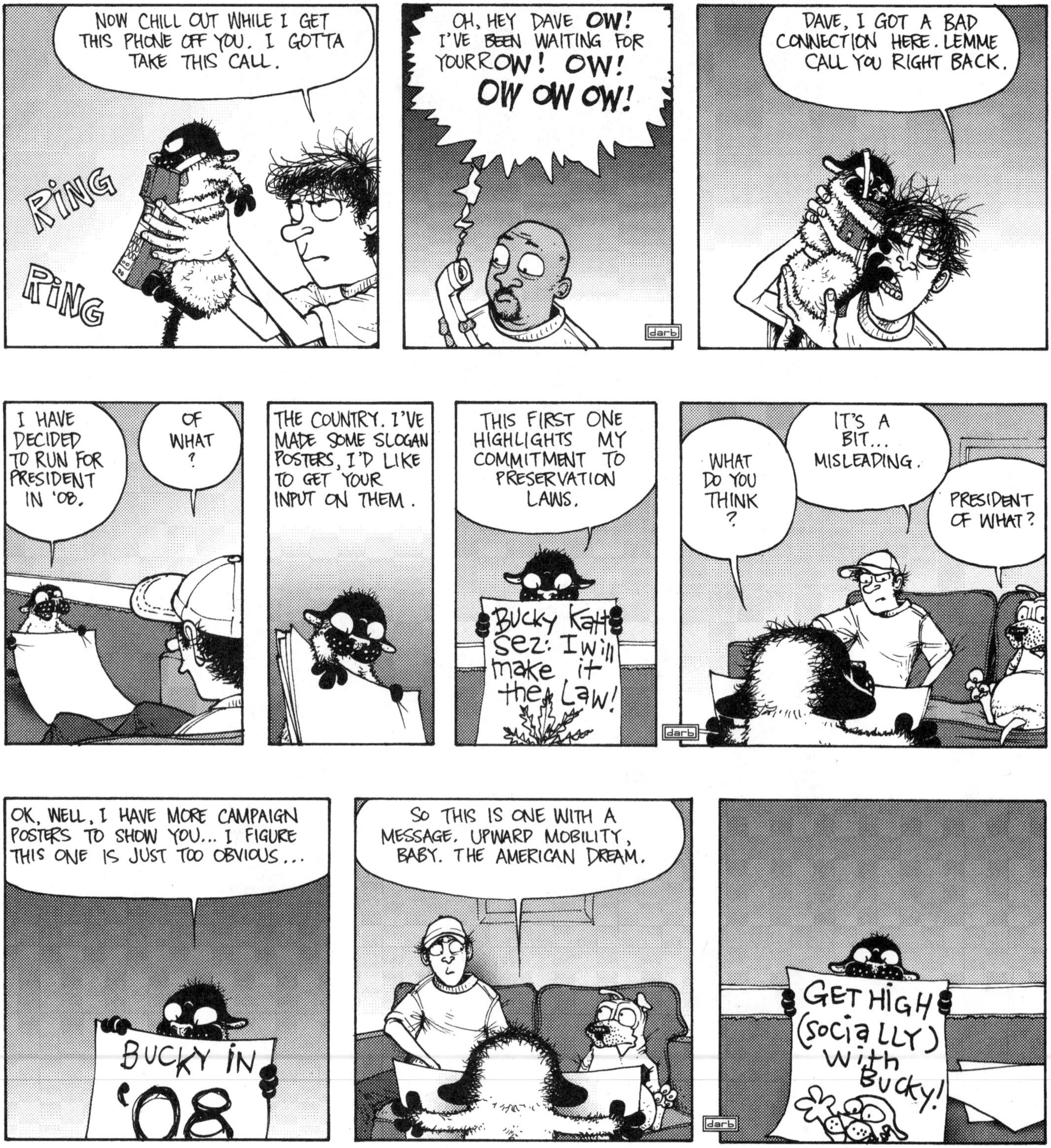
NOW CHILL OUT WHILE I GET THIS PHONE OFF YOU. I GOTTA TAKE THIS CALL.
RING
RING
OH, HEY DAVE OW! I'VE BEEN WAITING FOR YOURROW! OW! OW OW OW!
DAVE, I GOT A BAD CONNECTION HERE. LEMME CALL YOU RIGHT BACK.
darb
I HAVE DECIDED TO RUN FOR PRESIDENT IN '08.
OF WHAT?
THE COUNTRY. I'VE MADE SOME SLOGAN POSTERS, I'D LIKE TO GET YOUR INPUT ON THEM.
THIS FIRST ONE HIGHLIGHTS MY COMMITMENT TO PRESERVATION LAWS.
Bucky Katt sez: I will make it the Law!
WHAT DO YOU THINK?
IT'S A BIT... MISLEADING.
PRESIDENT OF WHAT?
darb
OK, WELL, I HAVE MORE CAMPAIGN POSTERS TO SHOW YOU... I FIGURE THIS ONE IS JUST TOO OBVIOUS...
BUCKY IN '08
SO THIS IS ONE WITH A MESSAGE. UPWARD MOBILITY, BABY. THE AMERICAN DREAM.
GET HIGH (socially) with Bucky!
darb

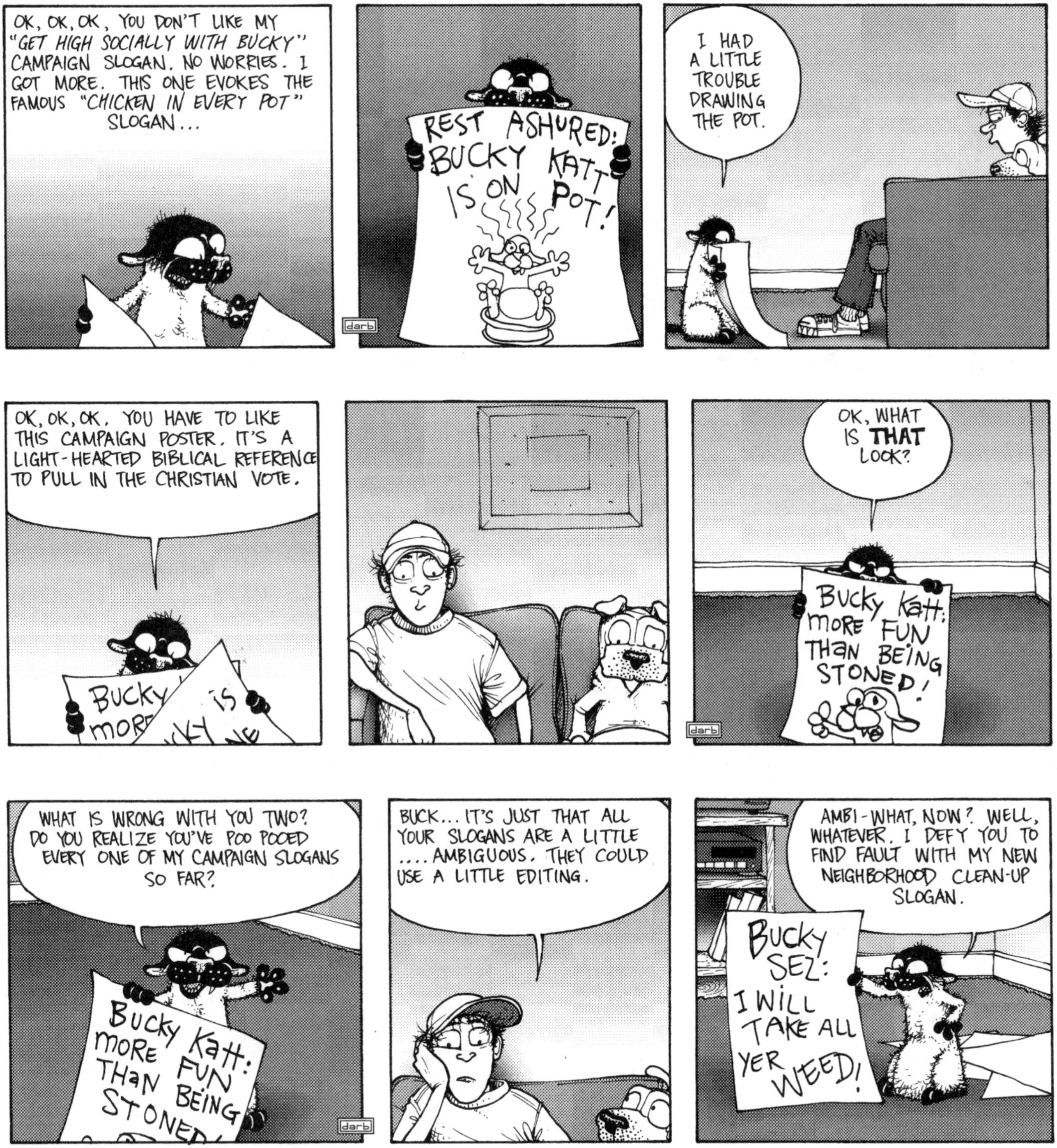

OK, OK, OK, YOU DON'T LIKE MY "GET HIGH SOCIALLY WITH BUCKY" CAMPAIGN SLOGAN. NO WORRIES. I GOT MORE. THIS ONE EVOKES THE FAMOUS "CHICKEN IN EVERY POT" SLOGAN...
REST ASHURED: BUCKY KATT IS ON POT!
darb
I HAD A LITTLE TROUBLE DRAWING THE POT.
OK, OK, OK. YOU HAVE TO LIKE THIS CAMPAIGN POSTER. IT'S A LIGHT-HEARTED BIBLICAL REFERENCE TO PULL IN THE CHRISTIAN VOTE.
BUCKY
IS
OK, WHAT IS **THAT** LOOK?
Bucky Katt: more FUN Than BEING STONED!
darb
WHAT IS WRONG WITH YOU TWO? DO YOU REALIZE YOU'VE POO POOED EVERY ONE OF MY CAMPAIGN SLOGANS SO FAR?
Bucky Katt: more FUN Than BEING
darb
BUCK... IT'S JUST THAT ALL YOUR SLOGANS ARE A LITTLE ....AMBIGUOUS. THEY COULD USE A LITTLE EDITING.
AMBI-WHAT, NOW? WELL, WHATEVER. I DEFY YOU TO FIND FAULT WITH MY NEW NEIGHBORHOOD CLEAN-UP SLOGAN.
Bucky SEZ: I WILL TAKE ALL YER WEED!

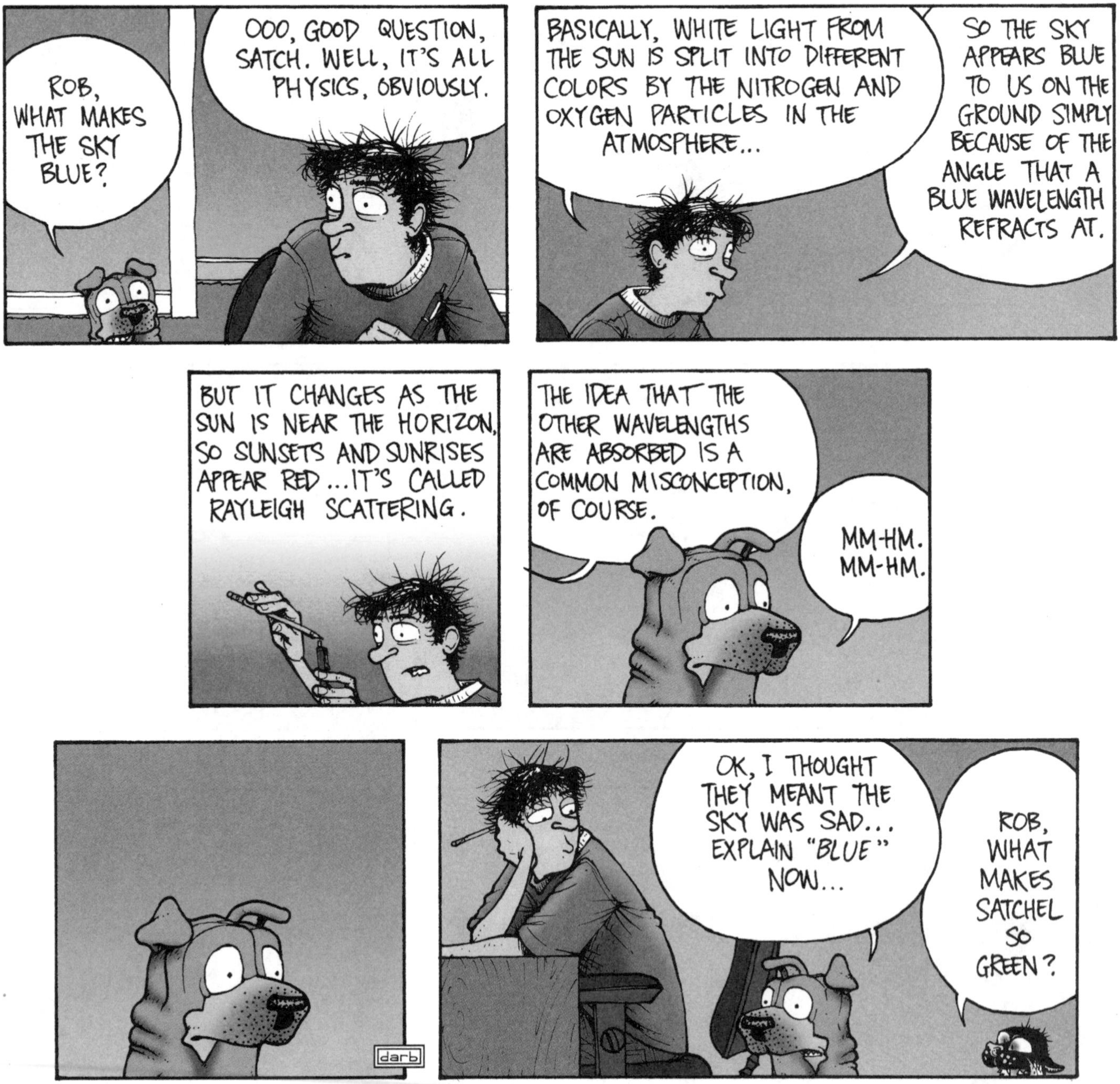
ROB, WHAT MAKES THE SKY BLUE?
OOO, GOOD QUESTION, SATCH. WELL, IT'S ALL PHYSICS, OBVIOUSLY.
BASICALLY, WHITE LIGHT FROM THE SUN IS SPLIT INTO DIFFERENT COLORS BY THE NITROGEN AND OXYGEN PARTICLES IN THE ATMOSPHERE...
SO THE SKY APPEARS BLUE TO US ON THE GROUND SIMPLY BECAUSE OF THE ANGLE THAT A BLUE WAVELENGTH REFRACTS AT.
BUT IT CHANGES AS THE SUN IS NEAR THE HORIZON, SO SUNSETS AND SUNRISES APPEAR RED...IT'S CALLED RAYLEIGH SCATTERING.
THE IDEA THAT THE OTHER WAVELENGTHS ARE ABSORBED IS A COMMON MISCONCEPTION, OF COURSE.
MM-HM. MM-HM.
darb
OK, I THOUGHT THEY MEANT THE SKY WAS SAD... EXPLAIN "BLUE" NOW...
ROB, WHAT MAKES SATCHEL SO GREEN?

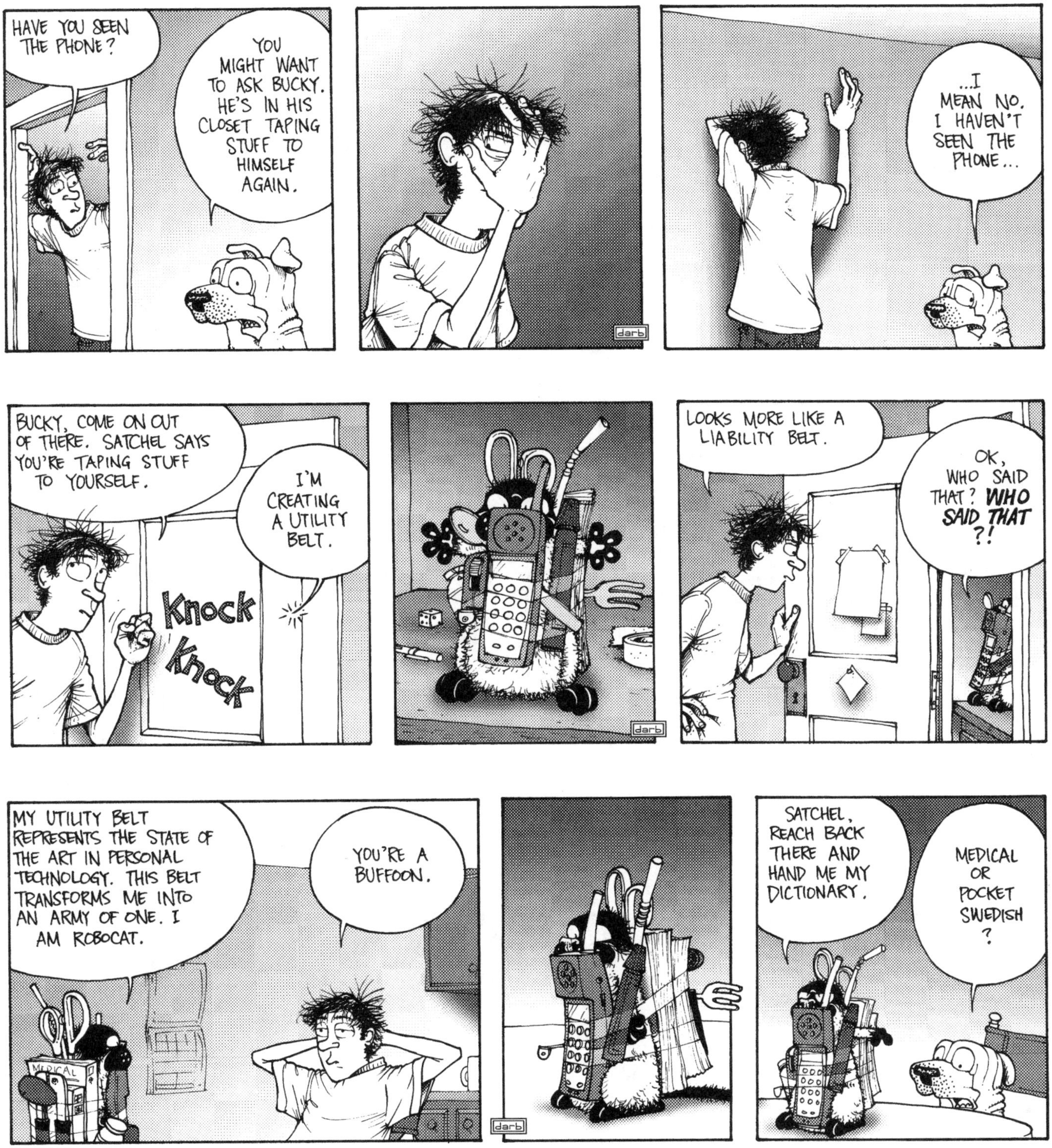
HAVE YOU SEEN THE PHONE?
YOU MIGHT WANT TO ASK BUCKY. HE'S IN HIS CLOSET TAPING STUFF TO HIMSELF AGAIN.
...I MEAN NO. I HAVEN'T SEEN THE PHONE...
BUCKY, COME ON OUT OF THERE. SATCHEL SAYS YOU'RE TAPING STUFF TO YOURSELF.
I'M CREATING A UTILITY BELT.
Knock Knock
LOOKS MORE LIKE A LIABILITY BELT.
OK, WHO SAID THAT? WHO SAID THAT?!
MY UTILITY BELT REPRESENTS THE STATE OF THE ART IN PERSONAL TECHNOLOGY. THIS BELT TRANSFORMS ME INTO AN ARMY OF ONE. I AM ROBOCAT.
YOU'RE A BUFFOON.
MEDICAL
SATCHEL, REACH BACK THERE AND HAND ME MY DICTIONARY.
MEDICAL OR POCKET SWEDISH?
darb

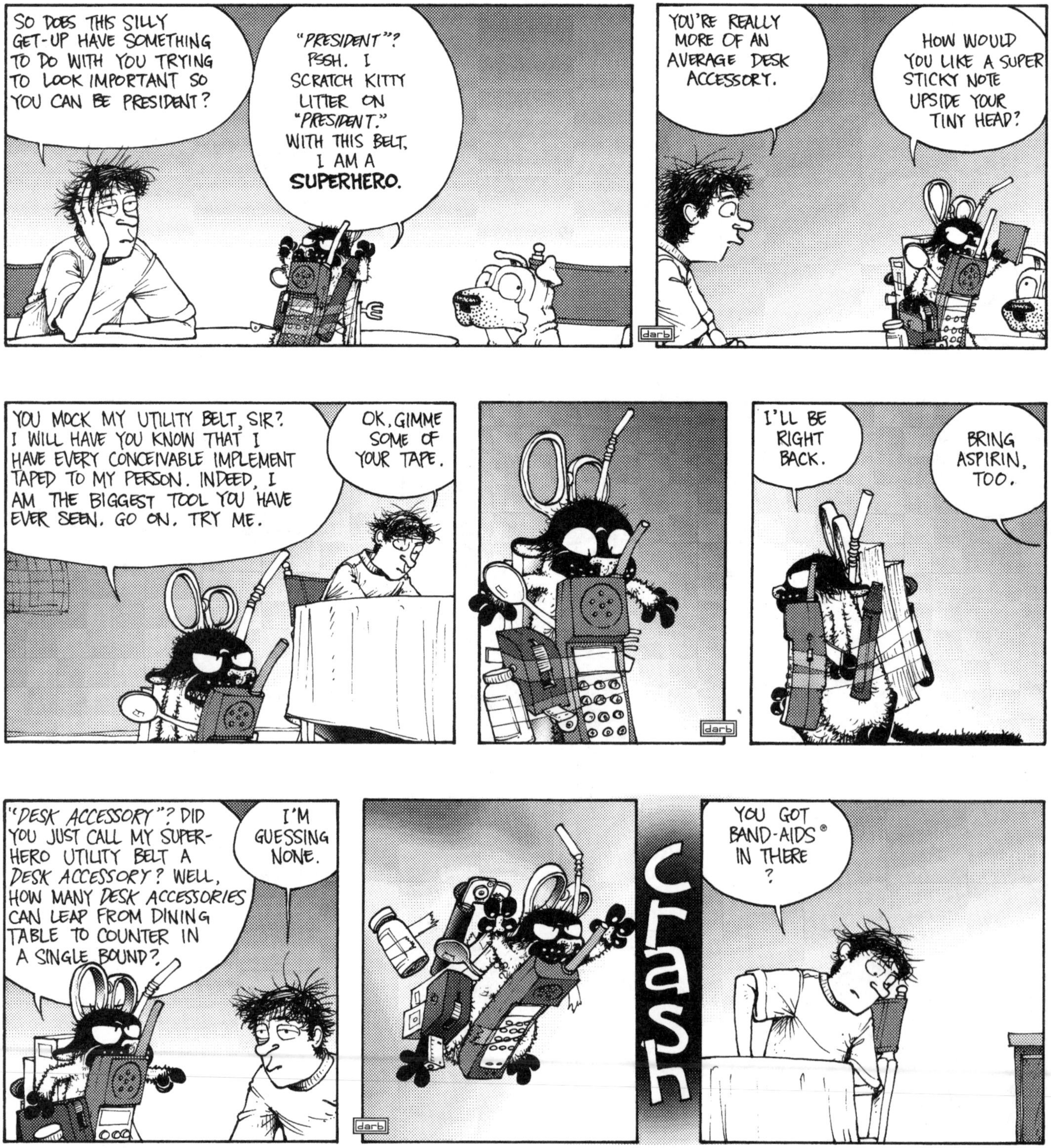
SO DOES THIS SILLY GET-UP HAVE SOMETHING TO DO WITH YOU TRYING TO LOOK IMPORTANT SO YOU CAN BE PRESIDENT?
"PRESIDENT"? PSSH. I SCRATCH KITTY LITTER ON "PRESIDENT." WITH THIS BELT, I AM A SUPERHERO.
YOU'RE REALLY MORE OF AN AVERAGE DESK ACCESSORY.
HOW WOULD YOU LIKE A SUPER STICKY NOTE UPSIDE YOUR TINY HEAD?
darb
YOU MOCK MY UTILITY BELT, SIR? I WILL HAVE YOU KNOW THAT I HAVE EVERY CONCEIVABLE IMPLEMENT TAPED TO MY PERSON. INDEED, I AM THE BIGGEST TOOL YOU HAVE EVER SEEN. GO ON. TRY ME.
OK, GIMME SOME OF YOUR TAPE.
darb
I'LL BE RIGHT BACK.
BRING ASPIRIN, TOO.
"DESK ACCESSORY"? DID YOU JUST CALL MY SUPER-HERO UTILITY BELT A DESK ACCESSORY? WELL, HOW MANY DESK ACCESSORIES CAN LEAP FROM DINING TABLE TO COUNTER IN A SINGLE BOUND?
I'M GUESSING NONE.
darb
Crash
YOU GOT BAND-AIDS® IN THERE ?

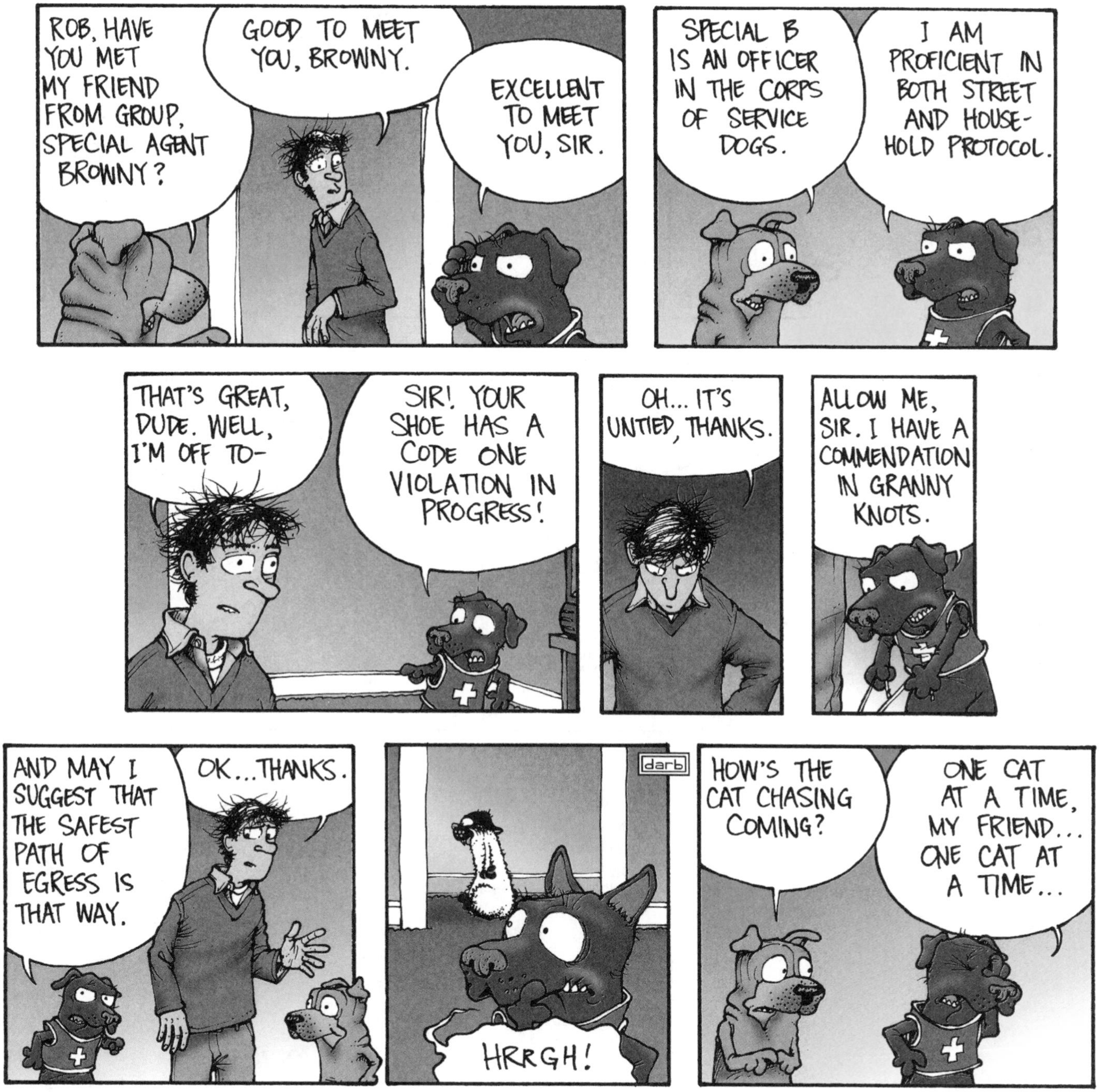
ROB, HAVE YOU MET MY FRIEND FROM GROUP, SPECIAL AGENT BROWNY?
GOOD TO MEET YOU, BROWNY.
EXCELLENT TO MEET YOU, SIR.
SPECIAL B IS AN OFFICER IN THE CORPS OF SERVICE DOGS.
I AM PROFICIENT IN BOTH STREET AND HOUSE-HOLD PROTOCOL.
THAT'S GREAT, DUDE. WELL, I'M OFF TO-
SIR! YOUR SHOE HAS A CODE ONE VIOLATION IN PROGRESS!
OH... IT'S UNTIED, THANKS.
ALLOW ME, SIR. I HAVE A COMMENDATION IN GRANNY KNOTS.
AND MAY I SUGGEST THAT THE SAFEST PATH OF EGRESS IS THAT WAY.
OK... THANKS.
darb
HRRGH!
HOW'S THE CAT CHASING COMING?
ONE CAT AT A TIME, MY FRIEND... ONE CAT AT A TIME...

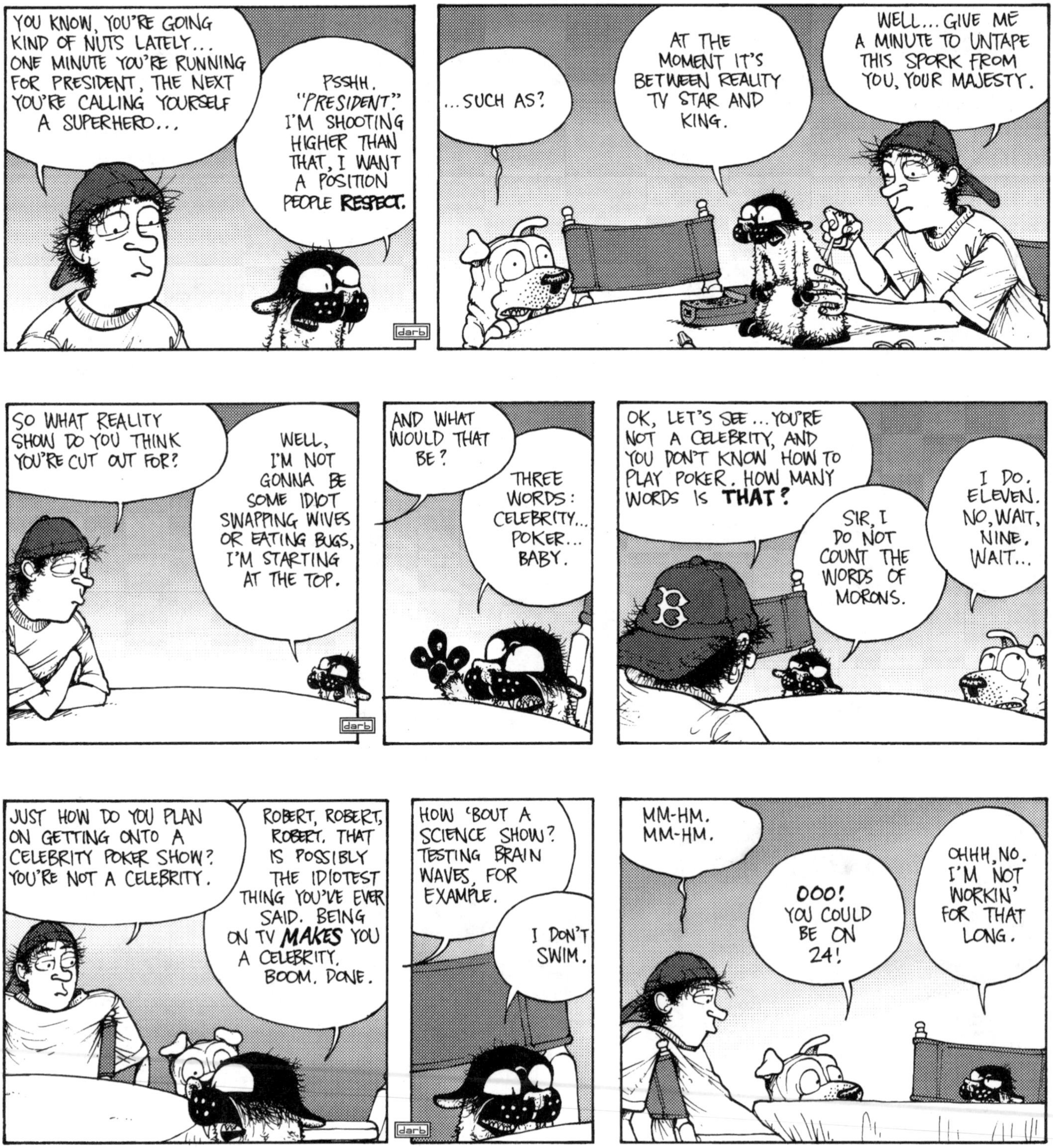
YOU KNOW, YOU'RE GOING KIND OF NUTS LATELY... ONE MINUTE YOU'RE RUNNING FOR PRESIDENT, THE NEXT YOU'RE CALLING YOURSELF A SUPERHERO...
PSSHH. "PRESIDENT." I'M SHOOTING HIGHER THAN THAT, I WANT A POSITION PEOPLE RESPECT.
...SUCH AS?
AT THE MOMENT IT'S BETWEEN REALITY TV STAR AND KING.
WELL... GIVE ME A MINUTE TO UNTAPE THIS SPORK FROM YOU, YOUR MAJESTY.
darb
SO WHAT REALITY SHOW DO YOU THINK YOU'RE CUT OUT FOR?
WELL, I'M NOT GONNA BE SOME IDIOT SWAPPING WIVES OR EATING BUGS, I'M STARTING AT THE TOP.
AND WHAT WOULD THAT BE?
THREE WORDS: CELEBRITY... POKER... BABY.
OK, LET'S SEE... YOU'RE NOT A CELEBRITY, AND YOU DON'T KNOW HOW TO PLAY POKER. HOW MANY WORDS IS THAT?
SIR, I DO NOT COUNT THE WORDS OF MORONS.
I DO. ELEVEN. NO, WAIT, NINE. WAIT...
darb
JUST HOW DO YOU PLAN ON GETTING ONTO A CELEBRITY POKER SHOW? YOU'RE NOT A CELEBRITY.
ROBERT, ROBERT, ROBERT. THAT IS POSSIBLY THE IDIOTEST THING YOU'VE EVER SAID. BEING ON TV MAKES YOU A CELEBRITY. BOOM. DONE.
HOW 'BOUT A SCIENCE SHOW? TESTING BRAIN WAVES, FOR EXAMPLE.
I DON'T SWIM.
MM-HM. MM-HM.
OOO! YOU COULD BE ON 24!
OHHH, NO. I'M NOT WORKIN' FOR THAT LONG.
darb

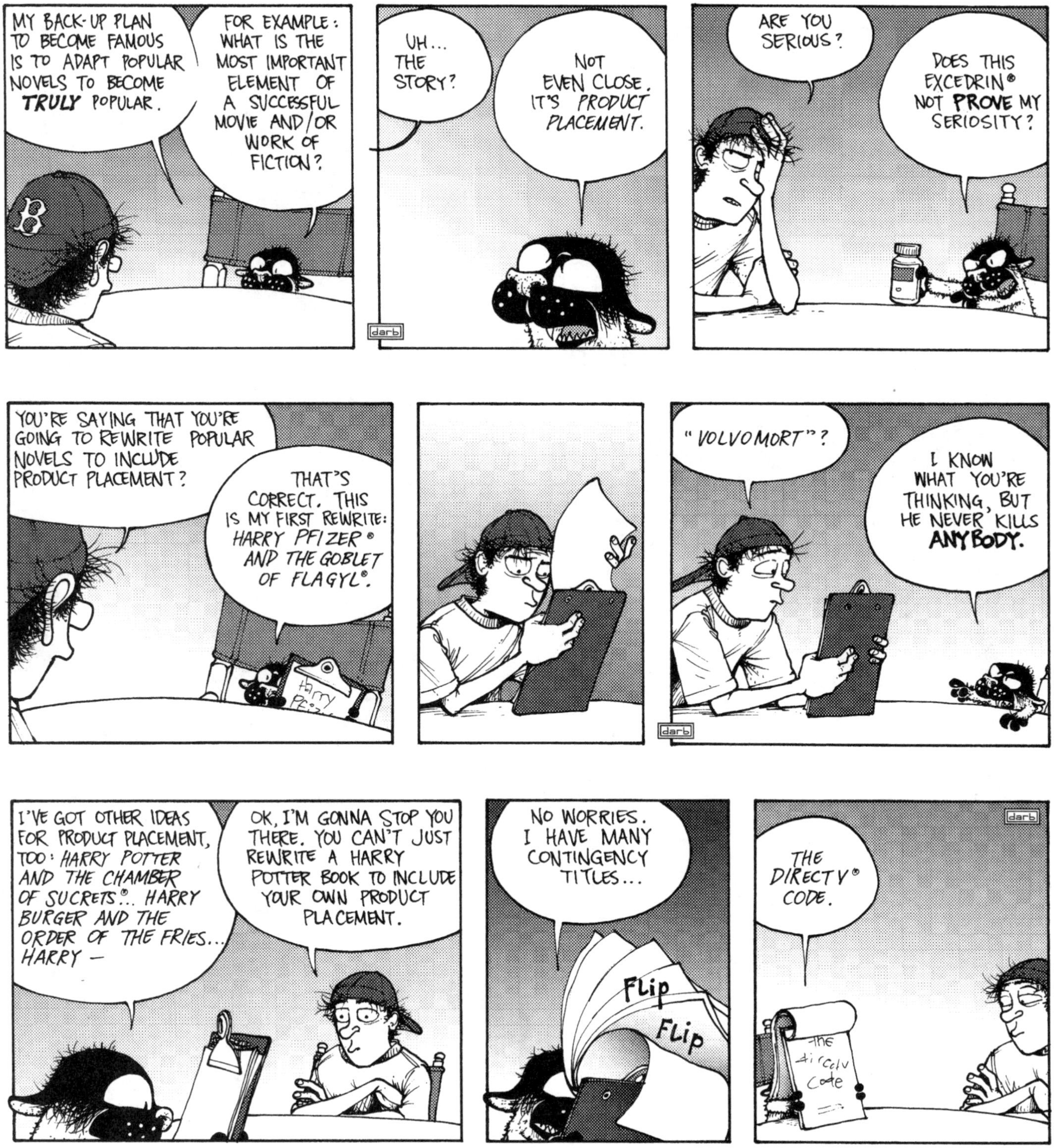
MY BACK-UP PLAN TO BECOME FAMOUS IS TO ADAPT POPULAR NOVELS TO BECOME TRULY POPULAR.
FOR EXAMPLE: WHAT IS THE MOST IMPORTANT ELEMENT OF A SUCCESSFUL MOVIE AND/OR WORK OF FICTION?
UH... THE STORY?
NOT EVEN CLOSE. IT'S PRODUCT PLACEMENT.
darb
ARE YOU SERIOUS?
DOES THIS EXCEDRIN® NOT PROVE MY SERIOSITY?
YOU'RE SAYING THAT YOU'RE GOING TO REWRITE POPULAR NOVELS TO INCLUDE PRODUCT PLACEMENT?
THAT'S CORRECT. THIS IS MY FIRST REWRITE: HARRY PFIZER® AND THE GOBLET OF FLAGYL®.
"VOLVOMORT"?
I KNOW WHAT YOU'RE THINKING, BUT HE NEVER KILLS ANYBODY.
darb
I'VE GOT OTHER IDEAS FOR PRODUCT PLACEMENT, TOO: HARRY POTTER AND THE CHAMBER OF SUCRETS®... HARRY BURGER AND THE ORDER OF THE FRIES... HARRY —
OK, I'M GONNA STOP YOU THERE. YOU CAN'T JUST REWRITE A HARRY POTTER BOOK TO INCLUDE YOUR OWN PRODUCT PLACEMENT.
NO WORRIES. I HAVE MANY CONTINGENCY TITLES...
FLIP
FLIP
darb
THE DIRECTV® CODE.
The directv code

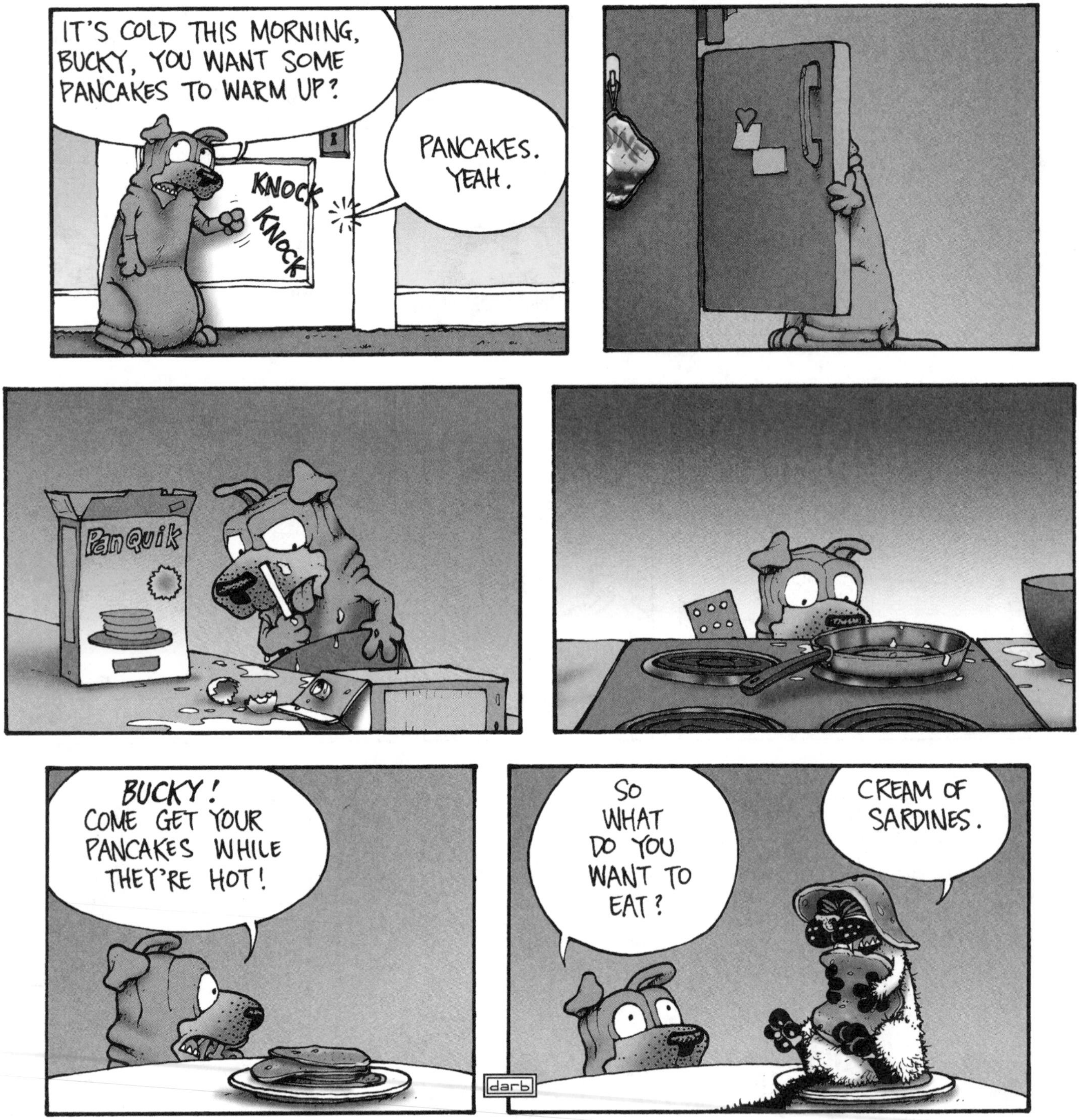
IT'S COLD THIS MORNING, BUCKY, YOU WANT SOME PANCAKES TO WARM UP?
KNOCK KNOCK
PANCAKES. YEAH.
PanQuik
BUCKY! COME GET YOUR PANCAKES WHILE THEY'RE HOT!
SO WHAT DO YOU WANT TO EAT?
CREAM OF SARDINES.
darb

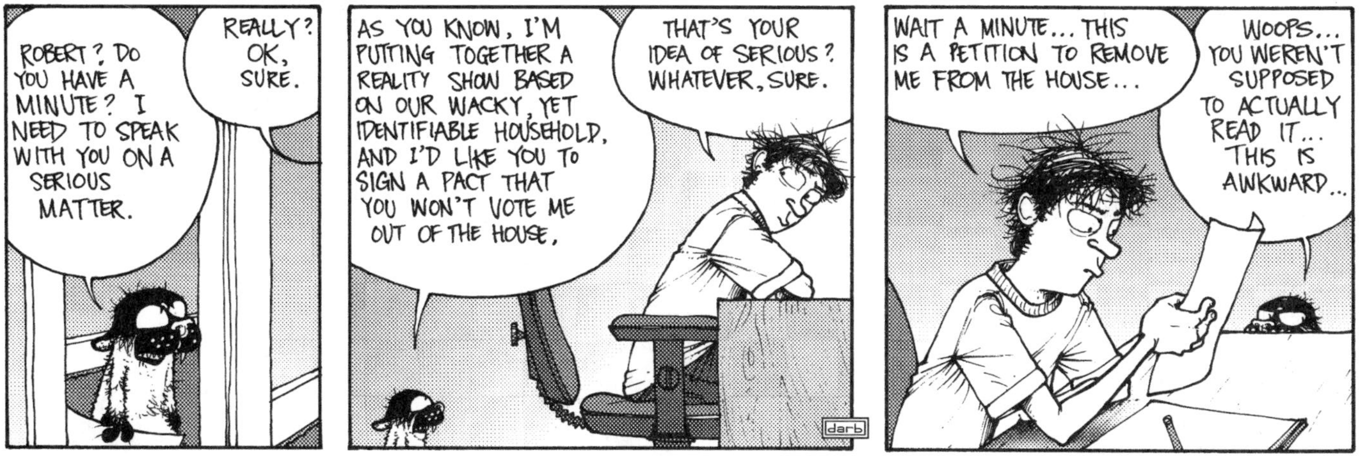
ROBERT? DO YOU HAVE A MINUTE? I NEED TO SPEAK WITH YOU ON A SERIOUS MATTER.
REALLY? OK, SURE.
AS YOU KNOW, I'M PUTTING TOGETHER A REALITY SHOW BASED ON OUR WACKY, YET IDENTIFIABLE HOUSEHOLD, AND I'D LIKE YOU TO SIGN A PACT THAT YOU WON'T VOTE ME OUT OF THE HOUSE.
THAT'S YOUR IDEA OF SERIOUS? WHATEVER, SURE.
darb
WAIT A MINUTE... THIS IS A PETITION TO REMOVE ME FROM THE HOUSE...
WOOPS... YOU WEREN'T SUPPOSED TO ACTUALLY READ IT... THIS IS AWKWARD...

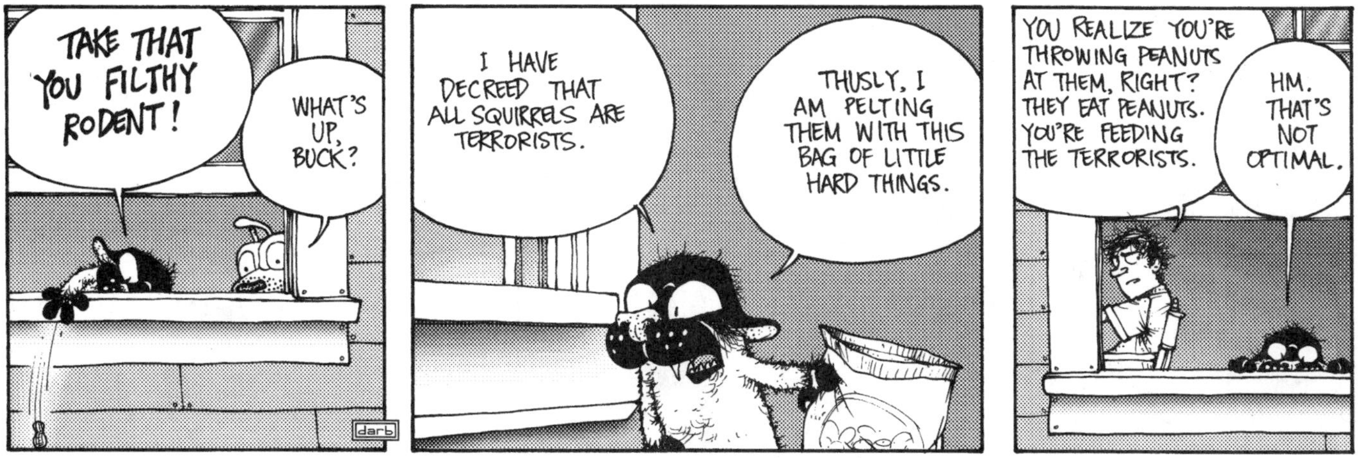
TAKE THAT YOU FILTHY RODENT!
WHAT'S UP, BUCK?
darb
I HAVE DECREED THAT ALL SQUIRRELS ARE TERRORISTS.
THUSLY, I AM PELTING THEM WITH THIS BAG OF LITTLE HARD THINGS.
YOU REALIZE YOU'RE THROWING PEANUTS AT THEM, RIGHT? THEY EAT PEANUTS. YOU'RE FEEDING THE TERRORISTS.
HM. THAT'S NOT OPTIMAL.

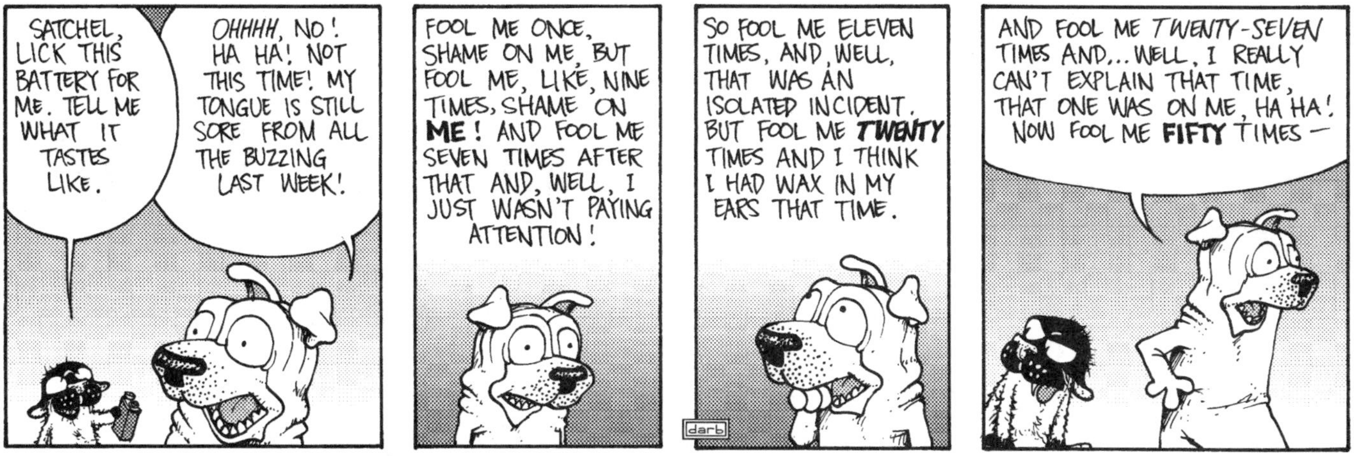
SATCHEL, LICK THIS BATTERY FOR ME. TELL ME WHAT IT TASTES LIKE.
OHHHH, NO! HA HA! NOT THIS TIME! MY TONGUE IS STILL SORE FROM ALL THE BUZZING LAST WEEK!
FOOL ME ONCE, SHAME ON ME, BUT FOOL ME, LIKE, NINE TIMES, SHAME ON ME! AND FOOL ME SEVEN TIMES AFTER THAT AND, WELL, I JUST WASN'T PAYING ATTENTION!
SO FOOL ME ELEVEN TIMES, AND, WELL, THAT WAS AN ISOLATED INCIDENT. BUT FOOL ME TWENTY TIMES AND I THINK I HAD WAX IN MY EARS THAT TIME.
darb
AND FOOL ME TWENTY-SEVEN TIMES AND... WELL, I REALLY CAN'T EXPLAIN THAT TIME, THAT ONE WAS ON ME, HA HA! NOW FOOL ME FIFTY TIMES —

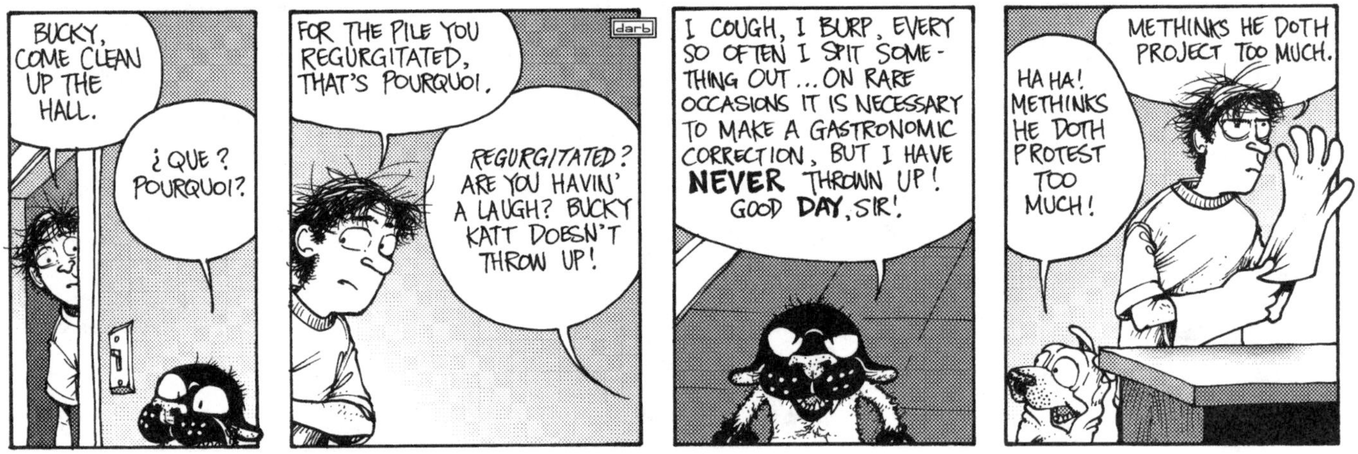
BUCKY, COME CLEAN UP THE HALL.
¿QUE? POURQUOI?
FOR THE PILE YOU REGURGITATED, THAT'S POURQUOI.
REGURGITATED? ARE YOU HAVIN' A LAUGH? BUCKY KATT DOESN'T THROW UP!
I COUGH, I BURP, EVERY SO OFTEN I SPIT SOMETHING OUT... ON RARE OCCASIONS IT IS NECESSARY TO MAKE A GASTRONOMIC CORRECTION, BUT I HAVE **NEVER** THROWN UP! GOOD **DAY**, SIR!
HA HA! METHINKS HE DOTH PROTEST TOO MUCH!
METHINKS HE DOTH PROJECT TOO MUCH.

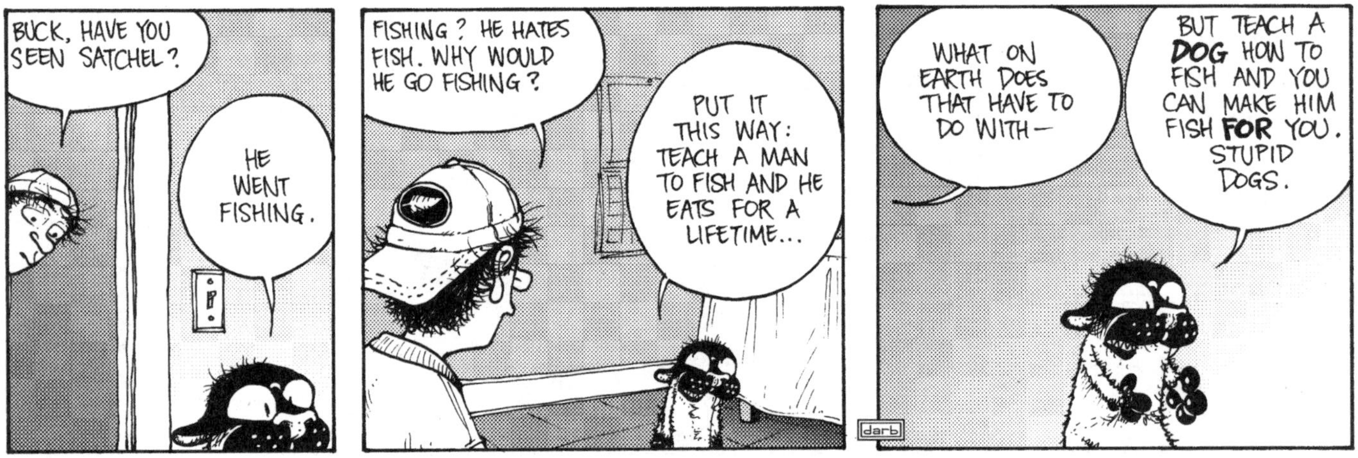
BUCK, HAVE YOU SEEN SATCHEL?
HE WENT FISHING.
FISHING? HE HATES FISH. WHY WOULD HE GO FISHING?
PUT IT THIS WAY: TEACH A MAN TO FISH AND HE EATS FOR A LIFETIME...
WHAT ON EARTH DOES THAT HAVE TO DO WITH—
BUT TEACH A **DOG** HOW TO FISH AND YOU CAN MAKE HIM FISH **FOR** YOU. STUPID DOGS.

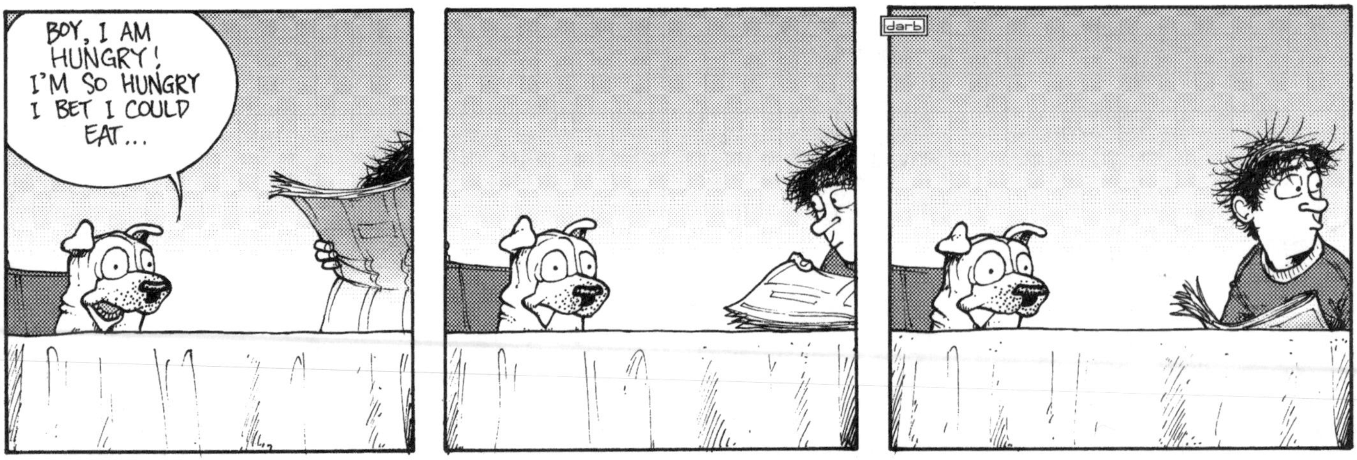
BOY, I AM HUNGRY! I'M SO HUNGRY I BET I COULD EAT...

WHATCHA WATCHIN' ?
HISTORY CHANNEL. PROGRAM ON GOEBBELS.
THE HISTORY CHANNEL HAS A PROGRAM ON GERBILS ?
GOEBBELS WAS A NAZI.
GERBILS ARE **NAZIS** ?
PSSH, FIGURES. FILTHY, FASCIST VERMIN.
darb
I KNEW A SQUIRREL NAMED NUTSY ONCE...HE NEVER HURT ANYBODY, THOUGH.
OH, YEAH? GO ASK A NUT.
OK, I'LL BE..... SOME-WHERE ELSE.

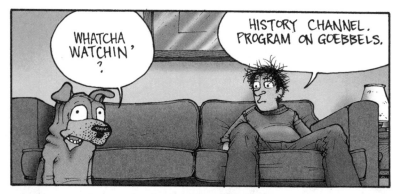

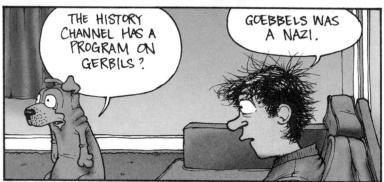

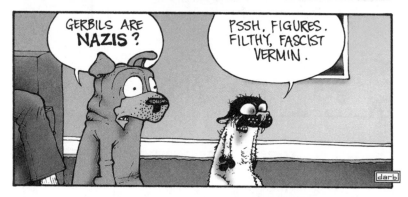

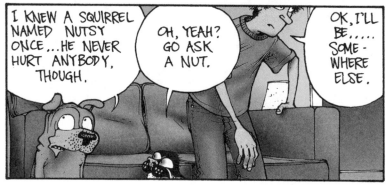

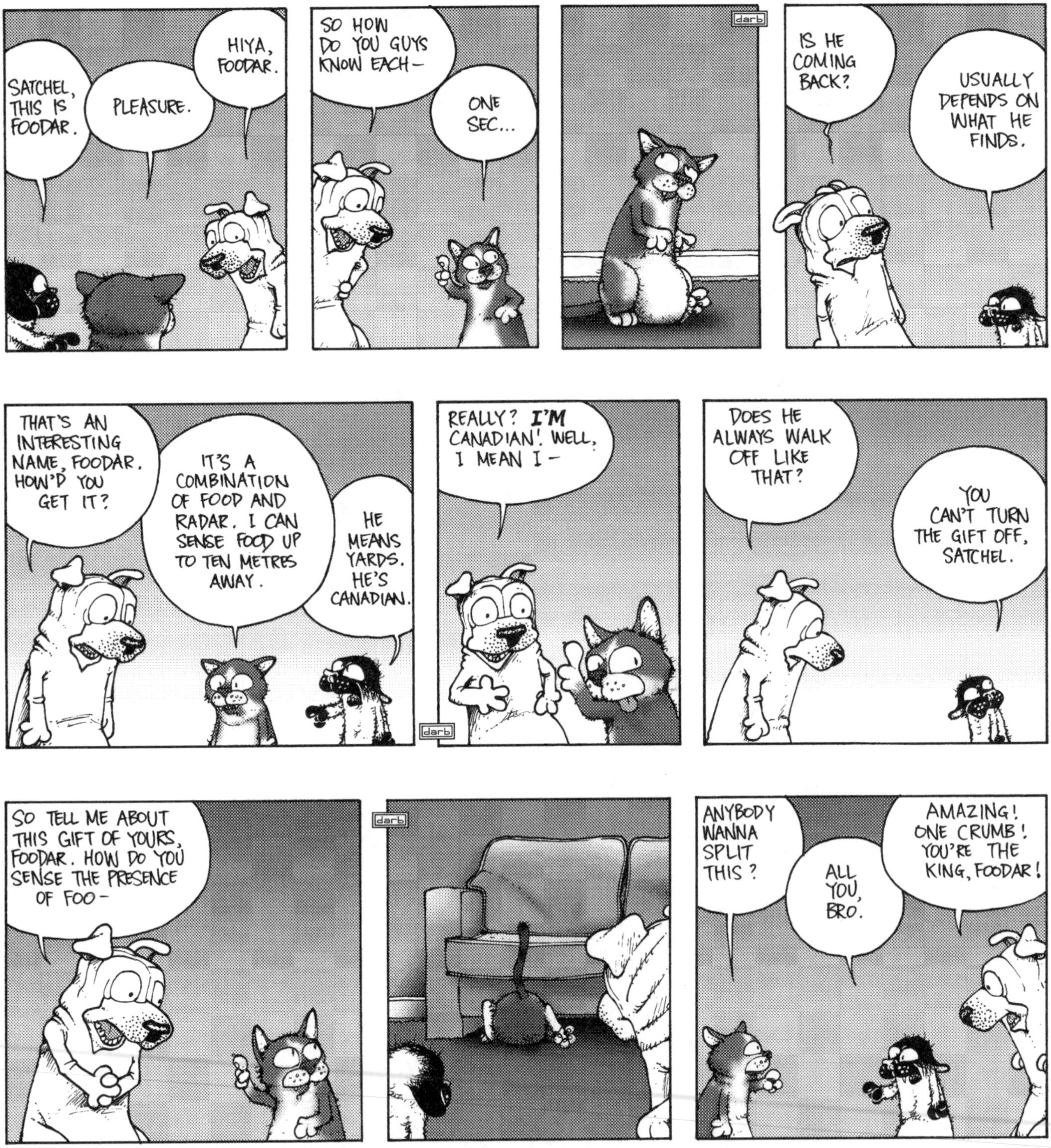
SATCHEL, THIS IS FOODAR.
PLEASURE.
HIYA, FOODAR.
SO HOW DO YOU GUYS KNOW EACH–
ONE SEC...
IS HE COMING BACK?
USUALLY DEPENDS ON WHAT HE FINDS.
THAT'S AN INTERESTING NAME, FOODAR. HOW'D YOU GET IT?
IT'S A COMBINATION OF FOOD AND RADAR. I CAN SENSE FOOD UP TO TEN METRES AWAY.
HE MEANS YARDS. HE'S CANADIAN.
REALLY? I'M CANADIAN! WELL, I MEAN I–
DOES HE ALWAYS WALK OFF LIKE THAT?
YOU CAN'T TURN THE GIFT OFF, SATCHEL.
SO TELL ME ABOUT THIS GIFT OF YOURS, FOODAR. HOW DO YOU SENSE THE PRESENCE OF FOO–
ANYBODY WANNA SPLIT THIS?
ALL YOU, BRO.
AMAZING! ONE CRUMB! YOU'RE THE KING, FOODAR!

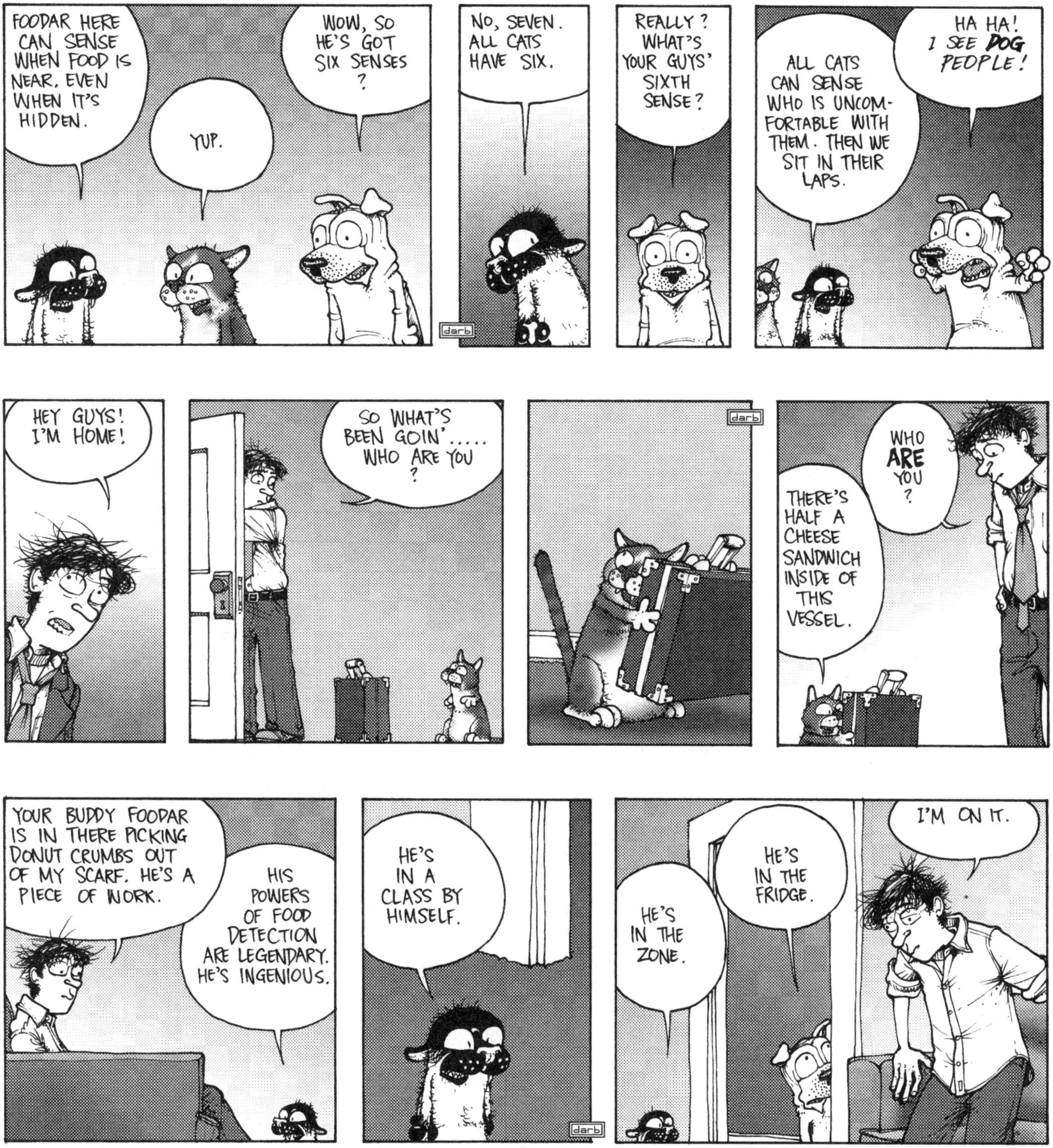
FOODAR HERE CAN SENSE WHEN FOOD IS NEAR. EVEN WHEN IT'S HIDDEN.
YUP.
WOW, SO HE'S GOT SIX SENSES ?
NO, SEVEN. ALL CATS HAVE SIX.
REALLY ? WHAT'S YOUR GUYS' SIXTH SENSE ?
ALL CATS CAN SENSE WHO IS UNCOMFORTABLE WITH THEM. THEN WE SIT IN THEIR LAPS.
HA HA! I SEE DOG PEOPLE!
darb
HEY GUYS! I'M HOME!
SO WHAT'S BEEN GOIN'..... WHO ARE YOU ?
WHO ARE YOU ?
THERE'S HALF A CHEESE SANDWICH INSIDE OF THIS VESSEL.
darb
YOUR BUDDY FOODAR IS IN THERE PICKING DONUT CRUMBS OUT OF MY SCARF. HE'S A PIECE OF WORK.
HIS POWERS OF FOOD DETECTION ARE LEGENDARY. HE'S INGENIOUS.
HE'S IN A CLASS BY HIMSELF.
HE'S IN THE ZONE.
HE'S IN THE FRIDGE.
I'M ON IT.
darb

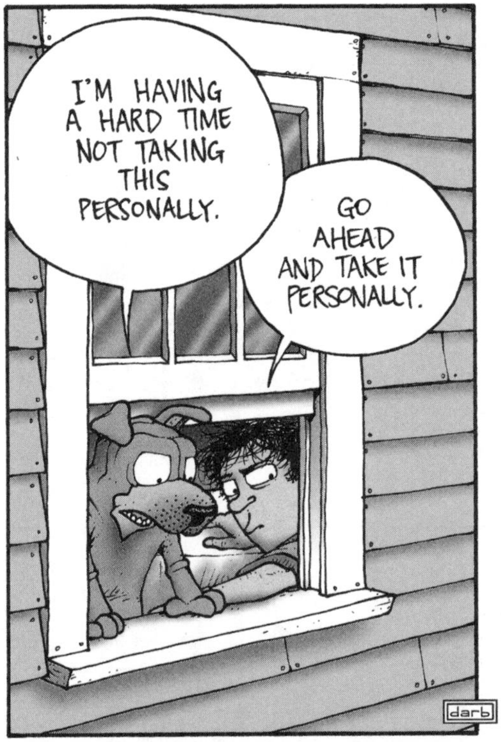
I'M HAVING A HARD TIME NOT TAKING THIS PERSONALLY.
GO AHEAD AND TAKE IT PERSONALLY.
darb

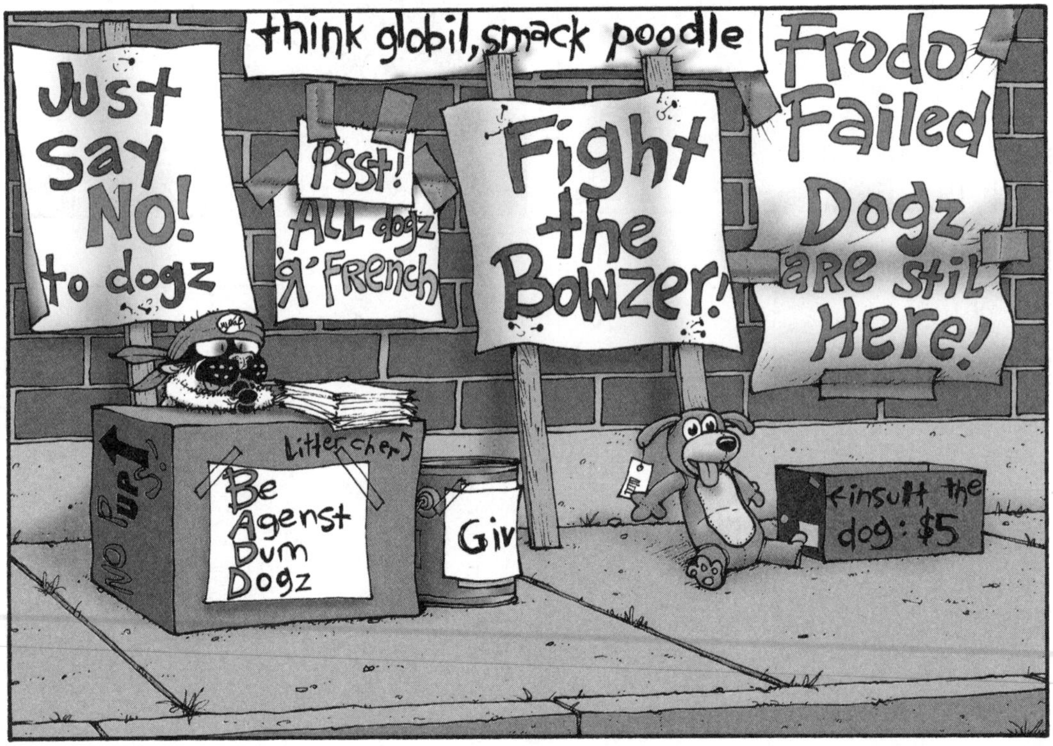
think globil, smack poodle
Just say NO! to dogz
Psst! ALL dogz 'r' French
Fight the Bowzer!
Frodo Failed
Dogz are stil Here!
Litter cher5
NO PUPS!
Be Agenst Dum Dogz
Giv
insult the dog: $5

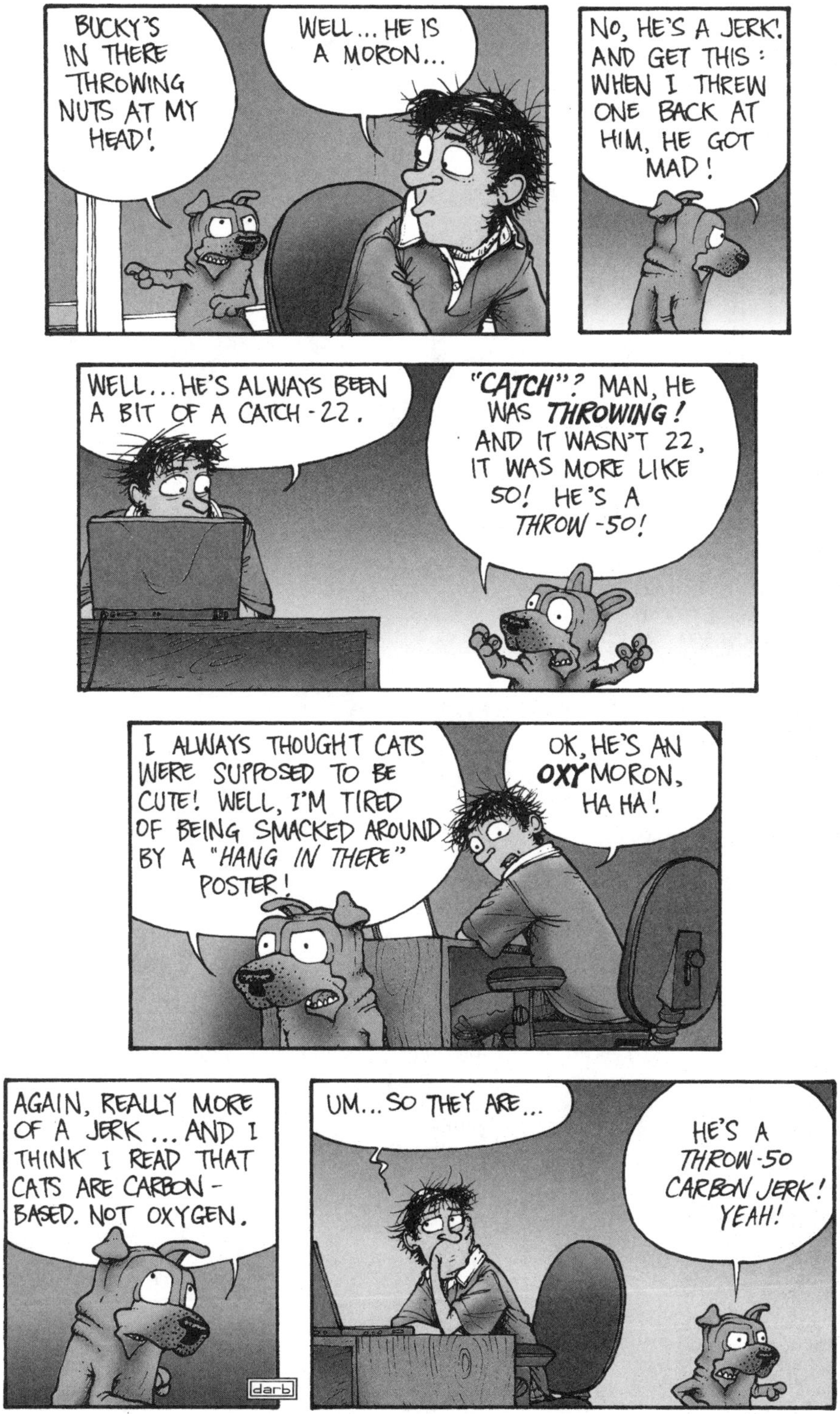
BUCKY'S IN THERE THROWING NUTS AT MY HEAD!
WELL... HE IS A MORON...
NO, HE'S A JERK! AND GET THIS: WHEN I THREW ONE BACK AT HIM, HE GOT MAD!
WELL... HE'S ALWAYS BEEN A BIT OF A CATCH-22.
"CATCH"? MAN, HE WAS THROWING! AND IT WASN'T 22, IT WAS MORE LIKE 50! HE'S A THROW-50!
I ALWAYS THOUGHT CATS WERE SUPPOSED TO BE CUTE! WELL, I'M TIRED OF BEING SMACKED AROUND BY A "HANG IN THERE" POSTER!
OK, HE'S AN OXYMORON, HA HA!
AGAIN, REALLY MORE OF A JERK... AND I THINK I READ THAT CATS ARE CARBON-BASED. NOT OXYGEN.
darb
UM... SO THEY ARE...
HE'S A THROW-50 CARBON JERK! YEAH!

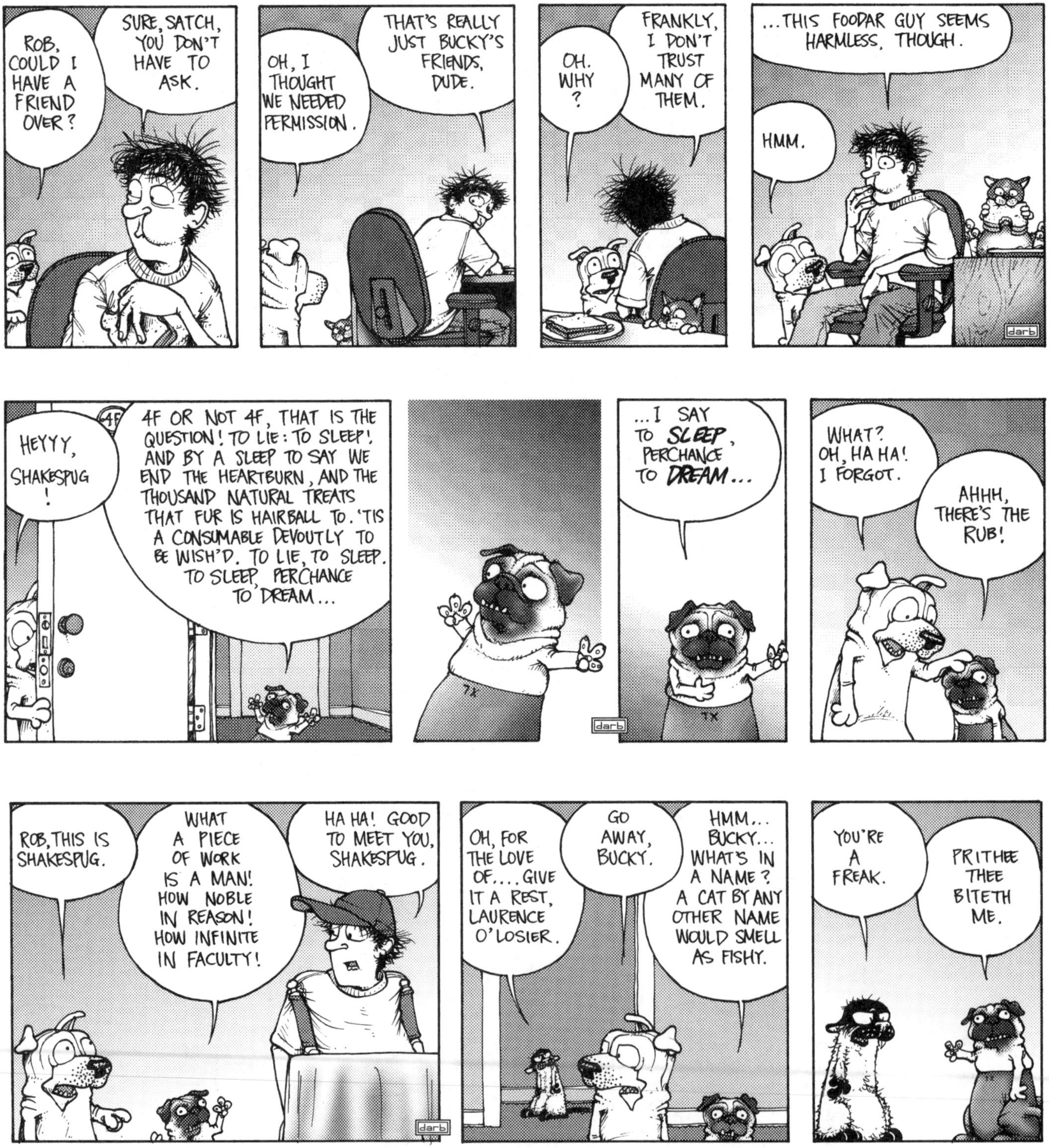

ROB, COULD I HAVE A FRIEND OVER?
SURE, SATCH, YOU DON'T HAVE TO ASK.
OH, I THOUGHT WE NEEDED PERMISSION.
THAT'S REALLY JUST BUCKY'S FRIENDS, DUDE.
OH. WHY?
FRANKLY, I DON'T TRUST MANY OF THEM.
...THIS FOODAR GUY SEEMS HARMLESS, THOUGH.
HMM.
darb
HEYYY, SHAKESPUG!
4F
4F OR NOT 4F, THAT IS THE QUESTION! TO LIE: TO SLEEP! AND BY A SLEEP TO SAY WE END THE HEARTBURN, AND THE THOUSAND NATURAL TREATS THAT FUR IS HAIRBALL TO. 'TIS A CONSUMABLE DEVOUTLY TO BE WISH'D. TO LIE, TO SLEEP. TO SLEEP, PERCHANCE TO DREAM...
darb
...I SAY TO **SLEEP**, PERCHANCE TO **DREAM**...
WHAT? OH, HA HA! I FORGOT.
AHHH, THERE'S THE RUB!
ROB, THIS IS SHAKESPUG.
WHAT A PIECE OF WORK IS A MAN! HOW NOBLE IN REASON! HOW INFINITE IN FACULTY!
HA HA! GOOD TO MEET YOU, SHAKESPUG.
darb
OH, FOR THE LOVE OF.... GIVE IT A REST, LAURENCE O'LOSIER.
GO AWAY, BUCKY.
HMM... BUCKY... WHAT'S IN A NAME? A CAT BY ANY OTHER NAME WOULD SMELL AS FISHY.
YOU'RE A FREAK.
PRITHEE THEE BITETH ME.

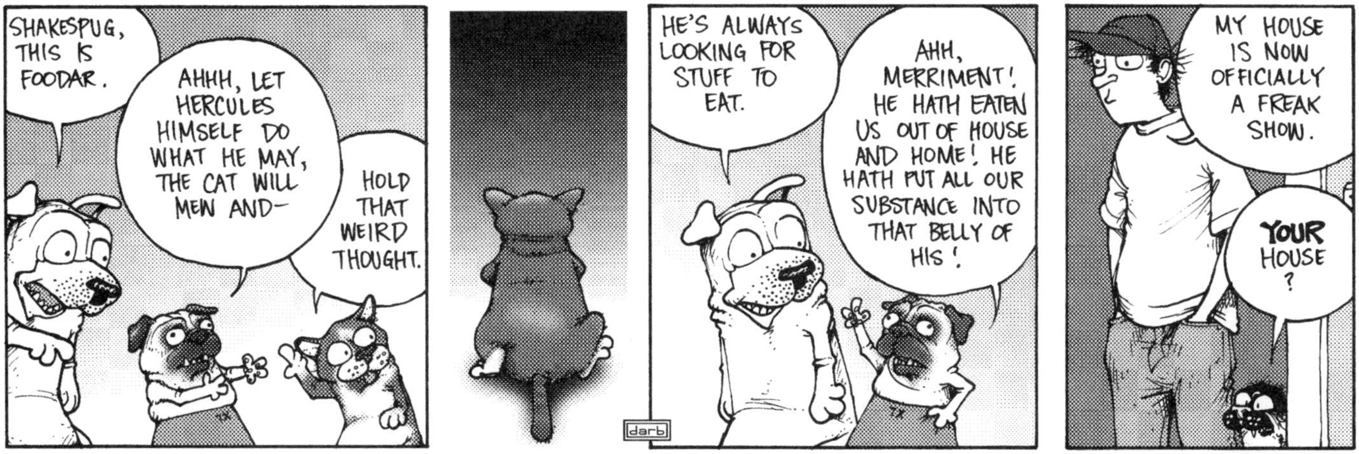
SHAKESPUG, THIS IS FOODAR.
AHHH, LET HERCULES HIMSELF DO WHAT HE MAY, THE CAT WILL MEW AND—
HOLD THAT WEIRD THOUGHT.
HE'S ALWAYS LOOKING FOR STUFF TO EAT.
AHH, MERRIMENT! HE HATH EATEN US OUT OF HOUSE AND HOME! HE HATH PUT ALL OUR SUBSTANCE INTO THAT BELLY OF HIS!
MY HOUSE IS NOW OFFICIALLY A FREAK SHOW.
YOUR HOUSE?

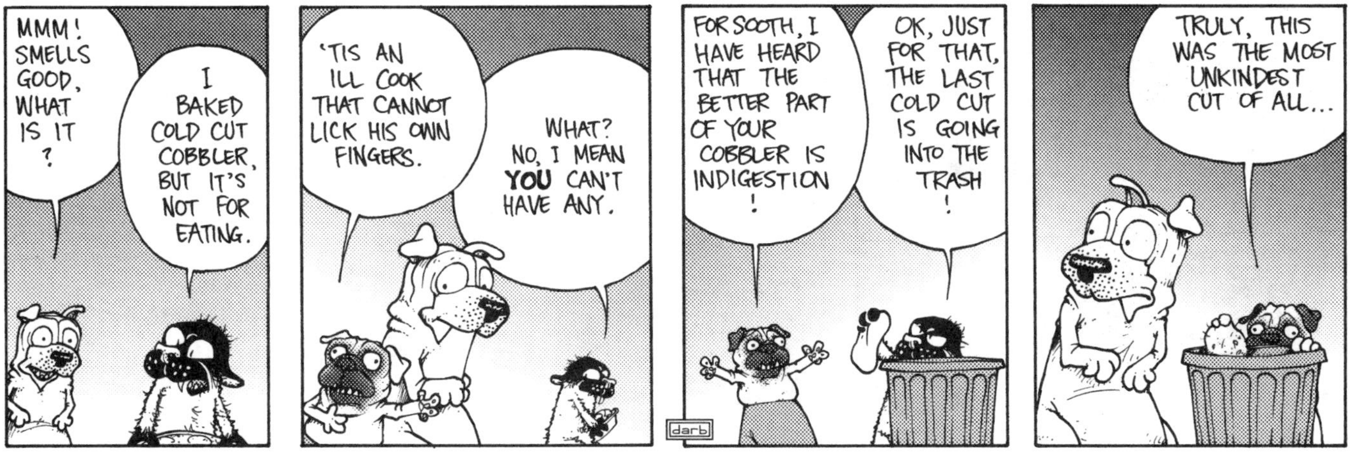
MMM! SMELLS GOOD, WHAT IS IT?
I BAKED COLD CUT COBBLER, BUT IT'S NOT FOR EATING.
'TIS AN ILL COOK THAT CANNOT LICK HIS OWN FINGERS.
WHAT? NO, I MEAN **YOU** CAN'T HAVE ANY.
FORSOOTH, I HAVE HEARD THAT THE BETTER PART OF YOUR COBBLER IS INDIGESTION!
OK, JUST FOR THAT, THE LAST COLD CUT IS GOING INTO THE TRASH!
TRULY, THIS WAS THE MOST UNKINDEST CUT OF ALL...

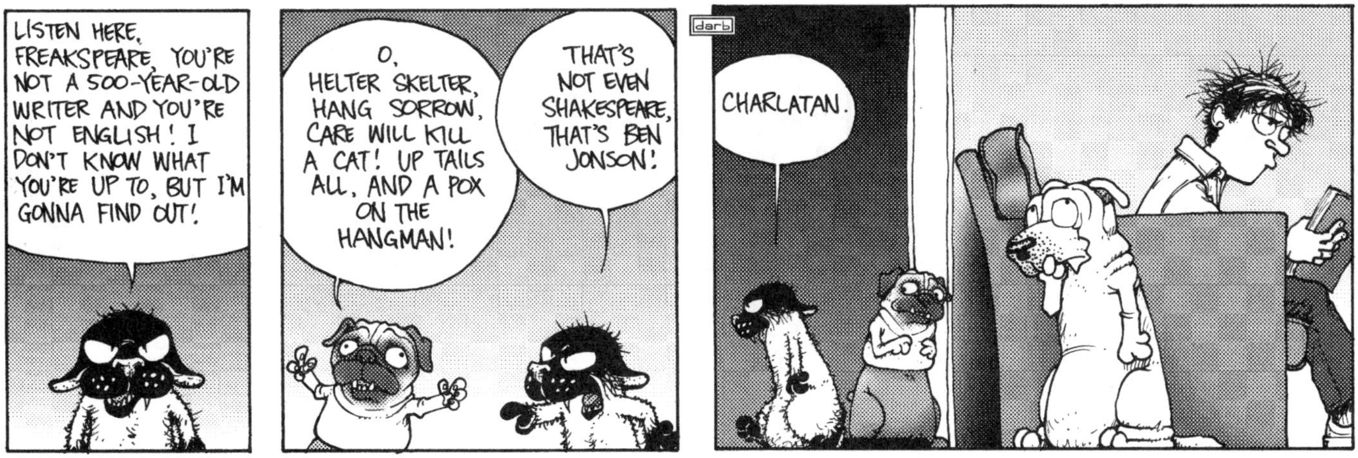
LISTEN HERE, FREAKSPEARE, YOU'RE NOT A 500-YEAR-OLD WRITER AND YOU'RE NOT ENGLISH! I DON'T KNOW WHAT YOU'RE UP TO, BUT I'M GONNA FIND OUT!
O, HELTER SKELTER, HANG SORROW, CARE WILL KILL A CAT! UP TAILS ALL, AND A POX ON THE HANGMAN!
THAT'S NOT EVEN SHAKESPEARE, THAT'S BEN JONSON!
CHARLATAN.

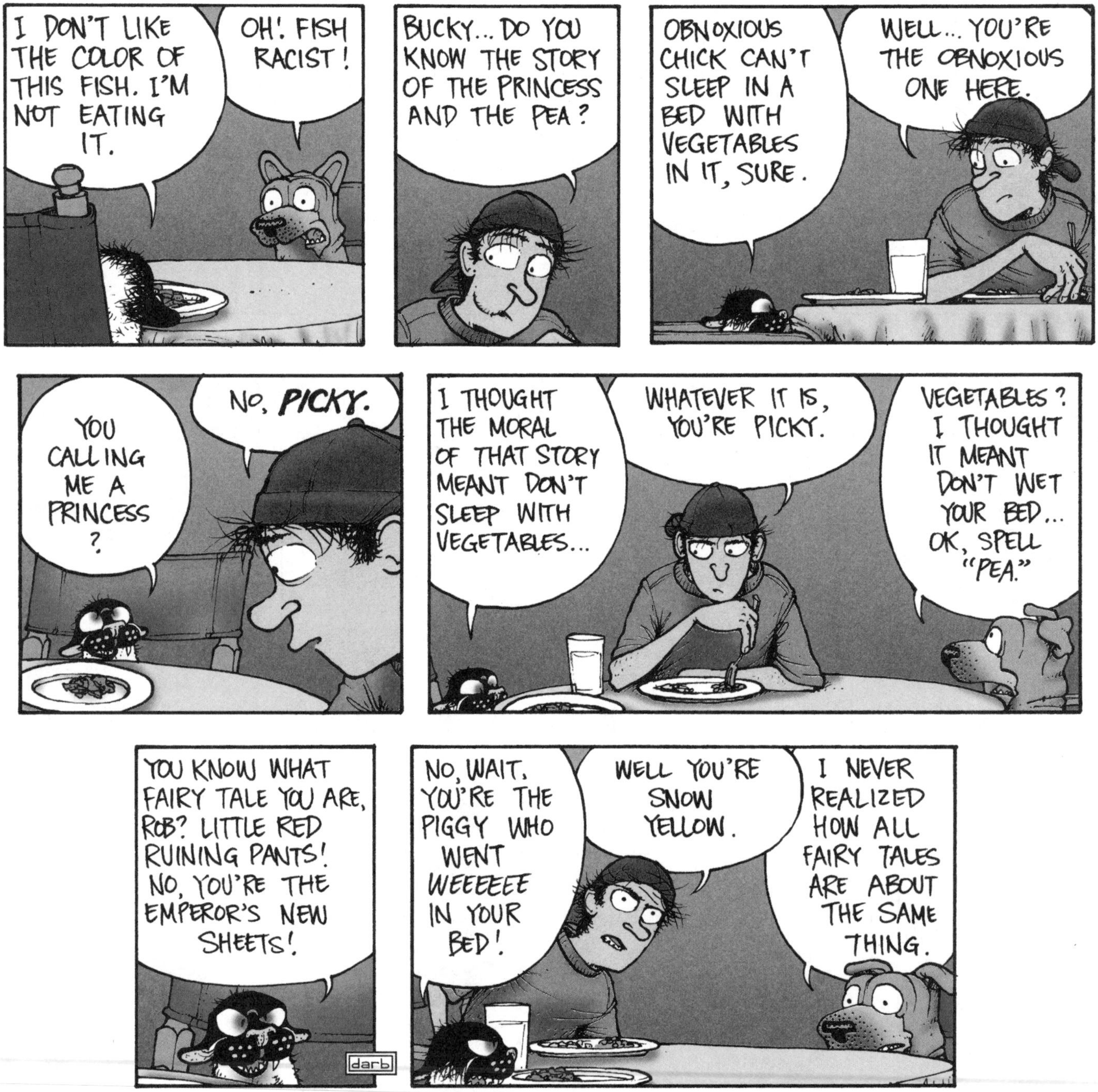
I DON'T LIKE THE COLOR OF THIS FISH. I'M NOT EATING IT.
OH! FISH RACIST!
BUCKY... DO YOU KNOW THE STORY OF THE PRINCESS AND THE PEA?
OBNOXIOUS CHICK CAN'T SLEEP IN A BED WITH VEGETABLES IN IT, SURE.
WELL... YOU'RE THE OBNOXIOUS ONE HERE.
YOU CALLING ME A PRINCESS?
NO, PICKY.
I THOUGHT THE MORAL OF THAT STORY MEANT DON'T SLEEP WITH VEGETABLES...
WHATEVER IT IS, YOU'RE PICKY.
VEGETABLES? I THOUGHT IT MEANT DON'T WET YOUR BED... OK, SPELL "PEA."
YOU KNOW WHAT FAIRY TALE YOU ARE, ROB? LITTLE RED RUINING PANTS! NO, YOU'RE THE EMPEROR'S NEW SHEETS!
darb
NO, WAIT, YOU'RE THE PIGGY WHO WENT WEEEEEE IN YOUR BED!
WELL YOU'RE SNOW YELLOW.
I NEVER REALIZED HOW ALL FAIRY TALES ARE ABOUT THE SAME THING.

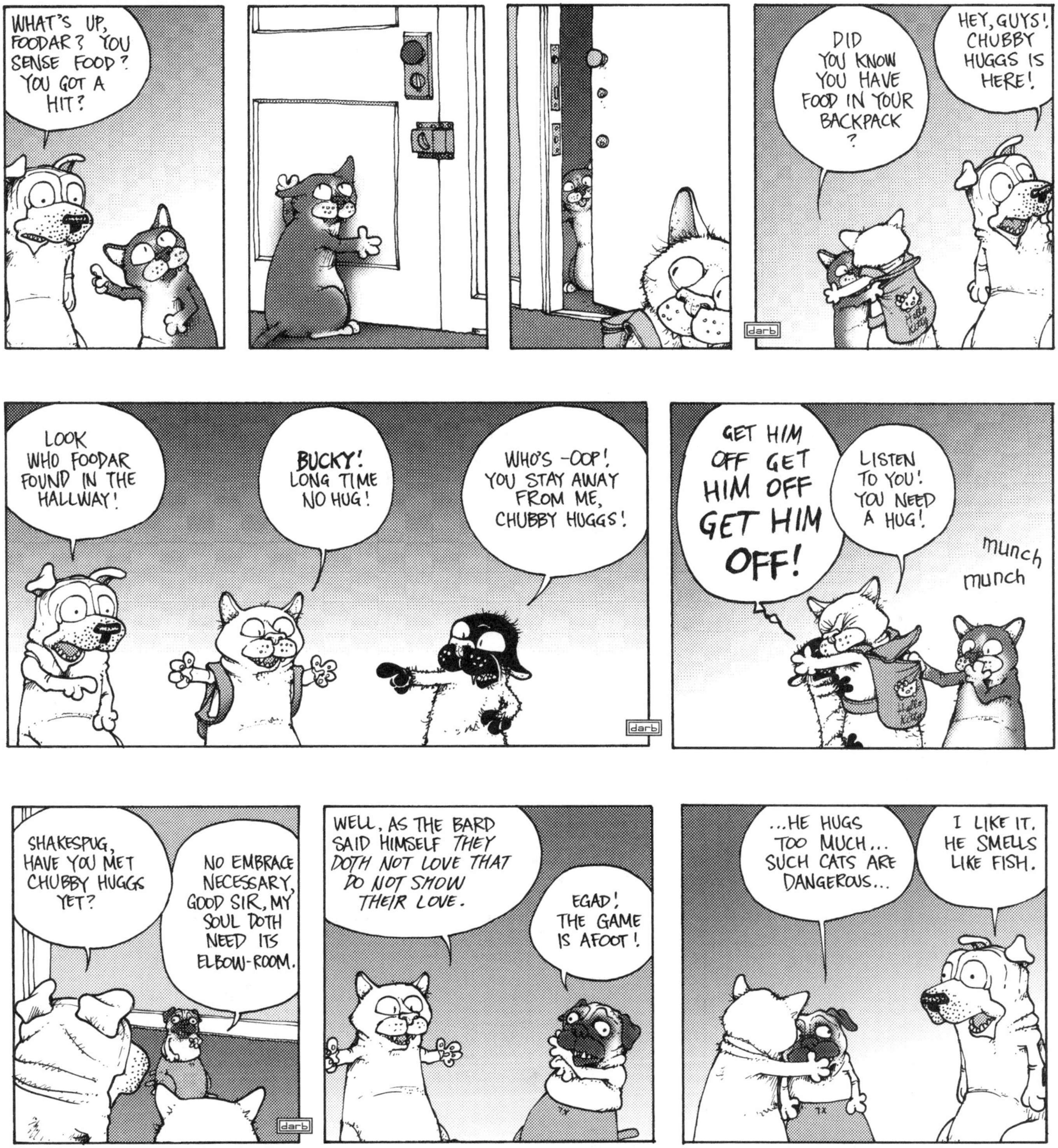
WHAT'S UP, FOODAR? YOU SENSE FOOD? YOU GOT A HIT?
DID YOU KNOW YOU HAVE FOOD IN YOUR BACKPACK?
HEY, GUYS! CHUBBY HUGGS IS HERE!
LOOK WHO FOODAR FOUND IN THE HALLWAY!
BUCKY! LONG TIME NO HUG!
WHO'S -OOP! YOU STAY AWAY FROM ME, CHUBBY HUGGS!
GET HIM OFF GET HIM OFF GET HIM OFF!
LISTEN TO YOU! YOU NEED A HUG!
munch munch
SHAKESPUG, HAVE YOU MET CHUBBY HUGGS YET?
NO EMBRACE NECESSARY, GOOD SIR, MY SOUL DOTH NEED ITS ELBOW-ROOM.
WELL, AS THE BARD SAID HIMSELF *THEY DOTH NOT LOVE THAT DO NOT SHOW THEIR LOVE.*
EGAD! THE GAME IS AFOOT!
...HE HUGS TOO MUCH... SUCH CATS ARE DANGEROUS...
I LIKE IT. HE SMELLS LIKE FISH.

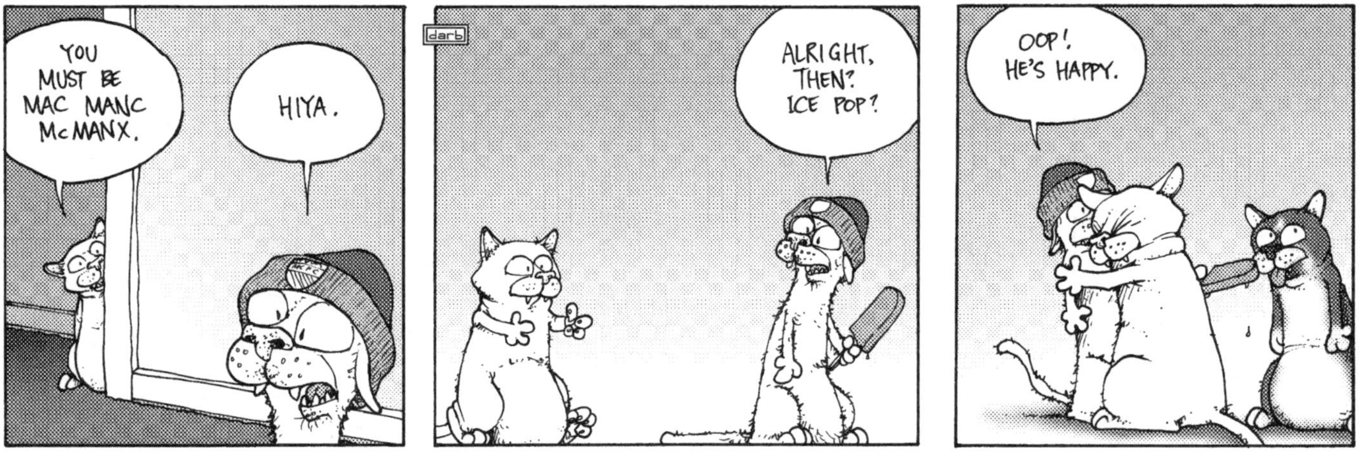
YOU MUST BE MAC MANC McMANX.
HIYA.
ALRIGHT, THEN? ICE POP?
OOP! HE'S HAPPY.

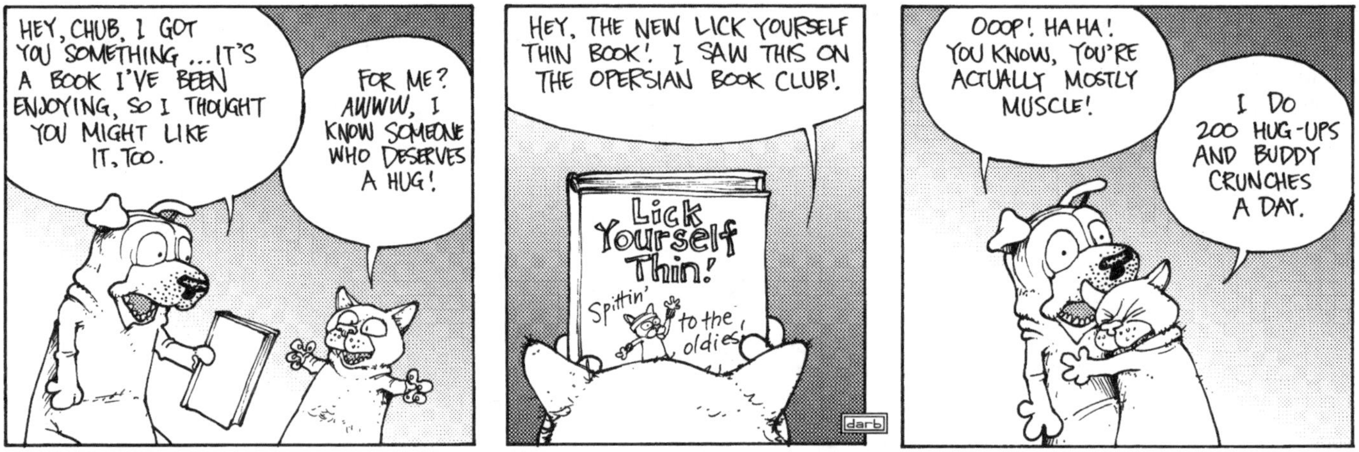
HEY, CHUB, I GOT YOU SOMETHING ... IT'S A BOOK I'VE BEEN ENJOYING, SO I THOUGHT YOU MIGHT LIKE IT, TOO.
FOR ME? AWWW, I KNOW SOMEONE WHO DESERVES A HUG!
HEY, THE NEW LICK YOURSELF THIN BOOK! I SAW THIS ON THE OPERSIAN BOOK CLUB!
Lick Yourself Thin!
Spittin' to the oldies!
OOOP! HA HA! YOU KNOW, YOU'RE ACTUALLY MOSTLY MUSCLE!
I DO 200 HUG-UPS AND BUDDY CRUNCHES A DAY.

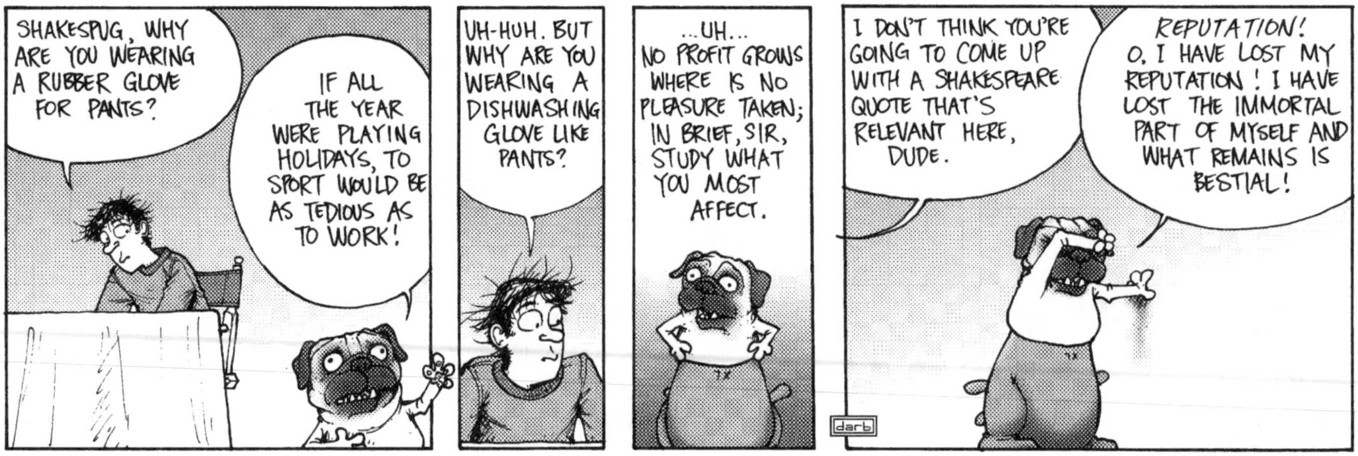
SHAKESPUG, WHY ARE YOU WEARING A RUBBER GLOVE FOR PANTS?
IF ALL THE YEAR WERE PLAYING HOLIDAYS, TO SPORT WOULD BE AS TEDIOUS AS TO WORK!
UH-HUH. BUT WHY ARE YOU WEARING A DISHWASHING GLOVE LIKE PANTS?
...UH... NO PROFIT GROWS WHERE IS NO PLEASURE TAKEN; IN BRIEF, SIR, STUDY WHAT YOU MOST AFFECT.
I DON'T THINK YOU'RE GOING TO COME UP WITH A SHAKESPEARE QUOTE THAT'S RELEVANT HERE, DUDE.
REPUTATION! O, I HAVE LOST MY REPUTATION! I HAVE LOST THE IMMORTAL PART OF MYSELF AND WHAT REMAINS IS BESTIAL!

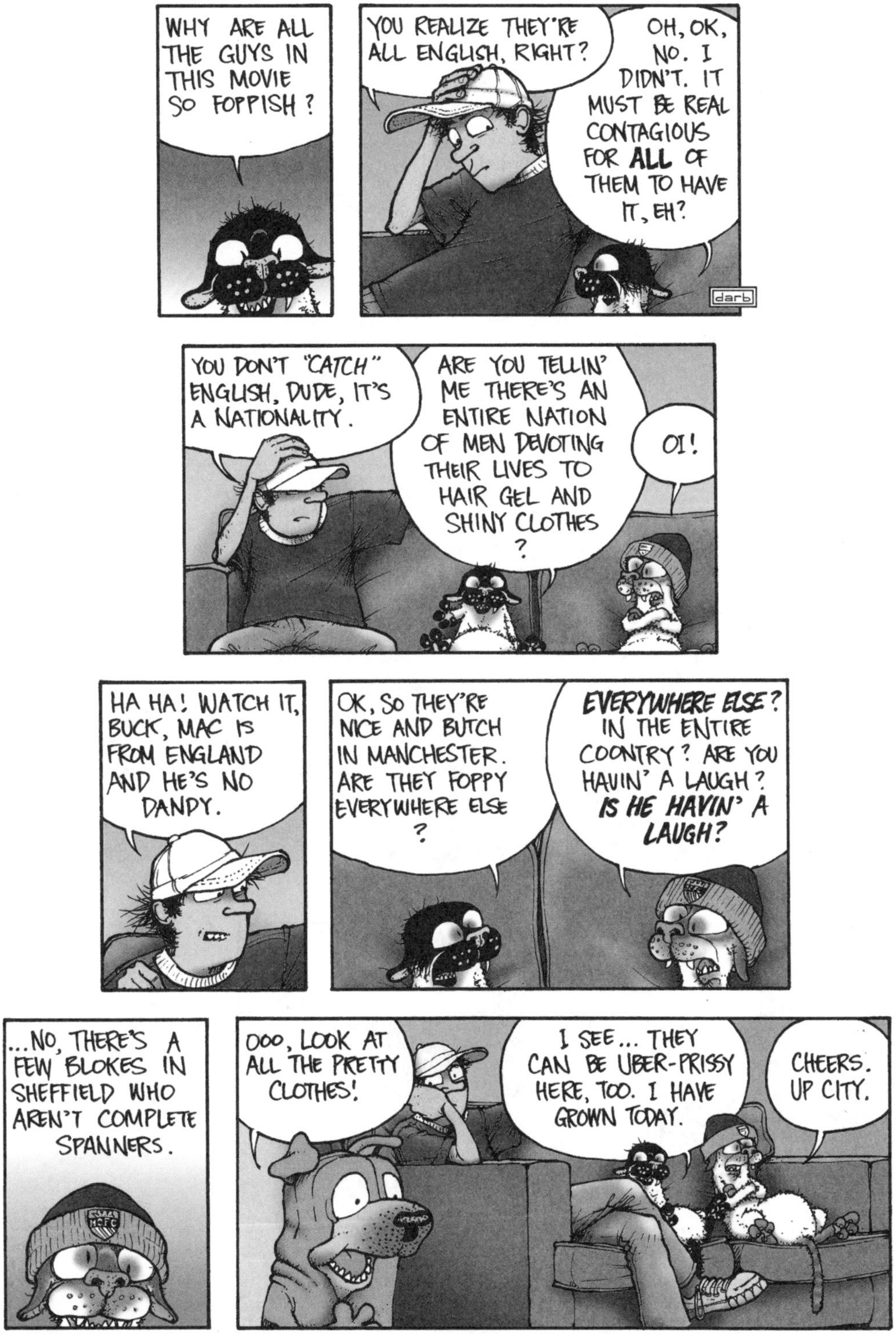
WHY ARE ALL THE GUYS IN THIS MOVIE SO FOPPISH?
YOU REALIZE THEY'RE ALL ENGLISH, RIGHT?
OH, OK, NO. I DIDN'T. IT MUST BE REAL CONTAGIOUS FOR **ALL** OF THEM TO HAVE IT, EH?
darb
YOU DON'T "CATCH" ENGLISH, DUDE, IT'S A NATIONALITY.
ARE YOU TELLIN' ME THERE'S AN ENTIRE NATION OF MEN DEVOTING THEIR LIVES TO HAIR GEL AND SHINY CLOTHES?
OI!
HA HA! WATCH IT, BUCK, MAC IS FROM ENGLAND AND HE'S NO DANDY.
OK, SO THEY'RE NICE AND BUTCH IN MANCHESTER. ARE THEY FOPPY EVERYWHERE ELSE?
EVERYWHERE ELSE? IN THE ENTIRE COONTRY? ARE YOU HAVIN' A LAUGH? ***IS HE HAVIN' A LAUGH?***
...NO, THERE'S A FEW BLOKES IN SHEFFIELD WHO AREN'T COMPLETE SPANNERS.
OOO, LOOK AT ALL THE PRETTY CLOTHES!
I SEE... THEY CAN BE UBER-PRISSY HERE, TOO. I HAVE GROWN TODAY.
CHEERS. UP CITY.

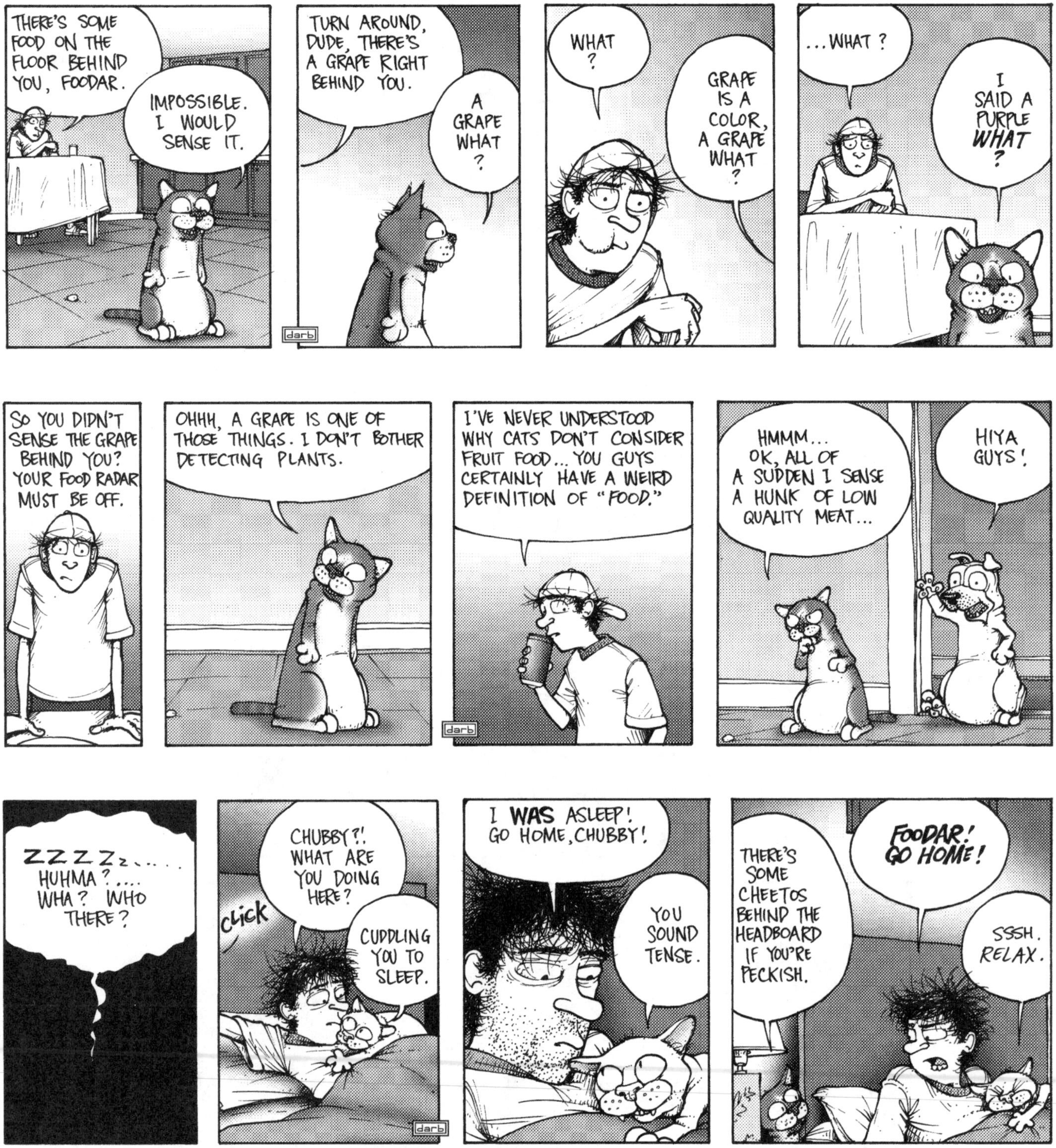

THERE'S SOME FOOD ON THE FLOOR BEHIND YOU, FOODAR.
IMPOSSIBLE. I WOULD SENSE IT.
TURN AROUND, DUDE, THERE'S A GRAPE RIGHT BEHIND YOU.
A GRAPE WHAT ?
WHAT ?
GRAPE IS A COLOR, A GRAPE WHAT ?
... WHAT ?
I SAID A PURPLE WHAT ?
darb
SO YOU DIDN'T SENSE THE GRAPE BEHIND YOU? YOUR FOOD RADAR MUST BE OFF.
OHHH, A GRAPE IS ONE OF THOSE THINGS. I DON'T BOTHER DETECTING PLANTS.
I'VE NEVER UNDERSTOOD WHY CATS DON'T CONSIDER FRUIT FOOD... YOU GUYS CERTAINLY HAVE A WEIRD DEFINITION OF "FOOD."
HMMM... OK, ALL OF A SUDDEN I SENSE A HUNK OF LOW QUALITY MEAT...
HIYA GUYS!
darb
ZZZZz.... HUHMA?.... WHA? WHO THERE?
CLICK
CHUBBY?! WHAT ARE YOU DOING HERE?
CUDDLING YOU TO SLEEP.
I WAS ASLEEP! GO HOME, CHUBBY!
YOU SOUND TENSE.
THERE'S SOME CHEETOS BEHIND THE HEADBOARD IF YOU'RE PECKISH.
FOODAR! GO HOME!
SSSH. RELAX.
darb

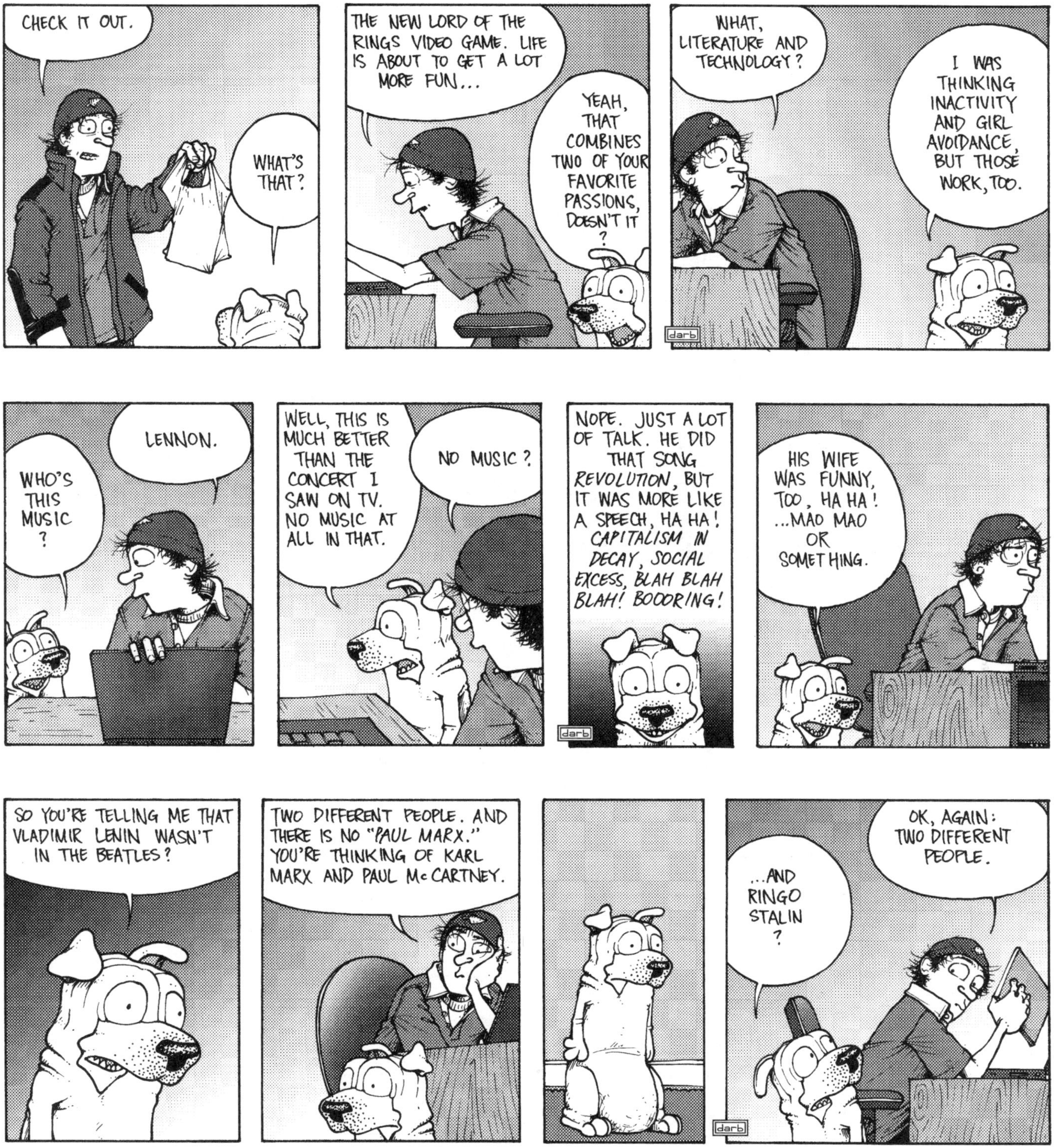
CHECK IT OUT.
WHAT'S THAT?
THE NEW LORD OF THE RINGS VIDEO GAME. LIFE IS ABOUT TO GET A LOT MORE FUN...
YEAH, THAT COMBINES TWO OF YOUR FAVORITE PASSIONS, DOESN'T IT?
WHAT, LITERATURE AND TECHNOLOGY?
I WAS THINKING INACTIVITY AND GIRL AVOIDANCE, BUT THOSE WORK, TOO.
darb
WHO'S THIS MUSIC?
LENNON.
WELL, THIS IS MUCH BETTER THAN THE CONCERT I SAW ON TV. NO MUSIC AT ALL IN THAT.
NO MUSIC?
NOPE. JUST A LOT OF TALK. HE DID THAT SONG *REVOLUTION*, BUT IT WAS MORE LIKE A SPEECH, HA HA! *CAPITALISM IN DECAY, SOCIAL EXCESS, BLAH BLAH BLAH! BOOORING!*
darb
HIS WIFE WAS FUNNY, TOO, HA HA! ...MAO MAO OR SOMETHING.
SO YOU'RE TELLING ME THAT VLADIMIR LENIN WASN'T IN THE BEATLES?
TWO DIFFERENT PEOPLE. AND THERE IS NO "*PAUL MARX.*" YOU'RE THINKING OF KARL MARX AND PAUL McCARTNEY.
darb
...AND RINGO STALIN?
OK, AGAIN: TWO DIFFERENT PEOPLE.

WHAT'S UP?
FOODAR IS SINGING SONGS ABOUT FOOD FOR TREATS. ANY REQUESTS?
ARE THERE ANY SONGS ABOUT TENNIS BALLS? I'M INTO TENNIS BALLS LATELY.
THOSE AREN'T FOOD, SATCHEL.
OH, I THINK YOU'RE WRONG...
OOO, SING THAT SONG ABOUT THE RAT! *BEN*, IT'S CALLED!
LOVE RATS. ALL FUZZY AND CHEWY AND CUTE. *MMMM*...
BUCKY, YOU'VE JUST DESCRIBED A TENNIS BALL!
THEY'RE NOT FOOD, YOU DUMB DOG!
THEN WHY DO THEY COME IN A PRINGLES CAN? WAIT, I'LL GO GET THEM.
MAN, I'M ABOUT TO LOSE IT, HE IS **SO STUPID.**
SOME YOGA WOULD PROBABLY BE GOOD FOR YOU.
NAW, I'M TRYING TO GIVE UP DAIRY.
darb

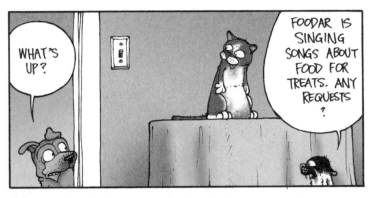

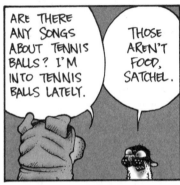

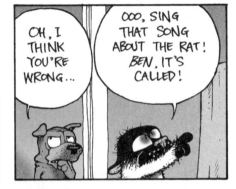

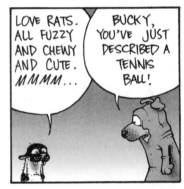

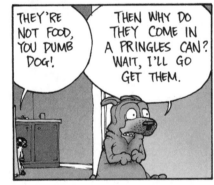

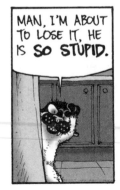

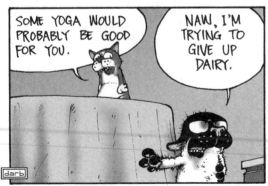

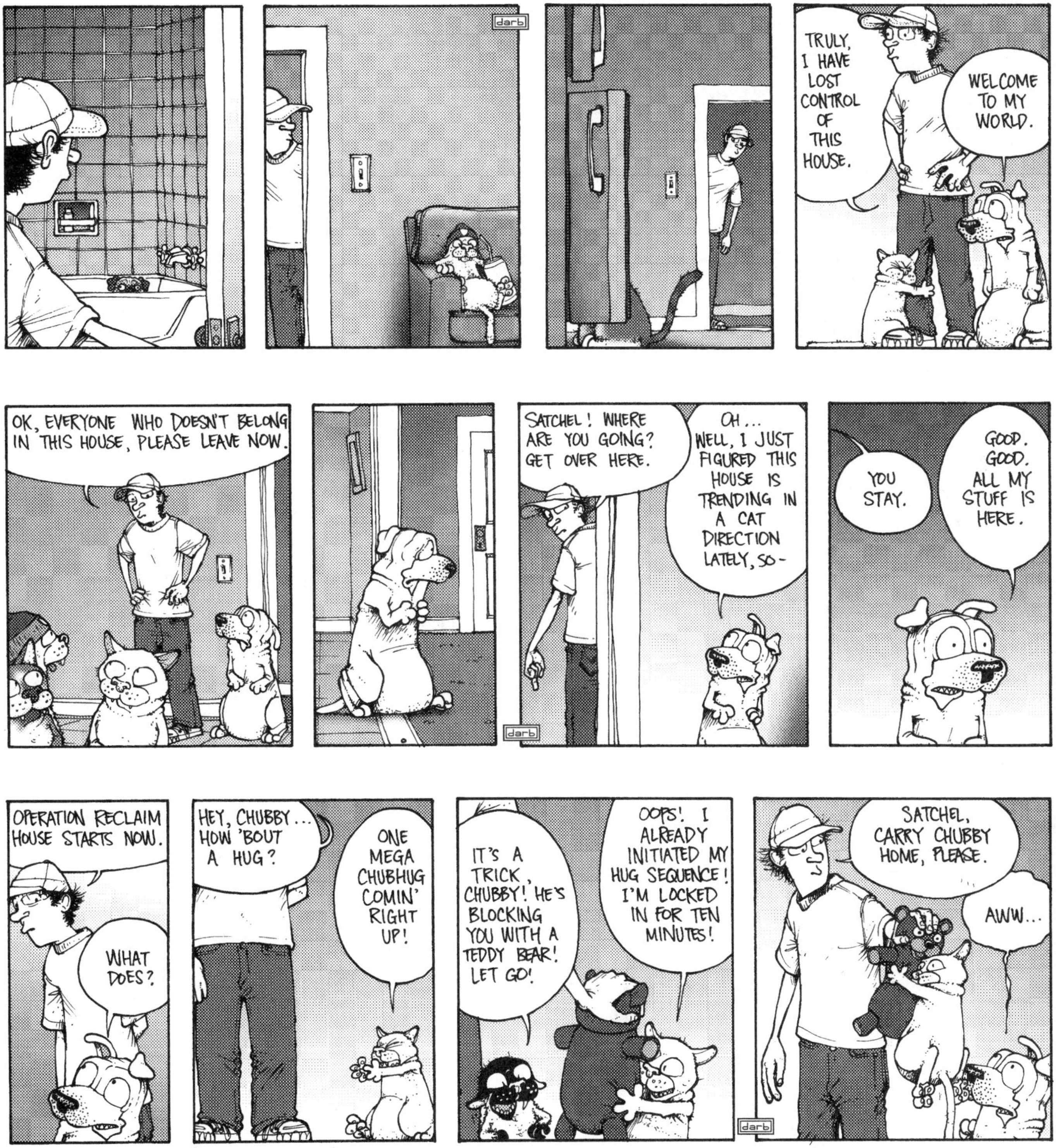
darb
TRULY, I HAVE LOST CONTROL OF THIS HOUSE.
WELCOME TO MY WORLD.
OK, EVERYONE WHO DOESN'T BELONG IN THIS HOUSE, PLEASE LEAVE NOW.
darb
SATCHEL! WHERE ARE YOU GOING? GET OVER HERE.
OH... WELL, I JUST FIGURED THIS HOUSE IS TRENDING IN A CAT DIRECTION LATELY, SO-
YOU STAY.
GOOD. GOOD. ALL MY STUFF IS HERE.
OPERATION RECLAIM HOUSE STARTS NOW.
WHAT DOES?
HEY, CHUBBY... HOW 'BOUT A HUG?
ONE MEGA CHUBHUG COMIN' RIGHT UP!
IT'S A TRICK, CHUBBY! HE'S BLOCKING YOU WITH A TEDDY BEAR! LET GO!
OOPS! I ALREADY INITIATED MY HUG SEQUENCE! I'M LOCKED IN FOR TEN MINUTES!
darb
SATCHEL, CARRY CHUBBY HOME, PLEASE.
AWW...

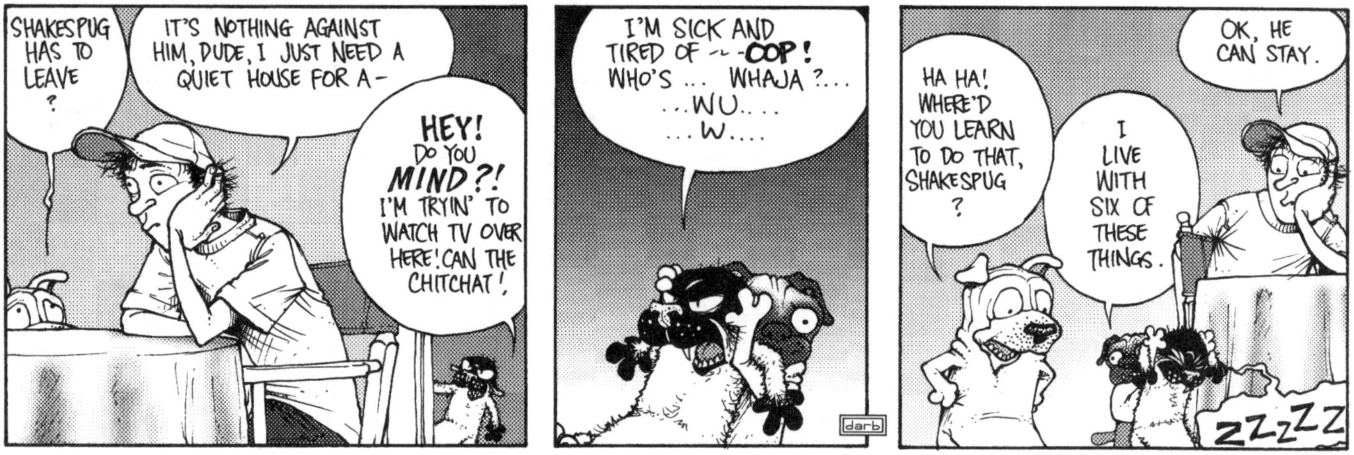
SHAKESPUG HAS TO LEAVE?
IT'S NOTHING AGAINST HIM, DUDE, I JUST NEED A QUIET HOUSE FOR A–
HEY! DO YOU MIND?! I'M TRYIN' TO WATCH TV OVER HERE! CAN THE CHITCHAT!
I'M SICK AND TIRED OF -- COP! WHO'S ... WHAJA?... ...WU... ...W....
darb
HA HA! WHERE'D YOU LEARN TO DO THAT, SHAKESPUG?
I LIVE WITH SIX OF THESE THINGS.
OK, HE CAN STAY.
ZZZZZ

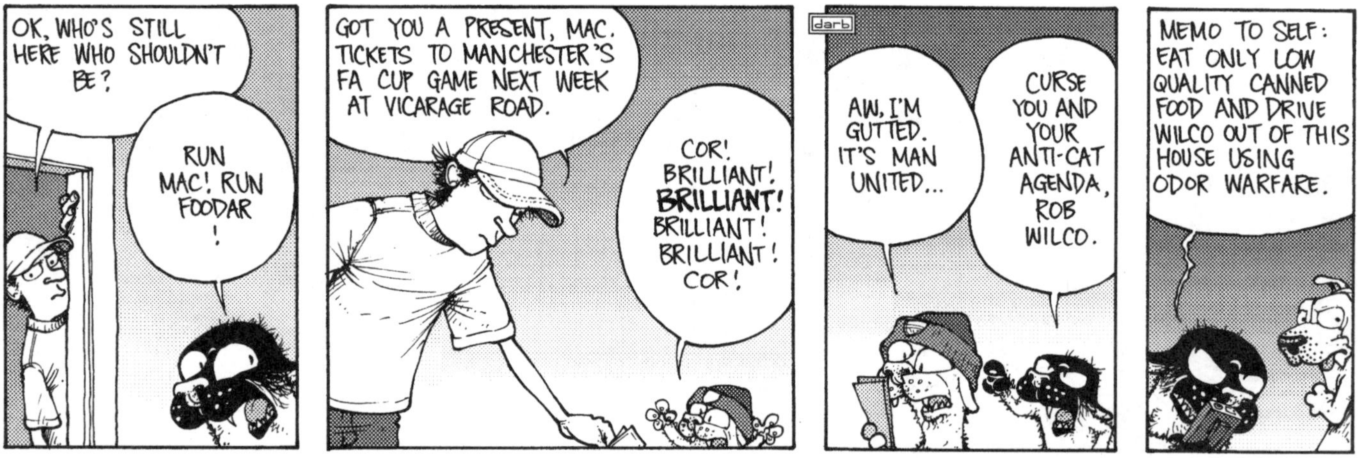
OK, WHO'S STILL HERE WHO SHOULDN'T BE?
RUN MAC! RUN FOODAR!
GOT YOU A PRESENT, MAC. TICKETS TO MANCHESTER'S FA CUP GAME NEXT WEEK AT VICARAGE ROAD.
COR! BRILLIANT! BRILLIANT! BRILLIANT! BRILLIANT! COR!
darb
AW, I'M GUTTED. IT'S MAN UNITED...
CURSE YOU AND YOUR ANTI-CAT AGENDA, ROB WILCO.
MEMO TO SELF: EAT ONLY LOW QUALITY CANNED FOOD AND DRIVE WILCO OUT OF THIS HOUSE USING ODOR WARFARE.

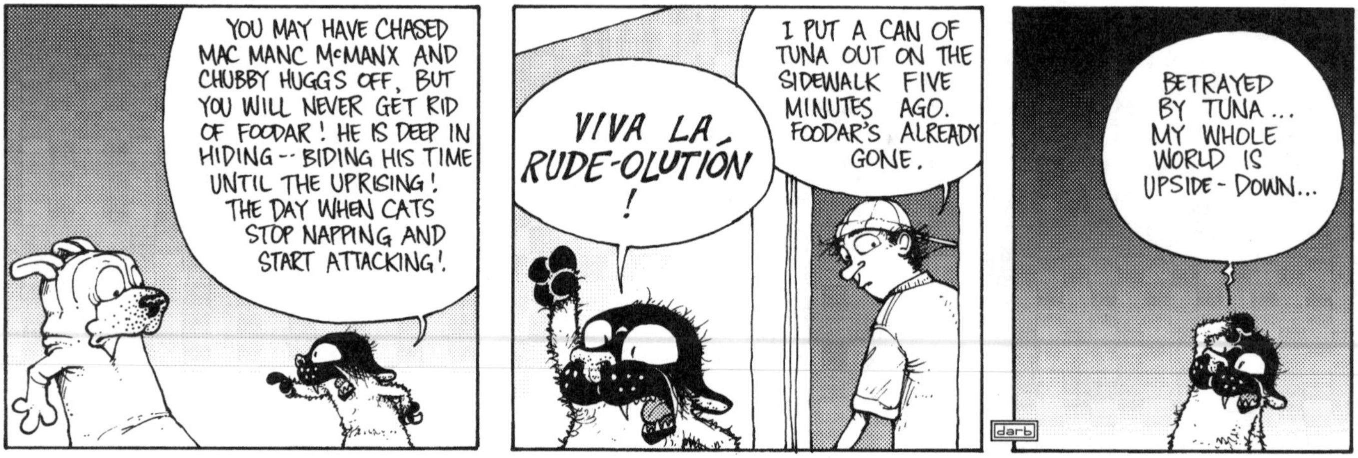
YOU MAY HAVE CHASED MAC MANC McMANX AND CHUBBY HUGGS OFF, BUT YOU WILL NEVER GET RID OF FOODAR! HE IS DEEP IN HIDING -- BIDING HIS TIME UNTIL THE UPRISING! THE DAY WHEN CATS STOP NAPPING AND START ATTACKING!
VIVA LA RUDE-OLUTIÓN!
I PUT A CAN OF TUNA OUT ON THE SIDEWALK FIVE MINUTES AGO. FOODAR'S ALREADY GONE.
darb
BETRAYED BY TUNA... MY WHOLE WORLD IS UPSIDE-DOWN...

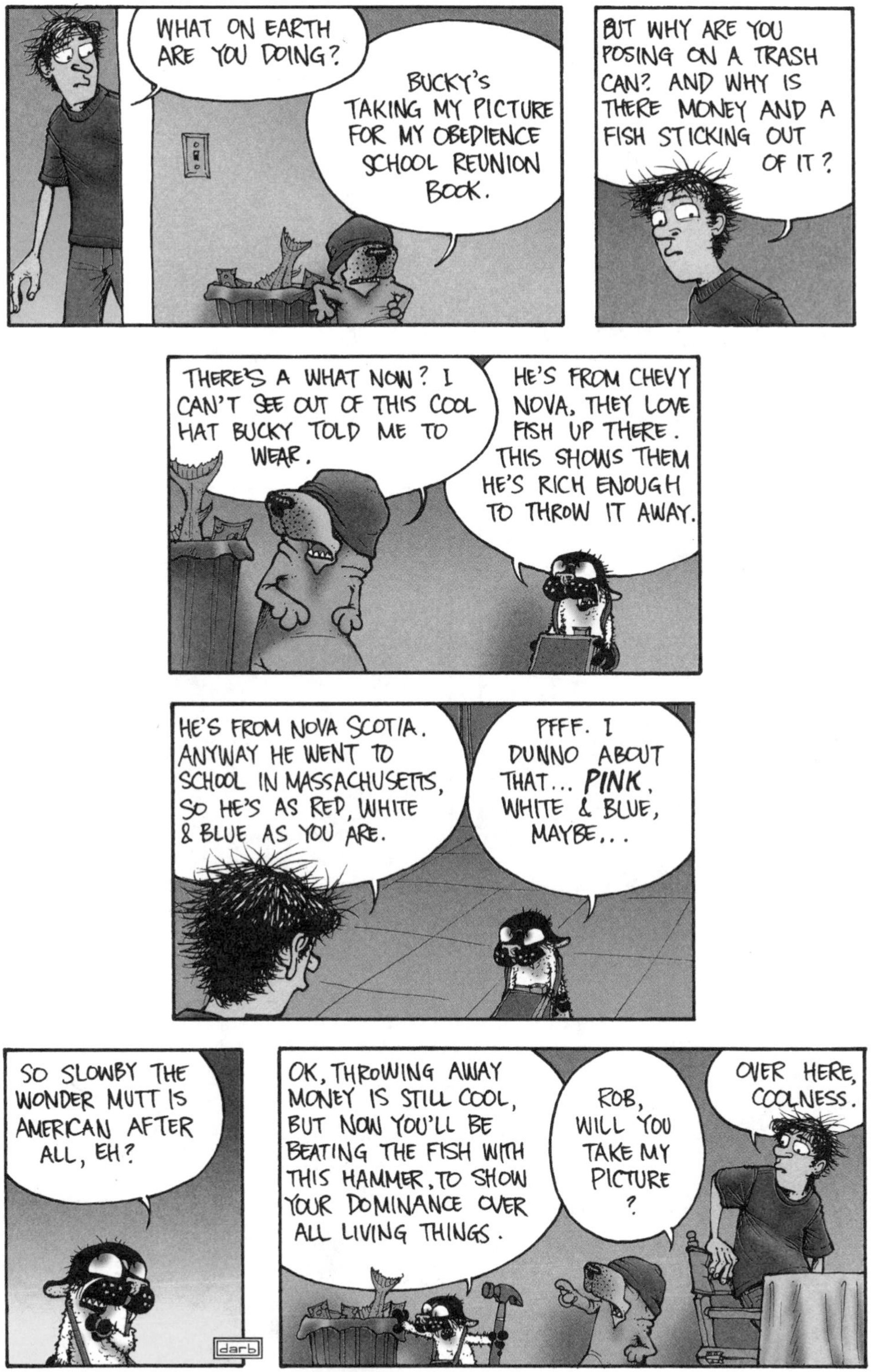
WHAT ON EARTH ARE YOU DOING?
BUCKY'S TAKING MY PICTURE FOR MY OBEDIENCE SCHOOL REUNION BOOK.
BUT WHY ARE YOU POSING ON A TRASH CAN? AND WHY IS THERE MONEY AND A FISH STICKING OUT OF IT?
THERE'S A WHAT NOW? I CAN'T SEE OUT OF THIS COOL HAT BUCKY TOLD ME TO WEAR.
HE'S FROM CHEVY NOVA, THEY LOVE FISH UP THERE. THIS SHOWS THEM HE'S RICH ENOUGH TO THROW IT AWAY.
HE'S FROM NOVA SCOTIA. ANYWAY HE WENT TO SCHOOL IN MASSACHUSETTS, SO HE'S AS RED, WHITE & BLUE AS YOU ARE.
PFFF. I DUNNO ABOUT THAT... PINK, WHITE & BLUE, MAYBE...
SO SLOWBY THE WONDER MUTT IS AMERICAN AFTER ALL, EH?
darb
OK, THROWING AWAY MONEY IS STILL COOL, BUT NOW YOU'LL BE BEATING THE FISH WITH THIS HAMMER, TO SHOW YOUR DOMINANCE OVER ALL LIVING THINGS.
ROB, WILL YOU TAKE MY PICTURE ?
OVER HERE, COOLNESS.

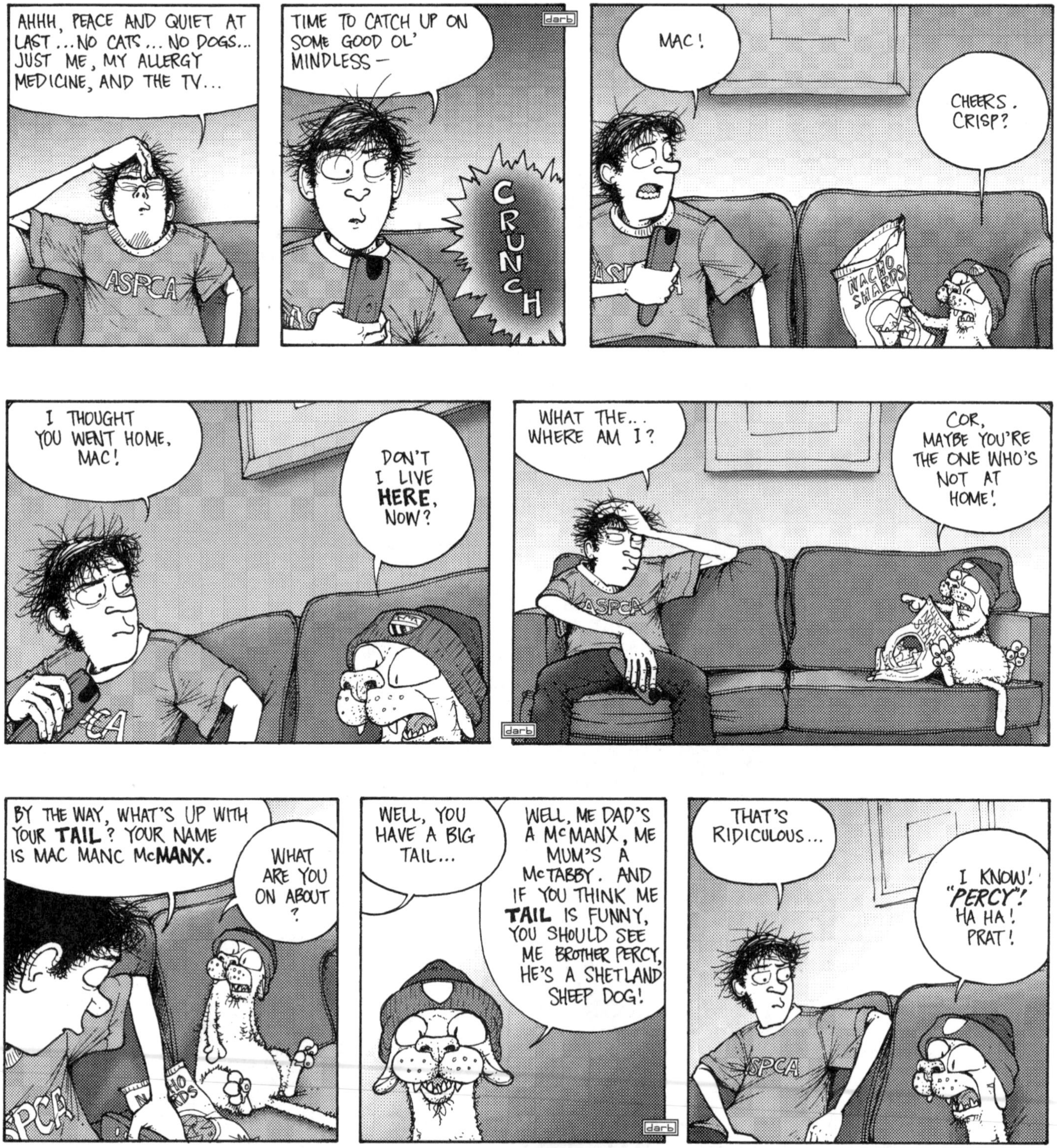
AHHH, PEACE AND QUIET AT LAST... NO CATS... NO DOGS... JUST ME, MY ALLERGY MEDICINE, AND THE TV...
ASPCA
TIME TO CATCH UP ON SOME GOOD OL' MINDLESS—
CRUNCH
darb
MAC!
CHEERS. CRISP?
NACHO SHARDS
I THOUGHT YOU WENT HOME, MAC!
DON'T I LIVE **HERE**, NOW?
darb
WHAT THE... WHERE AM I?
COR, MAYBE YOU'RE THE ONE WHO'S NOT AT HOME!
ASPCA
BY THE WAY, WHAT'S UP WITH YOUR **TAIL**? YOUR NAME IS MAC MANC Mc**MANX.**
WHAT ARE YOU ON ABOUT?
WELL, YOU HAVE A BIG TAIL...
WELL, ME DAD'S A McMANX, ME MUM'S A McTABBY. AND IF YOU THINK ME **TAIL** IS FUNNY, YOU SHOULD SEE ME BROTHER PERCY, HE'S A SHETLAND SHEEP DOG!
darb
THAT'S RIDICULOUS...
I KNOW! ***"PERCY"!*** HA HA! PRAT!

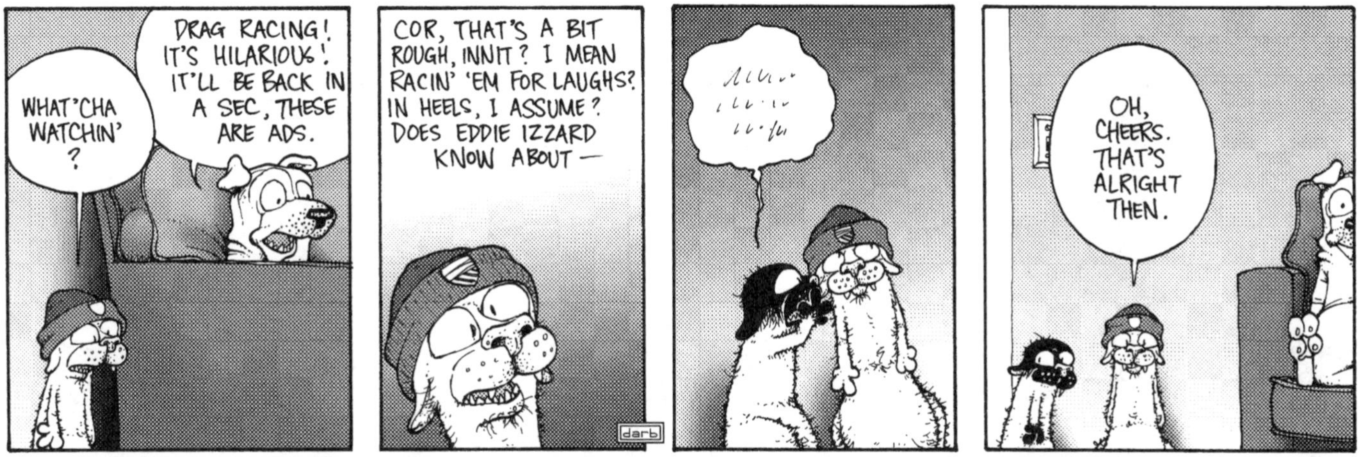
WHAT'CHA WATCHIN'?
DRAG RACING! IT'S HILARIOUS! IT'LL BE BACK IN A SEC, THESE ARE ADS.
COR, THAT'S A BIT ROUGH, INNIT? I MEAN RACIN' 'EM FOR LAUGHS? IN HEELS, I ASSUME? DOES EDDIE IZZARD KNOW ABOUT —
darb
OH, CHEERS. THAT'S ALRIGHT THEN.

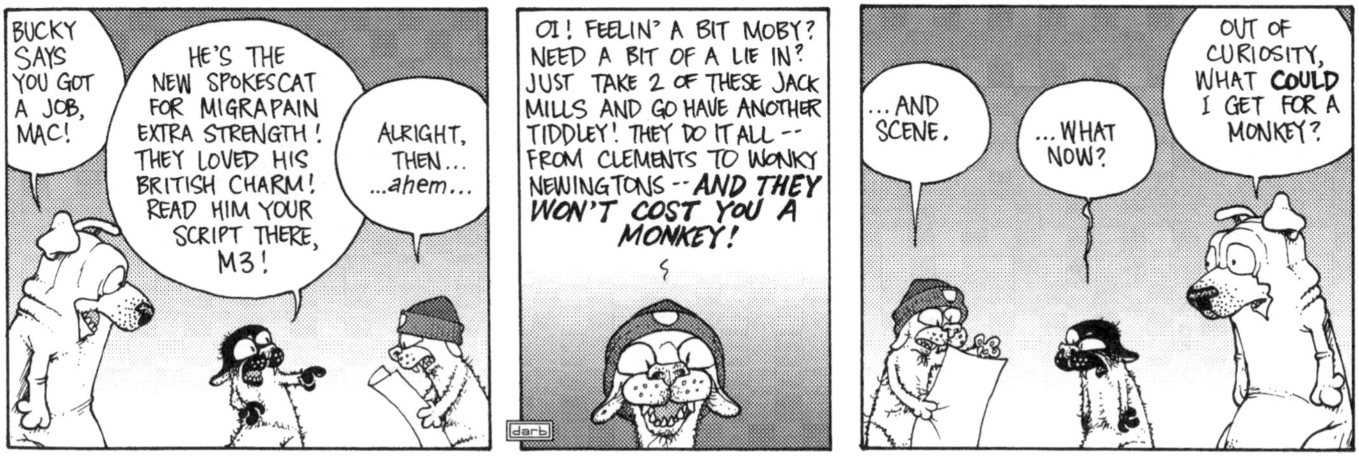
BUCKY SAYS YOU GOT A JOB, MAC!
HE'S THE NEW SPOKESCAT FOR MIGRAPAIN EXTRA STRENGTH! THEY LOVED HIS BRITISH CHARM! READ HIM YOUR SCRIPT THERE, M3!
ALRIGHT, THEN... ...ahem...
darb
OI! FEELIN' A BIT MOBY? NEED A BIT OF A LIE IN? JUST TAKE 2 OF THESE JACK MILLS AND GO HAVE ANOTHER TIDDLEY! THEY DO IT ALL -- FROM CLEMENTS TO WONKY NEWINGTONS -- AND THEY WON'T COST YOU A MONKEY!
...AND SCENE.
...WHAT NOW?
OUT OF CURIOSITY, WHAT COULD I GET FOR A MONKEY?

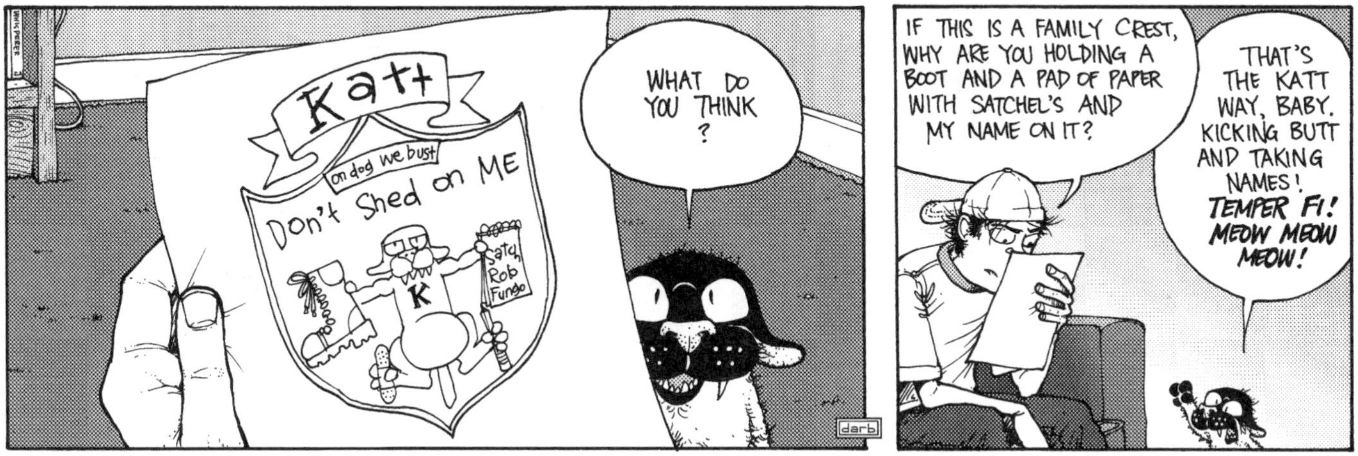
Katt
on dog we bust
Don't Shed on ME
K
Satch, Rob Fungo
WHAT DO YOU THINK?
darb
IF THIS IS A FAMILY CREST, WHY ARE YOU HOLDING A BOOT AND A PAD OF PAPER WITH SATCHEL'S AND MY NAME ON IT?
THAT'S THE KATT WAY, BABY. KICKING BUTT AND TAKING NAMES! TEMPER FI! MEOW MEOW MEOW!

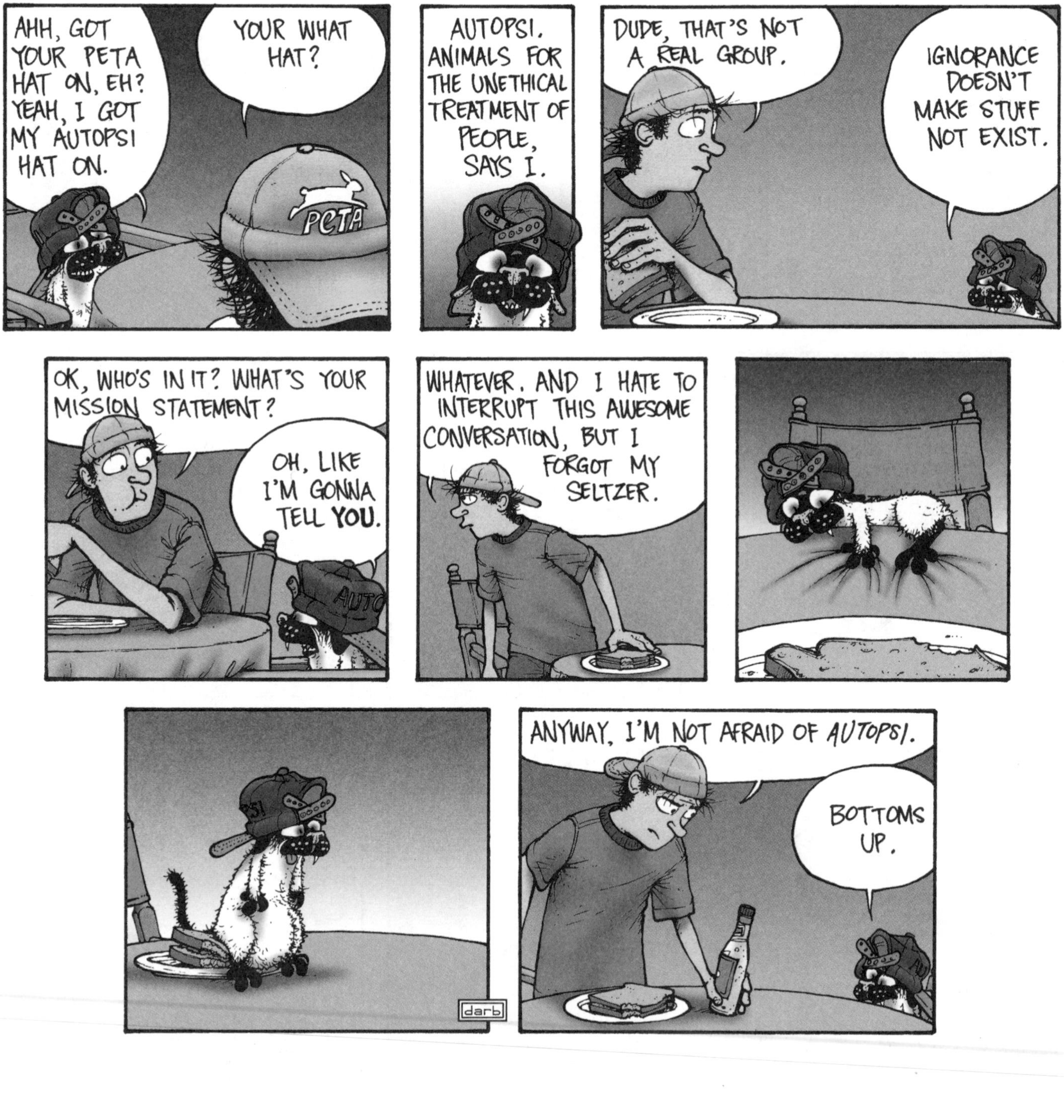
AHH, GOT YOUR PETA HAT ON, EH? YEAH, I GOT MY AUTOPSI HAT ON.
YOUR WHAT HAT?
PETA
AUTOPSI. ANIMALS FOR THE UNETHICAL TREATMENT OF PEOPLE, SAYS I.
DUDE, THAT'S NOT A REAL GROUP.
IGNORANCE DOESN'T MAKE STUFF NOT EXIST.
OK, WHO'S IN IT? WHAT'S YOUR MISSION STATEMENT?
OH, LIKE I'M GONNA TELL **YOU**.
AUTO
WHATEVER. AND I HATE TO INTERRUPT THIS AWESOME CONVERSATION, BUT I FORGOT MY SELTZER.
darb
ANYWAY, I'M NOT AFRAID OF *AUTOPSI*.
BOTTOMS UP.

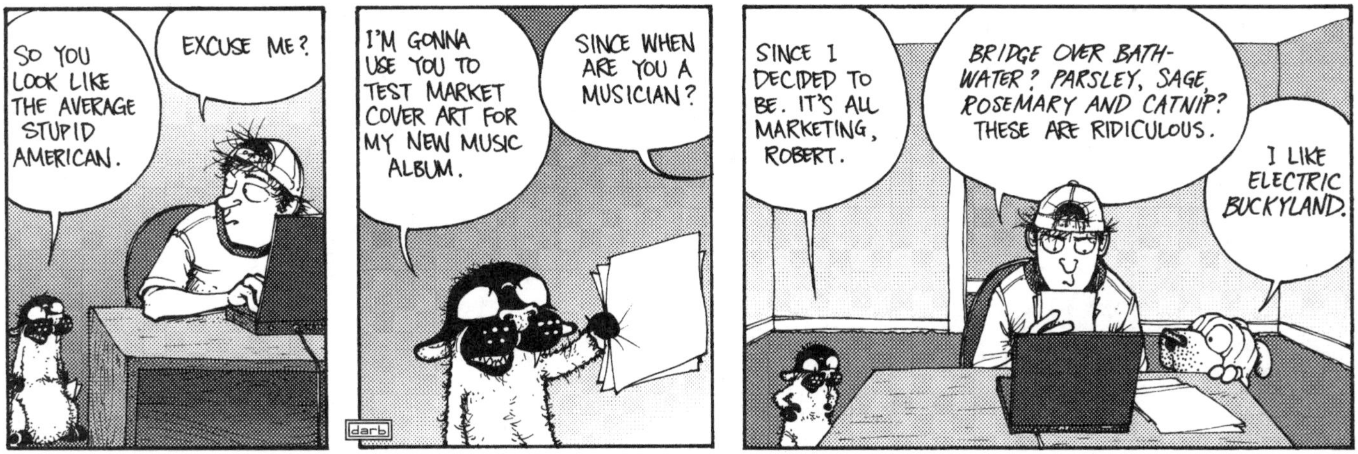
SO YOU LOOK LIKE THE AVERAGE STUPID AMERICAN.
EXCUSE ME?
I'M GONNA USE YOU TO TEST MARKET COVER ART FOR MY NEW MUSIC ALBUM.
SINCE WHEN ARE YOU A MUSICIAN?
SINCE I DECIDED TO BE. IT'S ALL MARKETING, ROBERT.
BRIDGE OVER BATH-WATER? PARSLEY, SAGE, ROSEMARY AND CATNIP? THESE ARE RIDICULOUS.
I LIKE ELECTRIC BUCKYLAND.

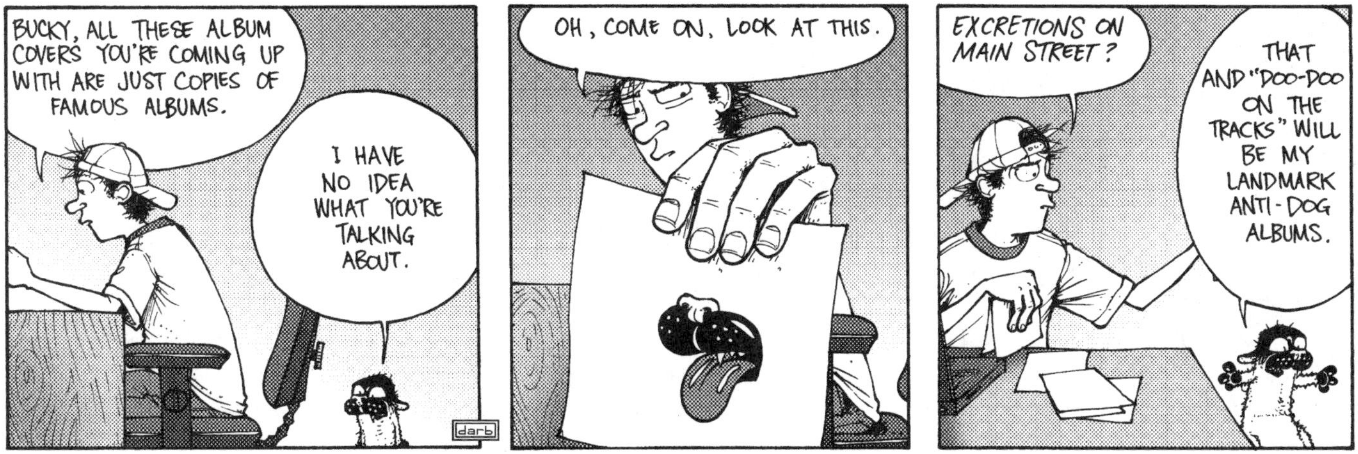
BUCKY, ALL THESE ALBUM COVERS YOU'RE COMING UP WITH ARE JUST COPIES OF FAMOUS ALBUMS.
I HAVE NO IDEA WHAT YOU'RE TALKING ABOUT.
OH, COME ON. LOOK AT THIS.
EXCRETIONS ON MAIN STREET?
THAT AND "DOO-DOO ON THE TRACKS" WILL BE MY LANDMARK ANTI-DOG ALBUMS.

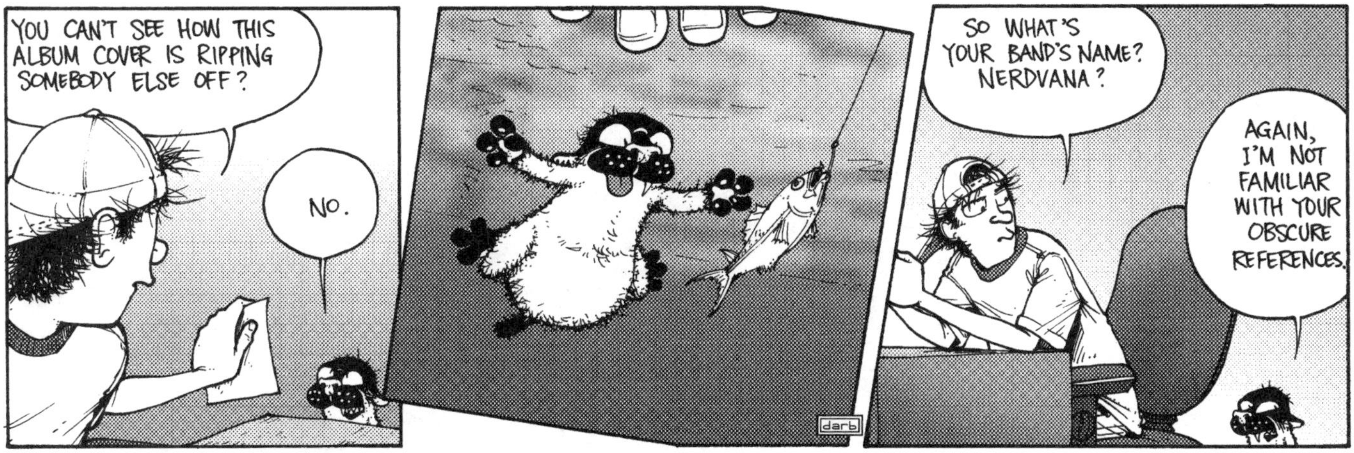
YOU CAN'T SEE HOW THIS ALBUM COVER IS RIPPING SOMEBODY ELSE OFF?
NO.
SO WHAT'S YOUR BAND'S NAME? NERDVANA?
AGAIN, I'M NOT FAMILIAR WITH YOUR OBSCURE REFERENCES.

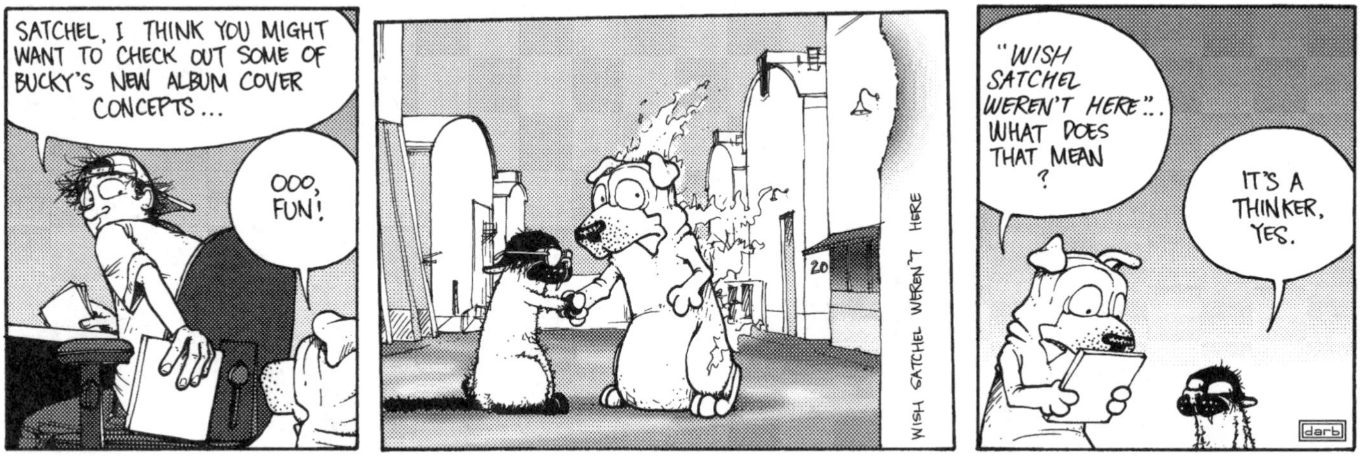
SATCHEL, I THINK YOU MIGHT WANT TO CHECK OUT SOME OF BUCKY'S NEW ALBUM COVER CONCEPTS...
OOO, FUN!
WISH SATCHEL WEREN'T HERE
"WISH SATCHEL WEREN'T HERE"... WHAT DOES THAT MEAN?
IT'S A THINKER, YES.
darb

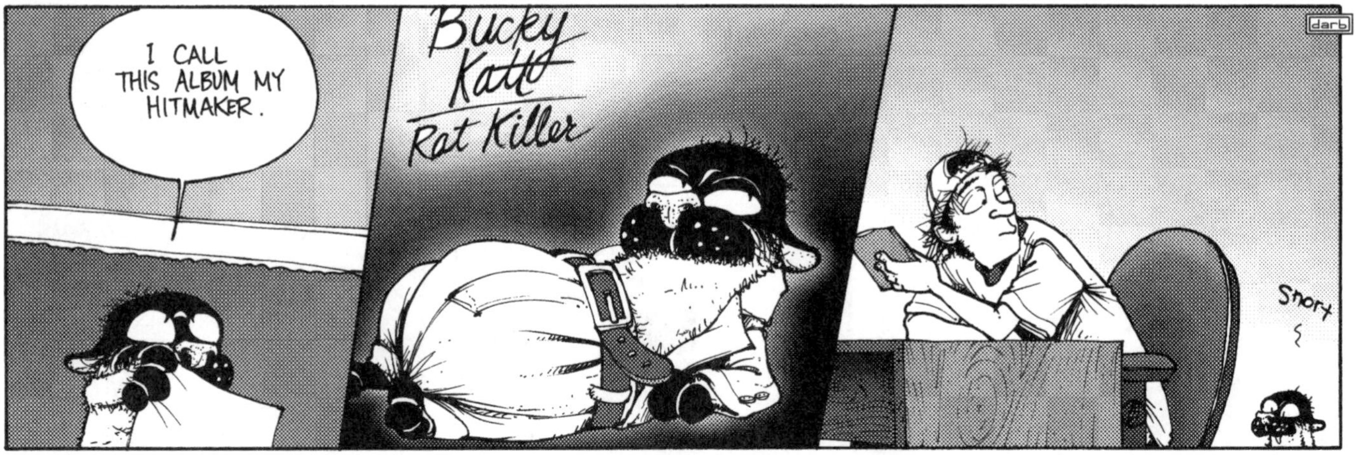
darb
I CALL THIS ALBUM MY HITMAKER.
Bucky Katt
Rat Killer
Snort

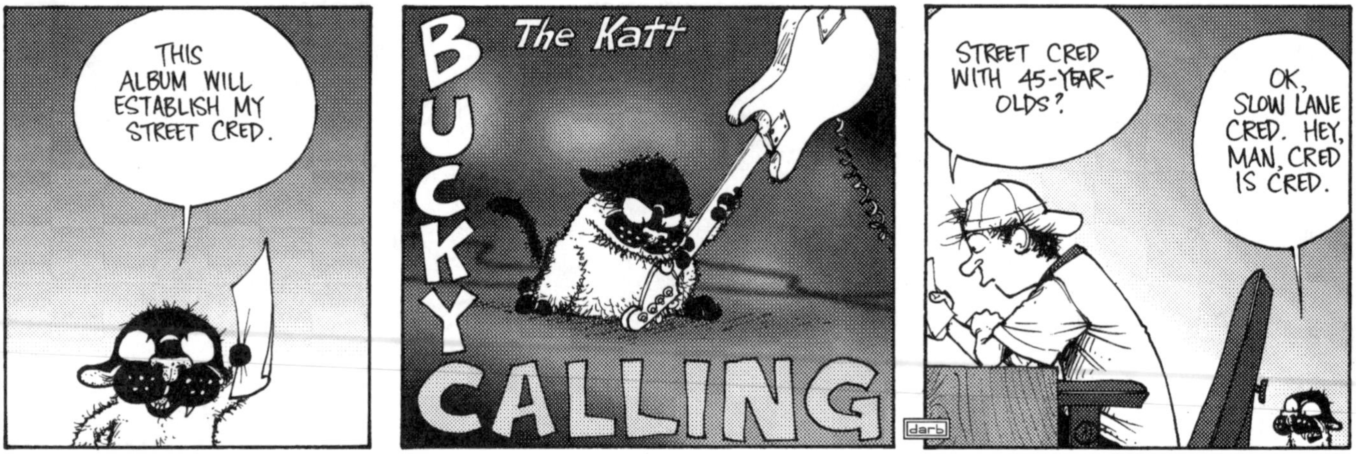
THIS ALBUM WILL ESTABLISH MY STREET CRED.
The Katt
BUCKY
CALLING
darb
STREET CRED WITH 45-YEAR-OLDS?
OK, SLOW LANE CRED. HEY, MAN, CRED IS CRED.

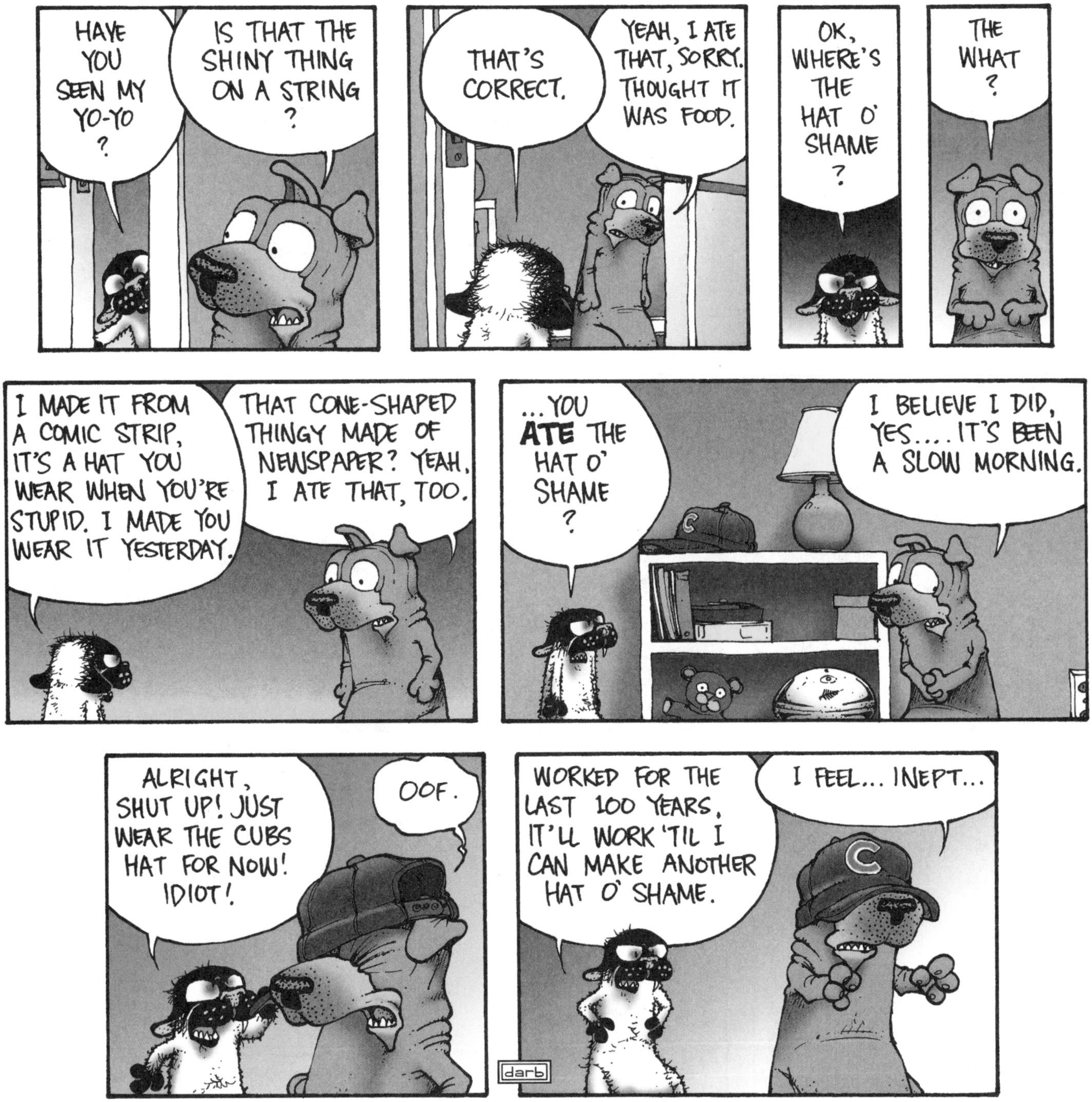
HAVE YOU SEEN MY YO-YO ?
IS THAT THE SHINY THING ON A STRING ?
THAT'S CORRECT.
YEAH, I ATE THAT, SORRY. THOUGHT IT WAS FOOD.
OK, WHERE'S THE HAT O' SHAME ?
THE WHAT ?
I MADE IT FROM A COMIC STRIP, IT'S A HAT YOU WEAR WHEN YOU'RE STUPID. I MADE YOU WEAR IT YESTERDAY.
THAT CONE-SHAPED THINGY MADE OF NEWSPAPER? YEAH, I ATE THAT, TOO.
...YOU **ATE** THE HAT O' SHAME ?
I BELIEVE I DID, YES.... IT'S BEEN A SLOW MORNING.
ALRIGHT, SHUT UP! JUST WEAR THE CUBS HAT FOR NOW! IDIOT!
OOF.
WORKED FOR THE LAST 100 YEARS, IT'LL WORK 'TIL I CAN MAKE ANOTHER HAT O' SHAME.
I FEEL... INEPT...
darb

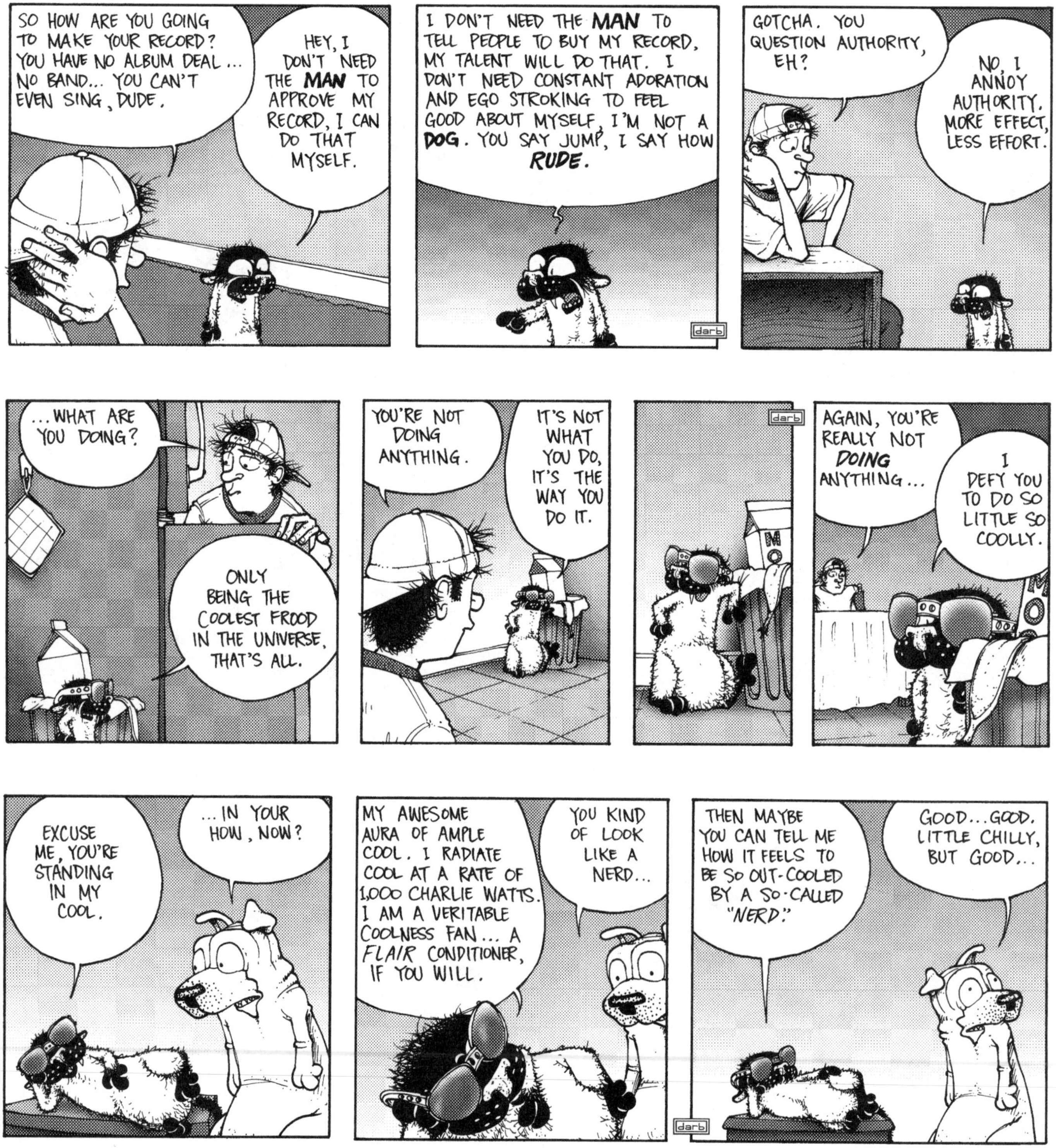
SO HOW ARE YOU GOING TO MAKE YOUR RECORD? YOU HAVE NO ALBUM DEAL... NO BAND... YOU CAN'T EVEN SING, DUDE.
HEY, I DON'T NEED THE **MAN** TO APPROVE MY RECORD, I CAN DO THAT MYSELF.
I DON'T NEED THE **MAN** TO TELL PEOPLE TO BUY MY RECORD, MY TALENT WILL DO THAT. I DON'T NEED CONSTANT ADORATION AND EGO STROKING TO FEEL GOOD ABOUT MYSELF, I'M NOT A **DOG**. YOU SAY JUMP, I SAY HOW ***RUDE***.
darb
GOTCHA. YOU QUESTION AUTHORITY, EH?
NO, I ANNOY AUTHORITY. MORE EFFECT, LESS EFFORT.
...WHAT ARE YOU DOING?
ONLY BEING THE COOLEST FROOD IN THE UNIVERSE, THAT'S ALL.
YOU'RE NOT DOING ANYTHING.
IT'S NOT WHAT YOU DO, IT'S THE WAY YOU DO IT.
darb
AGAIN, YOU'RE REALLY NOT ***DOING*** ANYTHING...
I DEFY YOU TO DO SO LITTLE SO COOLLY.
EXCUSE ME, YOU'RE STANDING IN MY COOL.
...IN YOUR HOW, NOW?
MY AWESOME AURA OF AMPLE COOL. I RADIATE COOL AT A RATE OF 1,000 CHARLIE WATTS. I AM A VERITABLE COOLNESS FAN... A *FLAIR* CONDITIONER, IF YOU WILL.
YOU KIND OF LOOK LIKE A NERD...
darb
THEN MAYBE YOU CAN TELL ME HOW IT FEELS TO BE SO OUT-COOLED BY A SO-CALLED *"NERD."*
GOOD...GOOD. LITTLE CHILLY, BUT GOOD...

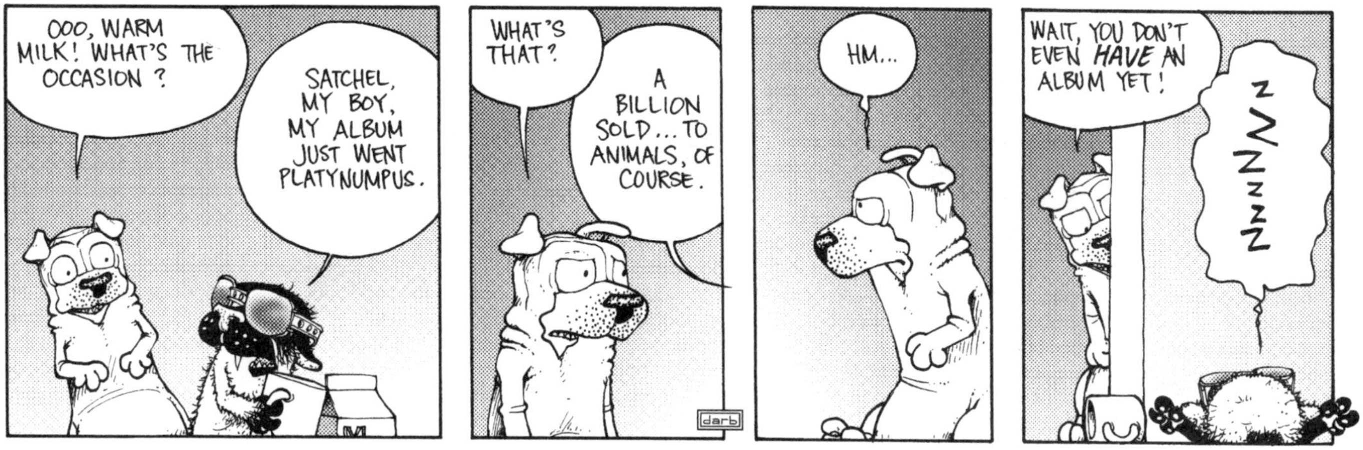
OOO, WARM MILK! WHAT'S THE OCCASION ?
SATCHEL, MY BOY, MY ALBUM JUST WENT PLATYNUMPUS.
WHAT'S THAT?
A BILLION SOLD... TO ANIMALS, OF COURSE.
HM...
WAIT, YOU DON'T EVEN **HAVE** AN ALBUM YET!
NNNNZZZ

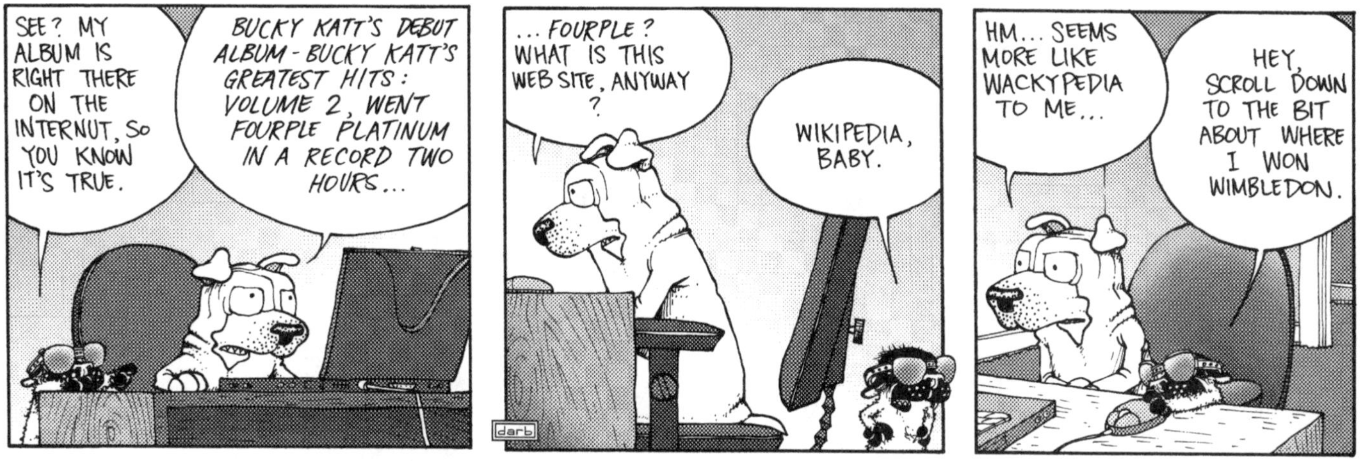
SEE? MY ALBUM IS RIGHT THERE ON THE INTERNUT, SO YOU KNOW IT'S TRUE.
BUCKY KATT'S DEBUT ALBUM - BUCKY KATT'S GREATEST HITS: VOLUME 2, WENT FOURPLE PLATINUM IN A RECORD TWO HOURS...
... *FOURPLE?* WHAT IS THIS WEB SITE, ANYWAY ?
WIKIPEDIA, BABY.
HM... SEEMS MORE LIKE WACKYPEDIA TO ME...
HEY, SCROLL DOWN TO THE BIT ABOUT WHERE I WON WIMBLEDON.

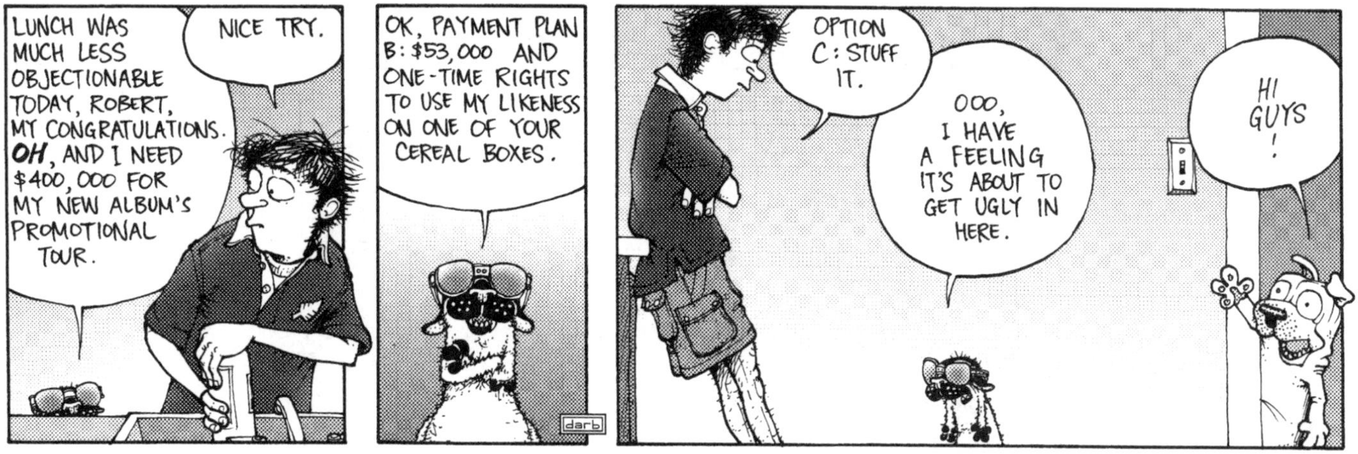
LUNCH WAS MUCH LESS OBJECTIONABLE TODAY, ROBERT, MY CONGRATULATIONS. **OH**, AND I NEED $400,000 FOR MY NEW ALBUM'S PROMOTIONAL TOUR.
NICE TRY.
OK, PAYMENT PLAN B: $53,000 AND ONE-TIME RIGHTS TO USE MY LIKENESS ON ONE OF YOUR CEREAL BOXES.
OPTION C: STUFF IT.
OOO, I HAVE A FEELING IT'S ABOUT TO GET UGLY IN HERE.
HI GUYS!

WATCHIN' THE FOOD NETWORK, EH? GOOD STUFF.

THIS IS THE ECO CHANNEL, YOU FREAK.

OH...MY...HEAD. THAT IS PERHAPS THE SINGLE MOST SUCCULENT PRIMATE I HAVE EVER SEEN...LOOK AT THAT **TAIL.**

darb

WITH THAT TAIL, I BET YOU COULD FREEZE IT AND EAT IT LIKE A POPSICLE... MMMM... MONKEY ON A STICK... A GIBBONSICLE... A LEMURPOP... SHISH KEBABOON...

THAT'S A RHESUS MONKEY. AND YOU'RE NOT ALLOWED TO EAT MONKEYS.

WELL, IF HE'S A RACIST MONKEY, WHY **CAN'T** I EAT HIM?!

RHESUS. **RHESUS.**

WOW, MONKEY **AND** CHOCOLATE? DOUBLE WHAMMY. THE MOST FORBIDDEN FOOD IN THE WORLD.

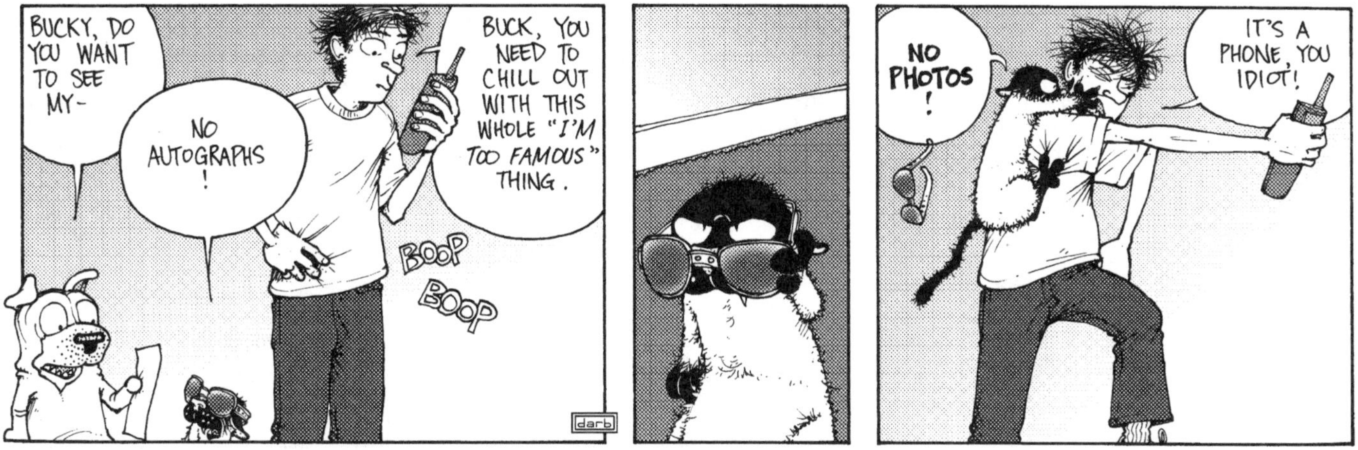
BUCKY, DO YOU WANT TO SEE MY-
NO AUTOGRAPHS!
BUCK, YOU NEED TO CHILL OUT WITH THIS WHOLE "*I'M TOO FAMOUS*" THING.
BOOP
BOOP
darb
NO PHOTOS!
IT'S A PHONE, YOU IDIOT!

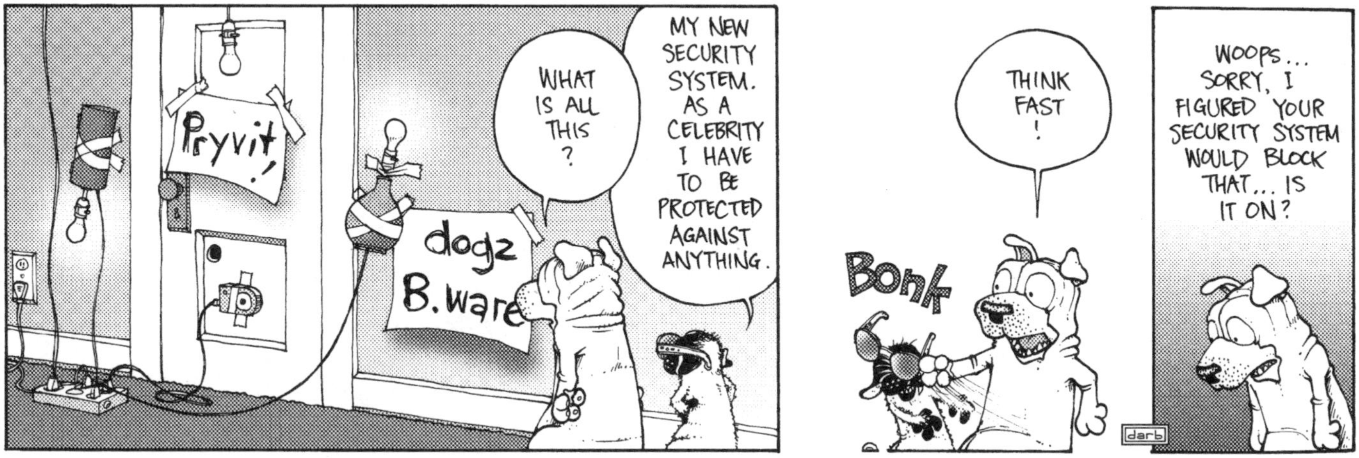
Pryvit!
dogz B.ware
WHAT IS ALL THIS?
MY NEW SECURITY SYSTEM. AS A CELEBRITY I HAVE TO BE PROTECTED AGAINST ANYTHING.
THINK FAST!
Bonk
darb
WOOPS... SORRY, I FIGURED YOUR SECURITY SYSTEM WOULD BLOCK THAT... IS IT ON?

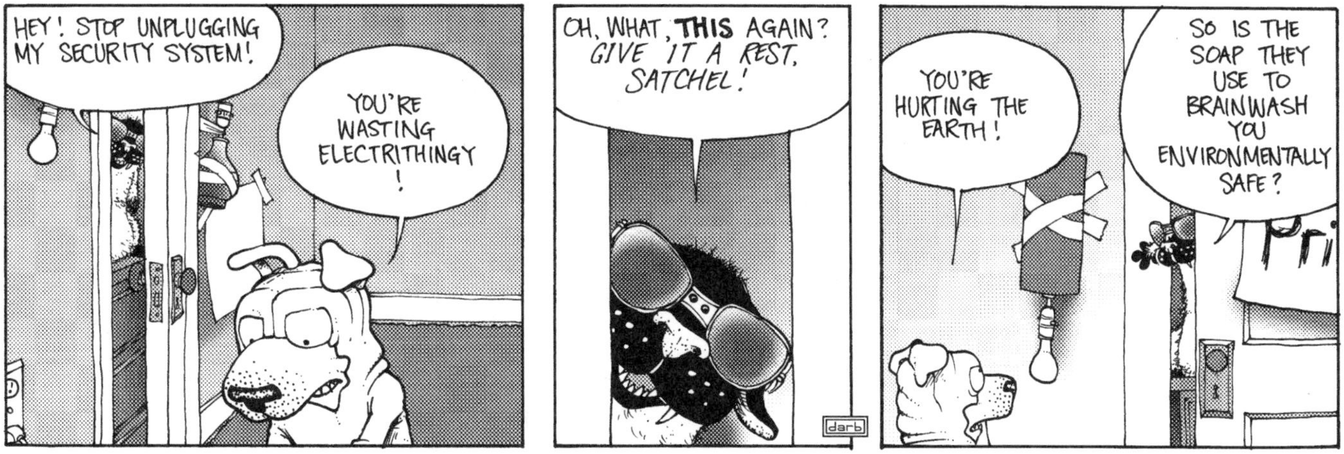
HEY! STOP UNPLUGGING MY SECURITY SYSTEM!
YOU'RE WASTING ELECTRITHINGY!
OH, WHAT, **THIS** AGAIN? *GIVE IT A REST, SATCHEL!*
darb
YOU'RE HURTING THE EARTH!
SO IS THE SOAP THEY USE TO BRAINWASH YOU ENVIRONMENTALLY SAFE?

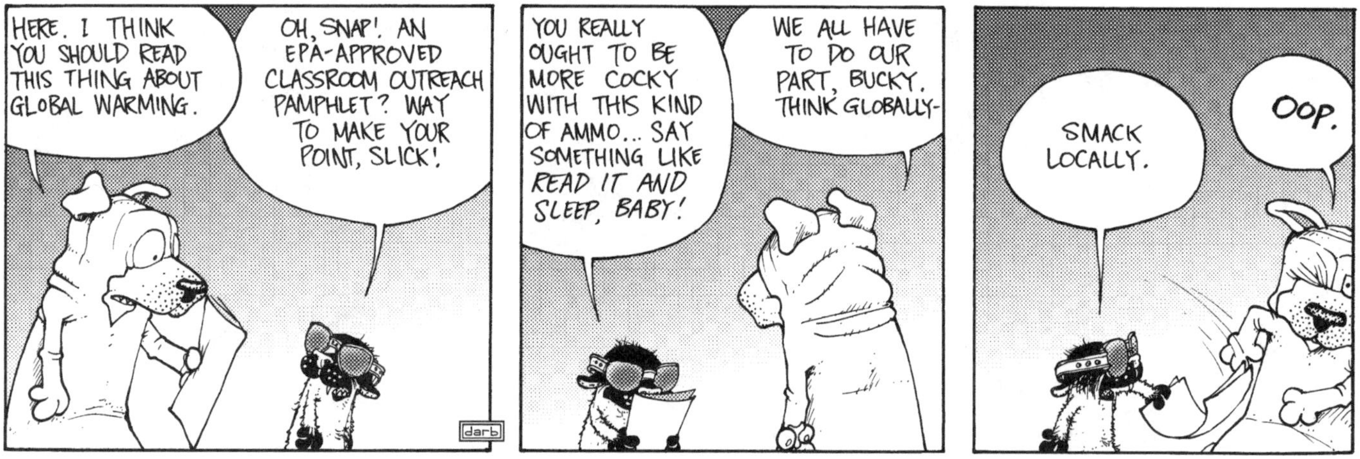
HERE. I THINK YOU SHOULD READ THIS THING ABOUT GLOBAL WARMING.
OH, SNAP! AN EPA-APPROVED CLASSROOM OUTREACH PAMPHLET? WAY TO MAKE YOUR POINT, SLICK!
YOU REALLY OUGHT TO BE MORE COCKY WITH THIS KIND OF AMMO... SAY SOMETHING LIKE *READ IT AND SLEEP, BABY!*
WE ALL HAVE TO DO OUR PART, BUCKY. THINK GLOBALLY-
SMACK LOCALLY.
OOP.
darb

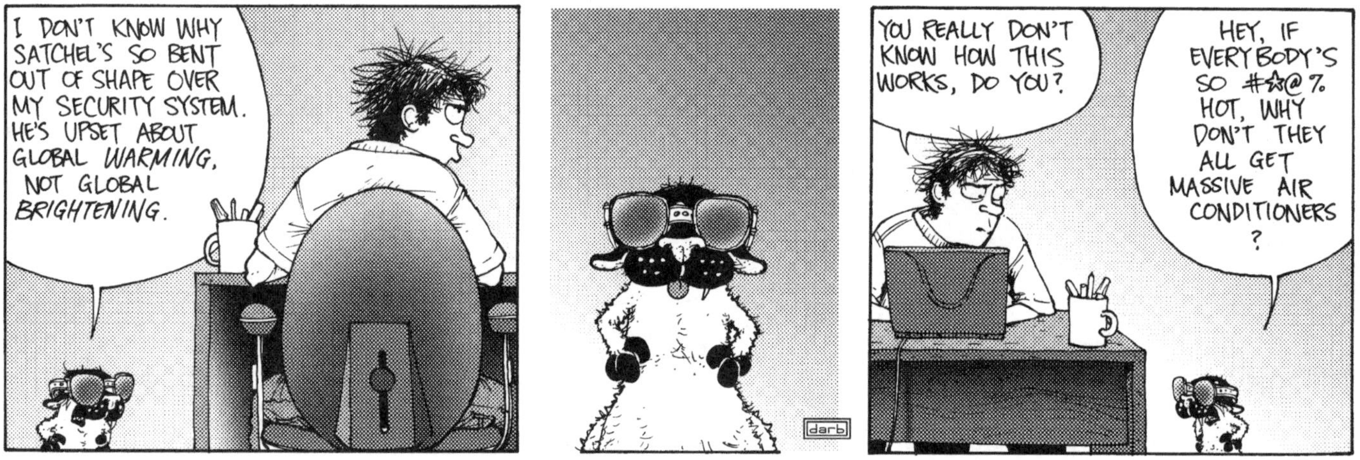
I DON'T KNOW WHY SATCHEL'S SO BENT OUT OF SHAPE OVER MY SECURITY SYSTEM. HE'S UPSET ABOUT GLOBAL *WARMING*, NOT GLOBAL *BRIGHTENING*.
darb
YOU REALLY DON'T KNOW HOW THIS WORKS, DO YOU?
HEY, IF EVERYBODY'S SO #☆@% HOT, WHY DON'T THEY ALL GET MASSIVE AIR CONDITIONERS?

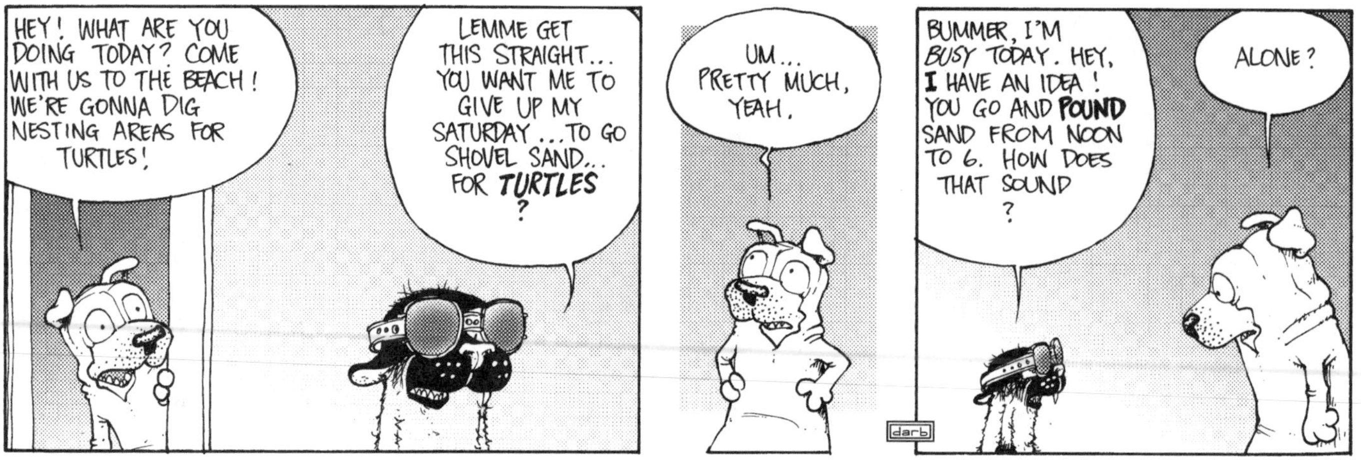
HEY! WHAT ARE YOU DOING TODAY? COME WITH US TO THE BEACH! WE'RE GONNA DIG NESTING AREAS FOR TURTLES!
LEMME GET THIS STRAIGHT... YOU WANT ME TO GIVE UP MY SATURDAY ... TO GO SHOVEL SAND... FOR **TURTLES**?
UM... PRETTY MUCH, YEAH.
darb
BUMMER, I'M *BUSY* TODAY. HEY, **I** HAVE AN IDEA! YOU GO AND **POUND** SAND FROM NOON TO 6. HOW DOES THAT SOUND?
ALONE?

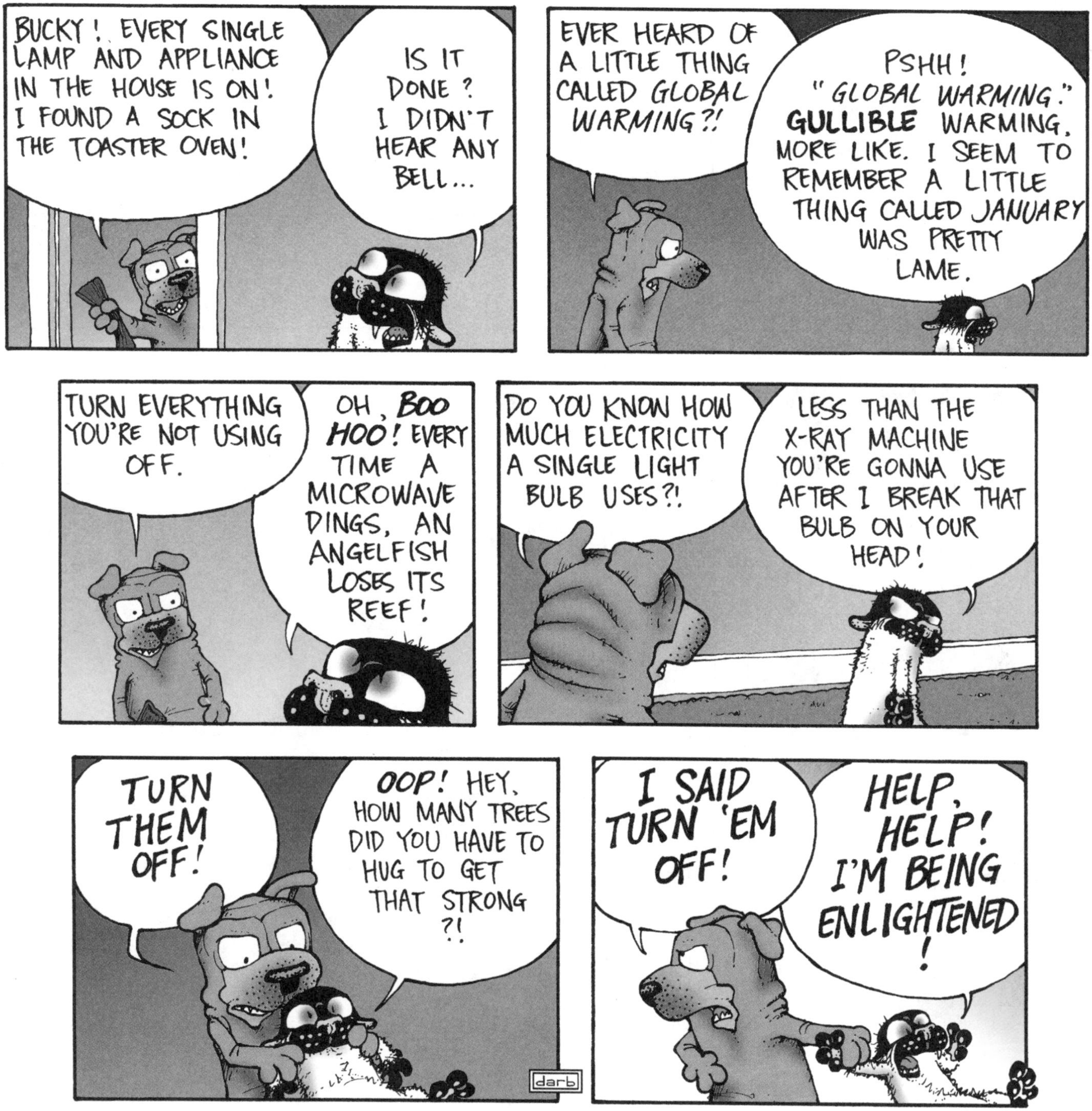
BUCKY! EVERY SINGLE LAMP AND APPLIANCE IN THE HOUSE IS ON! I FOUND A SOCK IN THE TOASTER OVEN!
IS IT DONE? I DIDN'T HEAR ANY BELL...
EVER HEARD OF A LITTLE THING CALLED GLOBAL WARMING?!
PSHH! "GLOBAL WARMING." GULLIBLE WARMING, MORE LIKE. I SEEM TO REMEMBER A LITTLE THING CALLED JANUARY WAS PRETTY LAME.
TURN EVERYTHING YOU'RE NOT USING OFF.
OH, BOO HOO! EVERY TIME A MICROWAVE DINGS, AN ANGELFISH LOSES ITS REEF!
DO YOU KNOW HOW MUCH ELECTRICITY A SINGLE LIGHT BULB USES?!
LESS THAN THE X-RAY MACHINE YOU'RE GONNA USE AFTER I BREAK THAT BULB ON YOUR HEAD!
TURN THEM OFF!
OOP! HEY, HOW MANY TREES DID YOU HAVE TO HUG TO GET THAT STRONG?!
darb
I SAID TURN 'EM OFF!
HELP, HELP! I'M BEING ENLIGHTENED!

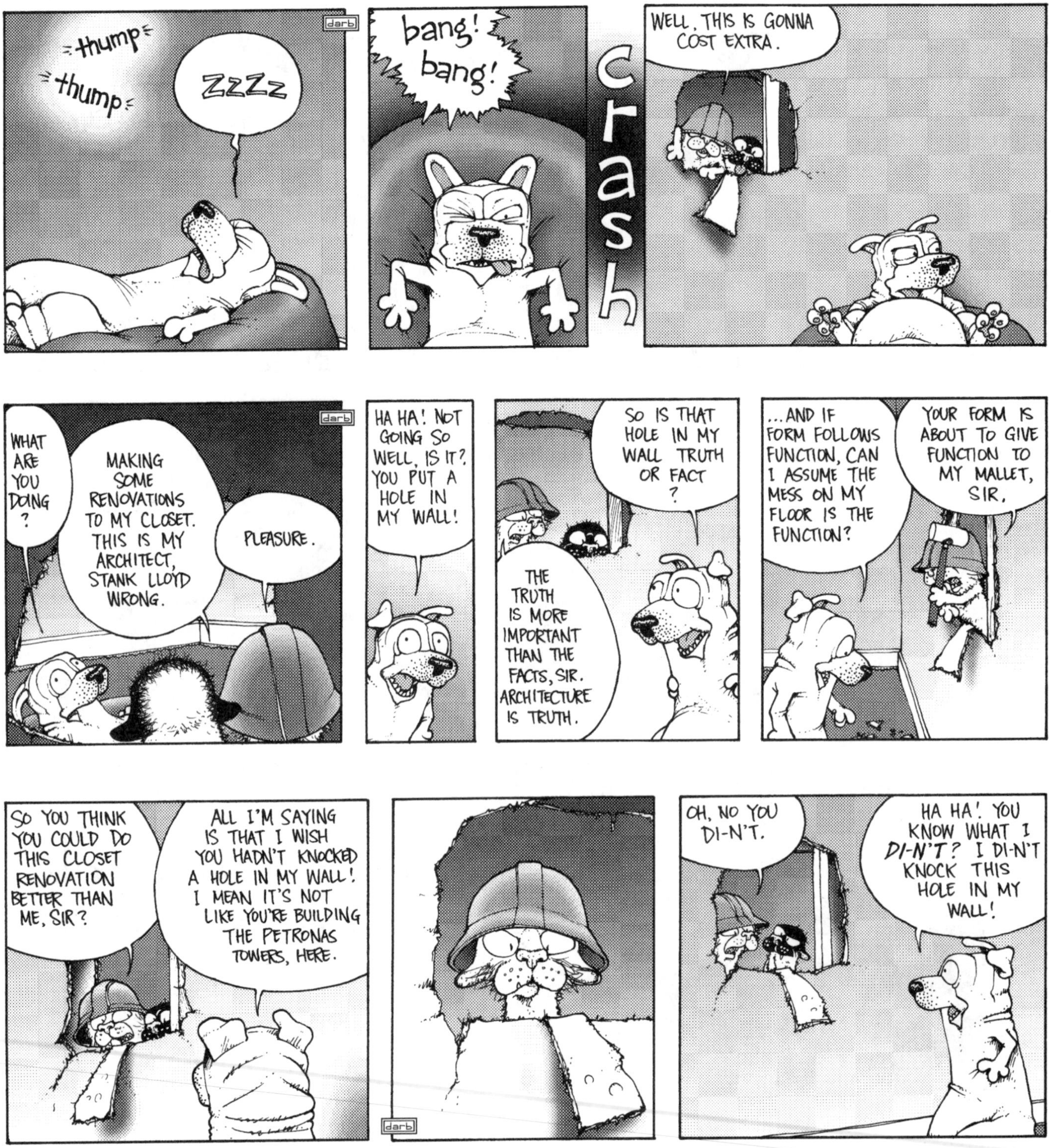
darb
thump
thump
ZzZz
bang!
bang!
crash
WELL, THIS IS GONNA COST EXTRA.
darb
WHAT ARE YOU DOING?
MAKING SOME RENOVATIONS TO MY CLOSET. THIS IS MY ARCHITECT, STANK LLOYD WRONG.
PLEASURE.
HA HA! NOT GOING SO WELL, IS IT? YOU PUT A HOLE IN MY WALL!
SO IS THAT HOLE IN MY WALL TRUTH OR FACT?
THE TRUTH IS MORE IMPORTANT THAN THE FACTS, SIR. ARCHITECTURE IS TRUTH.
...AND IF FORM FOLLOWS FUNCTION, CAN I ASSUME THE MESS ON MY FLOOR IS THE FUNCTION?
YOUR FORM IS ABOUT TO GIVE FUNCTION TO MY MALLET, SIR.
SO YOU THINK YOU COULD DO THIS CLOSET RENOVATION BETTER THAN ME, SIR?
ALL I'M SAYING IS THAT I WISH YOU HADN'T KNOCKED A HOLE IN MY WALL! I MEAN IT'S NOT LIKE YOU'RE BUILDING THE PETRONAS TOWERS, HERE.
darb
OH, NO YOU DI-N'T.
HA HA! YOU KNOW WHAT I DI-N'T? I DI-N'T KNOCK THIS HOLE IN MY WALL!

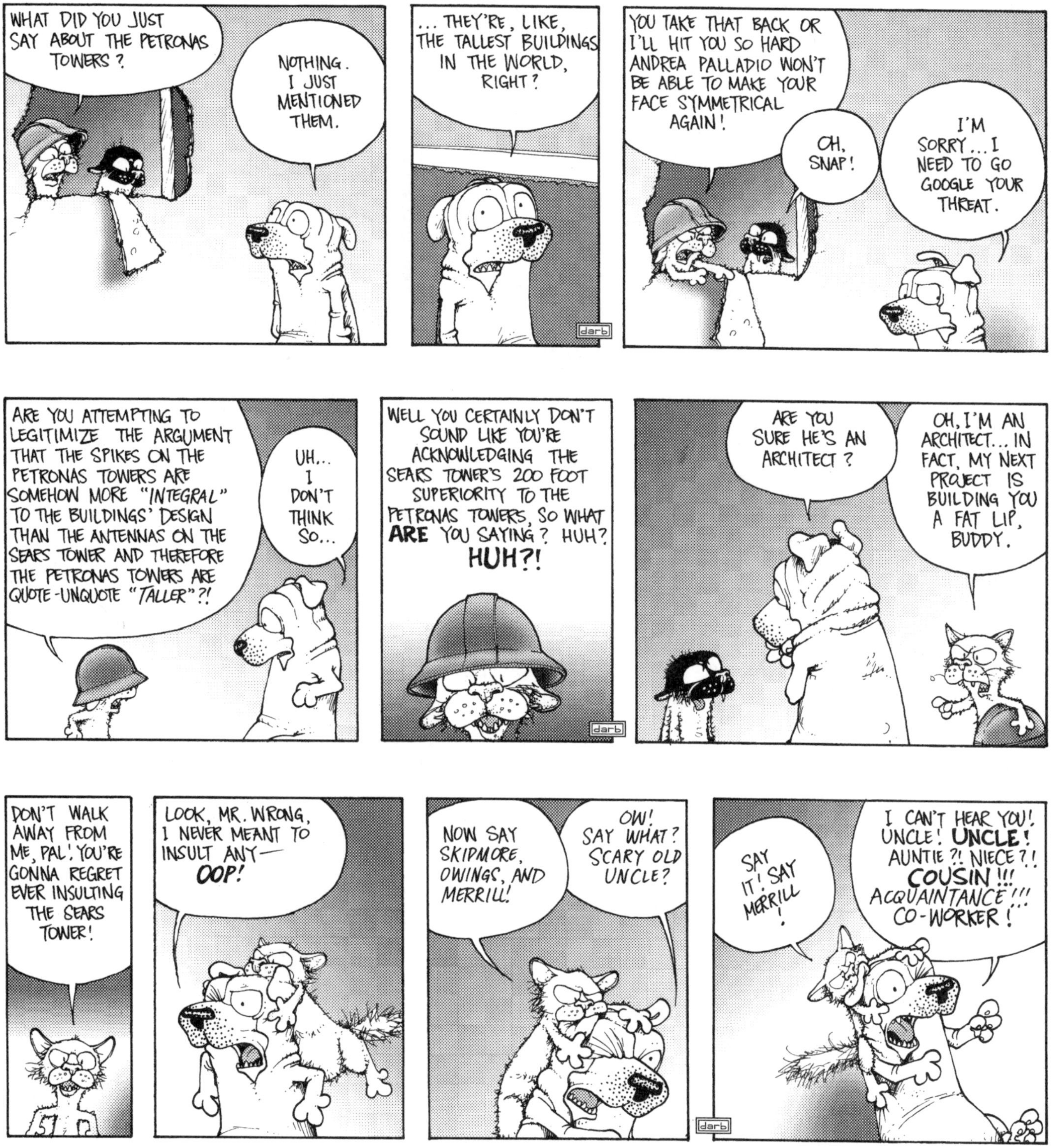
WHAT DID YOU JUST SAY ABOUT THE PETRONAS TOWERS?
NOTHING. I JUST MENTIONED THEM.
... THEY'RE, LIKE, THE TALLEST BUILDINGS IN THE WORLD, RIGHT?
YOU TAKE THAT BACK OR I'LL HIT YOU SO HARD ANDREA PALLADIO WON'T BE ABLE TO MAKE YOUR FACE SYMMETRICAL AGAIN!
OH, SNAP!
I'M SORRY... I NEED TO GO GOOGLE YOUR THREAT.
ARE YOU ATTEMPTING TO LEGITIMIZE THE ARGUMENT THAT THE SPIKES ON THE PETRONAS TOWERS ARE SOMEHOW MORE "INTEGRAL" TO THE BUILDINGS' DESIGN THAN THE ANTENNAS ON THE SEARS TOWER AND THEREFORE THE PETRONAS TOWERS ARE QUOTE-UNQUOTE "TALLER"?!
UH... I DON'T THINK SO...
WELL YOU CERTAINLY DON'T SOUND LIKE YOU'RE ACKNOWLEDGING THE SEARS TOWER'S 200 FOOT SUPERIORITY TO THE PETRONAS TOWERS, SO WHAT ARE YOU SAYING? HUH? HUH?!
ARE YOU SURE HE'S AN ARCHITECT?
OH, I'M AN ARCHITECT... IN FACT, MY NEXT PROJECT IS BUILDING YOU A FAT LIP, BUDDY.
DON'T WALK AWAY FROM ME, PAL! YOU'RE GONNA REGRET EVER INSULTING THE SEARS TOWER!
LOOK, MR. WRONG, I NEVER MEANT TO INSULT ANY— OOP!
NOW SAY SKIDMORE, OWINGS, AND MERRILL!
OW! SAY WHAT? SCARY OLD UNCLE?
SAY IT! SAY MERRILL!
I CAN'T HEAR YOU! UNCLE! UNCLE! AUNTIE?! NIECE?! COUSIN!!! ACQUAINTANCE!!! CO-WORKER!!!

OK, HERE, TRY THIS ONE. TELL ME WHAT YOU THINK.
THIS NEXT ONE IS FROM THE BEACH.
NOW TRY THIS ONE, IT'S HUGE.
darb
food
not food
FOOD?
NOT SO MUCH.
Stuff i found

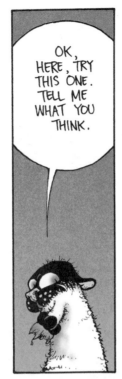

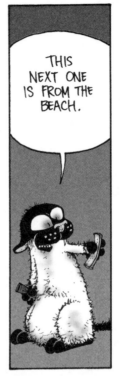

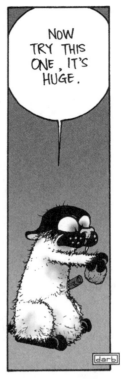

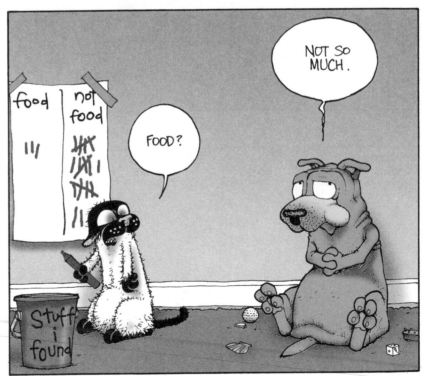

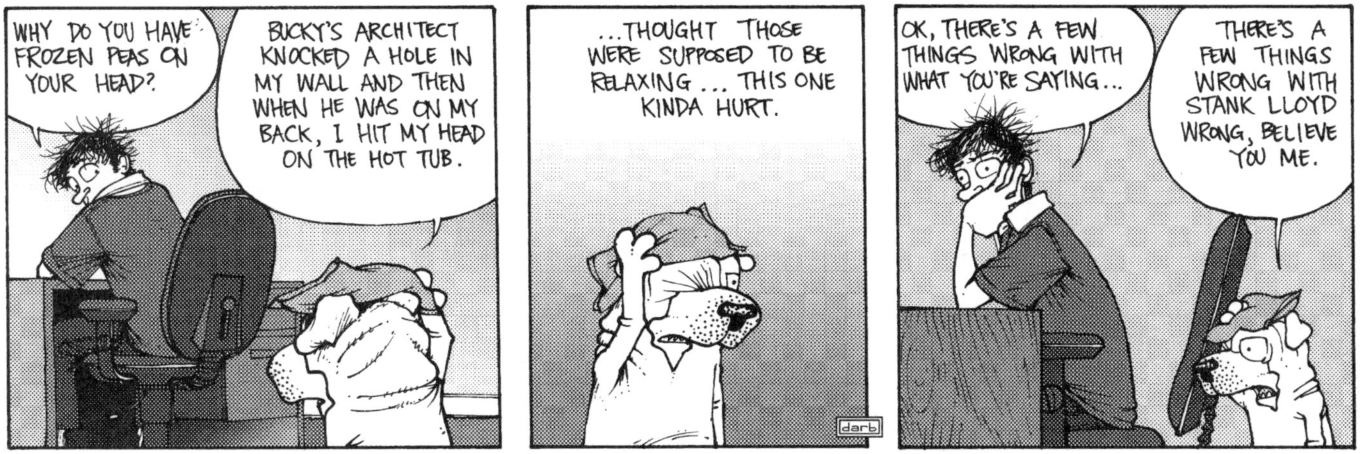
WHY DO YOU HAVE FROZEN PEAS ON YOUR HEAD?
BUCKY'S ARCHITECT KNOCKED A HOLE IN MY WALL AND THEN WHEN HE WAS ON MY BACK, I HIT MY HEAD ON THE HOT TUB.
...THOUGHT THOSE WERE SUPPOSED TO BE RELAXING ... THIS ONE KINDA HURT.
darb
OK, THERE'S A FEW THINGS WRONG WITH WHAT YOU'RE SAYING...
THERE'S A FEW THINGS WRONG WITH STANK LLOYD WRONG, BELIEVE YOU ME.

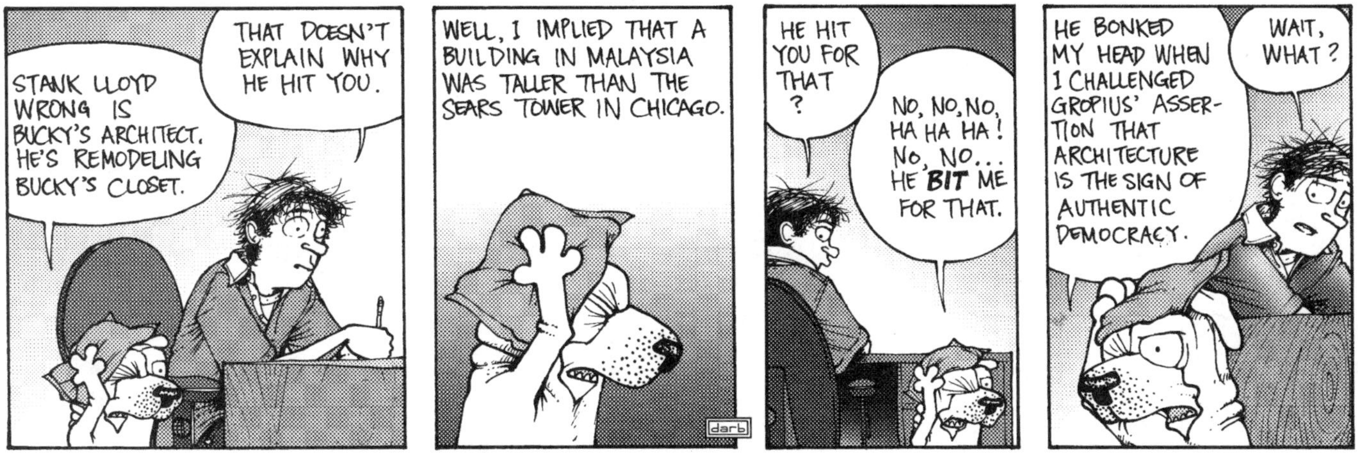
STANK LLOYD WRONG IS BUCKY'S ARCHITECT. HE'S REMODELING BUCKY'S CLOSET.
THAT DOESN'T EXPLAIN WHY HE HIT YOU.
WELL, I IMPLIED THAT A BUILDING IN MALAYSIA WAS TALLER THAN THE SEARS TOWER IN CHICAGO.
darb
HE HIT YOU FOR THAT ?
NO, NO, NO, HA HA HA! NO, NO... HE **BIT** ME FOR THAT.
HE BONKED MY HEAD WHEN I CHALLENGED GROPIUS' ASSERTION THAT ARCHITECTURE IS THE SIGN OF AUTHENTIC DEMOCRACY.
WAIT, WHAT?

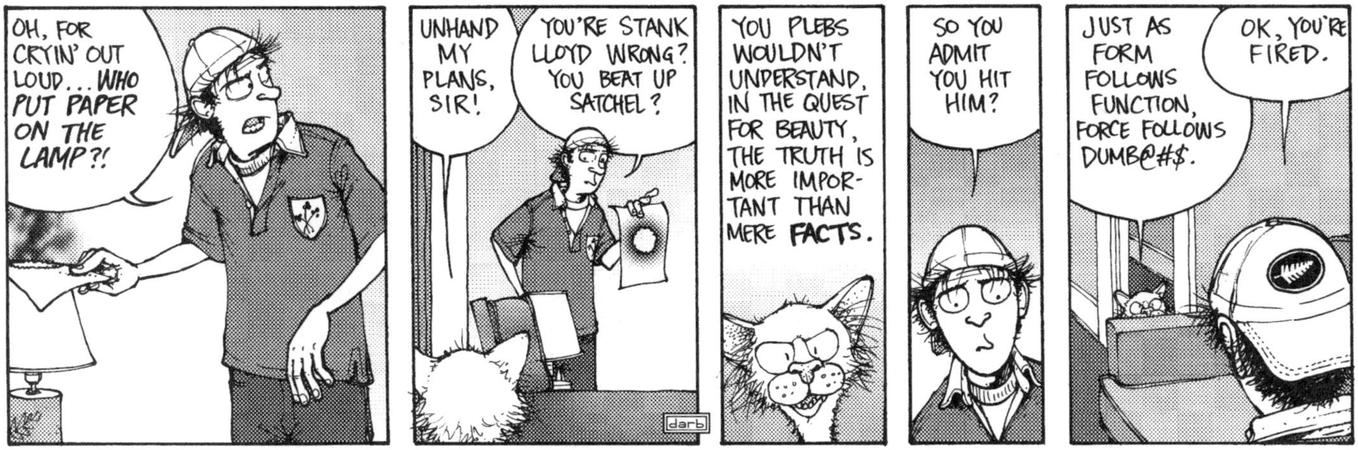
OH, FOR CRYIN' OUT LOUD... ***WHO PUT PAPER ON THE LAMP?!***
UNHAND MY PLANS, SIR!
YOU'RE STANK LLOYD WRONG? YOU BEAT UP SATCHEL?
darb
YOU PLEBS WOULDN'T UNDERSTAND. IN THE QUEST FOR BEAUTY, THE TRUTH IS MORE IMPORTANT THAN MERE **FACTS**.
SO YOU ADMIT YOU HIT HIM?
JUST AS FORM FOLLOWS FUNCTION, FORCE FOLLOWS DUMB@#$.
OK, YOU'RE FIRED.

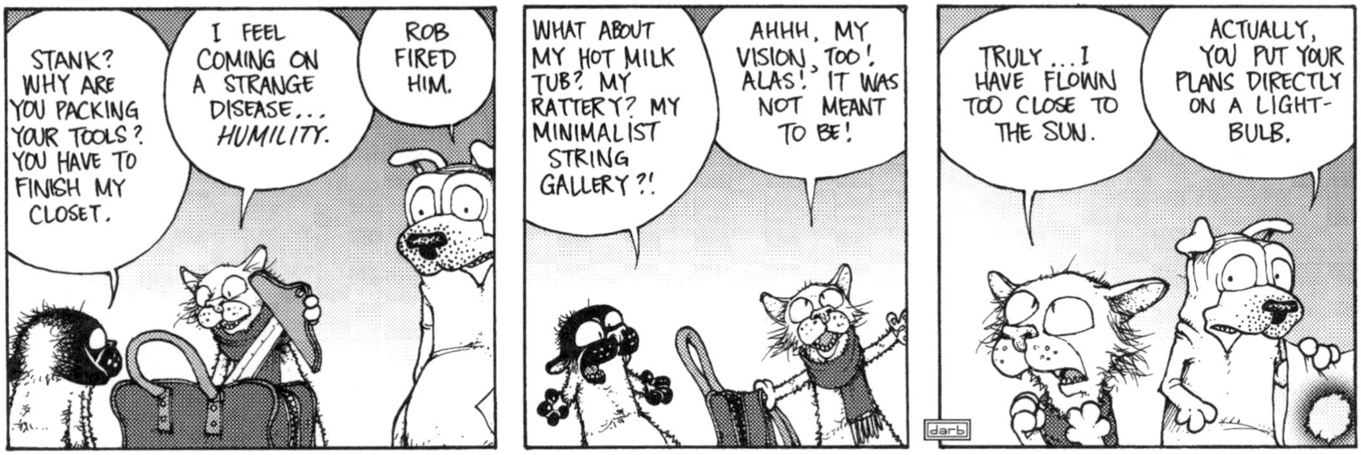
STANK? WHY ARE YOU PACKING YOUR TOOLS? YOU HAVE TO FINISH MY CLOSET.
I FEEL COMING ON A STRANGE DISEASE... *HUMILITY*.
ROB FIRED HIM.
WHAT ABOUT MY HOT MILK TUB? MY RATTERY? MY MINIMALIST STRING GALLERY?!
AHHH, MY VISION, TOO! ALAS! IT WAS NOT MEANT TO BE!
TRULY... I HAVE FLOWN TOO CLOSE TO THE SUN.
ACTUALLY, YOU PUT YOUR PLANS DIRECTLY ON A LIGHT-BULB.
darb

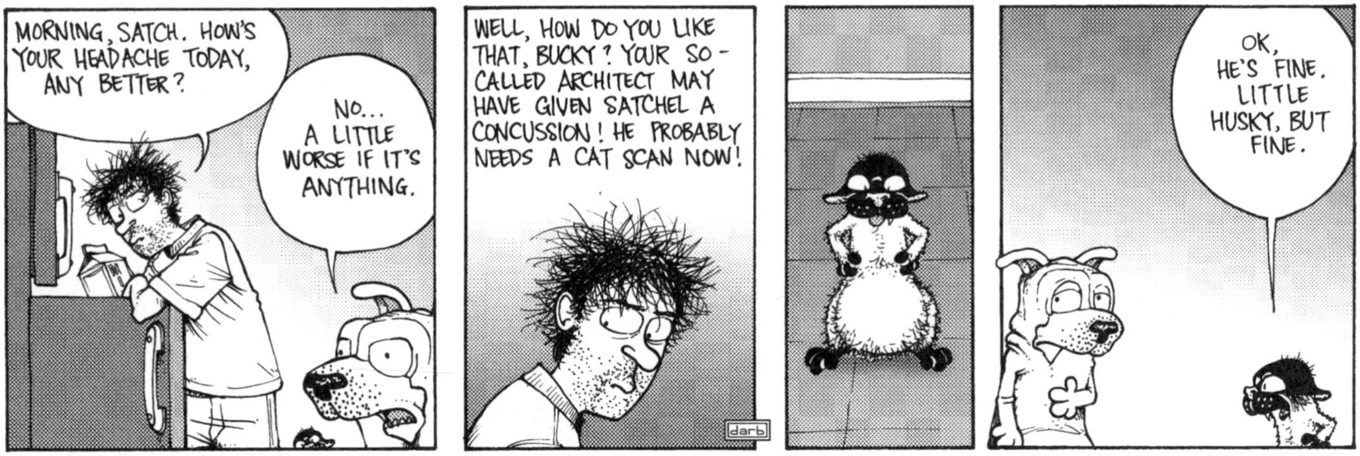
MORNING, SATCH. HOW'S YOUR HEADACHE TODAY, ANY BETTER?
NO... A LITTLE WORSE IF IT'S ANYTHING.
WELL, HOW DO YOU LIKE THAT, BUCKY? YOUR SO-CALLED ARCHITECT MAY HAVE GIVEN SATCHEL A CONCUSSION! HE PROBABLY NEEDS A CAT SCAN NOW!
darb
OK, HE'S FINE. LITTLE HUSKY, BUT FINE.

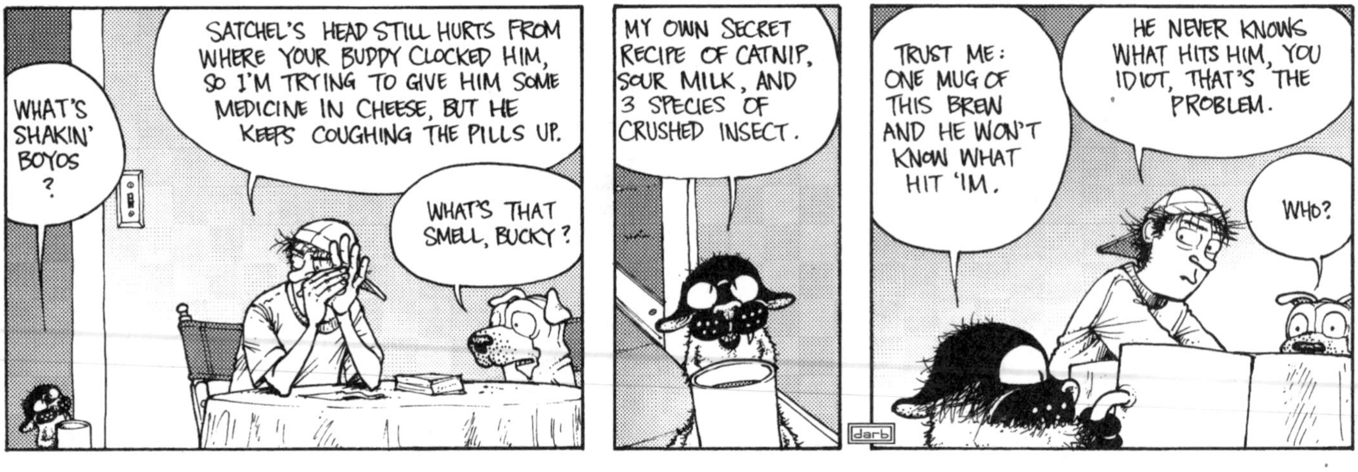
WHAT'S SHAKIN' BOYOS ?
SATCHEL'S HEAD STILL HURTS FROM WHERE YOUR BUDDY CLOCKED HIM, SO I'M TRYING TO GIVE HIM SOME MEDICINE IN CHEESE, BUT HE KEEPS COUGHING THE PILLS UP.
WHAT'S THAT SMELL, BUCKY?
MY OWN SECRET RECIPE OF CATNIP, SOUR MILK, AND 3 SPECIES OF CRUSHED INSECT.
darb
TRUST ME: ONE MUG OF THIS BREW AND HE WON'T KNOW WHAT HIT 'IM.
HE NEVER KNOWS WHAT HITS HIM, YOU IDIOT, THAT'S THE PROBLEM.
WHO?

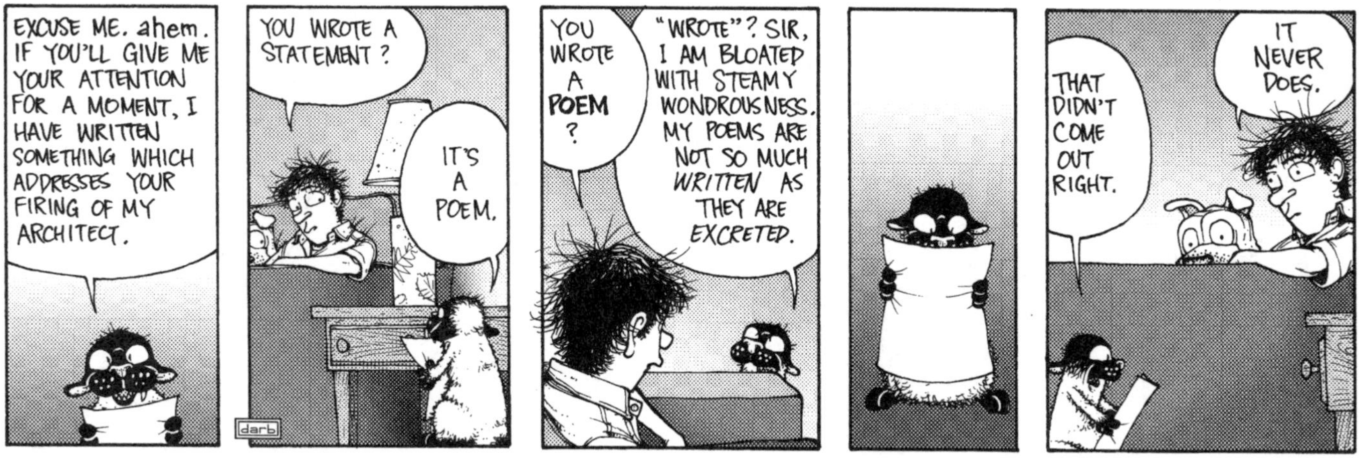
EXCUSE ME. ahem. IF YOU'LL GIVE ME YOUR ATTENTION FOR A MOMENT, I HAVE WRITTEN SOMETHING WHICH ADDRESSES YOUR FIRING OF MY ARCHITECT.
YOU WROTE A STATEMENT ?
IT'S A POEM.
darb
YOU WROTE A **POEM** ?
"WROTE"? SIR, I AM BLOATED WITH STEAMY WONDROUSNESS. MY POEMS ARE NOT SO MUCH *WRITTEN* AS THEY ARE *EXCRETED*.
IT NEVER DOES.
THAT DIDN'T COME OUT RIGHT.

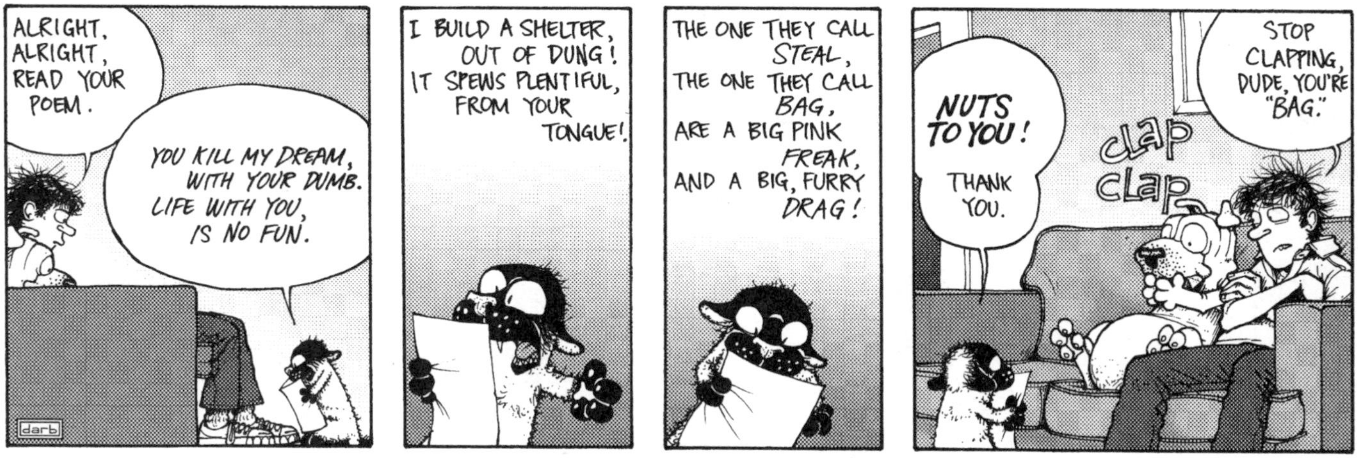
ALRIGHT, ALRIGHT, READ YOUR POEM.
YOU KILL MY DREAM, WITH YOUR DUMB. LIFE WITH YOU, IS NO FUN.
darb
I BUILD A SHELTER, OUT OF DUNG! IT SPEWS PLENTIFUL, FROM YOUR TONGUE!
THE ONE THEY CALL *STEAL*, THE ONE THEY CALL *BAG*, ARE A BIG PINK *FREAK*, AND A BIG, FURRY *DRAG*!
STOP CLAPPING, DUDE, YOU'RE "BAG."
NUTS TO YOU!
THANK YOU.
clap clap

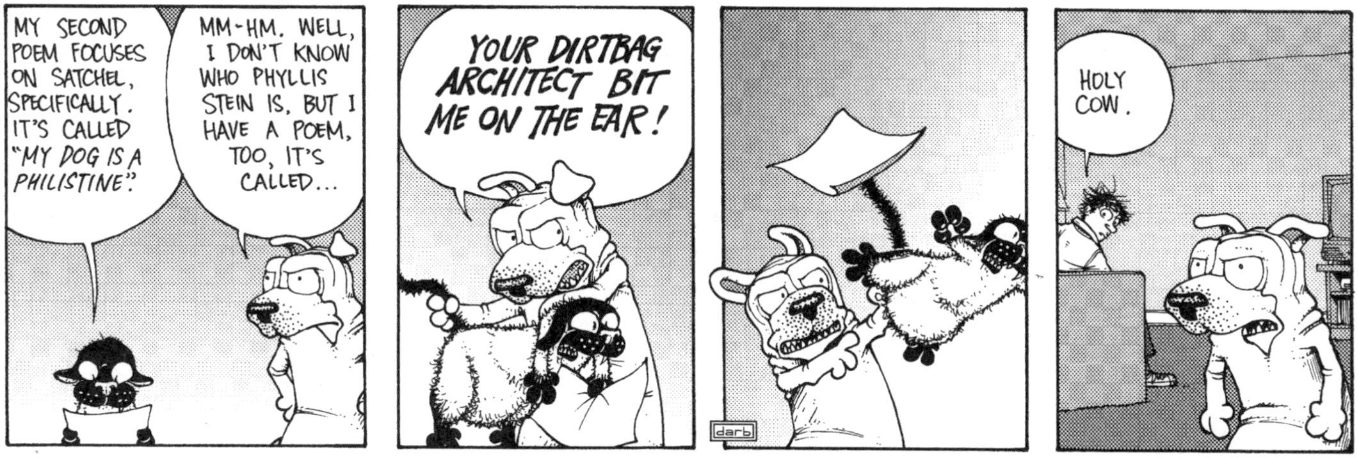
MY SECOND POEM FOCUSES ON SATCHEL, SPECIFICALLY. IT'S CALLED "*MY DOG IS A PHILISTINE*."
MM-HM. WELL, I DON'T KNOW WHO PHYLLIS STEIN IS, BUT I HAVE A POEM, TOO, IT'S CALLED...
YOUR DIRTBAG ARCHITECT BIT ME ON THE EAR!
darb
HOLY COW.

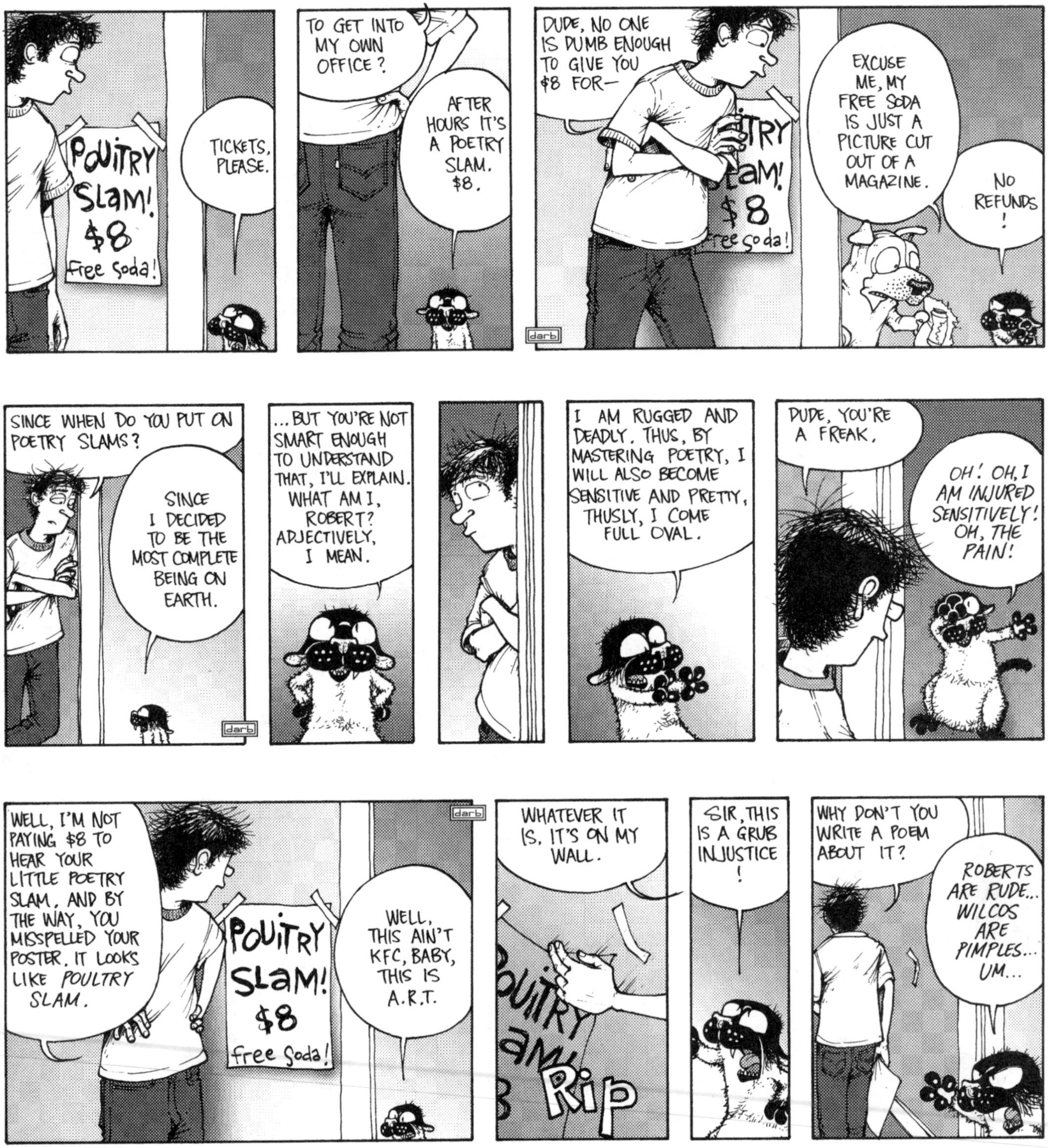

POUITRY SLAM! $8 Free soda!
TICKETS, PLEASE.
TO GET INTO MY OWN OFFICE?
AFTER HOURS IT'S A POETRY SLAM. $8.
DUDE, NO ONE IS DUMB ENOUGH TO GIVE YOU $8 FOR—
EXCUSE ME, MY FREE SODA IS JUST A PICTURE CUT OUT OF A MAGAZINE.
NO REFUNDS!
darb
SINCE WHEN DO YOU PUT ON POETRY SLAMS?
SINCE I DECIDED TO BE THE MOST COMPLETE BEING ON EARTH.
darb
...BUT YOU'RE NOT SMART ENOUGH TO UNDERSTAND THAT, I'LL EXPLAIN. WHAT AM I, ROBERT? ADJECTIVELY, I MEAN.
I AM RUGGED AND DEADLY. THUS, BY MASTERING POETRY, I WILL ALSO BECOME SENSITIVE AND PRETTY. THUSLY, I COME FULL OVAL.
DUDE, YOU'RE A FREAK.
OH! OH, I AM INJURED SENSITIVELY! OH, THE PAIN!
darb
WELL, I'M NOT PAYING $8 TO HEAR YOUR LITTLE POETRY SLAM. AND BY THE WAY, YOU MISSPELLED YOUR POSTER. IT LOOKS LIKE POULTRY SLAM.
POUITRY SLAM! $8 free soda!
WELL, THIS AIN'T KFC, BABY, THIS IS A.R.T.
WHATEVER IT IS, IT'S ON MY WALL.
RIP
SIR, THIS IS A GRUB INJUSTICE!
WHY DON'T YOU WRITE A POEM ABOUT IT?
ROBERTS ARE RUDE... WILCOS ARE PIMPLES... UM...

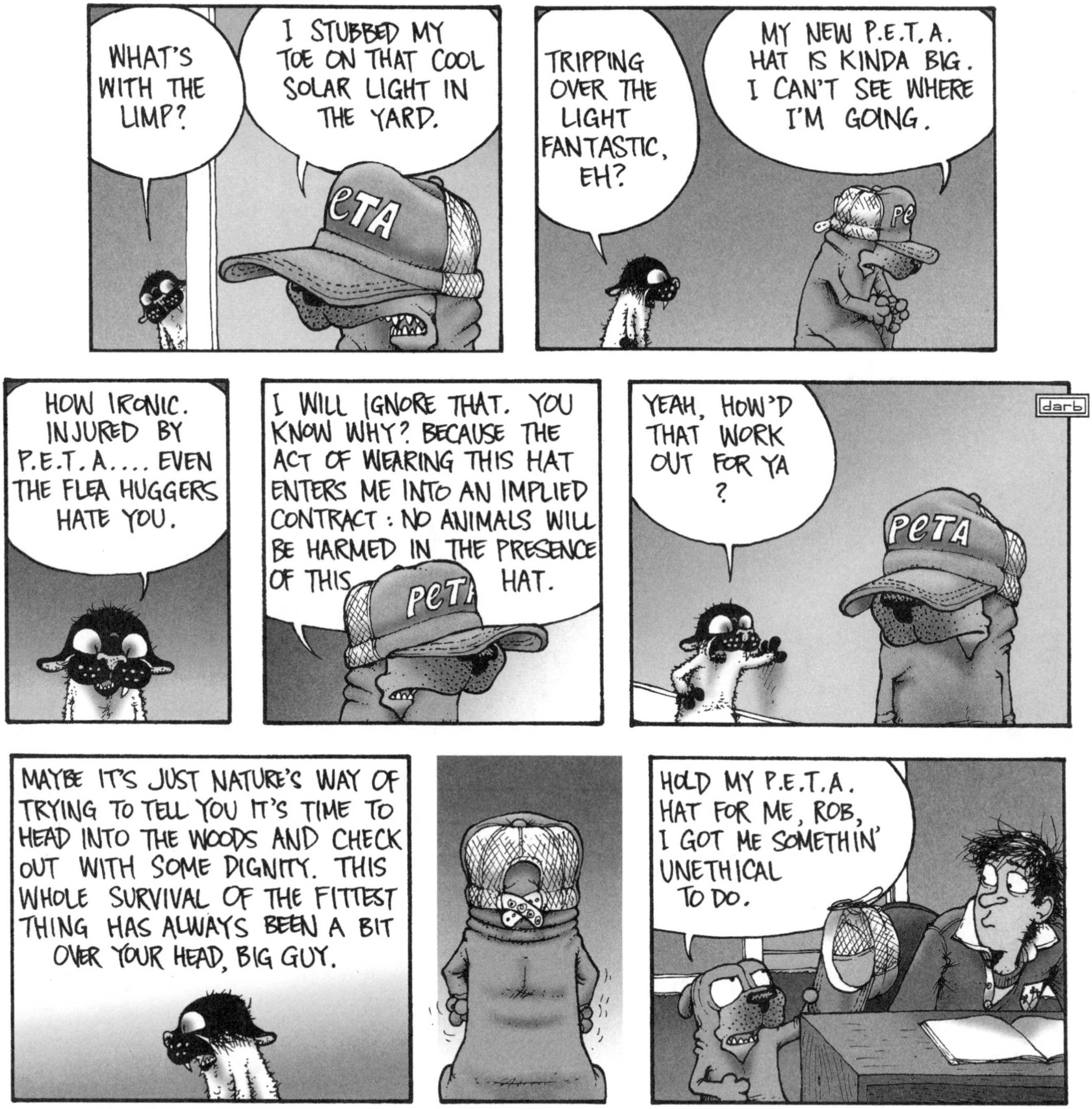
WHAT'S WITH THE LIMP?
I STUBBED MY TOE ON THAT COOL SOLAR LIGHT IN THE YARD.
TRIPPING OVER THE LIGHT FANTASTIC, EH?
MY NEW P.E.T.A. HAT IS KINDA BIG. I CAN'T SEE WHERE I'M GOING.
PETA
HOW IRONIC. INJURED BY P.E.T.A.... EVEN THE FLEA HUGGERS HATE YOU.
I WILL IGNORE THAT. YOU KNOW WHY? BECAUSE THE ACT OF WEARING THIS HAT ENTERS ME INTO AN IMPLIED CONTRACT: NO ANIMALS WILL BE HARMED IN THE PRESENCE OF THIS HAT.
YEAH, HOW'D THAT WORK OUT FOR YA?
PETA
darb
MAYBE IT'S JUST NATURE'S WAY OF TRYING TO TELL YOU IT'S TIME TO HEAD INTO THE WOODS AND CHECK OUT WITH SOME DIGNITY. THIS WHOLE SURVIVAL OF THE FITTEST THING HAS ALWAYS BEEN A BIT OVER YOUR HEAD, BIG GUY.
HOLD MY P.E.T.A. HAT FOR ME, ROB, I GOT ME SOMETHIN' UNETHICAL TO DO.

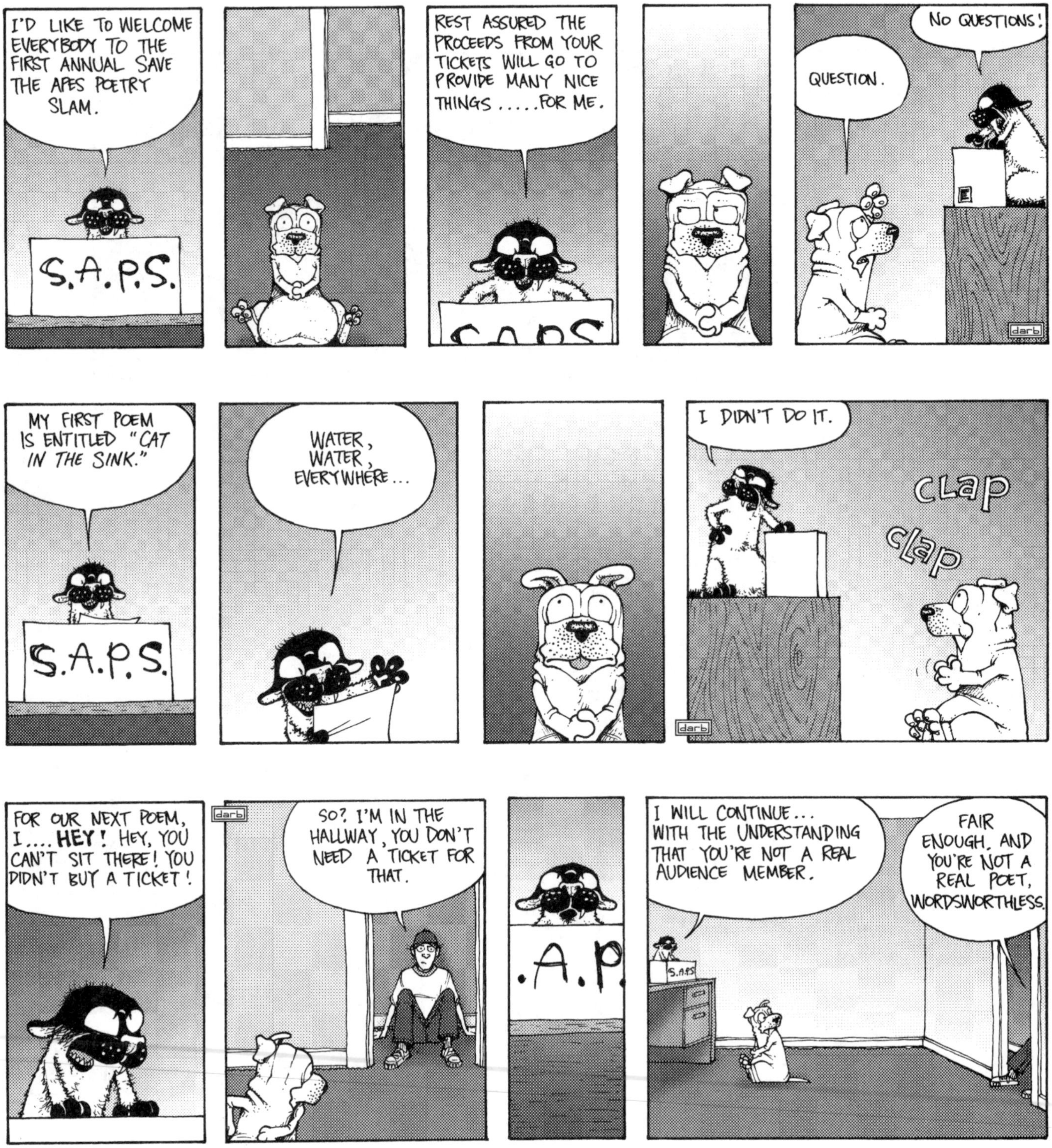
I'D LIKE TO WELCOME EVERYBODY TO THE FIRST ANNUAL SAVE THE APES POETRY SLAM.
S.A.P.S.
REST ASSURED THE PROCEEDS FROM YOUR TICKETS WILL GO TO PROVIDE MANY NICE THINGS .....FOR ME.
QUESTION.
NO QUESTIONS!
darb
MY FIRST POEM IS ENTITLED "CAT IN THE SINK."
S.A.P.S.
WATER, WATER, EVERYWHERE...
I DIDN'T DO IT.
CLAP
CLAP
darb
FOR OUR NEXT POEM, I.... HEY! HEY, YOU CAN'T SIT THERE! YOU DIDN'T BUY A TICKET!
darb
SO? I'M IN THE HALLWAY, YOU DON'T NEED A TICKET FOR THAT.
I WILL CONTINUE... WITH THE UNDERSTANDING THAT YOU'RE NOT A REAL AUDIENCE MEMBER.
FAIR ENOUGH. AND YOU'RE NOT A REAL POET, WORDSWORTHLESS.

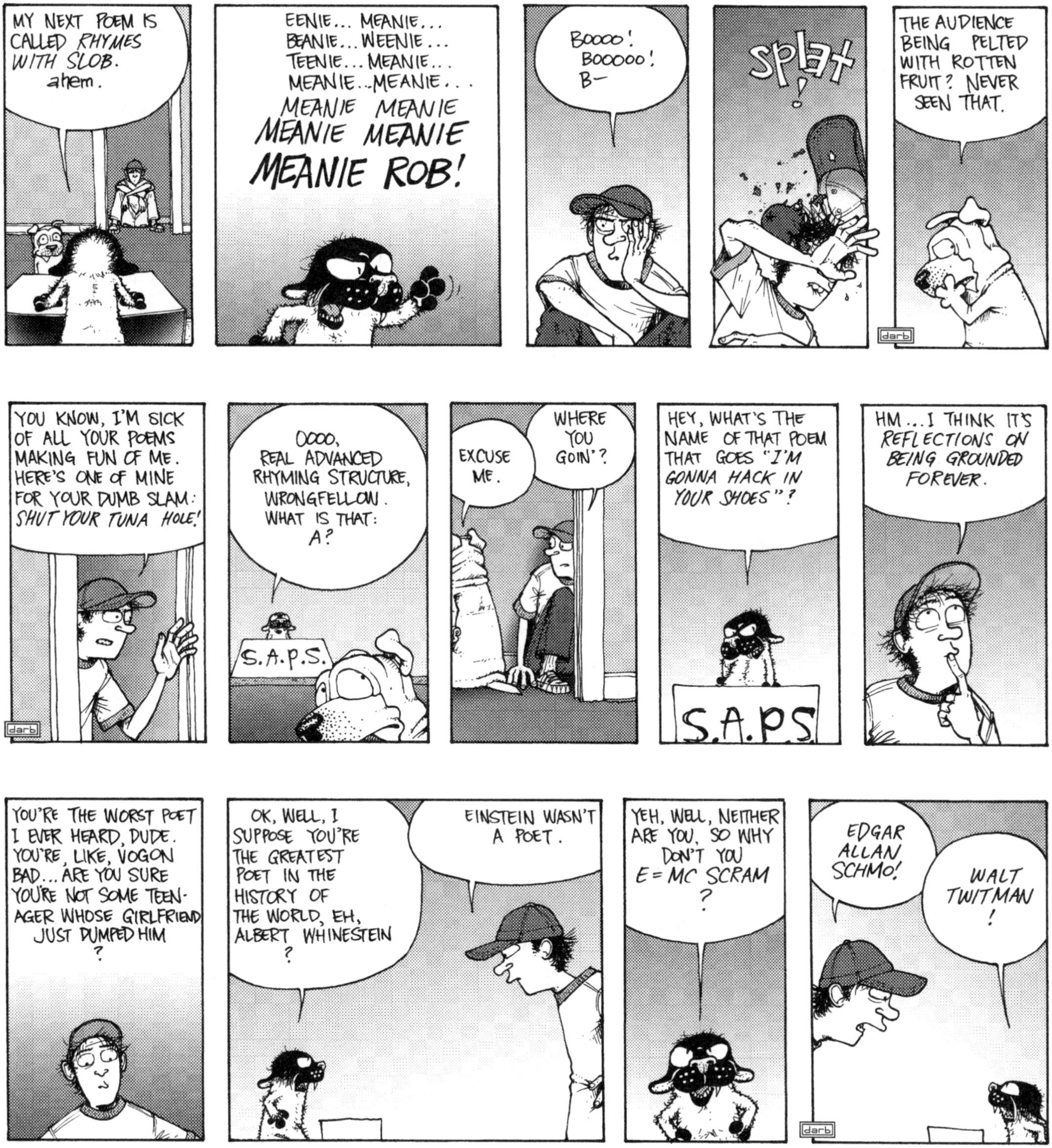
MY NEXT POEM IS CALLED *RHYMES WITH SLOB*. ahem.
EENIE... MEANIE... BEANIE... WEENIE... TEENIE... MEANIE... MEANIE...MEANIE... MEANIE MEANIE MEANIE MEANIE MEANIE ROB!
BOOOO! BOOOOO! B—
SPLAT
THE AUDIENCE BEING PELTED WITH ROTTEN FRUIT? NEVER SEEN THAT.
darb
YOU KNOW, I'M SICK OF ALL YOUR POEMS MAKING FUN OF ME. HERE'S ONE OF MINE FOR YOUR DUMB SLAM: *SHUT YOUR TUNA HOLE!*
darb
OOOO, REAL ADVANCED RHYMING STRUCTURE, WRONGFELLOW. WHAT IS THAT: A?
S.A.P.S.
EXCUSE ME.
WHERE YOU GOIN'?
HEY, WHAT'S THE NAME OF THAT POEM THAT GOES "*I'M GONNA HACK IN YOUR SHOES*"?
S.A.P.S
HM... I THINK IT'S *REFLECTIONS ON BEING GROUNDED FOREVER*.
YOU'RE THE WORST POET I EVER HEARD, DUDE. YOU'RE, LIKE, VOGON BAD... ARE YOU SURE YOU'RE NOT SOME TEEN-AGER WHOSE GIRLFRIEND JUST DUMPED HIM?
OK, WELL, I SUPPOSE YOU'RE THE GREATEST POET IN THE HISTORY OF THE WORLD, EH, ALBERT WHINESTEIN?
EINSTEIN WASN'T A POET.
YEH, WELL, NEITHER ARE YOU, SO WHY DON'T YOU *E = MC SCRAM*?
EDGAR ALLAN SCHMO!
WALT TWITMAN!
darb

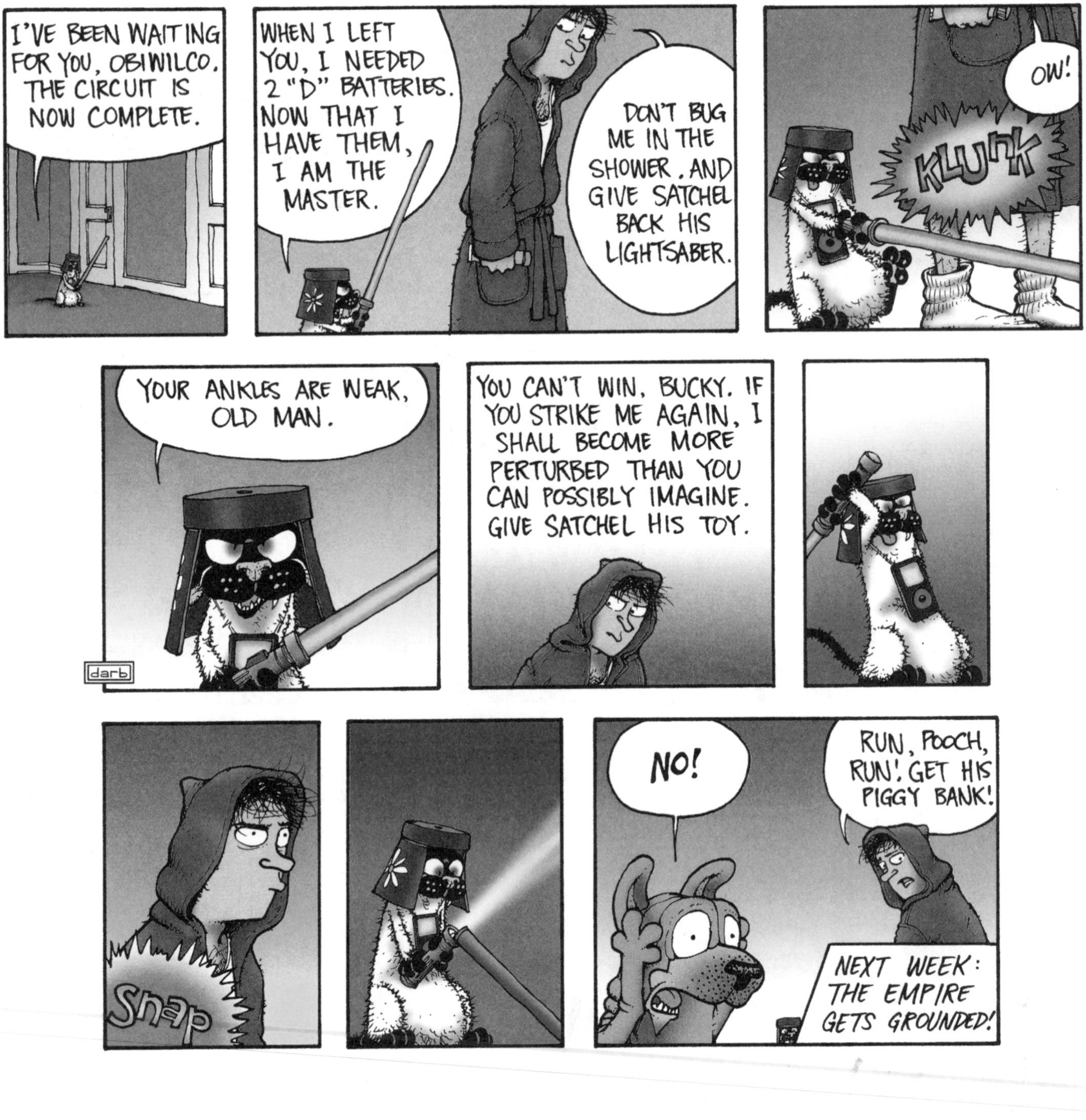
I'VE BEEN WAITING FOR YOU, OBIWILCO. THE CIRCUIT IS NOW COMPLETE.
WHEN I LEFT YOU, I NEEDED 2 "D" BATTERIES. NOW THAT I HAVE THEM, I AM THE MASTER.
DON'T BUG ME IN THE SHOWER. AND GIVE SATCHEL BACK HIS LIGHTSABER.
OW!
KLUNK
YOUR ANKLES ARE WEAK, OLD MAN.
darb
YOU CAN'T WIN, BUCKY. IF YOU STRIKE ME AGAIN, I SHALL BECOME MORE PERTURBED THAN YOU CAN POSSIBLY IMAGINE. GIVE SATCHEL HIS TOY.
Snap
NO!
RUN, POOCH, RUN! GET HIS PIGGY BANK!
NEXT WEEK: THE EMPIRE GETS GROUNDED!

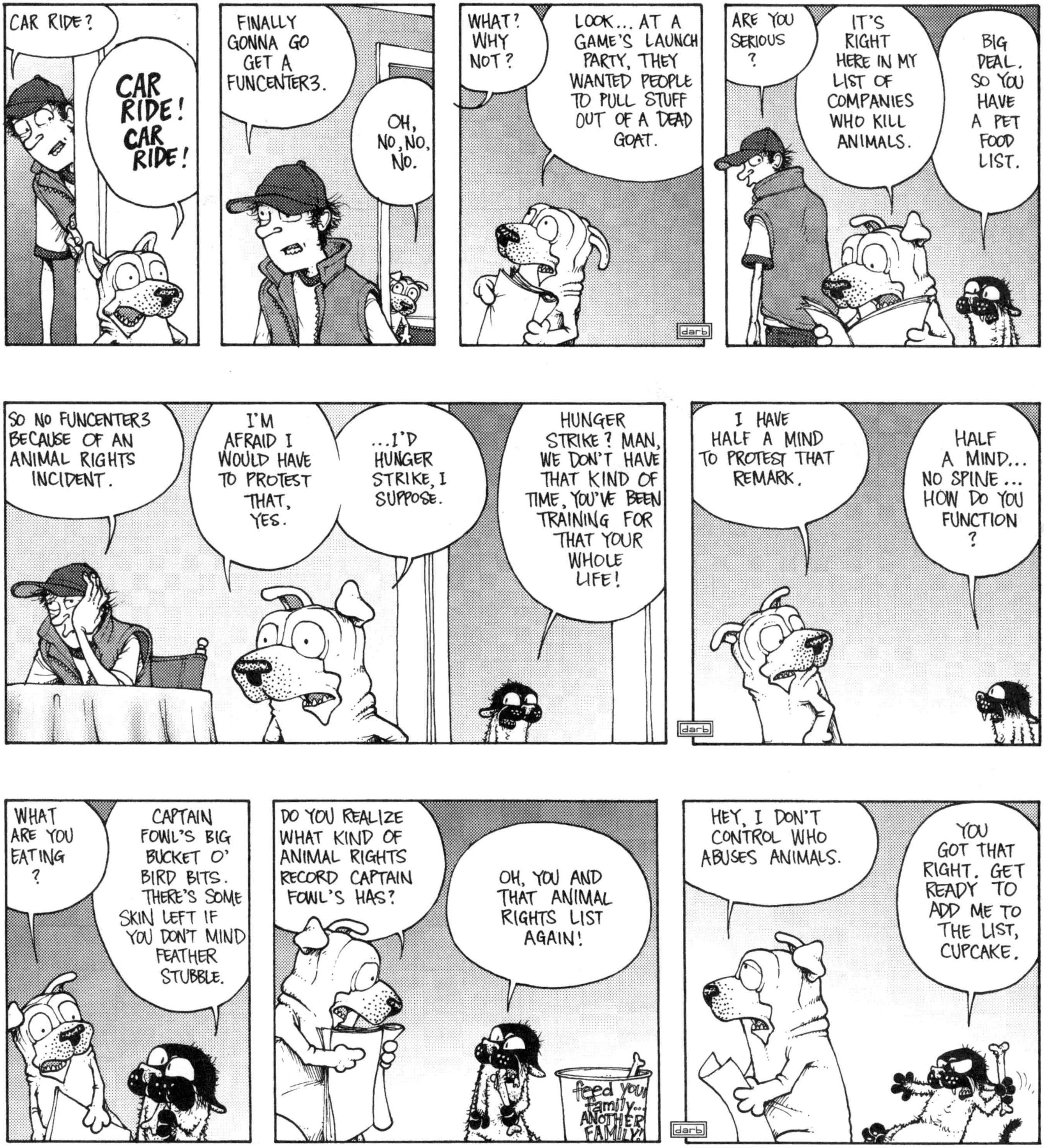
CAR RIDE?
CAR RIDE! CAR RIDE!
FINALLY GONNA GO GET A FUNCENTER3.
OH, NO, NO, NO.
WHAT? WHY NOT?
LOOK... AT A GAME'S LAUNCH PARTY, THEY WANTED PEOPLE TO PULL STUFF OUT OF A DEAD GOAT.
ARE YOU SERIOUS?
IT'S RIGHT HERE IN MY LIST OF COMPANIES WHO KILL ANIMALS.
BIG DEAL. SO YOU HAVE A PET FOOD LIST.
darb
SO NO FUNCENTER3 BECAUSE OF AN ANIMAL RIGHTS INCIDENT.
I'M AFRAID I WOULD HAVE TO PROTEST THAT, YES.
...I'D HUNGER STRIKE, I SUPPOSE.
HUNGER STRIKE? MAN, WE DON'T HAVE THAT KIND OF TIME, YOU'VE BEEN TRAINING FOR THAT YOUR WHOLE LIFE!
I HAVE HALF A MIND TO PROTEST THAT REMARK.
HALF A MIND... NO SPINE... HOW DO YOU FUNCTION?
darb
WHAT ARE YOU EATING?
CAPTAIN FOWL'S BIG BUCKET O' BIRD BITS. THERE'S SOME SKIN LEFT IF YOU DON'T MIND FEATHER STUBBLE.
DO YOU REALIZE WHAT KIND OF ANIMAL RIGHTS RECORD CAPTAIN FOWL'S HAS?
OH, YOU AND THAT ANIMAL RIGHTS LIST AGAIN!
feed your family... ANOTHER FAMILY!
HEY, I DON'T CONTROL WHO ABUSES ANIMALS.
YOU GOT THAT RIGHT. GET READY TO ADD ME TO THE LIST, CUPCAKE.
darb

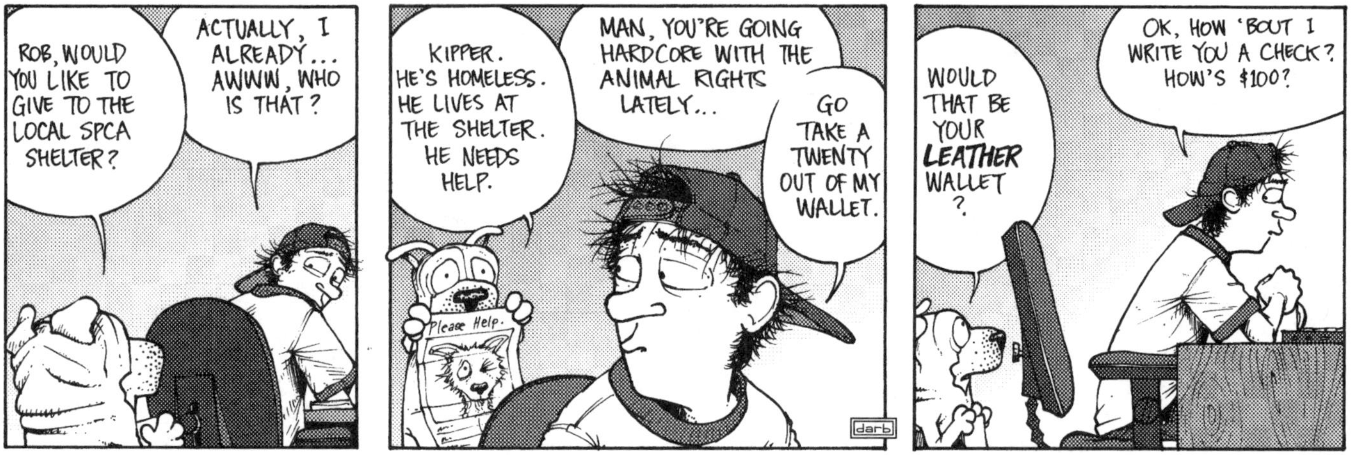
ROB, WOULD YOU LIKE TO GIVE TO THE LOCAL SPCA SHELTER?
ACTUALLY, I ALREADY... AWWW, WHO IS THAT?
KIPPER. HE'S HOMELESS. HE LIVES AT THE SHELTER. HE NEEDS HELP.
Please Help.
MAN, YOU'RE GOING HARDCORE WITH THE ANIMAL RIGHTS LATELY...
GO TAKE A TWENTY OUT OF MY WALLET.
darb
WOULD THAT BE YOUR **LEATHER** WALLET?
OK, HOW 'BOUT I WRITE YOU A CHECK? HOW'S $100?

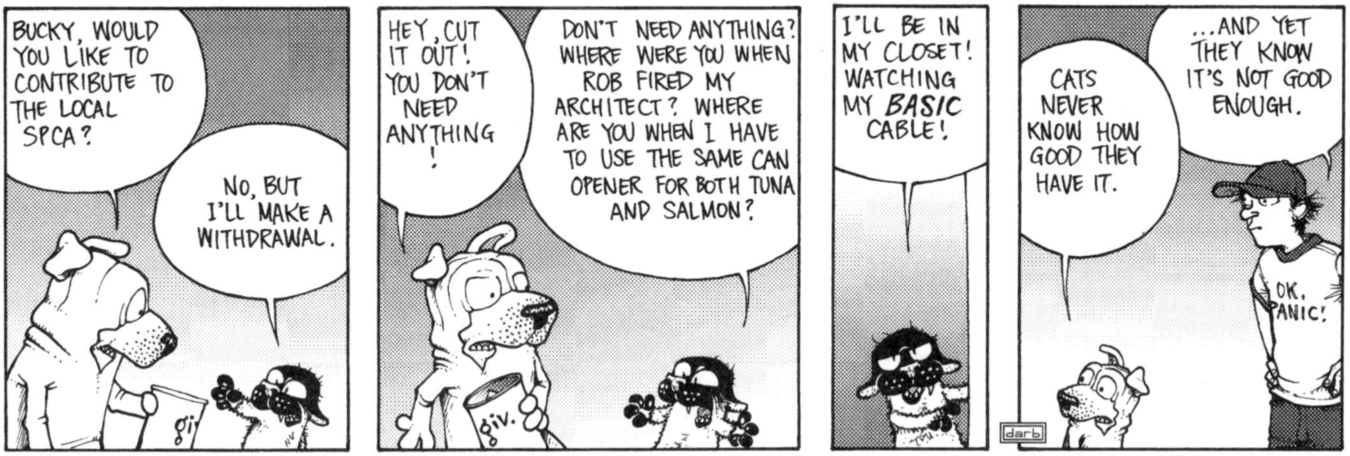
BUCKY, WOULD YOU LIKE TO CONTRIBUTE TO THE LOCAL SPCA?
NO, BUT I'LL MAKE A WITHDRAWAL.
HEY, CUT IT OUT! YOU DON'T NEED ANYTHING!
DON'T NEED ANYTHING? WHERE WERE YOU WHEN ROB FIRED MY ARCHITECT? WHERE ARE YOU WHEN I HAVE TO USE THE SAME CAN OPENER FOR BOTH TUNA AND SALMON?
giv.
I'LL BE IN MY CLOSET! WATCHING MY ***BASIC*** CABLE!
CATS NEVER KNOW HOW GOOD THEY HAVE IT.
...AND YET THEY KNOW IT'S NOT GOOD ENOUGH.
OK, PANIC!
darb

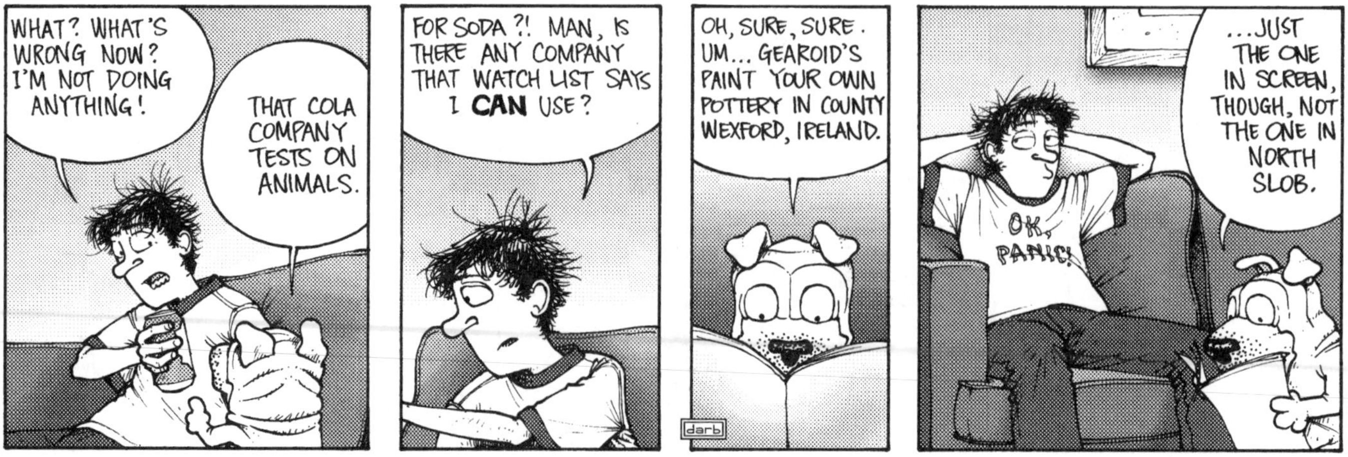
WHAT? WHAT'S WRONG NOW? I'M NOT DOING ANYTHING!
THAT COLA COMPANY TESTS ON ANIMALS.
FOR SODA?! MAN, IS THERE ANY COMPANY THAT WATCH LIST SAYS I **CAN** USE?
OH, SURE, SURE. UM... GEAROID'S PAINT YOUR OWN POTTERY IN COUNTY WEXFORD, IRELAND.
darb
...JUST THE ONE IN SCREEN, THOUGH, NOT THE ONE IN NORTH SLOB.
OK, PANIC!

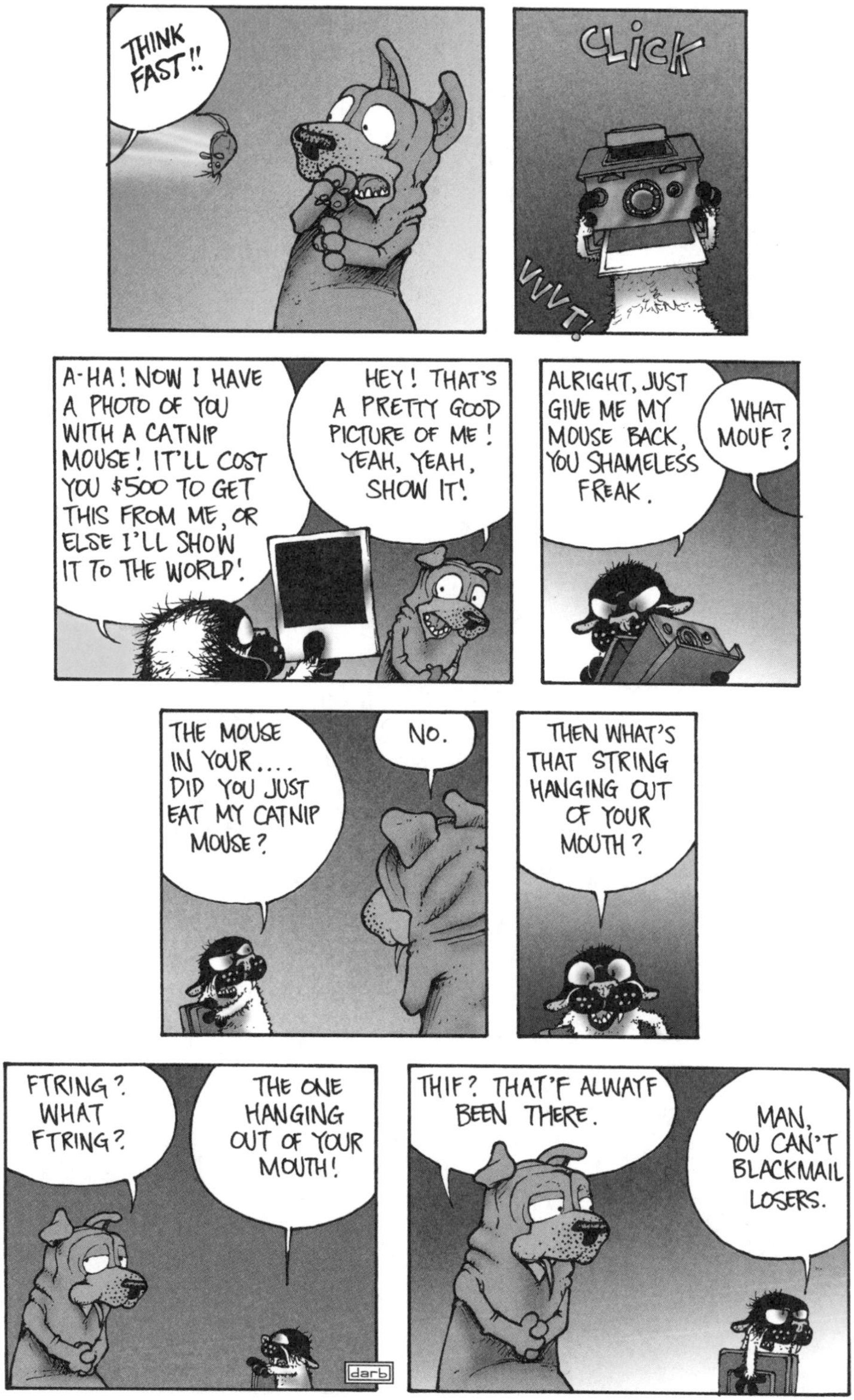
THINK FAST!!
CLICK
VVVT!
A-HA! NOW I HAVE A PHOTO OF YOU WITH A CATNIP MOUSE! IT'LL COST YOU $500 TO GET THIS FROM ME, OR ELSE I'LL SHOW IT TO THE WORLD!
HEY! THAT'S A PRETTY GOOD PICTURE OF ME! YEAH, YEAH, SHOW IT!
ALRIGHT, JUST GIVE ME MY MOUSE BACK, YOU SHAMELESS FREAK.
WHAT MOUF?
THE MOUSE IN YOUR.... DID YOU JUST EAT MY CATNIP MOUSE?
NO.
THEN WHAT'S THAT STRING HANGING OUT OF YOUR MOUTH?
FTRING? WHAT FTRING?
THE ONE HANGING OUT OF YOUR MOUTH!
darb
THIF? THAT'F ALWAYF BEEN THERE.
MAN, YOU CAN'T BLACKMAIL LOSERS.

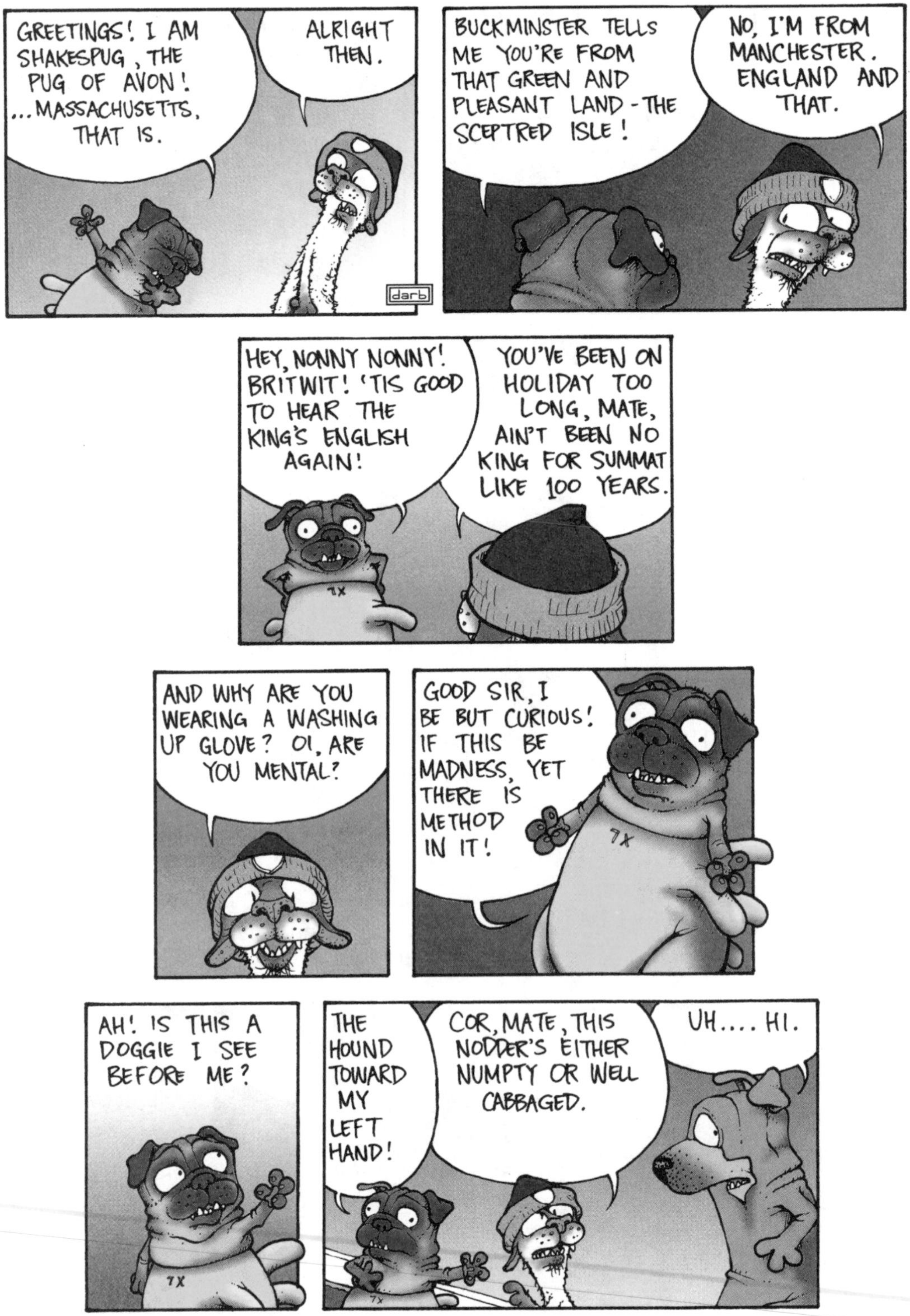

GREETINGS! I AM SHAKESPUG, THE PUG OF AVON! ...MASSACHUSETTS, THAT IS.
ALRIGHT THEN.
darb
BUCKMINSTER TELLS ME YOU'RE FROM THAT GREEN AND PLEASANT LAND - THE SCEPTRED ISLE!
NO, I'M FROM MANCHESTER. ENGLAND AND THAT.
HEY, NONNY NONNY! BRITWIT! 'TIS GOOD TO HEAR THE KING'S ENGLISH AGAIN!
YOU'VE BEEN ON HOLIDAY TOO LONG, MATE, AIN'T BEEN NO KING FOR SUMMAT LIKE 100 YEARS.
AND WHY ARE YOU WEARING A WASHING UP GLOVE? OI, ARE YOU MENTAL?
GOOD SIR, I BE BUT CURIOUS! IF THIS BE MADNESS, YET THERE IS METHOD IN IT!
AH! IS THIS A DOGGIE I SEE BEFORE ME?
THE HOUND TOWARD MY LEFT HAND!
COR, MATE, THIS NODDER'S EITHER NUMPTY OR WELL CABBAGED.
UH.... HI.

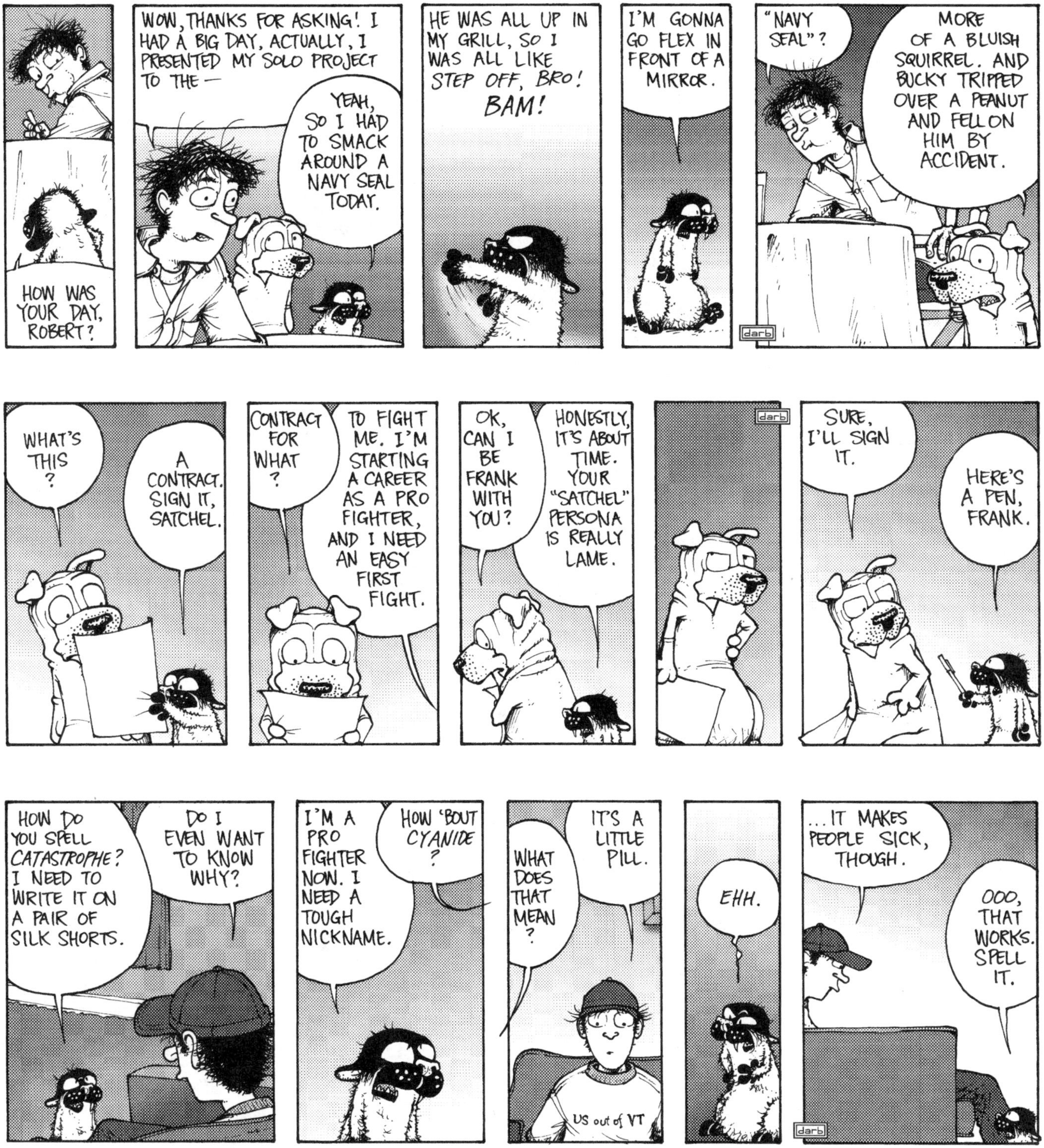
HOW WAS YOUR DAY, ROBERT?
WOW, THANKS FOR ASKING! I HAD A BIG DAY, ACTUALLY. I PRESENTED MY SOLO PROJECT TO THE —
YEAH, SO I HAD TO SMACK AROUND A NAVY SEAL TODAY.
HE WAS ALL UP IN MY GRILL, SO I WAS ALL LIKE STEP OFF, BRO! BAM!
I'M GONNA GO FLEX IN FRONT OF A MIRROR.
"NAVY SEAL"?
MORE OF A BLUISH SQUIRREL. AND BUCKY TRIPPED OVER A PEANUT AND FELL ON HIM BY ACCIDENT.
darb
WHAT'S THIS?
A CONTRACT. SIGN IT, SATCHEL.
CONTRACT FOR WHAT?
TO FIGHT ME. I'M STARTING A CAREER AS A PRO FIGHTER, AND I NEED AN EASY FIRST FIGHT.
OK, CAN I BE FRANK WITH YOU?
HONESTLY, IT'S ABOUT TIME. YOUR "SATCHEL" PERSONA IS REALLY LAME.
darb
SURE, I'LL SIGN IT.
HERE'S A PEN, FRANK.
HOW DO YOU SPELL CATASTROPHE? I NEED TO WRITE IT ON A PAIR OF SILK SHORTS.
DO I EVEN WANT TO KNOW WHY?
I'M A PRO FIGHTER NOW. I NEED A TOUGH NICKNAME.
HOW 'BOUT CYANIDE?
WHAT DOES THAT MEAN?
IT'S A LITTLE PILL.
US out of VT
EHH.
...IT MAKES PEOPLE SICK, THOUGH.
OOO, THAT WORKS. SPELL IT.
darb

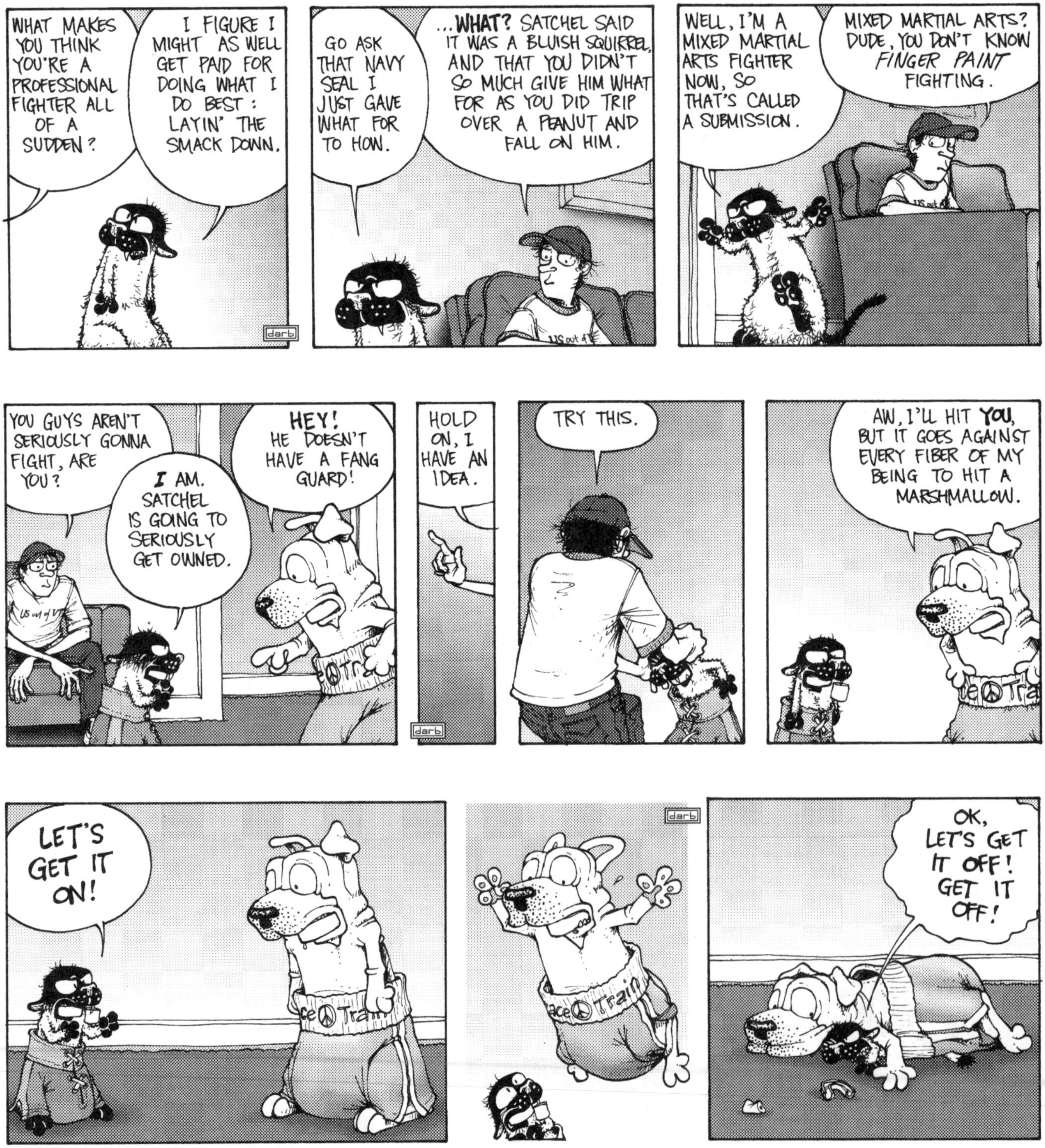
WHAT MAKES YOU THINK YOU'RE A PROFESSIONAL FIGHTER ALL OF A SUDDEN?
I FIGURE I MIGHT AS WELL GET PAID FOR DOING WHAT I DO BEST: LAYIN' THE SMACK DOWN.
GO ASK THAT NAVY SEAL I JUST GAVE WHAT FOR TO HOW.
...WHAT? SATCHEL SAID IT WAS A BLUISH SQUIRREL, AND THAT YOU DIDN'T SO MUCH GIVE HIM WHAT FOR AS YOU DID TRIP OVER A PEANUT AND FALL ON HIM.
WELL, I'M A MIXED MARTIAL ARTS FIGHTER NOW, SO THAT'S CALLED A SUBMISSION.
MIXED MARTIAL ARTS? DUDE, YOU DON'T KNOW FINGER PAINT FIGHTING.
YOU GUYS AREN'T SERIOUSLY GONNA FIGHT, ARE YOU?
I AM. SATCHEL IS GOING TO SERIOUSLY GET OWNED.
HEY! HE DOESN'T HAVE A FANG GUARD!
HOLD ON, I HAVE AN IDEA.
TRY THIS.
AW, I'LL HIT YOU, BUT IT GOES AGAINST EVERY FIBER OF MY BEING TO HIT A MARSHMALLOW.
LET'S GET IT ON!
OK, LET'S GET IT OFF! GET IT OFF!

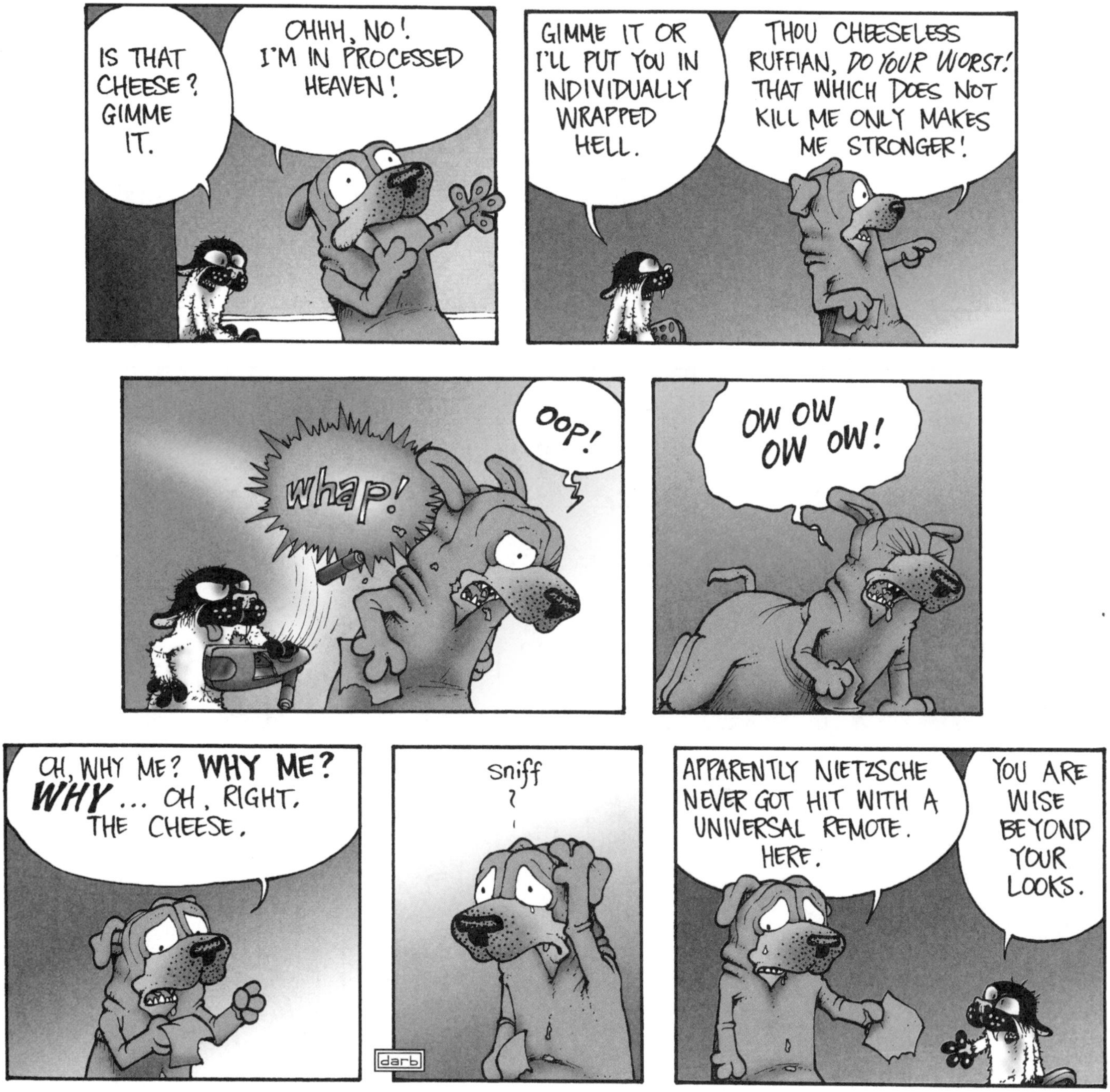
IS THAT CHEESE? GIMME IT.
OHHH, NO! I'M IN PROCESSED HEAVEN!
GIMME IT OR I'LL PUT YOU IN INDIVIDUALLY WRAPPED HELL.
THOU CHEESELESS RUFFIAN, DO YOUR WORST! THAT WHICH DOES NOT KILL ME ONLY MAKES ME STRONGER!
whap!
OOP!
OW OW OW OW!
OH, WHY ME? WHY ME? WHY... OH, RIGHT. THE CHEESE.
darb
sniff ?
APPARENTLY NIETZSCHE NEVER GOT HIT WITH A UNIVERSAL REMOTE. HERE.
YOU ARE WISE BEYOND YOUR LOOKS.

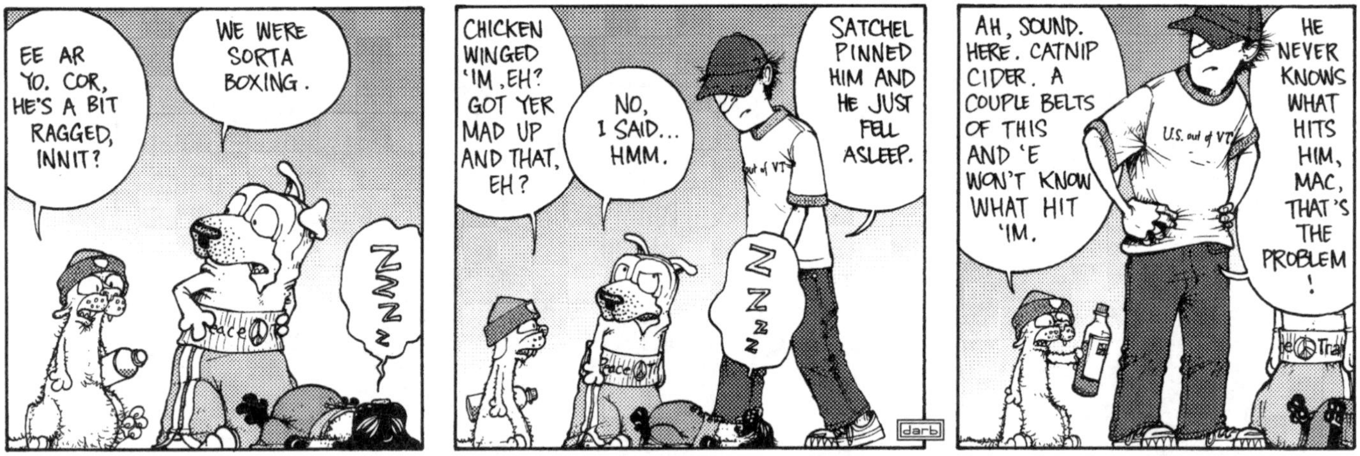
EE AR YO. COR, HE'S A BIT RAGGED, INNIT?
WE WERE SORTA BOXING.
ZZZZ
CHICKEN WINGED 'IM, EH? GOT YER MAD UP AND THAT, EH?
NO, I SAID... HMM.
SATCHEL PINNED HIM AND HE JUST FELL ASLEEP.
ZZZ
AH, SOUND. HERE. CATNIP CIDER. A COUPLE BELTS OF THIS AND 'E WON'T KNOW WHAT HIT 'IM.
HE NEVER KNOWS WHAT HITS HIM, MAC, THAT'S THE PROBLEM!
darb

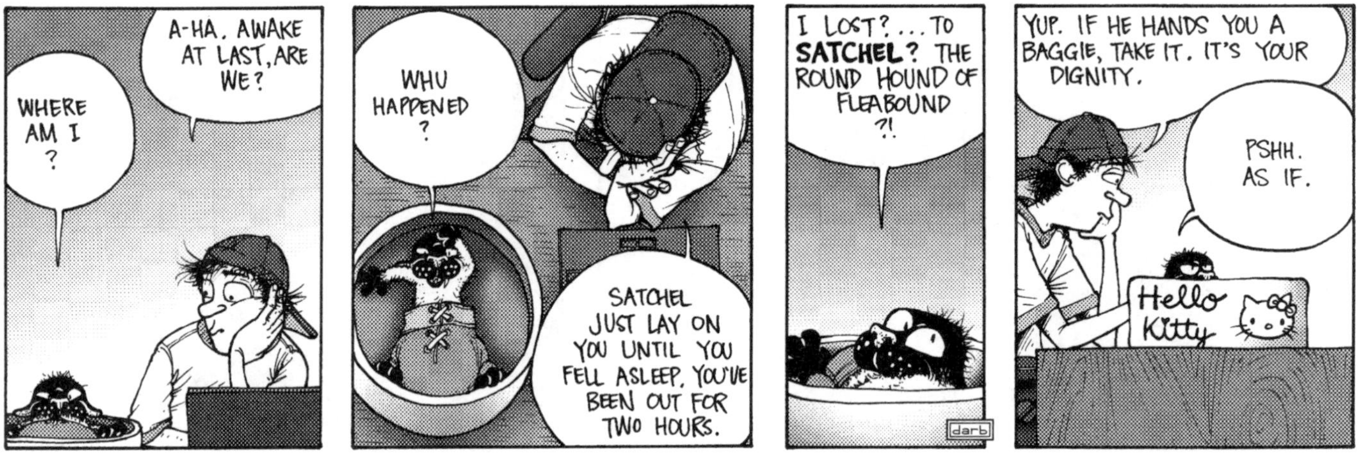
WHERE AM I?
A-HA. AWAKE AT LAST, ARE WE?
WHU HAPPENED?
SATCHEL JUST LAY ON YOU UNTIL YOU FELL ASLEEP. YOU'VE BEEN OUT FOR TWO HOURS.
I LOST?... TO **SATCHEL**? THE ROUND HOUND OF FLEABOUND?!
darb
YUP. IF HE HANDS YOU A BAGGIE, TAKE IT. IT'S YOUR DIGNITY.
PSHH. AS IF.
Hello Kitty

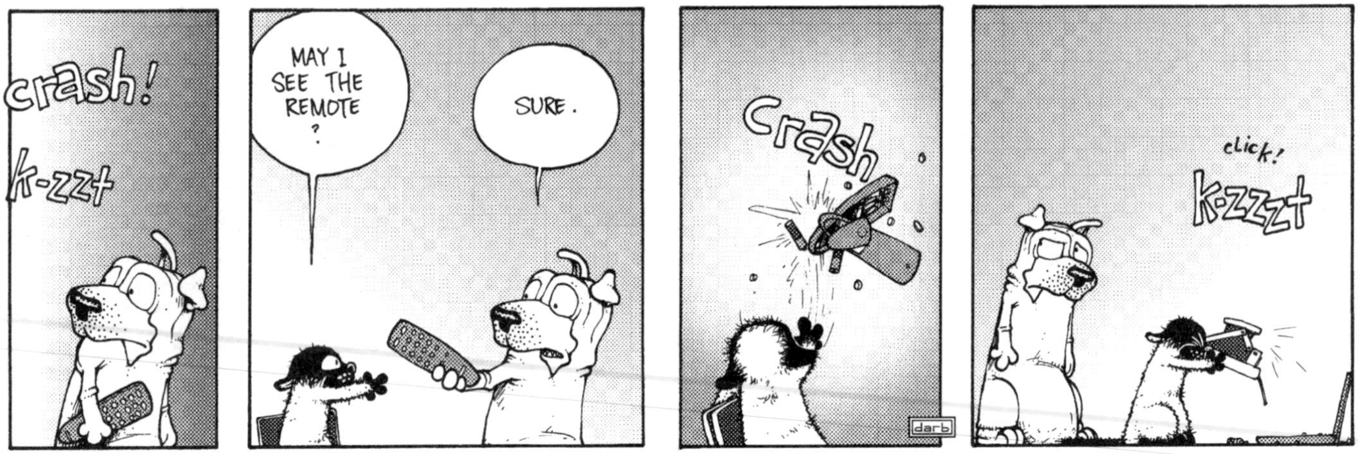
crash!
k-zzt
MAY I SEE THE REMOTE?
SURE.
crash
darb
click!
k-zzzt

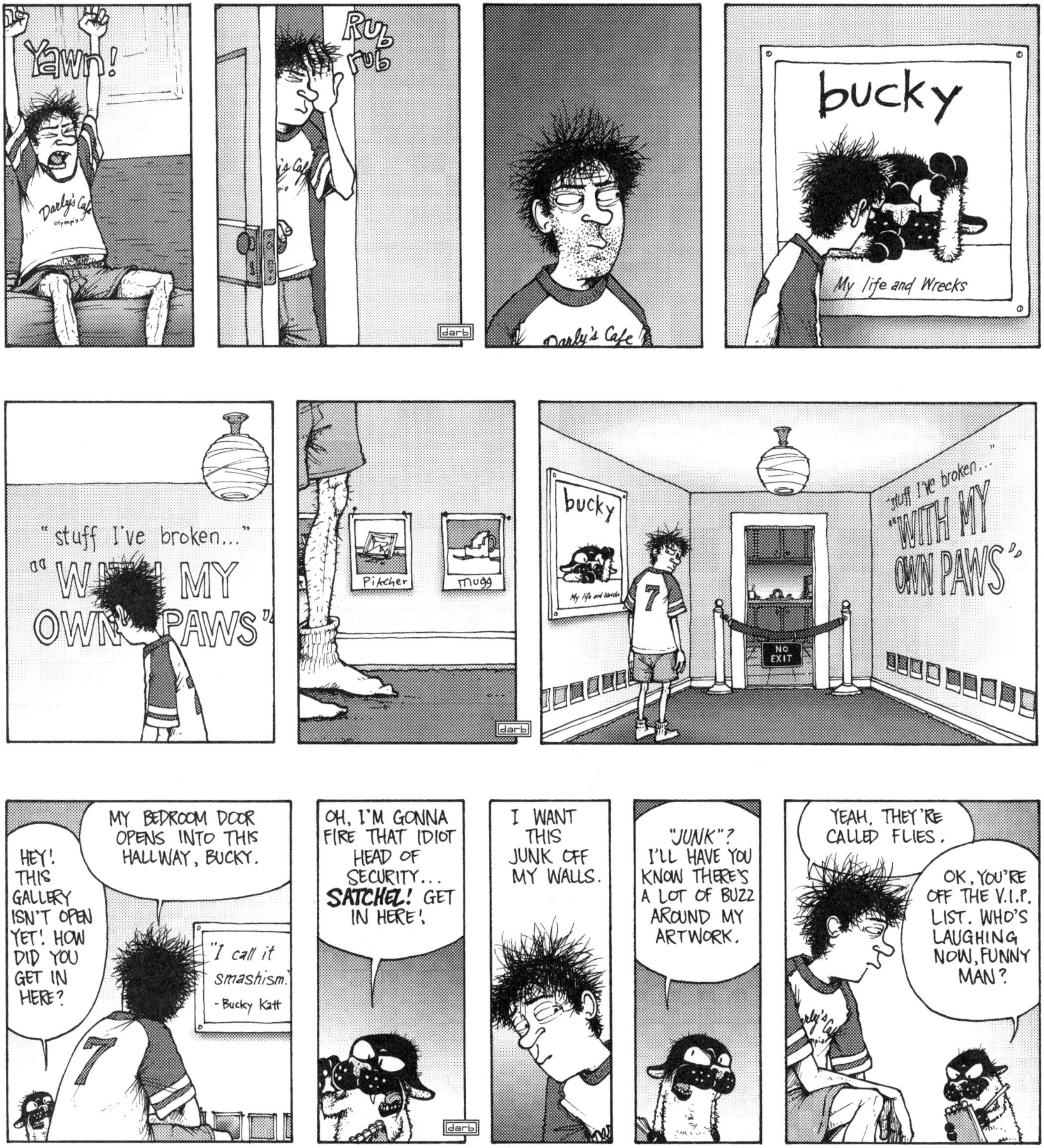
Yawn!
Rub rub
Darly's Cafe
bucky
My life and Wrecks
"stuff I've broken..."
"WITH MY OWN PAWS"
Pitcher
mugg
NO EXIT
HEY! THIS GALLERY ISN'T OPEN YET! HOW DID YOU GET IN HERE?
MY BEDROOM DOOR OPENS INTO THIS HALLWAY, BUCKY.
"I call it smashism." - Bucky Katt
OH, I'M GONNA FIRE THAT IDIOT HEAD OF SECURITY... SATCHEL! GET IN HERE!
I WANT THIS JUNK OFF MY WALLS.
"JUNK"? I'LL HAVE YOU KNOW THERE'S A LOT OF BUZZ AROUND MY ARTWORK.
YEAH, THEY'RE CALLED FLIES.
OK, YOU'RE OFF THE V.I.P. LIST. WHO'S LAUGHING NOW, FUNNY MAN?

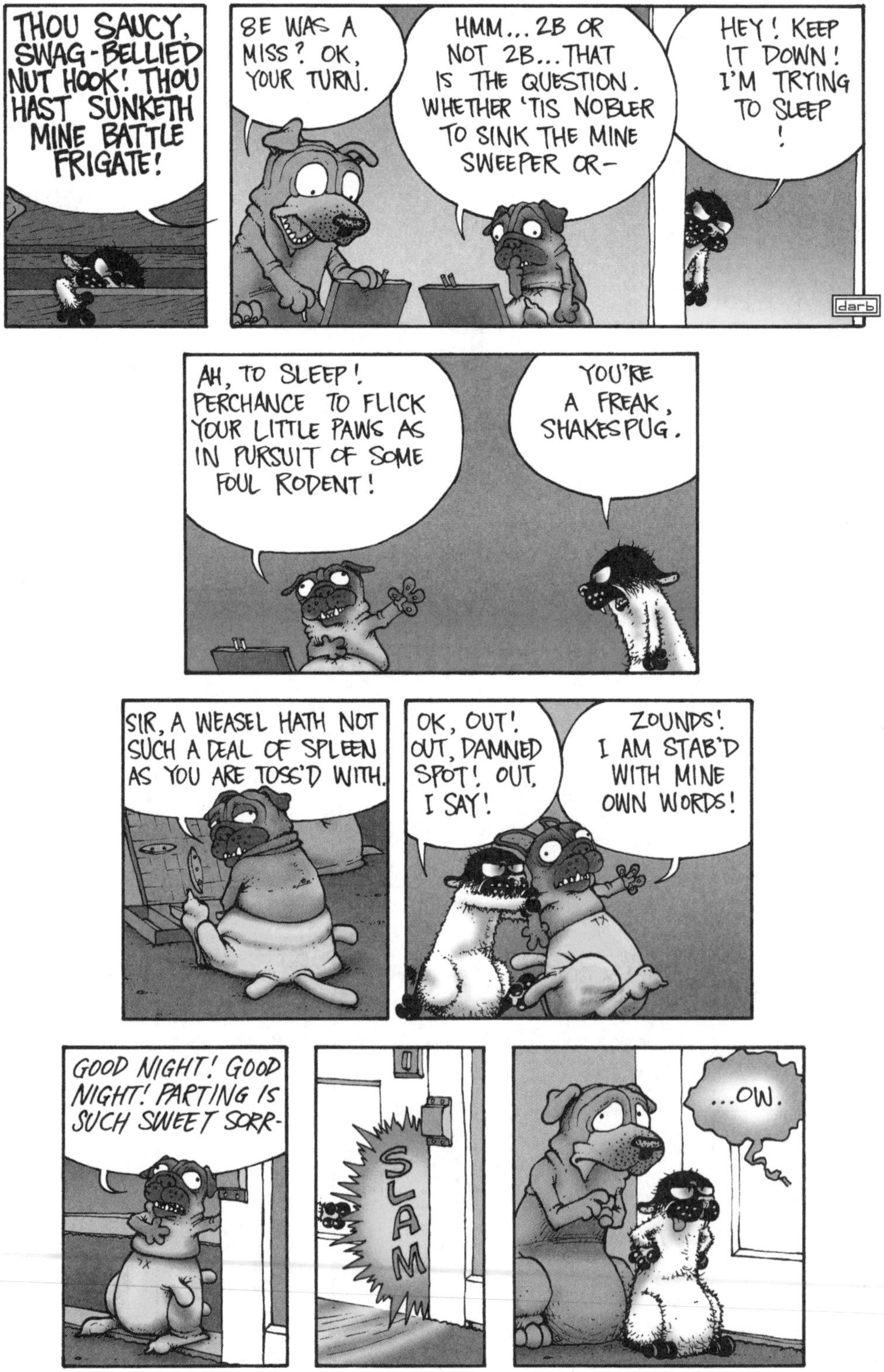
THOU SAUCY, SWAG-BELLIED NUT HOOK! THOU HAST SUNKETH MINE BATTLE FRIGATE!
8E WAS A MISS? OK, YOUR TURN.
HMM... 2B OR NOT 2B... THAT IS THE QUESTION. WHETHER 'TIS NOBLER TO SINK THE MINE SWEEPER OR-
HEY! KEEP IT DOWN! I'M TRYING TO SLEEP!
darb
AH, TO SLEEP! PERCHANCE TO FLICK YOUR LITTLE PAWS AS IN PURSUIT OF SOME FOUL RODENT!
YOU'RE A FREAK, SHAKESPUG.
SIR, A WEASEL HATH NOT SUCH A DEAL OF SPLEEN AS YOU ARE TOSS'D WITH.
OK, OUT! OUT, DAMNED SPOT! OUT, I SAY!
ZOUNDS! I AM STAB'D WITH MINE OWN WORDS!
GOOD NIGHT! GOOD NIGHT! PARTING IS SUCH SWEET SORR-
SLAM
...OW.

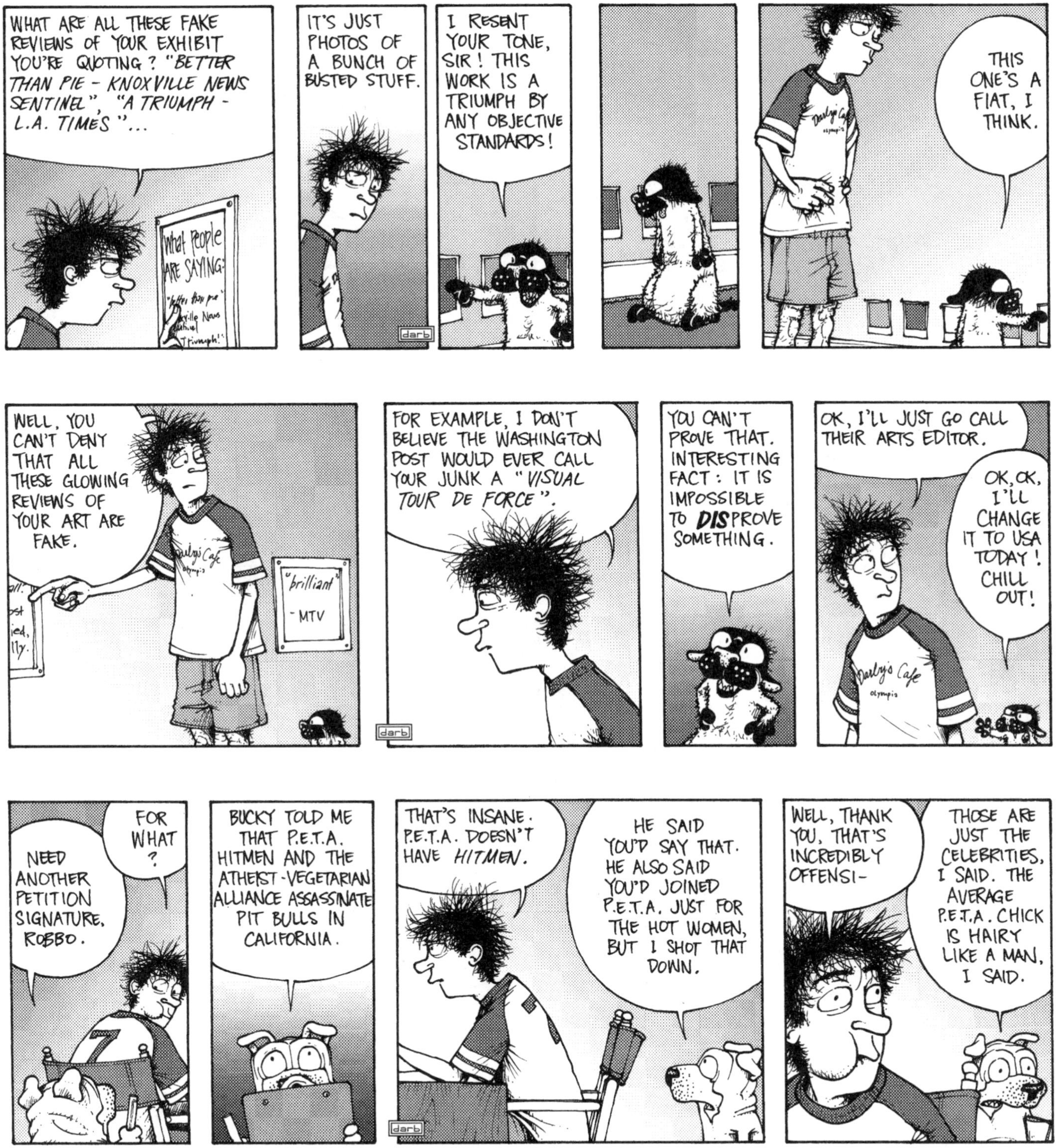
WHAT ARE ALL THESE FAKE REVIEWS OF YOUR EXHIBIT YOU'RE QUOTING? *"BETTER THAN PIE - KNOXVILLE NEWS SENTINEL", "A TRIUMPH - L.A. TIMES"*...
What People ARE SAYING:
IT'S JUST PHOTOS OF A BUNCH OF BUSTED STUFF.
I RESENT YOUR TONE, SIR! THIS WORK IS A TRIUMPH BY ANY OBJECTIVE STANDARDS!
THIS ONE'S A FIAT, I THINK.
WELL, YOU CAN'T DENY THAT ALL THESE GLOWING REVIEWS OF YOUR ART ARE FAKE.
"brilliant" - MTV
FOR EXAMPLE, I DON'T BELIEVE THE WASHINGTON POST WOULD EVER CALL YOUR JUNK A *"VISUAL TOUR DE FORCE"*.
YOU CAN'T PROVE THAT. INTERESTING FACT: IT IS IMPOSSIBLE TO ***DIS***PROVE SOMETHING.
OK, I'LL JUST GO CALL THEIR ARTS EDITOR.
OK, OK, I'LL CHANGE IT TO USA TODAY! CHILL OUT!
NEED ANOTHER PETITION SIGNATURE, ROBBO.
FOR WHAT?
BUCKY TOLD ME THAT P.E.T.A. HITMEN AND THE ATHEIST-VEGETARIAN ALLIANCE ASSASSINATE PIT BULLS IN CALIFORNIA.
THAT'S INSANE. P.E.T.A. DOESN'T HAVE *HITMEN*.
HE SAID YOU'D SAY THAT. HE ALSO SAID YOU'D JOINED P.E.T.A. JUST FOR THE HOT WOMEN, BUT I SHOT THAT DOWN.
WELL, THANK YOU, THAT'S INCREDIBLY OFFENSI-
THOSE ARE JUST THE CELEBRITIES, I SAID. THE AVERAGE P.E.T.A. CHICK IS HAIRY LIKE A MAN, I SAID.

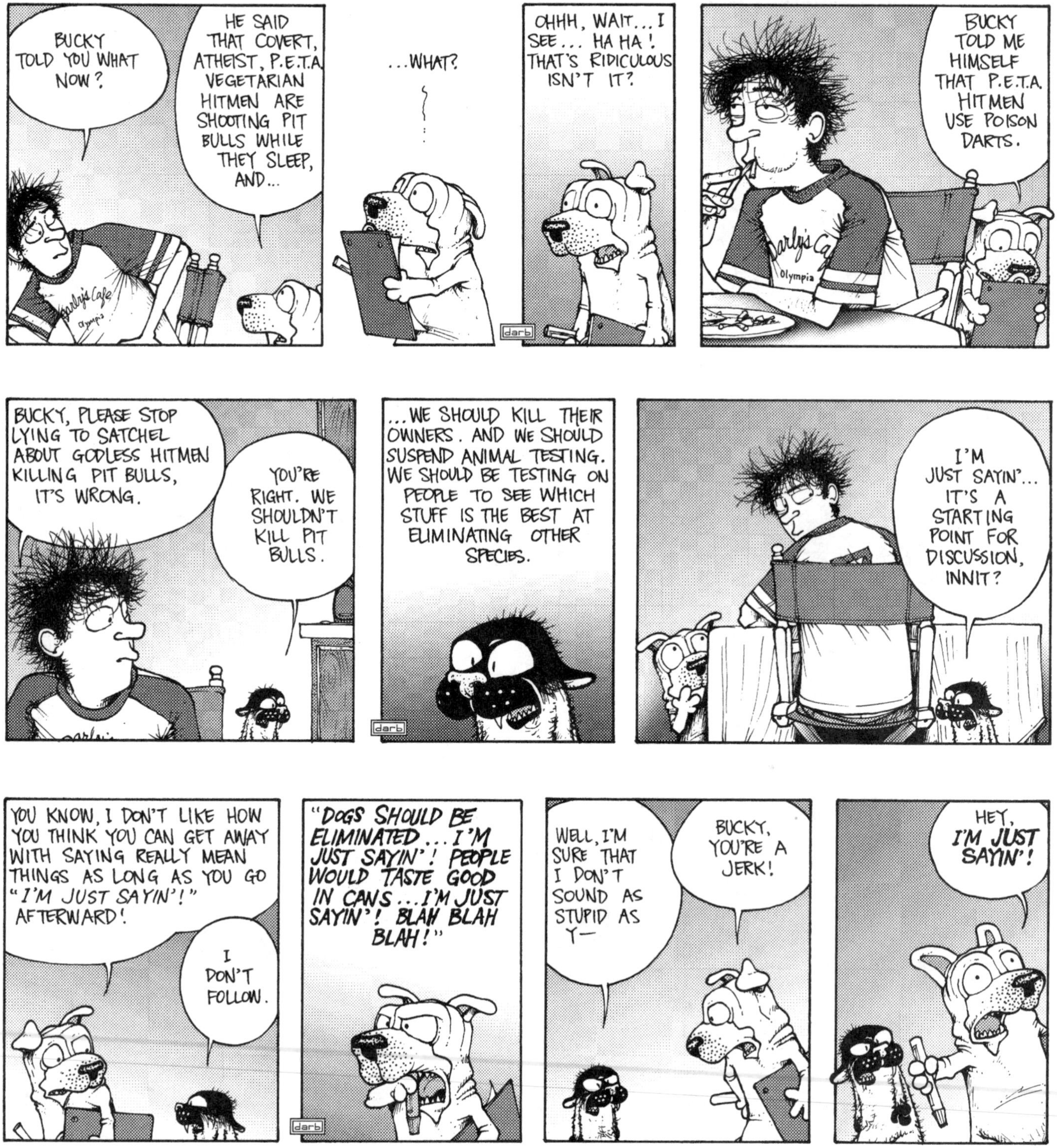
BUCKY TOLD YOU WHAT NOW?
HE SAID THAT COVERT, ATHEIST, P.E.T.A. VEGETARIAN HITMEN ARE SHOOTING PIT BULLS WHILE THEY SLEEP, AND...
...WHAT?
OHHH, WAIT... I SEE... HA HA! THAT'S RIDICULOUS ISN'T IT?
BUCKY TOLD ME HIMSELF THAT P.E.T.A. HITMEN USE POISON DARTS.
BUCKY, PLEASE STOP LYING TO SATCHEL ABOUT GODLESS HITMEN KILLING PIT BULLS, IT'S WRONG.
YOU'RE RIGHT. WE SHOULDN'T KILL PIT BULLS.
...WE SHOULD KILL THEIR OWNERS. AND WE SHOULD SUSPEND ANIMAL TESTING. WE SHOULD BE TESTING ON PEOPLE TO SEE WHICH STUFF IS THE BEST AT ELIMINATING OTHER SPECIES.
I'M JUST SAYIN'... IT'S A STARTING POINT FOR DISCUSSION, INNIT?
YOU KNOW, I DON'T LIKE HOW YOU THINK YOU CAN GET AWAY WITH SAYING REALLY MEAN THINGS AS LONG AS YOU GO "I'M JUST SAYIN'!" AFTERWARD!
I DON'T FOLLOW.
"DOGS SHOULD BE ELIMINATED... I'M JUST SAYIN'! PEOPLE WOULD TASTE GOOD IN CANS... I'M JUST SAYIN'! BLAH BLAH BLAH!"
WELL, I'M SURE THAT I DON'T SOUND AS STUPID AS Y—
BUCKY, YOU'RE A JERK!
HEY, I'M JUST SAYIN'!
darb

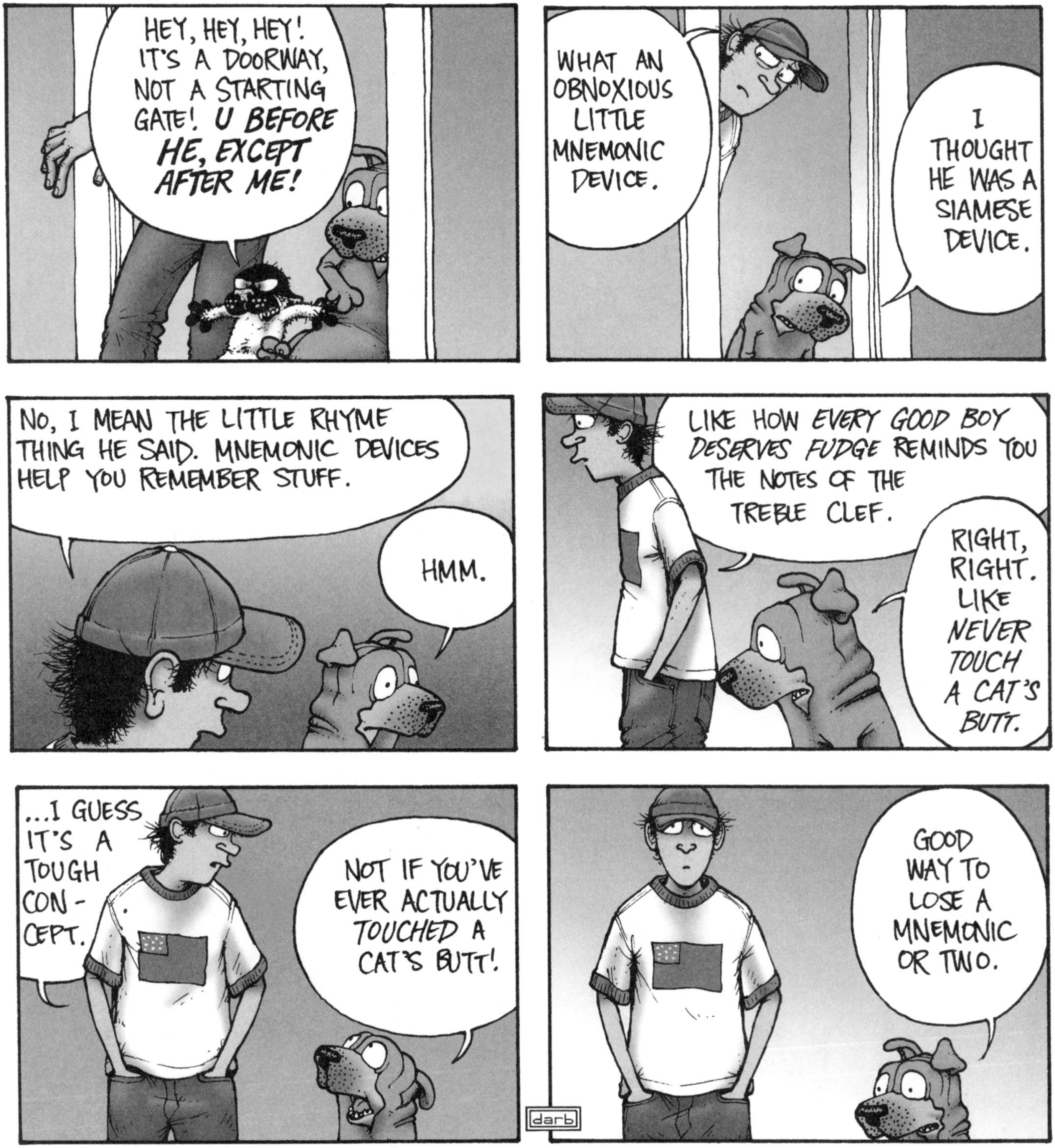
HEY, HEY, HEY! IT'S A DOORWAY, NOT A STARTING GATE! U BEFORE HE, EXCEPT AFTER ME!
WHAT AN OBNOXIOUS LITTLE MNEMONIC DEVICE.
I THOUGHT HE WAS A SIAMESE DEVICE.
NO, I MEAN THE LITTLE RHYME THING HE SAID. MNEMONIC DEVICES HELP YOU REMEMBER STUFF.
HMM.
LIKE HOW EVERY GOOD BOY DESERVES FUDGE REMINDS YOU THE NOTES OF THE TREBLE CLEF.
RIGHT, RIGHT. LIKE NEVER TOUCH A CAT'S BUTT.
...I GUESS IT'S A TOUGH CON-CEPT.
NOT IF YOU'VE EVER ACTUALLY TOUCHED A CAT'S BUTT!
darb
GOOD WAY TO LOSE A MNEMONIC OR TWO.

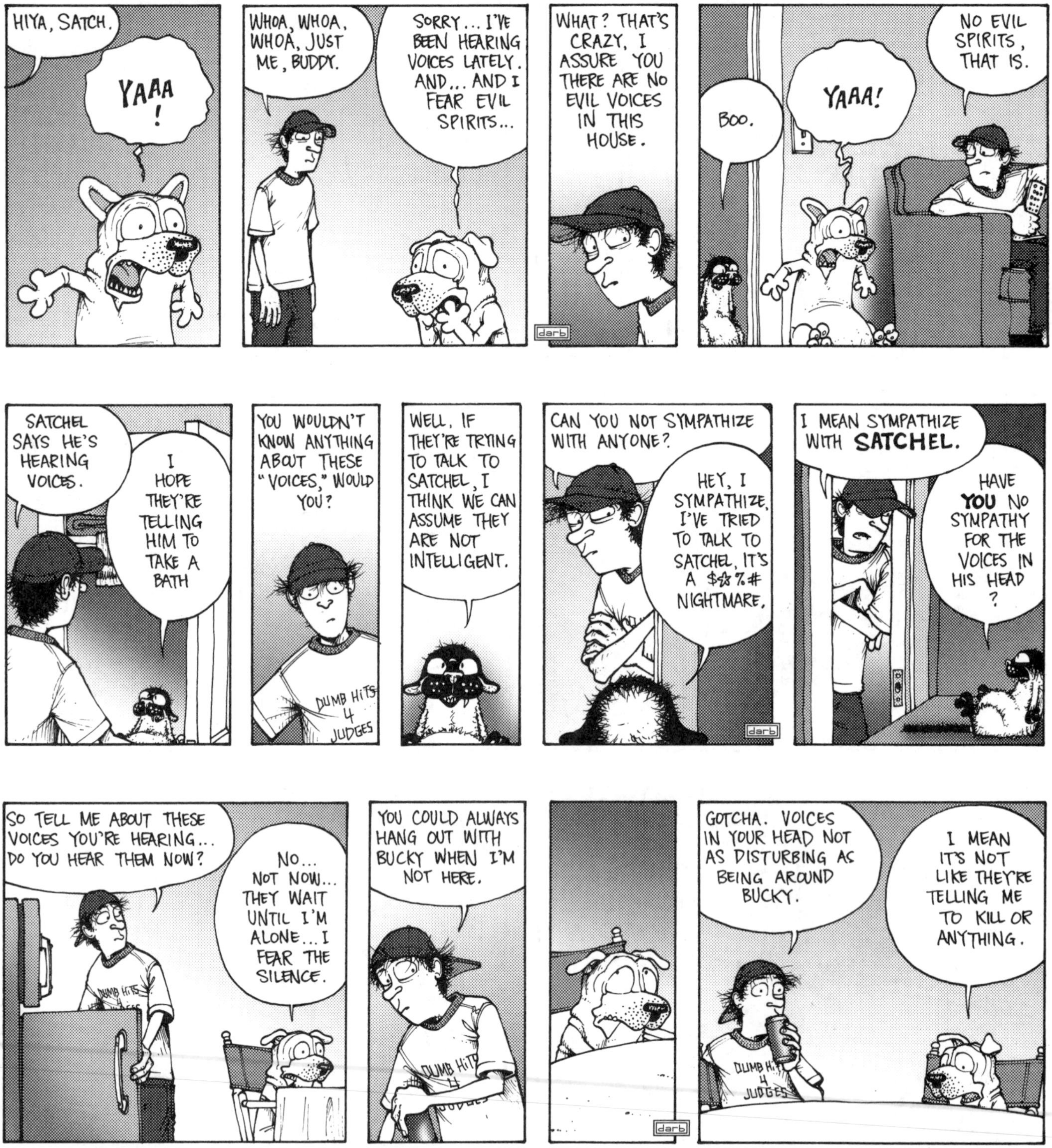

HIYA, SATCH.
YAAA!
WHOA, WHOA, WHOA, JUST ME, BUDDY.
SORRY... I'VE BEEN HEARING VOICES LATELY. AND... AND I FEAR EVIL SPIRITS...
WHAT? THAT'S CRAZY, I ASSURE YOU THERE ARE NO EVIL VOICES IN THIS HOUSE.
darb
BOO.
YAAA!
NO EVIL SPIRITS, THAT IS.
SATCHEL SAYS HE'S HEARING VOICES.
I HOPE THEY'RE TELLING HIM TO TAKE A BATH
YOU WOULDN'T KNOW ANYTHING ABOUT THESE "VOICES," WOULD YOU?
DUMB HITS 4 JUDGES
WELL, IF THEY'RE TRYING TO TALK TO SATCHEL, I THINK WE CAN ASSUME THEY ARE NOT INTELLIGENT.
CAN YOU NOT SYMPATHIZE WITH ANYONE?
HEY, I SYMPATHIZE, I'VE TRIED TO TALK TO SATCHEL, IT'S A $&%# NIGHTMARE.
darb
I MEAN SYMPATHIZE WITH **SATCHEL.**
HAVE **YOU** NO SYMPATHY FOR THE VOICES IN HIS HEAD?
SO TELL ME ABOUT THESE VOICES YOU'RE HEARING... DO YOU HEAR THEM NOW?
NO... NOT NOW... THEY WAIT UNTIL I'M ALONE... I FEAR THE SILENCE.
YOU COULD ALWAYS HANG OUT WITH BUCKY WHEN I'M NOT HERE.
darb
GOTCHA. VOICES IN YOUR HEAD NOT AS DISTURBING AS BEING AROUND BUCKY.
I MEAN IT'S NOT LIKE THEY'RE TELLING ME TO KILL OR ANYTHING.

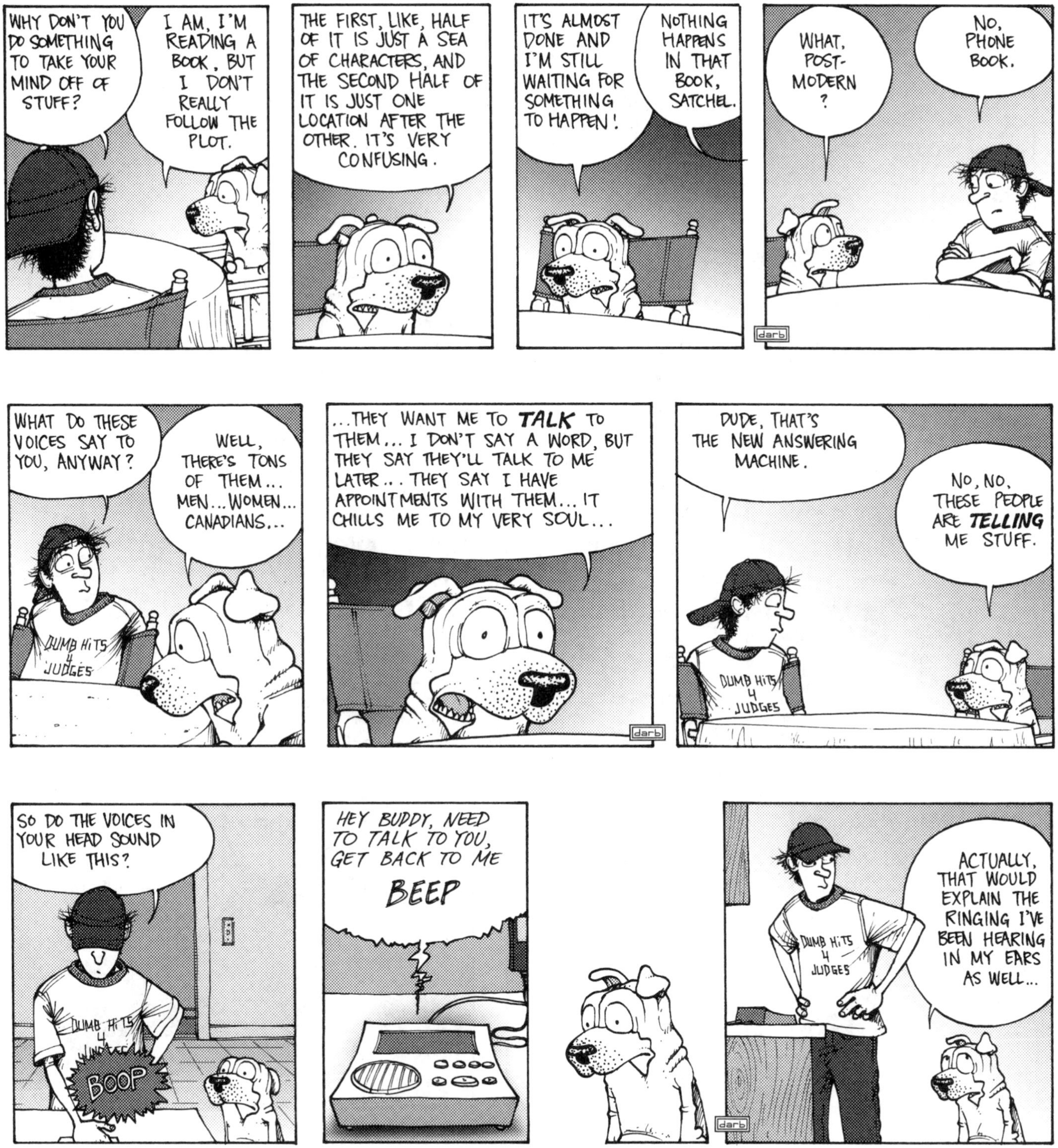
WHY DON'T YOU DO SOMETHING TO TAKE YOUR MIND OFF OF STUFF?
I AM, I'M READING A BOOK, BUT I DON'T REALLY FOLLOW THE PLOT.
THE FIRST, LIKE, HALF OF IT IS JUST A SEA OF CHARACTERS, AND THE SECOND HALF OF IT IS JUST ONE LOCATION AFTER THE OTHER. IT'S VERY CONFUSING.
IT'S ALMOST DONE AND I'M STILL WAITING FOR SOMETHING TO HAPPEN!
NOTHING HAPPENS IN THAT BOOK, SATCHEL.
WHAT, POST-MODERN?
NO, PHONE BOOK.
darb
WHAT DO THESE VOICES SAY TO YOU, ANYWAY?
WELL, THERE'S TONS OF THEM... MEN...WOMEN... CANADIANS...
DUMB HITS 4 JUDGES
...THEY WANT ME TO TALK TO THEM... I DON'T SAY A WORD, BUT THEY SAY THEY'LL TALK TO ME LATER... THEY SAY I HAVE APPOINTMENTS WITH THEM... IT CHILLS ME TO MY VERY SOUL...
darb
DUDE, THAT'S THE NEW ANSWERING MACHINE.
NO, NO, THESE PEOPLE ARE TELLING ME STUFF.
DUMB HITS 4 JUDGES
SO DO THE VOICES IN YOUR HEAD SOUND LIKE THIS?
BOOP
HEY BUDDY, NEED TO TALK TO YOU, GET BACK TO ME
BEEP
DUMB HITS 4 JUDGES
ACTUALLY, THAT WOULD EXPLAIN THE RINGING I'VE BEEN HEARING IN MY EARS AS WELL...
darb

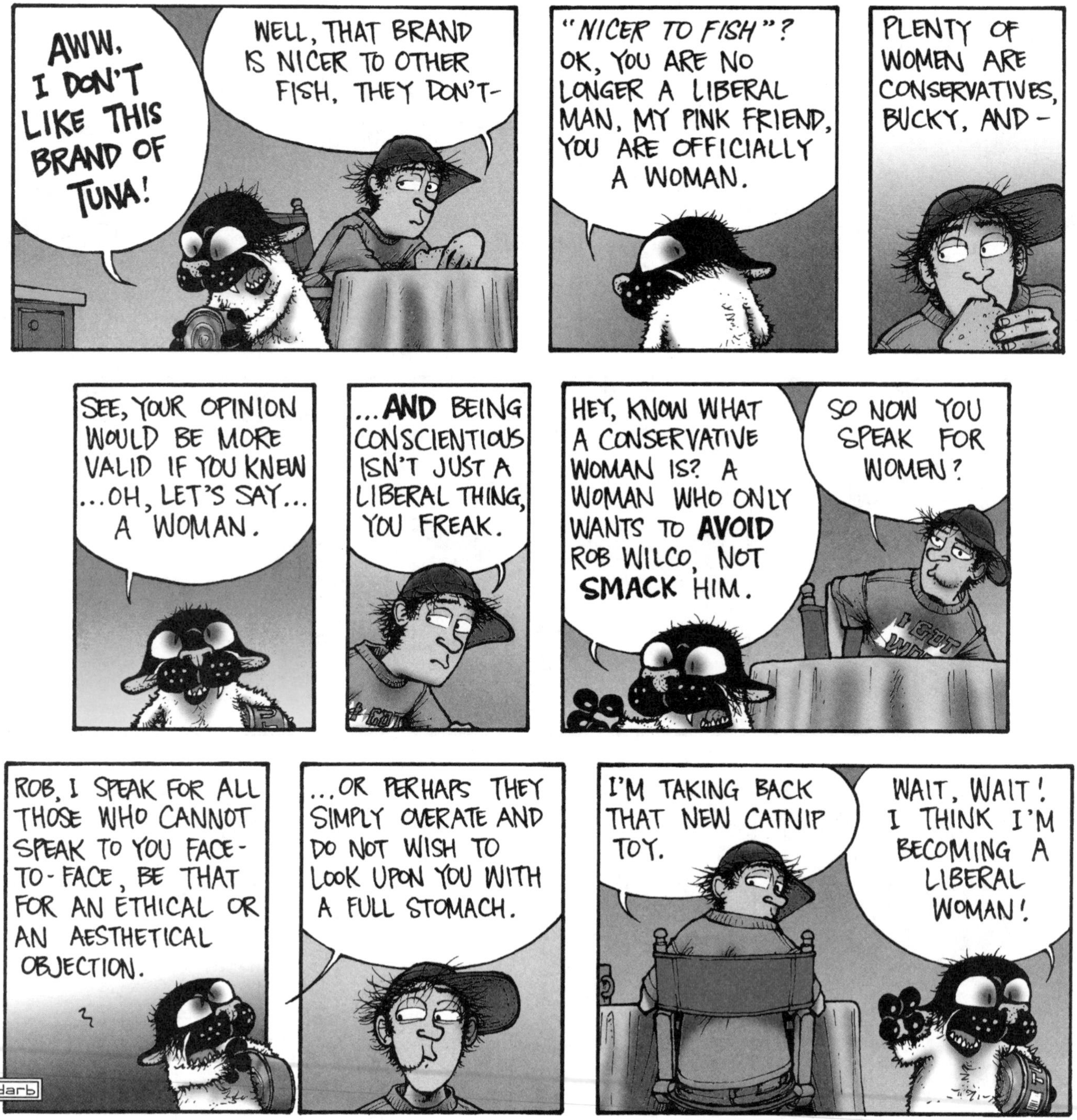
AWW, I DON'T LIKE THIS BRAND OF TUNA!
WELL, THAT BRAND IS NICER TO OTHER FISH. THEY DON'T-
"NICER TO FISH"? OK, YOU ARE NO LONGER A LIBERAL MAN, MY PINK FRIEND, YOU ARE OFFICIALLY A WOMAN.
PLENTY OF WOMEN ARE CONSERVATIVES, BUCKY, AND -
SEE, YOUR OPINION WOULD BE MORE VALID IF YOU KNEW ...OH, LET'S SAY... A WOMAN.
...AND BEING CONSCIENTIOUS ISN'T JUST A LIBERAL THING, YOU FREAK.
HEY, KNOW WHAT A CONSERVATIVE WOMAN IS? A WOMAN WHO ONLY WANTS TO AVOID ROB WILCO, NOT SMACK HIM.
SO NOW YOU SPEAK FOR WOMEN?
ROB, I SPEAK FOR ALL THOSE WHO CANNOT SPEAK TO YOU FACE-TO-FACE, BE THAT FOR AN ETHICAL OR AN AESTHETICAL OBJECTION.
...OR PERHAPS THEY SIMPLY OVERATE AND DO NOT WISH TO LOOK UPON YOU WITH A FULL STOMACH.
I'M TAKING BACK THAT NEW CATNIP TOY.
WAIT, WAIT! I THINK I'M BECOMING A LIBERAL WOMAN!
darb

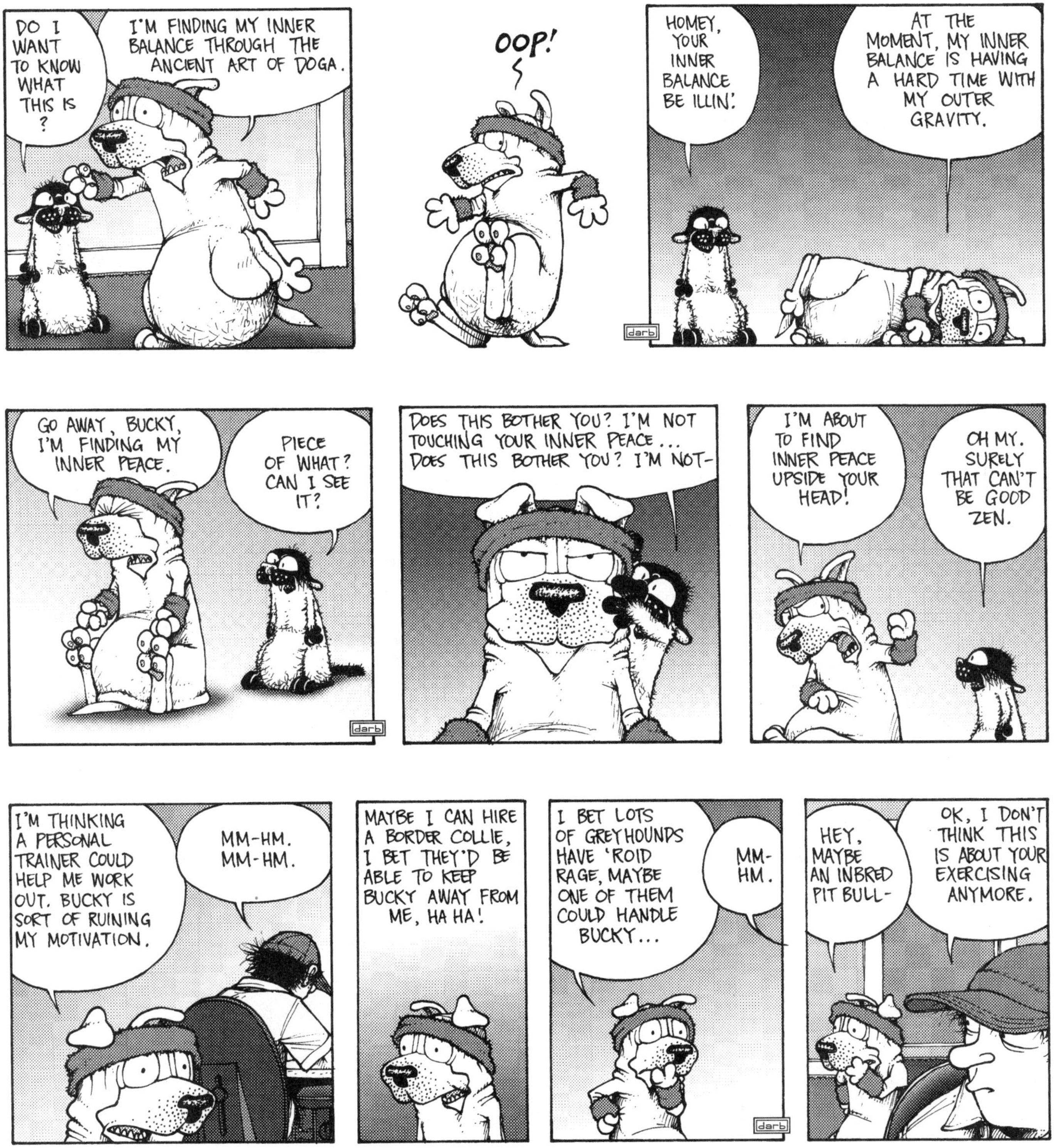
DO I WANT TO KNOW WHAT THIS IS ?
I'M FINDING MY INNER BALANCE THROUGH THE ANCIENT ART OF DOGA.
OOP!
HOMEY, YOUR INNER BALANCE BE ILLIN'.
AT THE MOMENT, MY INNER BALANCE IS HAVING A HARD TIME WITH MY OUTER GRAVITY.
darb
GO AWAY, BUCKY, I'M FINDING MY INNER PEACE.
PIECE OF WHAT? CAN I SEE IT?
darb
DOES THIS BOTHER YOU? I'M NOT TOUCHING YOUR INNER PEACE... DOES THIS BOTHER YOU? I'M NOT-
I'M ABOUT TO FIND INNER PEACE UPSIDE YOUR HEAD!
OH MY. SURELY THAT CAN'T BE GOOD ZEN.
I'M THINKING A PERSONAL TRAINER COULD HELP ME WORK OUT. BUCKY IS SORT OF RUINING MY MOTIVATION.
MM-HM. MM-HM.
MAYBE I CAN HIRE A BORDER COLLIE, I BET THEY'D BE ABLE TO KEEP BUCKY AWAY FROM ME, HA HA!
I BET LOTS OF GREYHOUNDS HAVE 'ROID RAGE, MAYBE ONE OF THEM COULD HANDLE BUCKY...
MM-HM.
darb
HEY, MAYBE AN INBRED PIT BULL-
OK, I DON'T THINK THIS IS ABOUT YOUR EXERCISING ANYMORE.

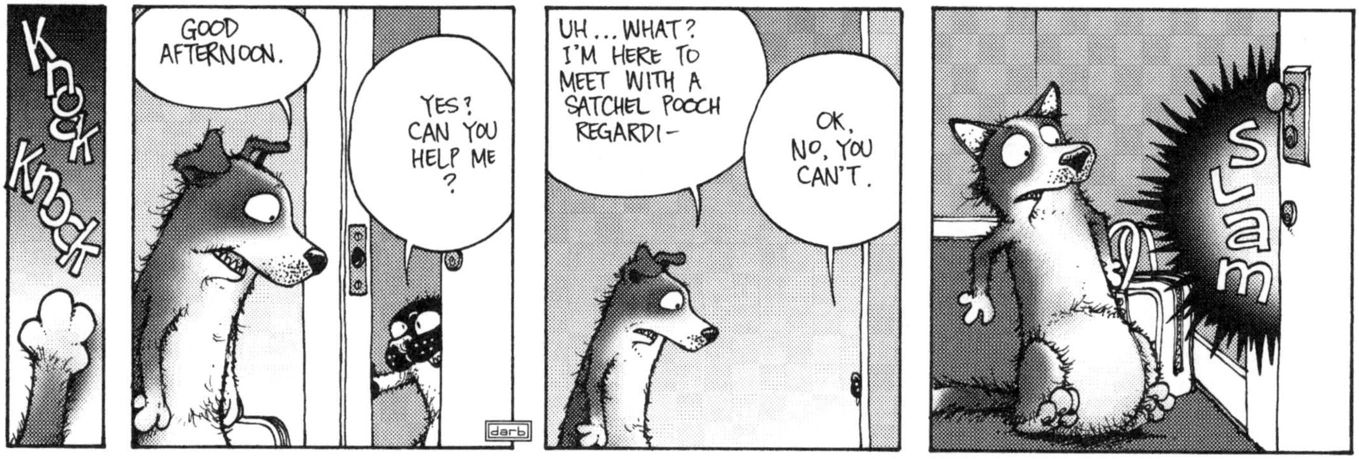
Knock Knock
GOOD AFTERNOON.
YES? CAN YOU HELP ME ?
darb
UH... WHAT? I'M HERE TO MEET WITH A SATCHEL POOCH REGARDI-
OK, NO, YOU CAN'T.
Slam

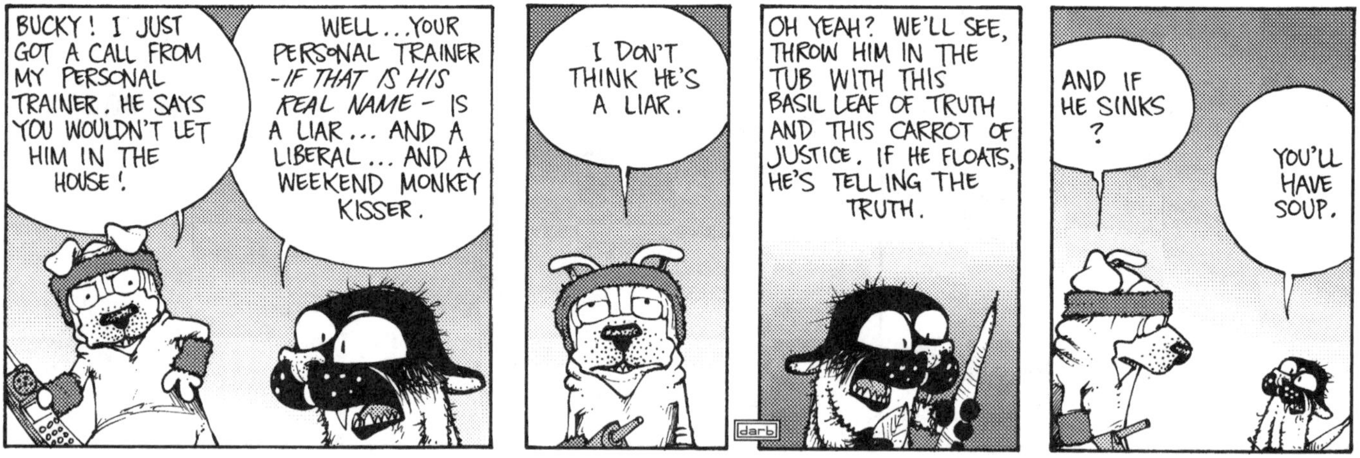
BUCKY! I JUST GOT A CALL FROM MY PERSONAL TRAINER. HE SAYS YOU WOULDN'T LET HIM IN THE HOUSE!
WELL...YOUR PERSONAL TRAINER -IF THAT IS HIS REAL NAME- IS A LIAR... AND A LIBERAL... AND A WEEKEND MONKEY KISSER.
I DON'T THINK HE'S A LIAR.
darb
OH YEAH? WE'LL SEE, THROW HIM IN THE TUB WITH THIS BASIL LEAF OF TRUTH AND THIS CARROT OF JUSTICE. IF HE FLOATS, HE'S TELLING THE TRUTH.
AND IF HE SINKS ?
YOU'LL HAVE SOUP.

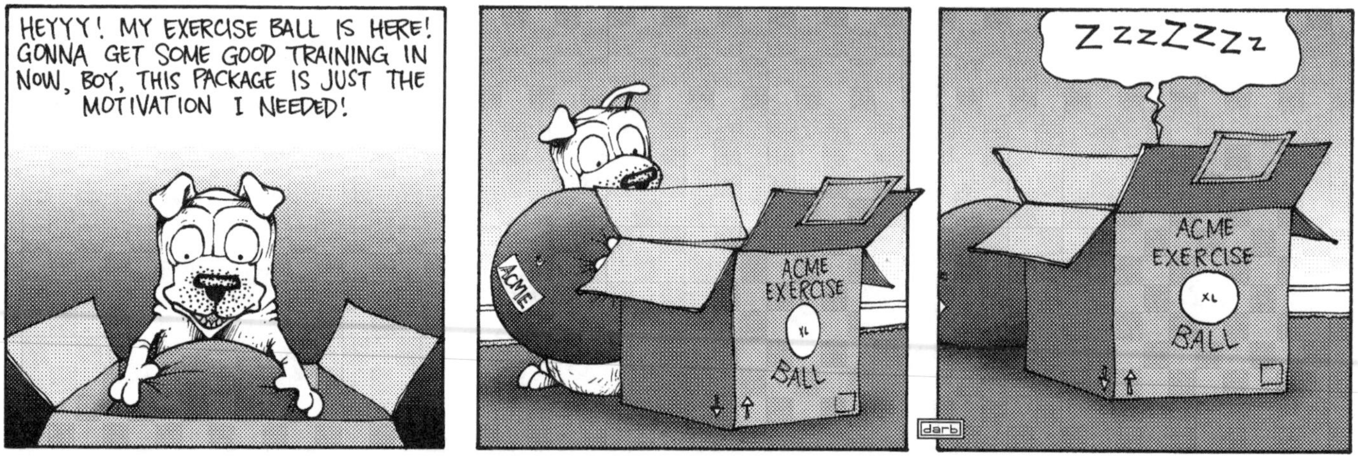
HEYYY! MY EXERCISE BALL IS HERE! GONNA GET SOME GOOD TRAINING IN NOW, BOY, THIS PACKAGE IS JUST THE MOTIVATION I NEEDED!
ACME
ACME EXERCISE XL BALL
darb
ZzzZZZz
ACME EXERCISE XL BALL

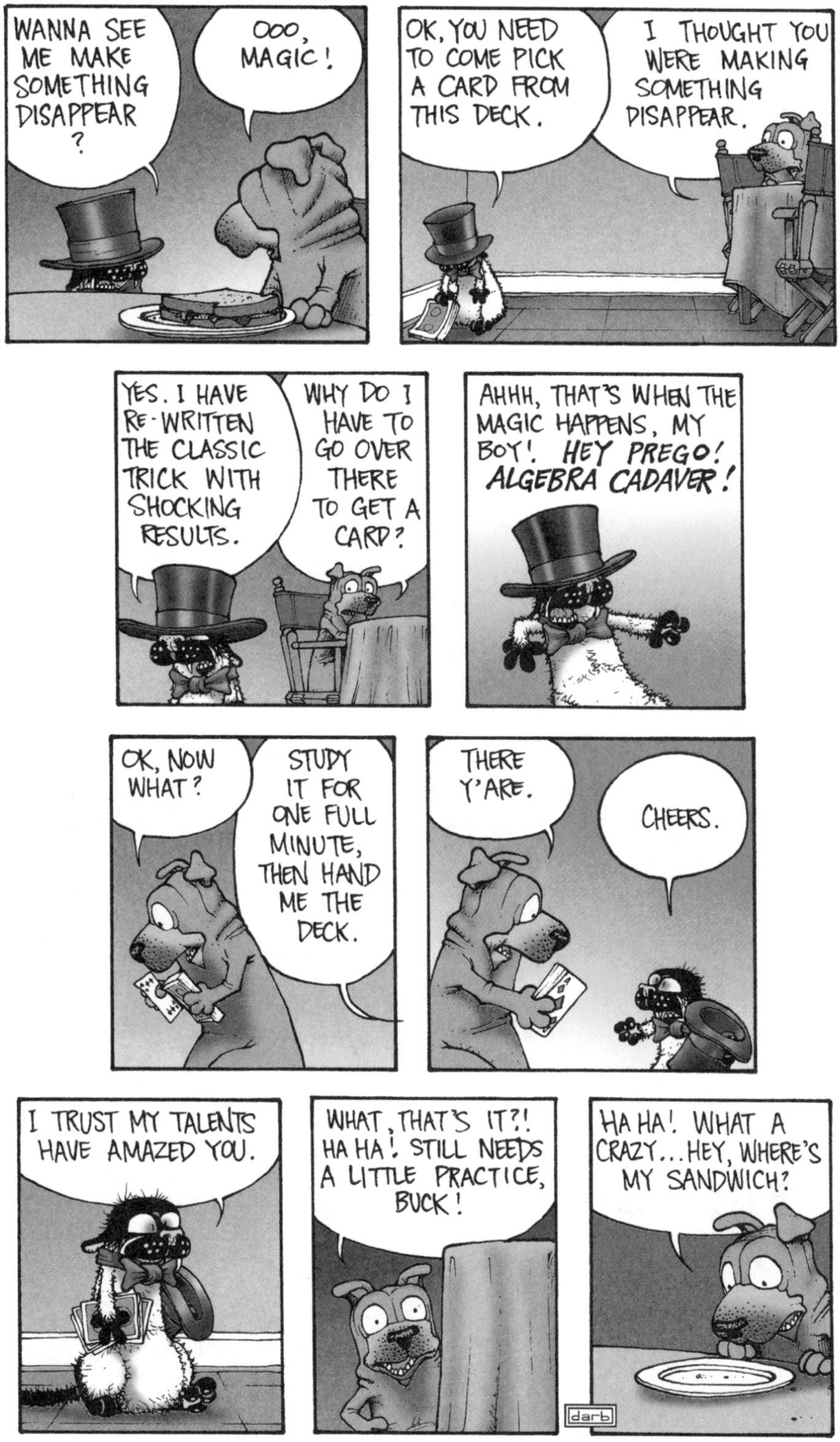
WANNA SEE ME MAKE SOMETHING DISAPPEAR ?
OOO, MAGIC!
OK, YOU NEED TO COME PICK A CARD FROM THIS DECK.
I THOUGHT YOU WERE MAKING SOMETHING DISAPPEAR.
YES. I HAVE RE-WRITTEN THE CLASSIC TRICK WITH SHOCKING RESULTS.
WHY DO I HAVE TO GO OVER THERE TO GET A CARD?
AHHH, THAT'S WHEN THE MAGIC HAPPENS, MY BOY! HEY PREGO! ALGEBRA CADAVER!
OK, NOW WHAT?
STUDY IT FOR ONE FULL MINUTE, THEN HAND ME THE DECK.
THERE Y'ARE.
CHEERS.
I TRUST MY TALENTS HAVE AMAZED YOU.
WHAT, THAT'S IT?! HA HA! STILL NEEDS A LITTLE PRACTICE, BUCK!
HA HA! WHAT A CRAZY... HEY, WHERE'S MY SANDWICH?
darb

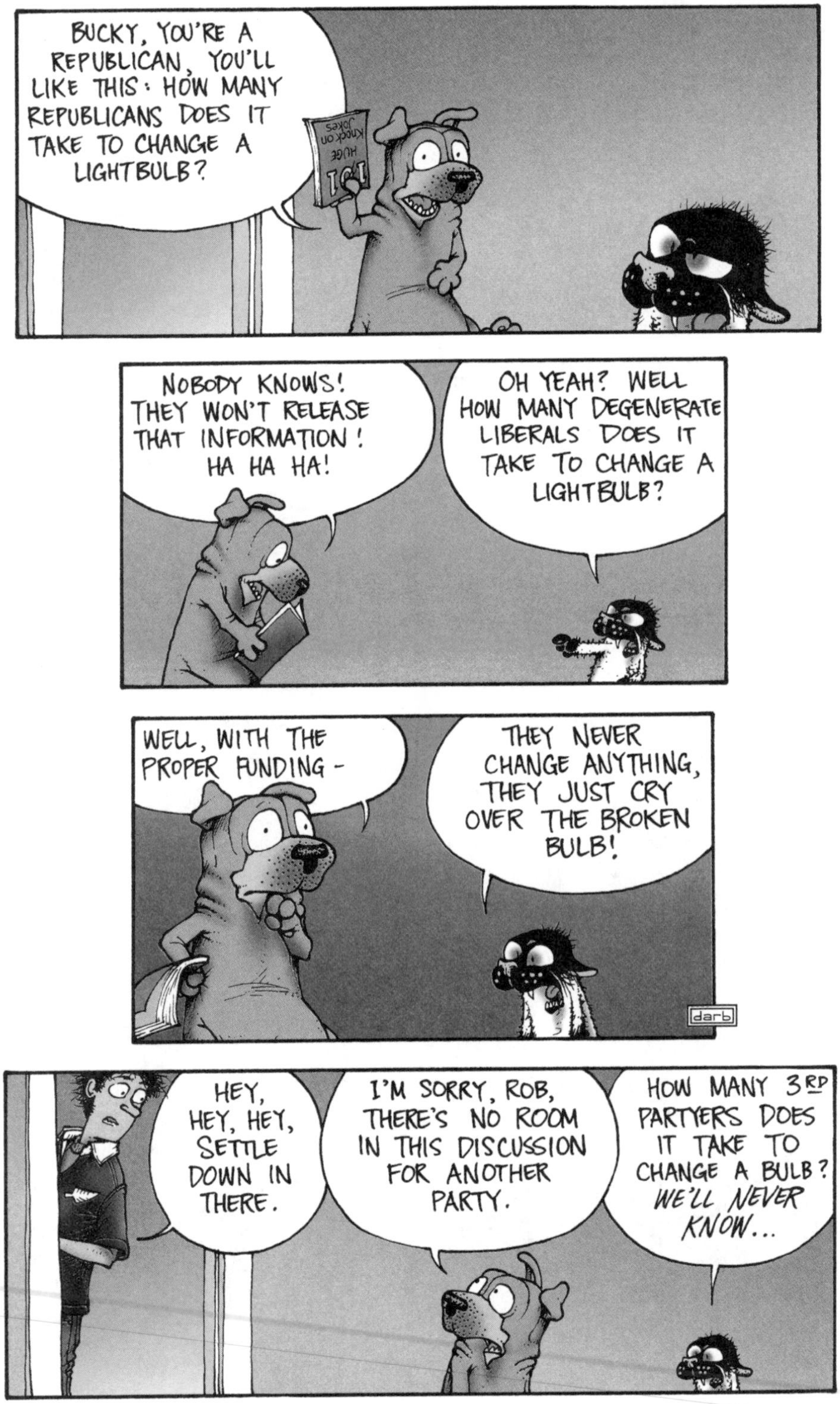
BUCKY, YOU'RE A REPUBLICAN, YOU'LL LIKE THIS: HOW MANY REPUBLICANS DOES IT TAKE TO CHANGE A LIGHTBULB?
NOBODY KNOWS! THEY WON'T RELEASE THAT INFORMATION! HA HA HA!
OH YEAH? WELL HOW MANY DEGENERATE LIBERALS DOES IT TAKE TO CHANGE A LIGHTBULB?
WELL, WITH THE PROPER FUNDING -
THEY NEVER CHANGE ANYTHING, THEY JUST CRY OVER THE BROKEN BULB!
darb
HEY, HEY, HEY, SETTLE DOWN IN THERE.
I'M SORRY, ROB, THERE'S NO ROOM IN THIS DISCUSSION FOR ANOTHER PARTY.
HOW MANY 3RD PARTYERS DOES IT TAKE TO CHANGE A BULB? *WE'LL NEVER KNOW...*

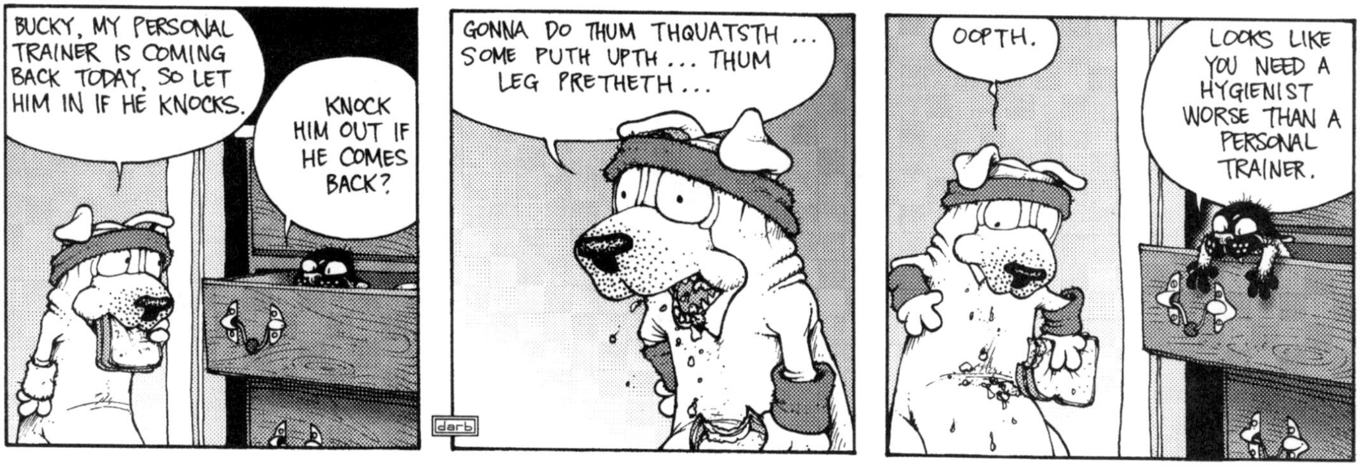
BUCKY, MY PERSONAL TRAINER IS COMING BACK TODAY, SO LET HIM IN IF HE KNOCKS.
KNOCK HIM OUT IF HE COMES BACK?
GONNA DO THUM THQUATSTH ... SOME PUTH UPTH ... THUM LEG PRETHETH ...
OOPTH.
LOOKS LIKE YOU NEED A HYGIENIST WORSE THAN A PERSONAL TRAINER.
darb

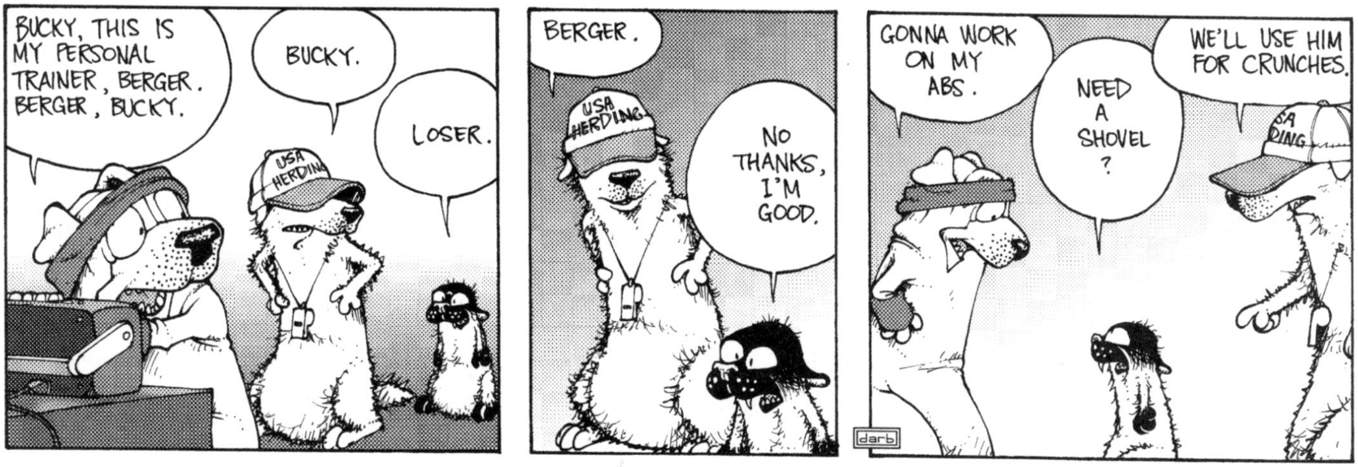
BUCKY, THIS IS MY PERSONAL TRAINER, BERGER. BERGER, BUCKY.
BUCKY.
LOSER.
USA HERDING
BERGER.
NO THANKS, I'M GOOD.
GONNA WORK ON MY ABS.
NEED A SHOVEL ?
WE'LL USE HIM FOR CRUNCHES.
darb

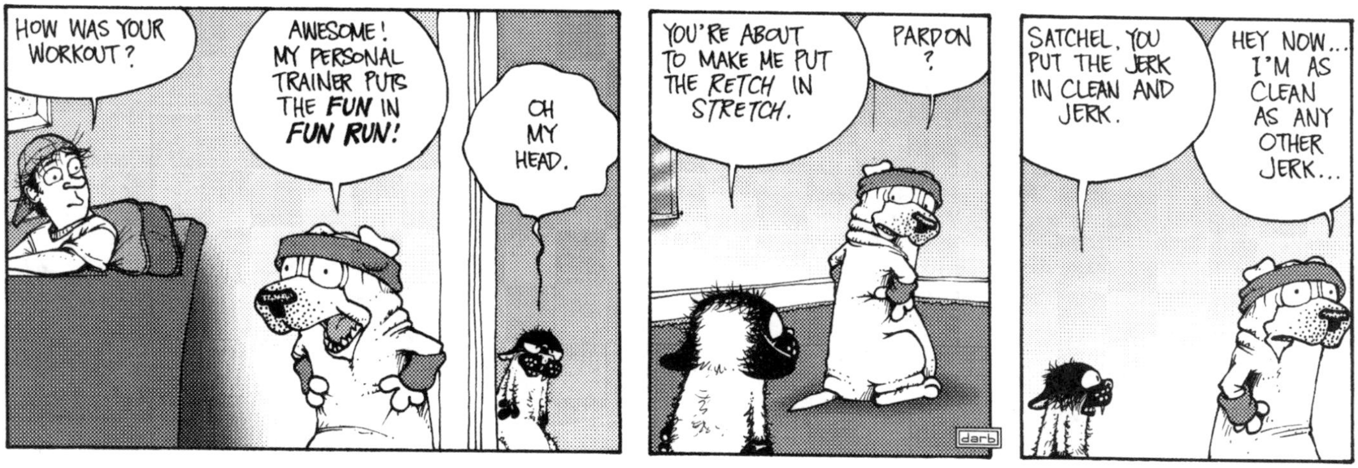
HOW WAS YOUR WORKOUT?
AWESOME! MY PERSONAL TRAINER PUTS THE FUN IN FUN RUN!
OH MY HEAD.
YOU'RE ABOUT TO MAKE ME PUT THE RETCH IN STRETCH.
PARDON ?
SATCHEL, YOU PUT THE JERK IN CLEAN AND JERK.
HEY NOW... I'M AS CLEAN AS ANY OTHER JERK...
darb

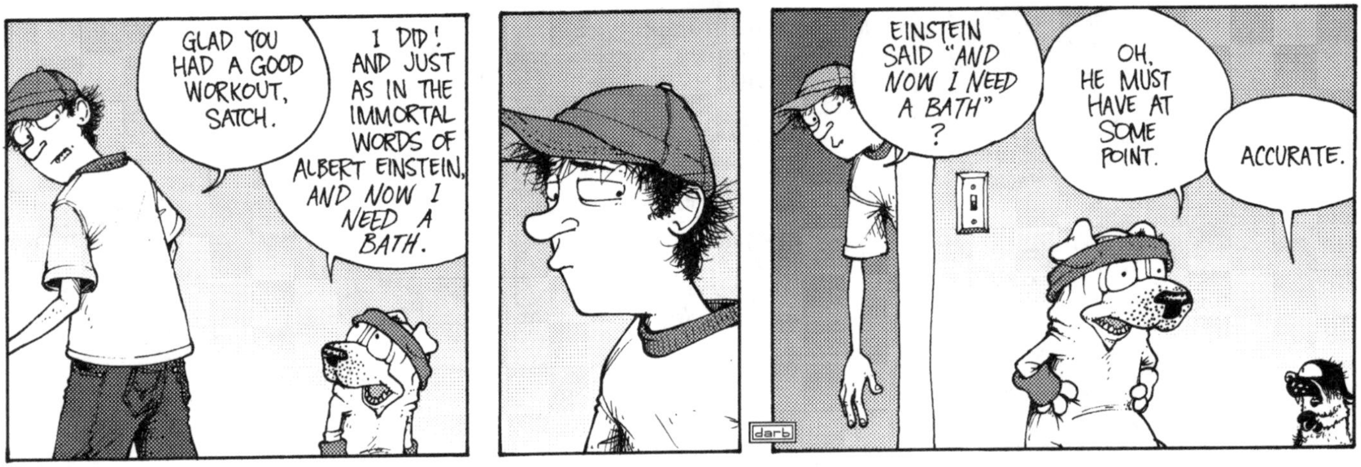
GLAD YOU HAD A GOOD WORKOUT, SATCH.
I DID! AND JUST AS IN THE IMMORTAL WORDS OF ALBERT EINSTEIN, AND NOW I NEED A BATH.
EINSTEIN SAID "AND NOW I NEED A BATH"?
OH, HE MUST HAVE AT SOME POINT.
ACCURATE.
darb

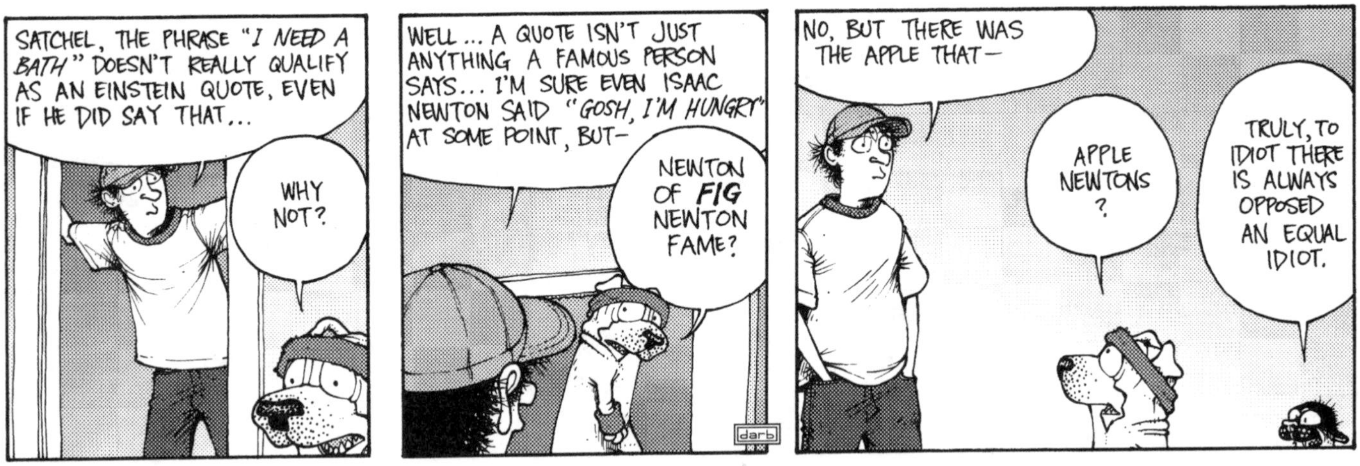
SATCHEL, THE PHRASE "I NEED A BATH" DOESN'T REALLY QUALIFY AS AN EINSTEIN QUOTE, EVEN IF HE DID SAY THAT...
WHY NOT?
WELL... A QUOTE ISN'T JUST ANYTHING A FAMOUS PERSON SAYS... I'M SURE EVEN ISAAC NEWTON SAID "GOSH, I'M HUNGRY" AT SOME POINT, BUT–
NEWTON OF FIG NEWTON FAME?
darb
NO, BUT THERE WAS THE APPLE THAT–
APPLE NEWTONS?
TRULY, TO IDIOT THERE IS ALWAYS OPPOSED AN EQUAL IDIOT.

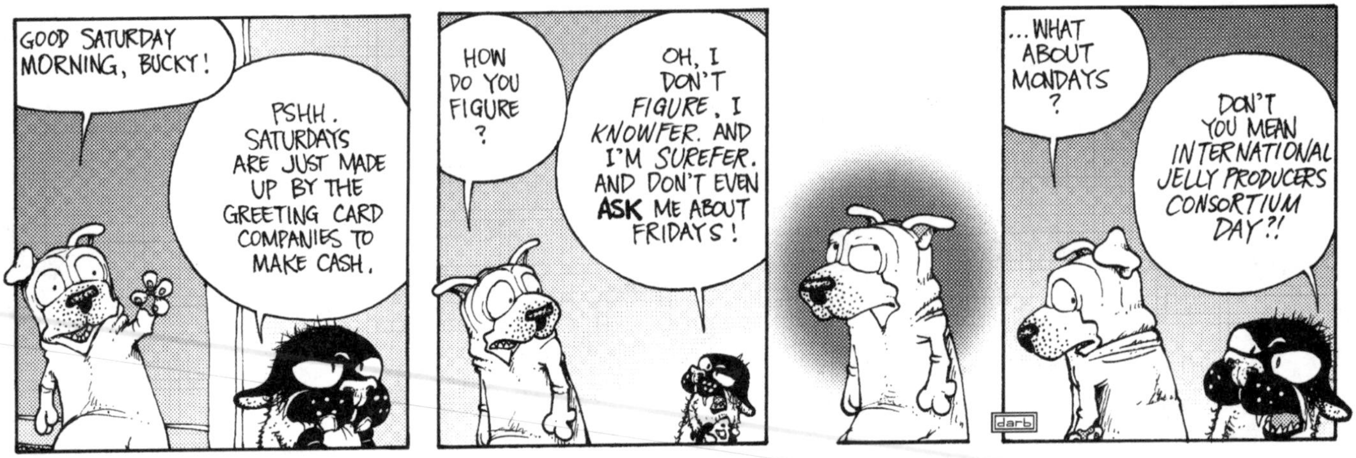
GOOD SATURDAY MORNING, BUCKY!
PSHH. SATURDAYS ARE JUST MADE UP BY THE GREETING CARD COMPANIES TO MAKE CASH.
HOW DO YOU FIGURE?
OH, I DON'T FIGURE, I KNOWFER. AND I'M SUREFER. AND DON'T EVEN ASK ME ABOUT FRIDAYS!
...WHAT ABOUT MONDAYS?
DON'T YOU MEAN INTERNATIONAL JELLY PRODUCERS CONSORTIUM DAY?!
darb

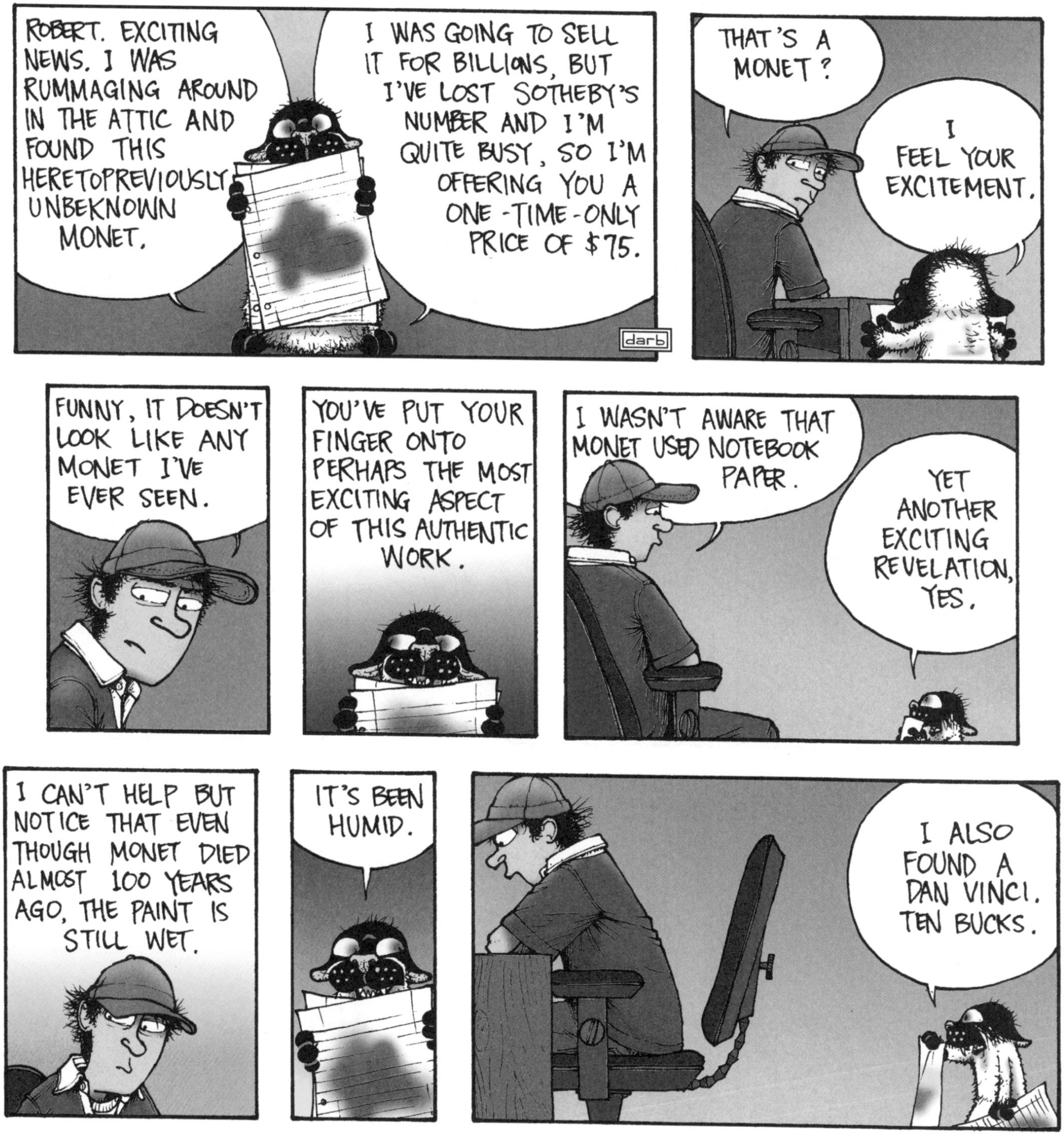
ROBERT. EXCITING NEWS. I WAS RUMMAGING AROUND IN THE ATTIC AND FOUND THIS HERETOPREVIOUSLY UNBEKNOWN MONET.
I WAS GOING TO SELL IT FOR BILLIONS, BUT I'VE LOST SOTHEBY'S NUMBER AND I'M QUITE BUSY, SO I'M OFFERING YOU A ONE-TIME-ONLY PRICE OF $75.
darb
THAT'S A MONET?
I FEEL YOUR EXCITEMENT.
FUNNY, IT DOESN'T LOOK LIKE ANY MONET I'VE EVER SEEN.
YOU'VE PUT YOUR FINGER ONTO PERHAPS THE MOST EXCITING ASPECT OF THIS AUTHENTIC WORK.
I WASN'T AWARE THAT MONET USED NOTEBOOK PAPER.
YET ANOTHER EXCITING REVELATION, YES.
I CAN'T HELP BUT NOTICE THAT EVEN THOUGH MONET DIED ALMOST 100 YEARS AGO, THE PAINT IS STILL WET.
IT'S BEEN HUMID.
I ALSO FOUND A DAN VINCI. TEN BUCKS.

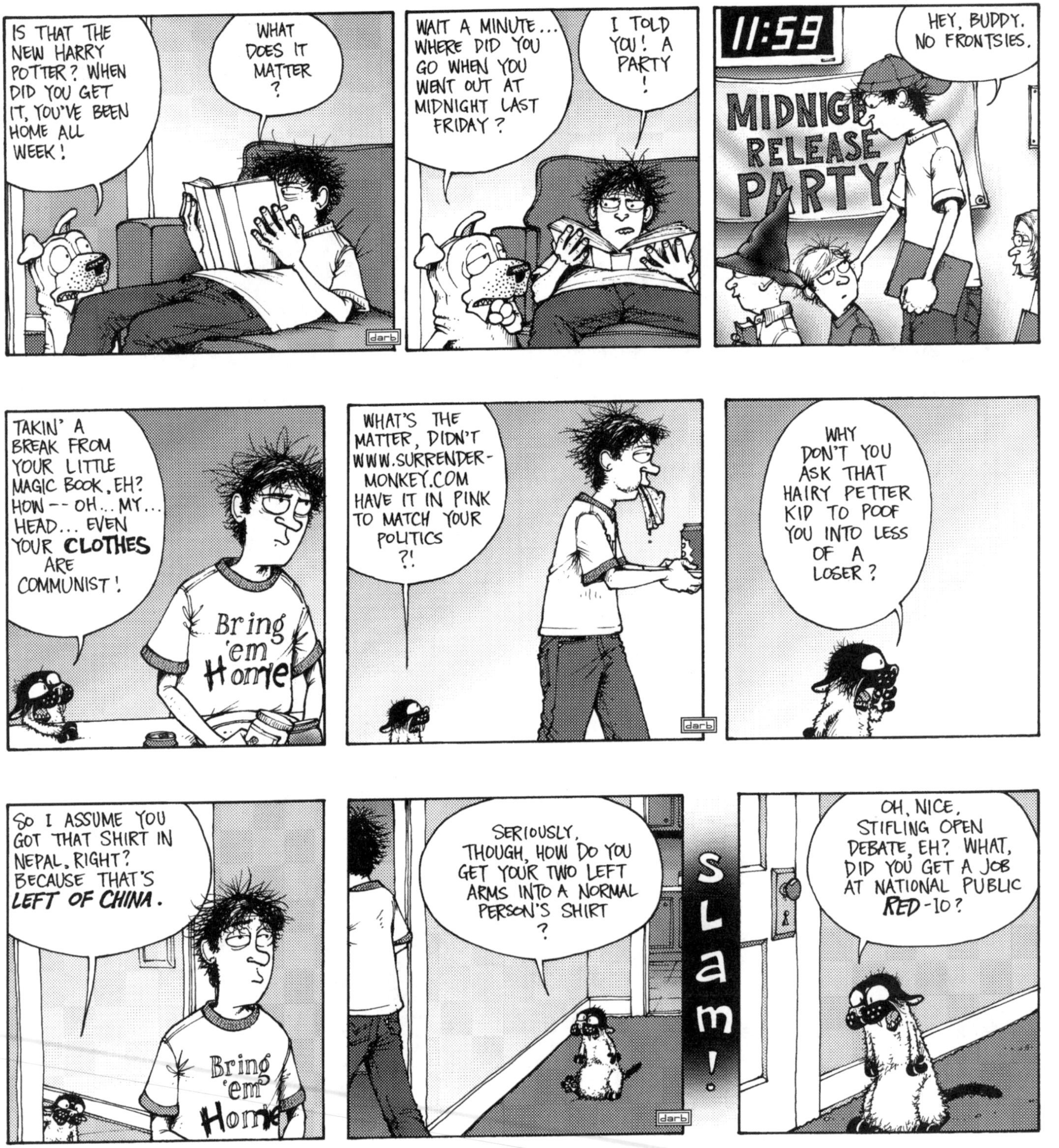

IS THAT THE NEW HARRY POTTER? WHEN DID YOU GET IT, YOU'VE BEEN HOME ALL WEEK!
WHAT DOES IT MATTER?
WAIT A MINUTE... WHERE DID YOU GO WHEN YOU WENT OUT AT MIDNIGHT LAST FRIDAY?
I TOLD YOU! A PARTY!
11:59
MIDNIGHT RELEASE PARTY
HEY, BUDDY. NO FRONTSIES.
TAKIN' A BREAK FROM YOUR LITTLE MAGIC BOOK, EH? HOW -- OH... MY... HEAD... EVEN YOUR **CLOTHES** ARE COMMUNIST!
Bring 'em Home
WHAT'S THE MATTER, DIDN'T WWW.SURRENDER-MONKEY.COM HAVE IT IN PINK TO MATCH YOUR POLITICS?!
WHY DON'T YOU ASK THAT HAIRY PETTER KID TO POOF YOU INTO LESS OF A LOSER?
SO I ASSUME YOU GOT THAT SHIRT IN NEPAL, RIGHT? BECAUSE THAT'S ***LEFT OF CHINA***.
Bring 'em Home
SERIOUSLY, THOUGH, HOW DO YOU GET YOUR TWO LEFT ARMS INTO A NORMAL PERSON'S SHIRT?
SLAM!
OH, NICE, STIFLING OPEN DEBATE, EH? WHAT, DID YOU GET A JOB AT NATIONAL PUBLIC ***RED***-IO?

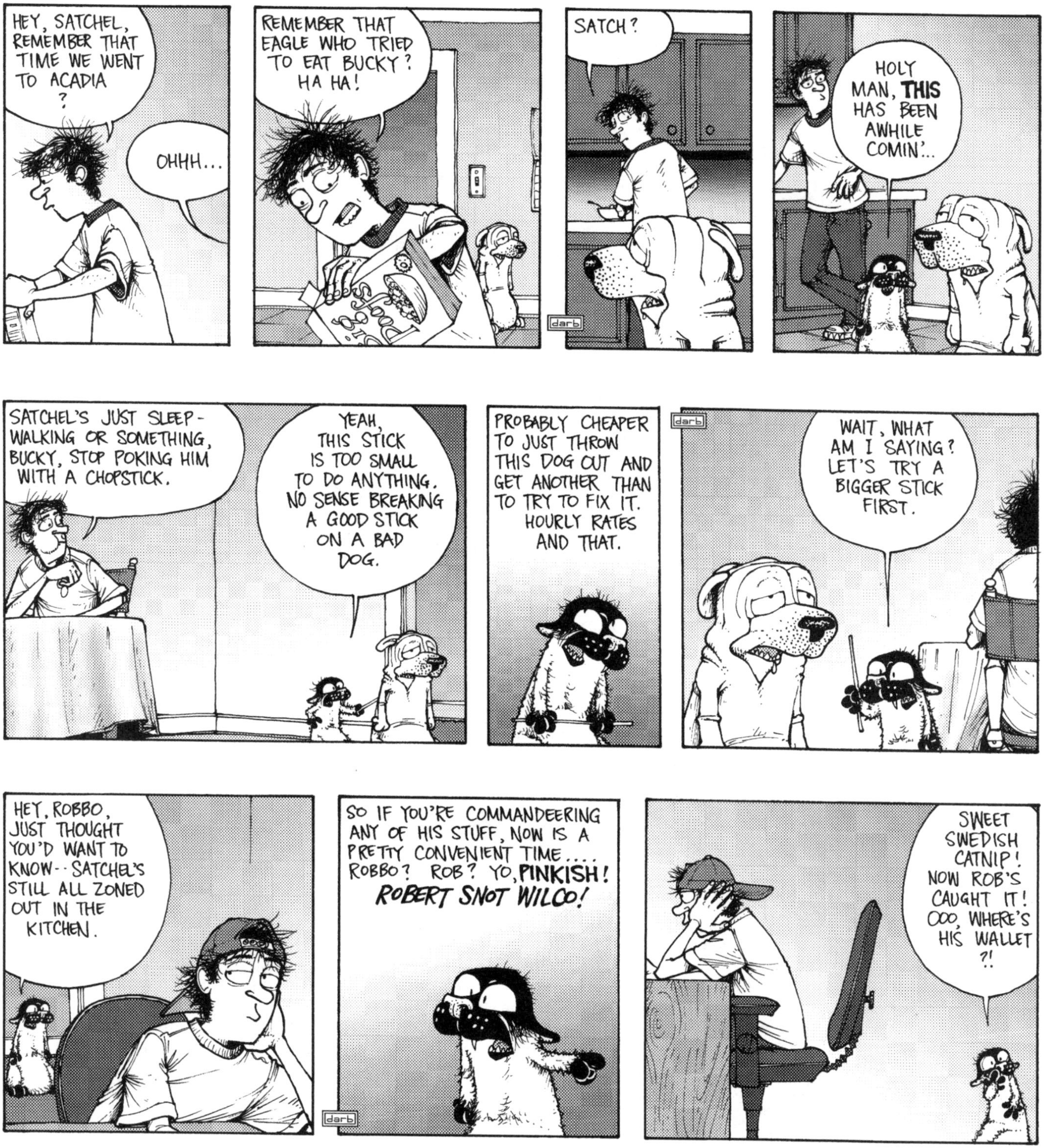
HEY, SATCHEL, REMEMBER THAT TIME WE WENT TO ACADIA ?
OHHH...
REMEMBER THAT EAGLE WHO TRIED TO EAT BUCKY? HA HA!
SATCH?
HOLY MAN, THIS HAS BEEN AWHILE COMIN'...
darb
SATCHEL'S JUST SLEEP-WALKING OR SOMETHING. BUCKY, STOP POKING HIM WITH A CHOPSTICK.
YEAH, THIS STICK IS TOO SMALL TO DO ANYTHING. NO SENSE BREAKING A GOOD STICK ON A BAD DOG.
PROBABLY CHEAPER TO JUST THROW THIS DOG OUT AND GET ANOTHER THAN TO TRY TO FIX IT. HOURLY RATES AND THAT.
WAIT, WHAT AM I SAYING? LET'S TRY A BIGGER STICK FIRST.
darb
HEY, ROBBO, JUST THOUGHT YOU'D WANT TO KNOW-- SATCHEL'S STILL ALL ZONED OUT IN THE KITCHEN.
SO IF YOU'RE COMMANDEERING ANY OF HIS STUFF, NOW IS A PRETTY CONVENIENT TIME.... ROBBO? ROB? YO, PINKISH! ROBERT SNOT WILCO!
SWEET SWEDISH CATNIP! NOW ROB'S CAUGHT IT! OOO, WHERE'S HIS WALLET ?!
darb

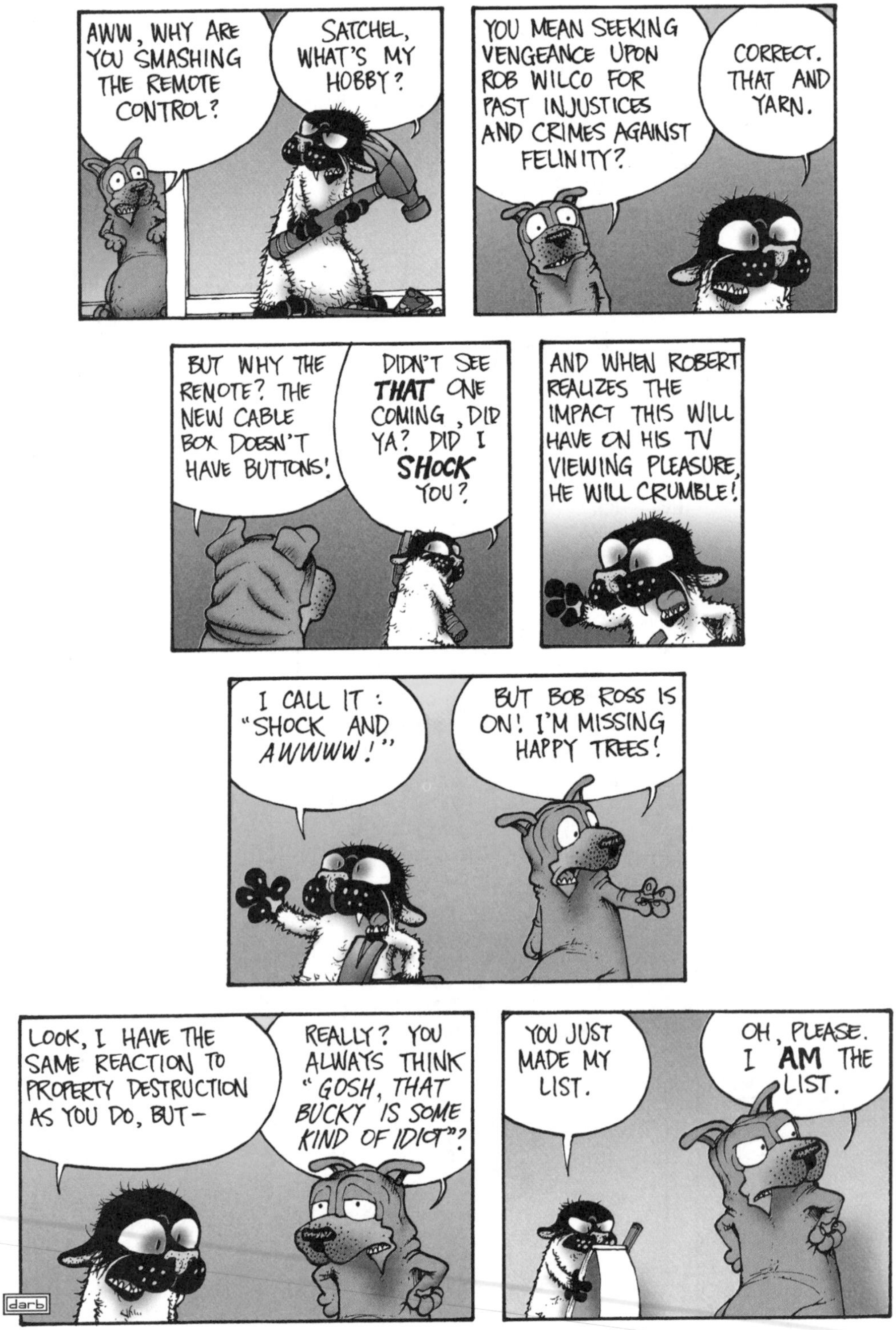
AWW, WHY ARE YOU SMASHING THE REMOTE CONTROL?
SATCHEL, WHAT'S MY HOBBY?
YOU MEAN SEEKING VENGEANCE UPON ROB WILCO FOR PAST INJUSTICES AND CRIMES AGAINST FELINITY?
CORRECT. THAT AND YARN.
BUT WHY THE REMOTE? THE NEW CABLE BOX DOESN'T HAVE BUTTONS!
DIDN'T SEE **THAT** ONE COMING, DID YA? DID I **SHOCK** YOU?
AND WHEN ROBERT REALIZES THE IMPACT THIS WILL HAVE ON HIS TV VIEWING PLEASURE, HE WILL CRUMBLE!
I CALL IT: "SHOCK AND *AWWWW!*"
BUT BOB ROSS IS ON! I'M MISSING HAPPY TREES!
LOOK, I HAVE THE SAME REACTION TO PROPERTY DESTRUCTION AS YOU DO, BUT–
REALLY? YOU ALWAYS THINK "*GOSH, THAT BUCKY IS SOME KIND OF IDIOT*"?
darb
YOU JUST MADE MY LIST.
OH, PLEASE. I **AM** THE LIST.

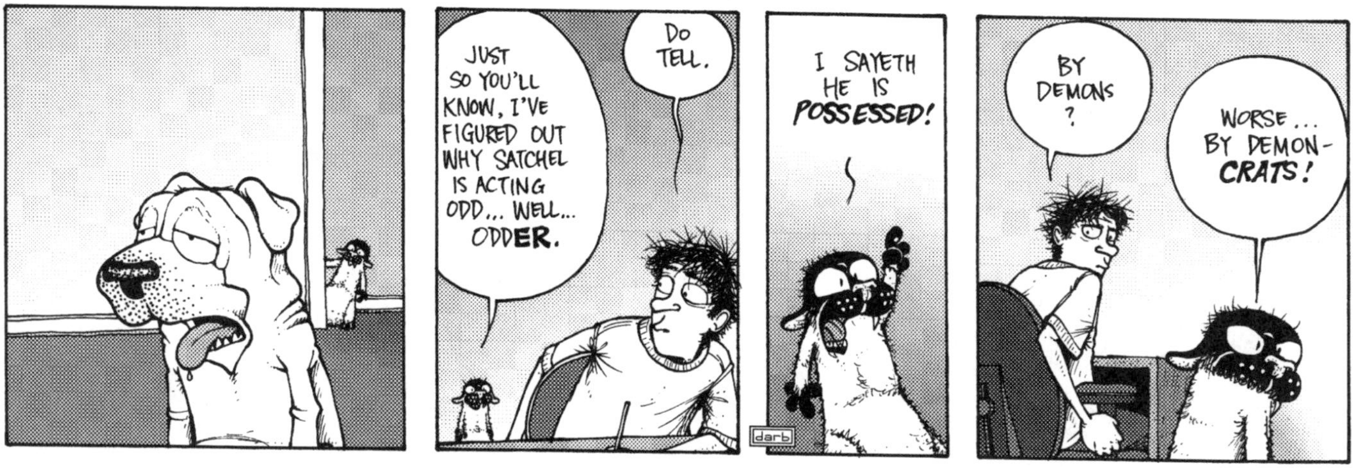
JUST SO YOU'LL KNOW, I'VE FIGURED OUT WHY SATCHEL IS ACTING ODD... WELL... ODDER.
DO TELL.
I SAYETH HE IS POSSESSED!
BY DEMONS?
WORSE... BY DEMON-CRATS!
darb

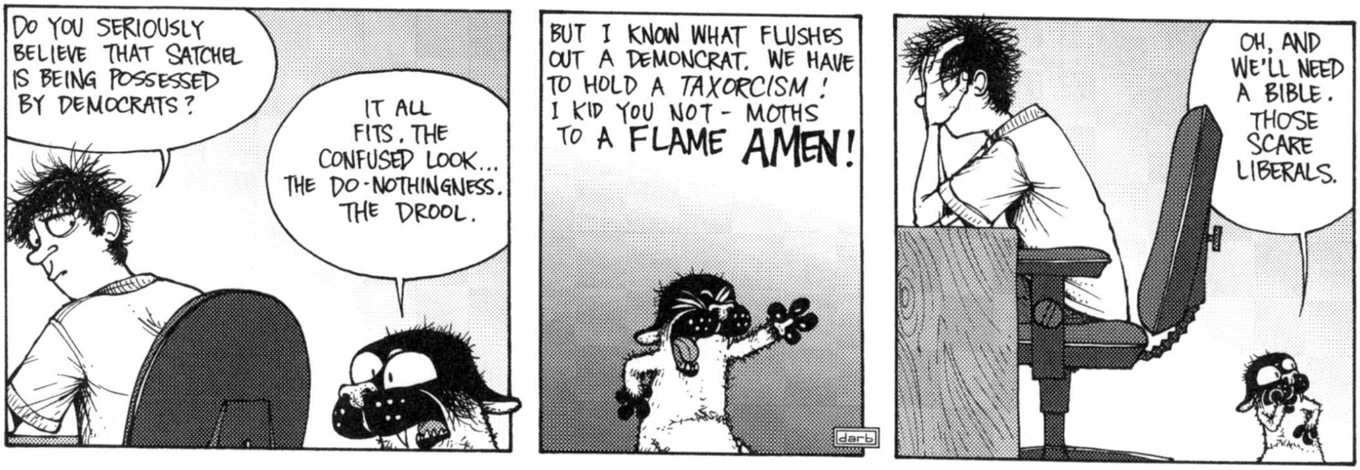
DO YOU SERIOUSLY BELIEVE THAT SATCHEL IS BEING POSSESSED BY DEMOCRATS?
IT ALL FITS. THE CONFUSED LOOK... THE DO-NOTHINGNESS. THE DROOL.
BUT I KNOW WHAT FLUSHES OUT A DEMONCRAT. WE HAVE TO HOLD A TAXORCISM! I KID YOU NOT- MOTHS TO A FLAME AMEN!
OH, AND WE'LL NEED A BIBLE. THOSE SCARE LIBERALS.
darb

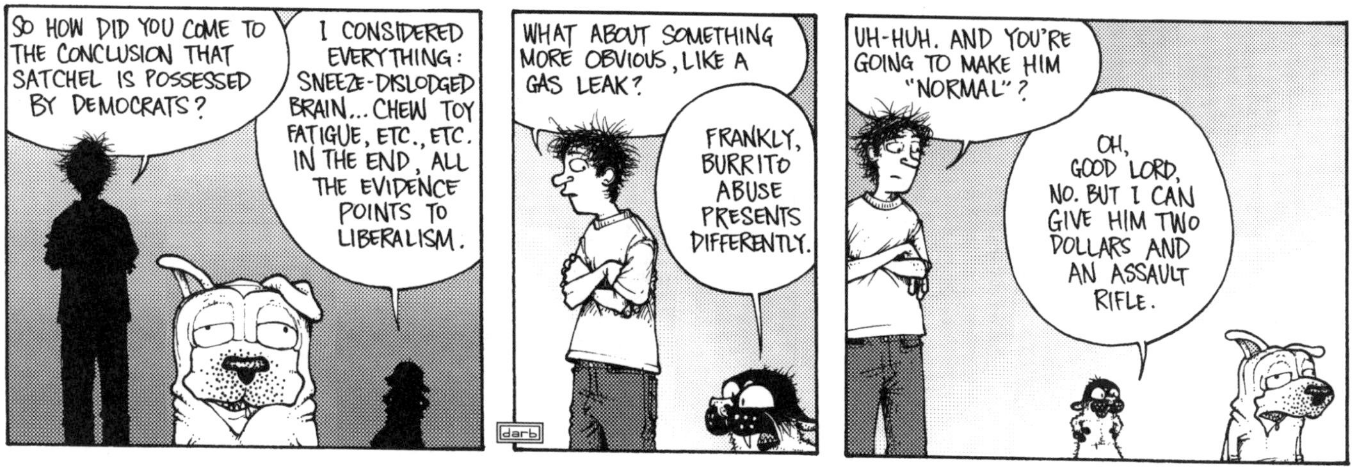
SO HOW DID YOU COME TO THE CONCLUSION THAT SATCHEL IS POSSESSED BY DEMOCRATS?
I CONSIDERED EVERYTHING: SNEEZE-DISLODGED BRAIN... CHEW TOY FATIGUE, ETC., ETC. IN THE END, ALL THE EVIDENCE POINTS TO LIBERALISM.
WHAT ABOUT SOMETHING MORE OBVIOUS, LIKE A GAS LEAK?
FRANKLY, BURRITO ABUSE PRESENTS DIFFERENTLY.
UH-HUH. AND YOU'RE GOING TO MAKE HIM "NORMAL"?
OH, GOOD LORD, NO. BUT I CAN GIVE HIM TWO DOLLARS AND AN ASSAULT RIFLE.
darb

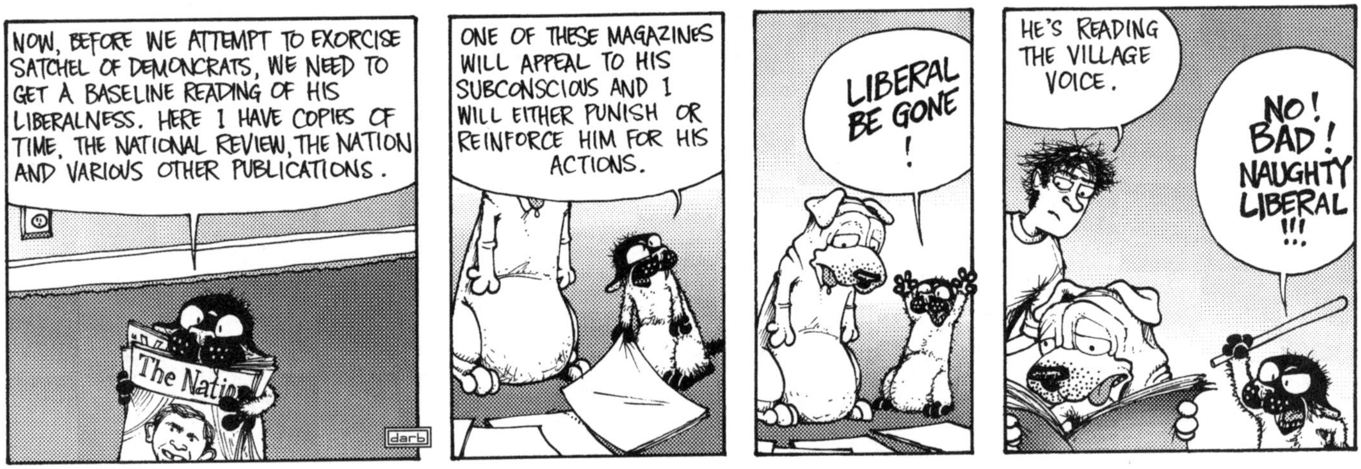
NOW, BEFORE WE ATTEMPT TO EXORCISE SATCHEL OF DEMONCRATS, WE NEED TO GET A BASELINE READING OF HIS LIBERALNESS. HERE I HAVE COPIES OF TIME, THE NATIONAL REVIEW, THE NATION AND VARIOUS OTHER PUBLICATIONS.
darb
ONE OF THESE MAGAZINES WILL APPEAL TO HIS SUBCONSCIOUS AND I WILL EITHER PUNISH OR REINFORCE HIM FOR HIS ACTIONS.
LIBERAL BE GONE!
HE'S READING THE VILLAGE VOICE.
NO! BAD! NAUGHTY LIBERAL!!!

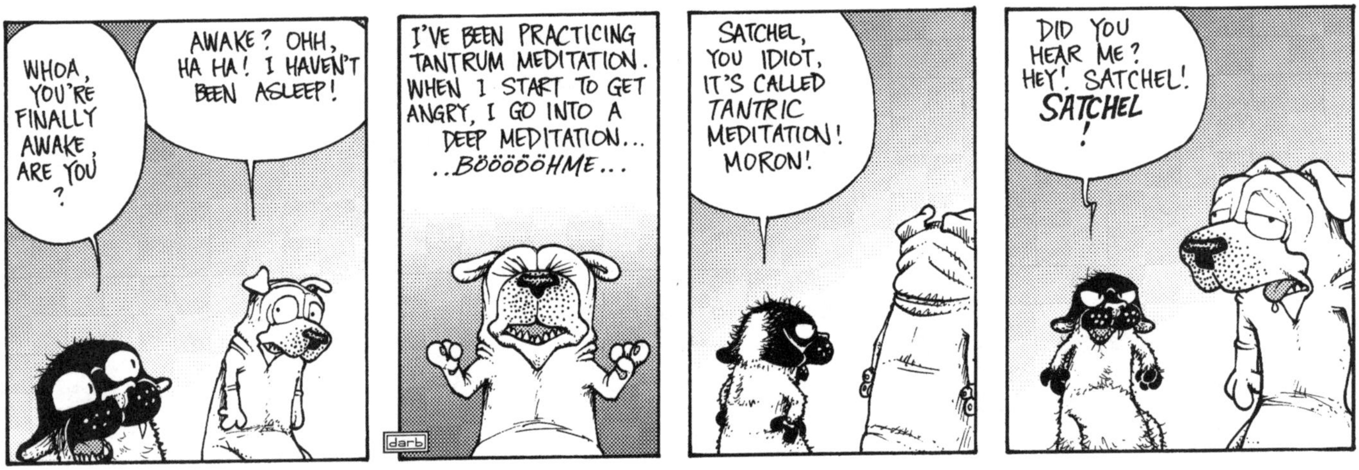
WHOA, YOU'RE FINALLY AWAKE, ARE YOU?
AWAKE? OHH, HA HA! I HAVEN'T BEEN ASLEEP!
darb
I'VE BEEN PRACTICING TANTRUM MEDITATION. WHEN I START TO GET ANGRY, I GO INTO A DEEP MEDITATION... ..BÖÖÖÖÖHME...
SATCHEL, YOU IDIOT, IT'S CALLED TANTRIC MEDITATION! MORON!
DID YOU HEAR ME? HEY! SATCHEL! SATCHEL!

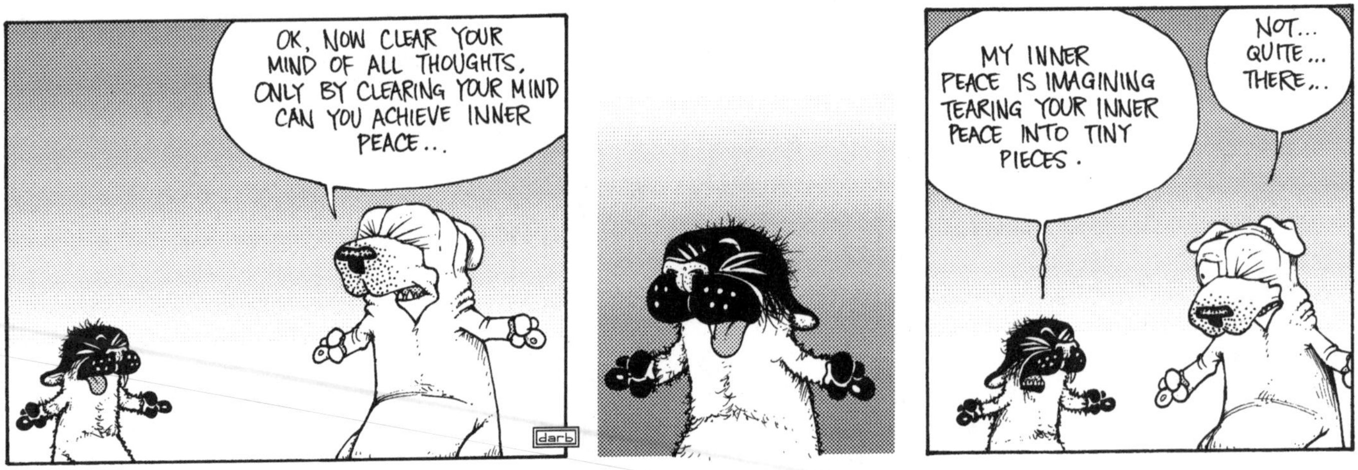
OK, NOW CLEAR YOUR MIND OF ALL THOUGHTS. ONLY BY CLEARING YOUR MIND CAN YOU ACHIEVE INNER PEACE...
darb
MY INNER PEACE IS IMAGINING TEARING YOUR INNER PEACE INTO TINY PIECES.
NOT... QUITE... THERE...

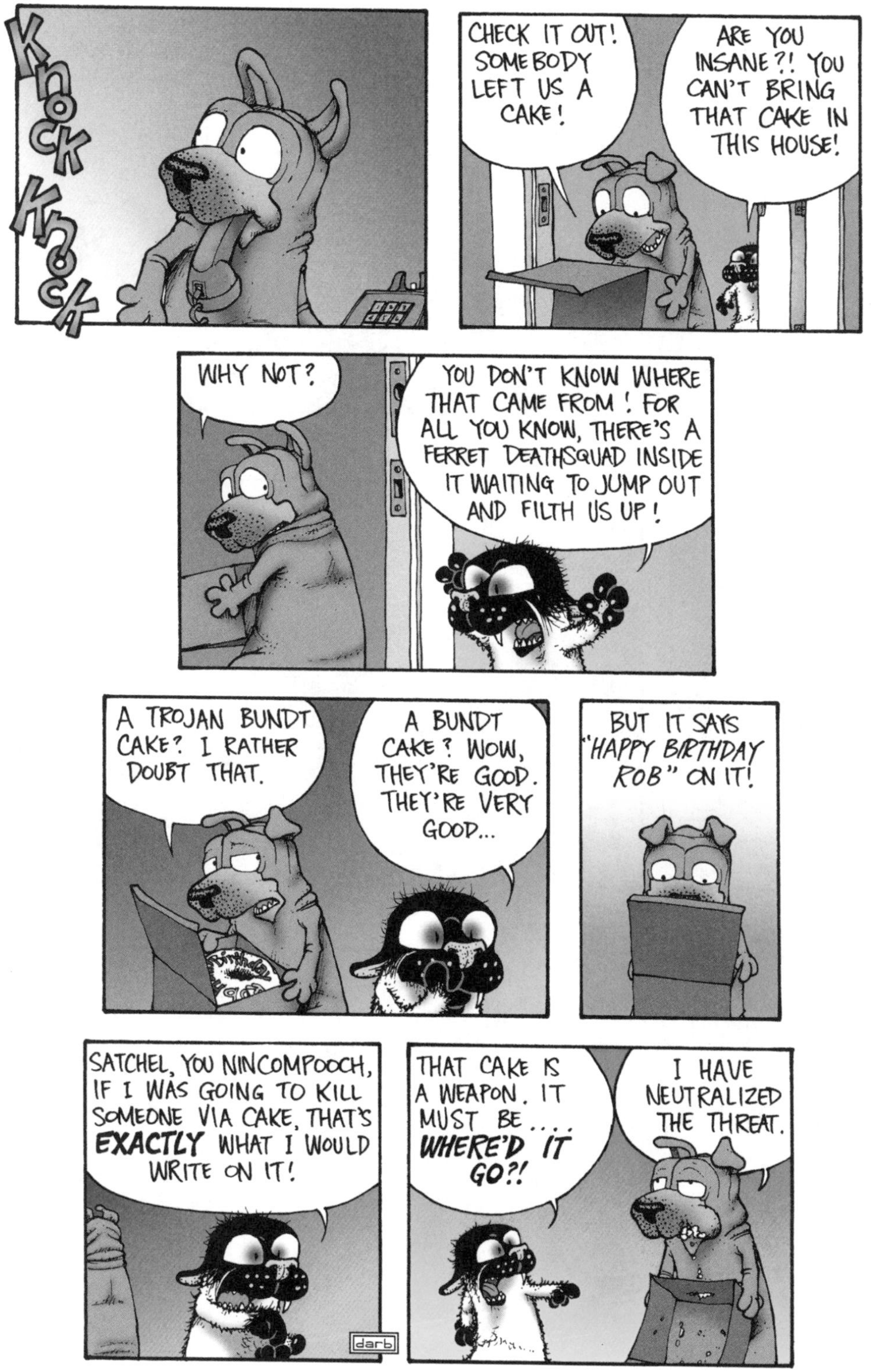
Knock Knock Knock
CHECK IT OUT! SOMEBODY LEFT US A CAKE!
ARE YOU INSANE?! YOU CAN'T BRING THAT CAKE IN THIS HOUSE!
WHY NOT?
YOU DON'T KNOW WHERE THAT CAME FROM! FOR ALL YOU KNOW, THERE'S A FERRET DEATHSQUAD INSIDE IT WAITING TO JUMP OUT AND FILTH US UP!
A TROJAN BUNDT CAKE? I RATHER DOUBT THAT.
A BUNDT CAKE? WOW, THEY'RE GOOD. THEY'RE VERY GOOD...
BUT IT SAYS "HAPPY BIRTHDAY ROB" ON IT!
SATCHEL, YOU NINCOMPOOCH, IF I WAS GOING TO KILL SOMEONE VIA CAKE, THAT'S EXACTLY WHAT I WOULD WRITE ON IT!
THAT CAKE IS A WEAPON. IT MUST BE.... WHERE'D IT GO?!
I HAVE NEUTRALIZED THE THREAT.
darb

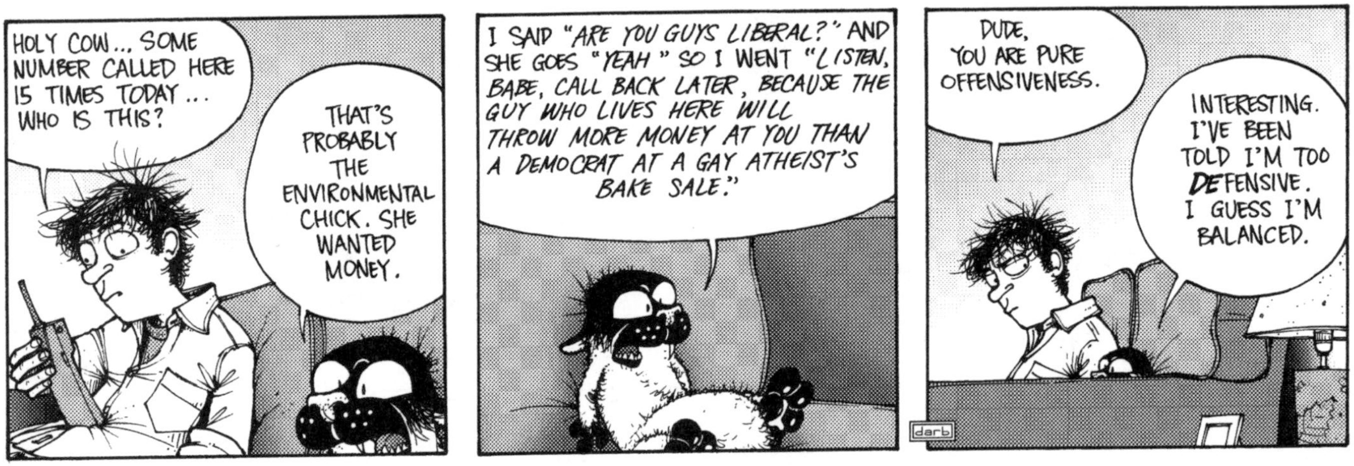
HOLY COW... SOME NUMBER CALLED HERE 15 TIMES TODAY... WHO IS THIS?
THAT'S PROBABLY THE ENVIRONMENTAL CHICK. SHE WANTED MONEY.
I SAID "ARE YOU GUYS LIBERAL?" AND SHE GOES "YEAH" SO I WENT "LISTEN, BABE, CALL BACK LATER, BECAUSE THE GUY WHO LIVES HERE WILL THROW MORE MONEY AT YOU THAN A DEMOCRAT AT A GAY ATHEIST'S BAKE SALE."
DUDE, YOU ARE PURE OFFENSIVENESS.
INTERESTING. I'VE BEEN TOLD I'M TOO DEFENSIVE. I GUESS I'M BALANCED.
darb

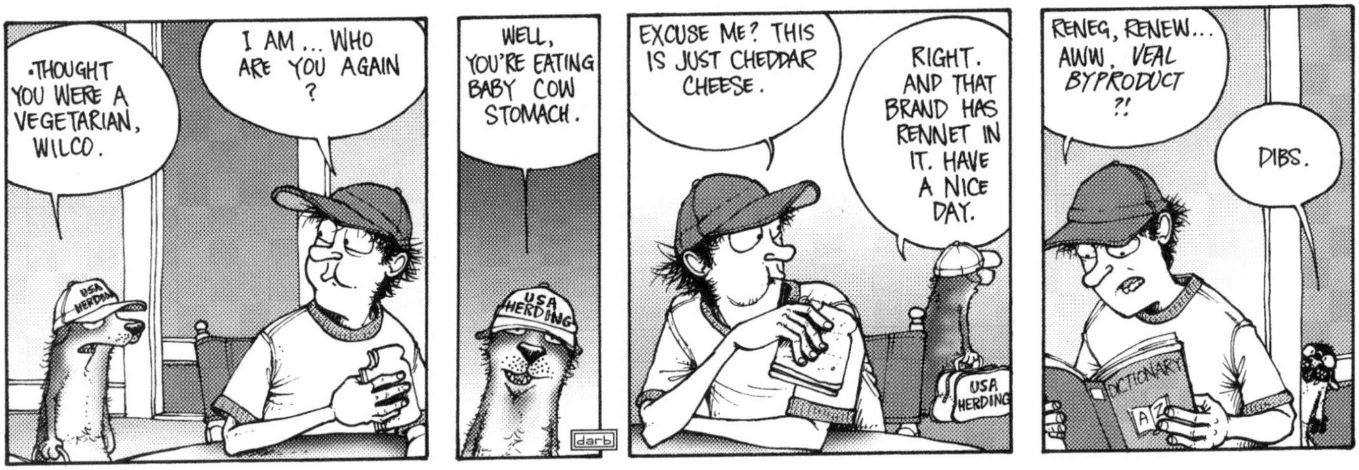
THOUGHT YOU WERE A VEGETARIAN, WILCO.
I AM... WHO ARE YOU AGAIN?
USA HERDING
WELL, YOU'RE EATING BABY COW STOMACH.
darb
EXCUSE ME? THIS IS JUST CHEDDAR CHEESE.
RIGHT. AND THAT BRAND HAS RENNET IN IT. HAVE A NICE DAY.
RENEG, RENEW... AWW, VEAL BYPRODUCT?!
DIBS.
DICTIONARY
A-Z

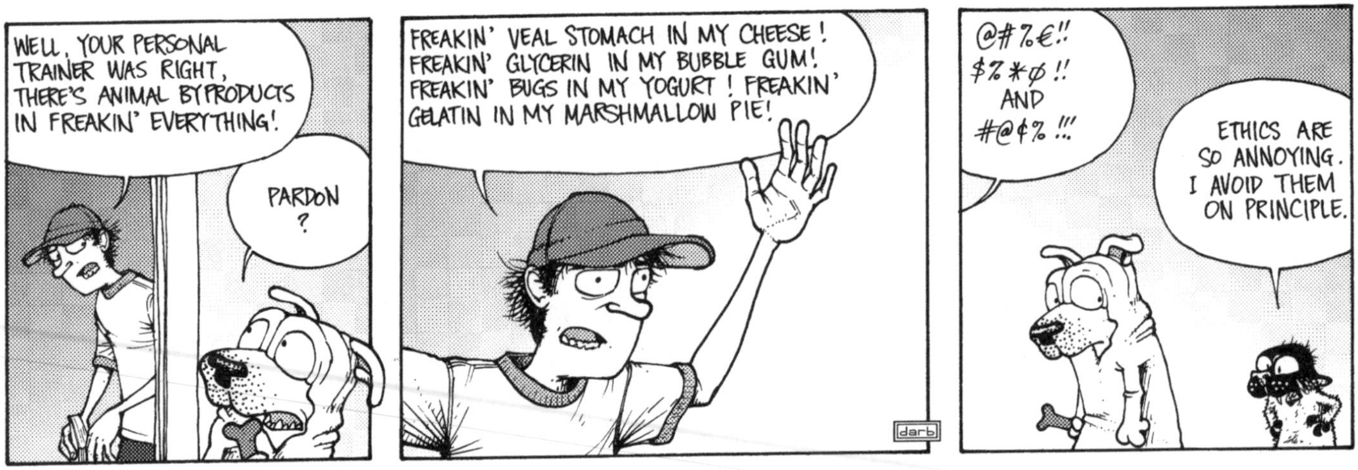
WELL, YOUR PERSONAL TRAINER WAS RIGHT, THERE'S ANIMAL BYPRODUCTS IN FREAKIN' EVERYTHING!
PARDON?
FREAKIN' VEAL STOMACH IN MY CHEESE! FREAKIN' GLYCERIN IN MY BUBBLE GUM! FREAKIN' BUGS IN MY YOGURT! FREAKIN' GELATIN IN MY MARSHMALLOW PIE!
darb
@#%€!! $%*¢!! AND #@¢%!!!
ETHICS ARE SO ANNOYING. I AVOID THEM ON PRINCIPLE.

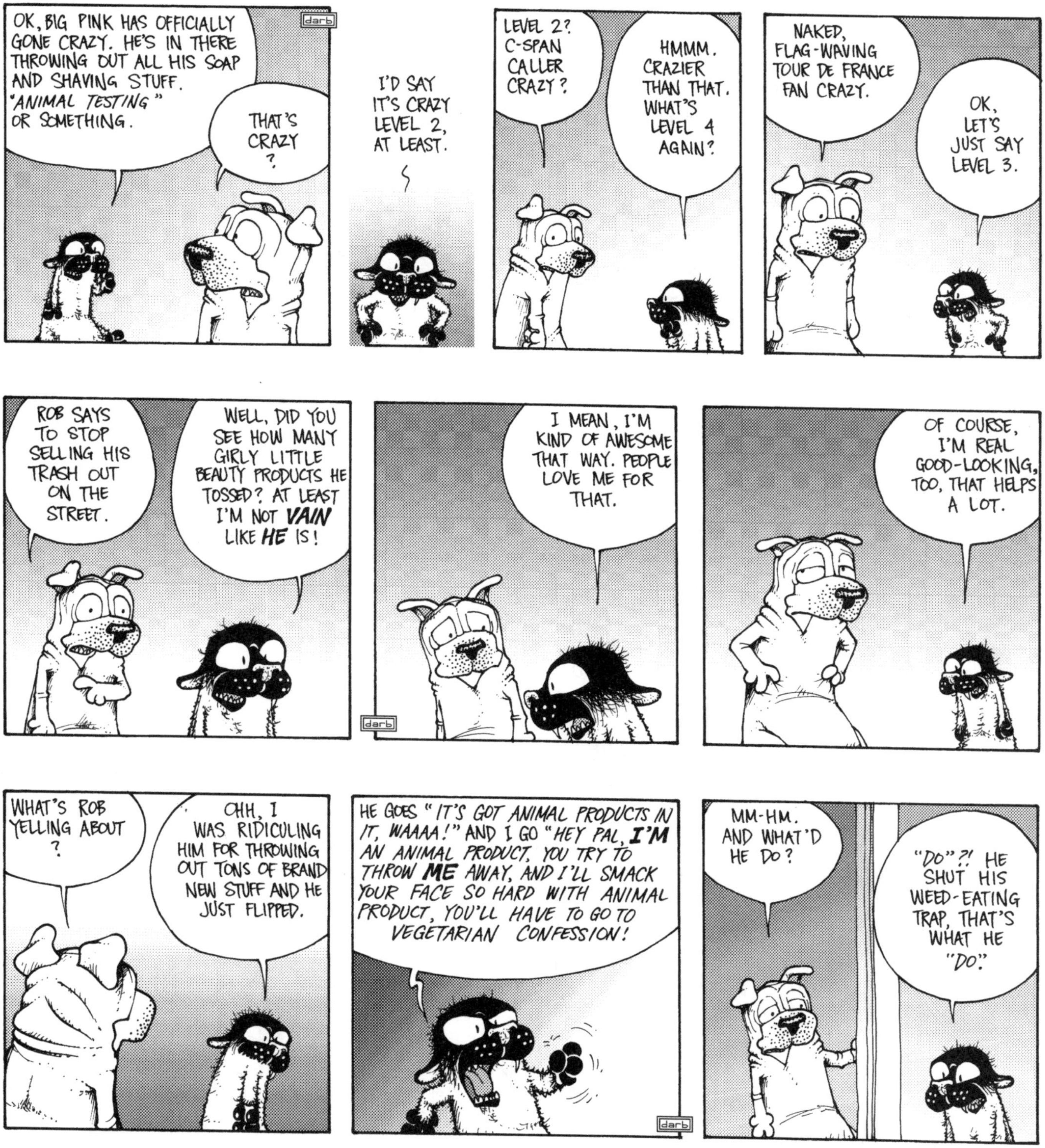
darb
OK, BIG PINK HAS OFFICIALLY GONE CRAZY. HE'S IN THERE THROWING OUT ALL HIS SOAP AND SHAVING STUFF. "ANIMAL TESTING" OR SOMETHING.
THAT'S CRAZY?
I'D SAY IT'S CRAZY LEVEL 2, AT LEAST.
LEVEL 2? C-SPAN CALLER CRAZY?
HMMM. CRAZIER THAN THAT. WHAT'S LEVEL 4 AGAIN?
NAKED, FLAG-WAVING TOUR DE FRANCE FAN CRAZY.
OK, LET'S JUST SAY LEVEL 3.
ROB SAYS TO STOP SELLING HIS TRASH OUT ON THE STREET.
WELL, DID YOU SEE HOW MANY GIRLY LITTLE BEAUTY PRODUCTS HE TOSSED? AT LEAST I'M NOT VAIN LIKE HE IS!
I MEAN, I'M KIND OF AWESOME THAT WAY. PEOPLE LOVE ME FOR THAT.
darb
OF COURSE, I'M REAL GOOD-LOOKING, TOO, THAT HELPS A LOT.
WHAT'S ROB YELLING ABOUT?
OHH, I WAS RIDICULING HIM FOR THROWING OUT TONS OF BRAND NEW STUFF AND HE JUST FLIPPED.
HE GOES "IT'S GOT ANIMAL PRODUCTS IN IT, WAAAA!" AND I GO "HEY PAL, I'M AN ANIMAL PRODUCT. YOU TRY TO THROW ME AWAY, AND I'LL SMACK YOUR FACE SO HARD WITH ANIMAL PRODUCT, YOU'LL HAVE TO GO TO VEGETARIAN CONFESSION!
darb
MM-HM. AND WHAT'D HE DO?
"DO"?! HE SHUT HIS WEED-EATING TRAP, THAT'S WHAT HE "DO."

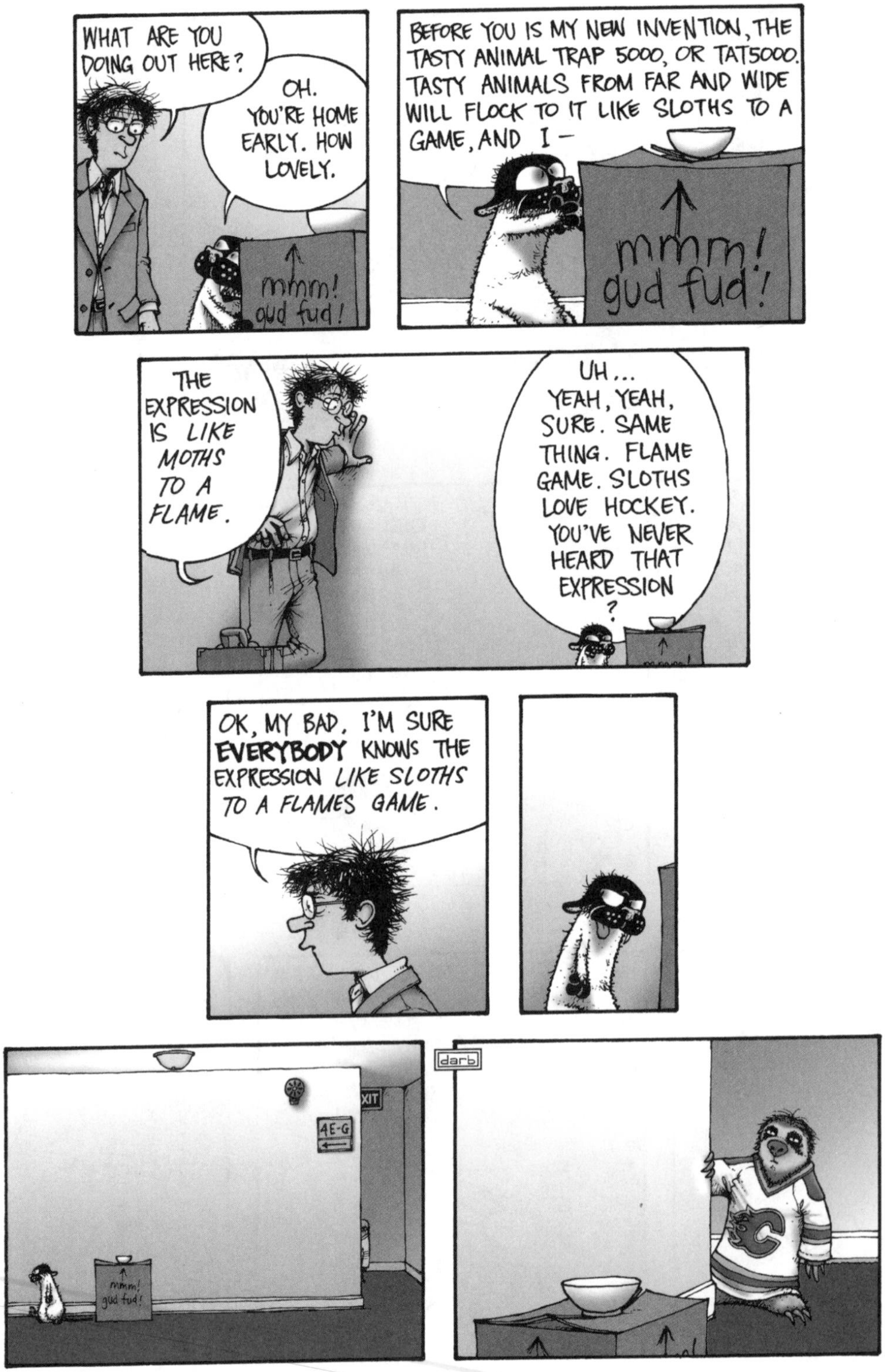
WHAT ARE YOU DOING OUT HERE?
OH. YOU'RE HOME EARLY. HOW LOVELY.
mmm! gud fud!
BEFORE YOU IS MY NEW INVENTION, THE TASTY ANIMAL TRAP 5000, OR TAT5000. TASTY ANIMALS FROM FAR AND WIDE WILL FLOCK TO IT LIKE SLOTHS TO A GAME, AND I –
mmm! gud fud!
THE EXPRESSION IS *LIKE MOTHS TO A FLAME.*
UH... YEAH, YEAH, SURE. SAME THING. FLAME GAME. SLOTHS LOVE HOCKEY. YOU'VE NEVER HEARD THAT EXPRESSION?
OK, MY BAD. I'M SURE **EVERYBODY** KNOWS THE EXPRESSION *LIKE SLOTHS TO A FLAMES GAME.*
EXIT
4E-G
mmm! gud fud!
darb

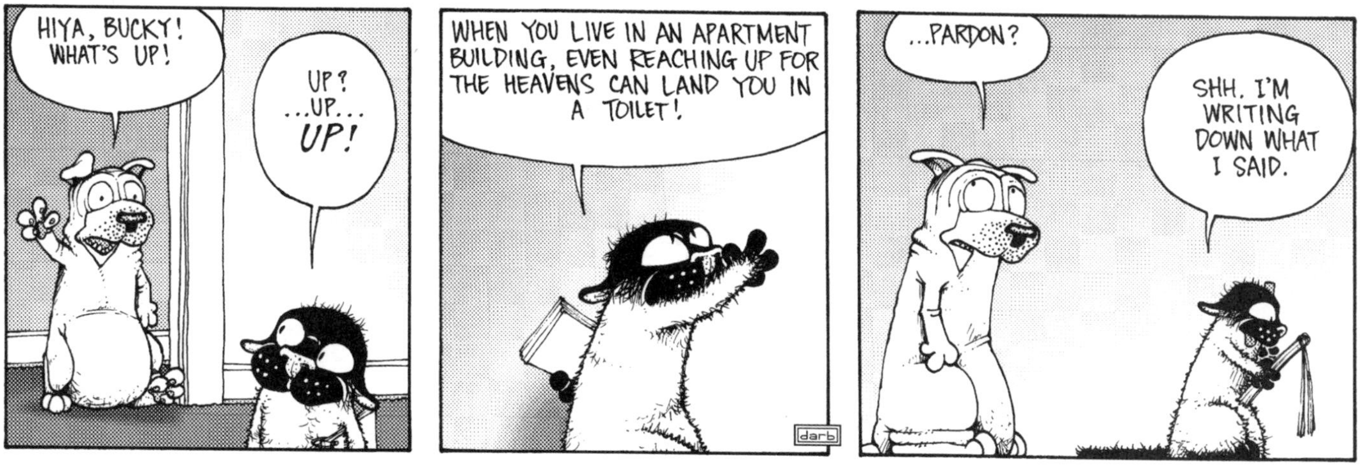
HIYA, BUCKY! WHAT'S UP!
UP? ...UP... UP!
WHEN YOU LIVE IN AN APARTMENT BUILDING, EVEN REACHING UP FOR THE HEAVENS CAN LAND YOU IN A TOILET!
darb
...PARDON?
SHH. I'M WRITING DOWN WHAT I SAID.

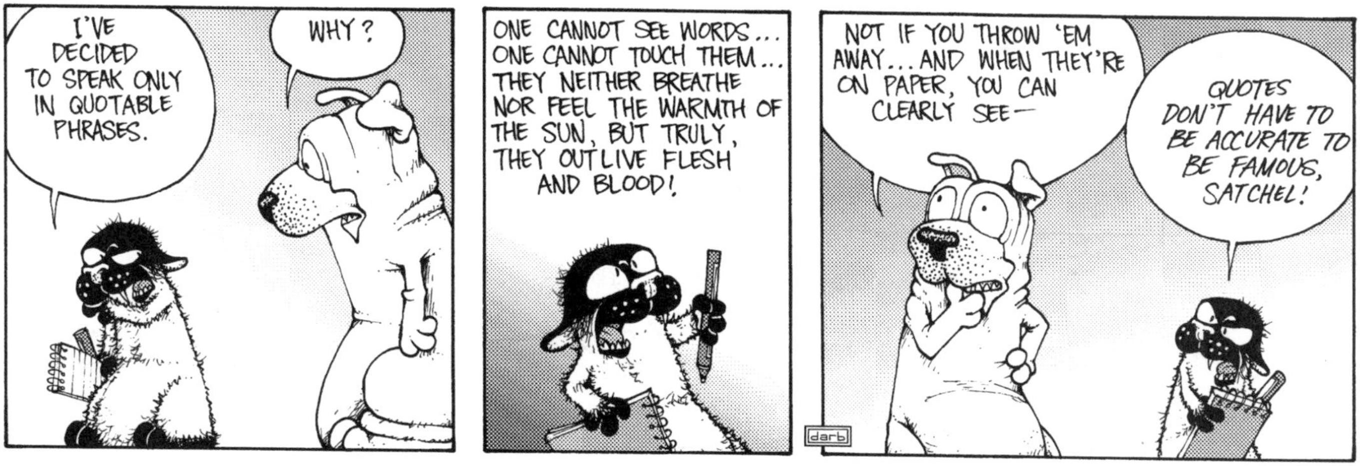
I'VE DECIDED TO SPEAK ONLY IN QUOTABLE PHRASES.
WHY?
ONE CANNOT SEE WORDS... ONE CANNOT TOUCH THEM... THEY NEITHER BREATHE NOR FEEL THE WARMTH OF THE SUN, BUT TRULY, THEY OUTLIVE FLESH AND BLOOD!
darb
NOT IF YOU THROW 'EM AWAY... AND WHEN THEY'RE ON PAPER, YOU CAN CLEARLY SEE—
QUOTES DON'T HAVE TO BE ACCURATE TO BE FAMOUS, SATCHEL!

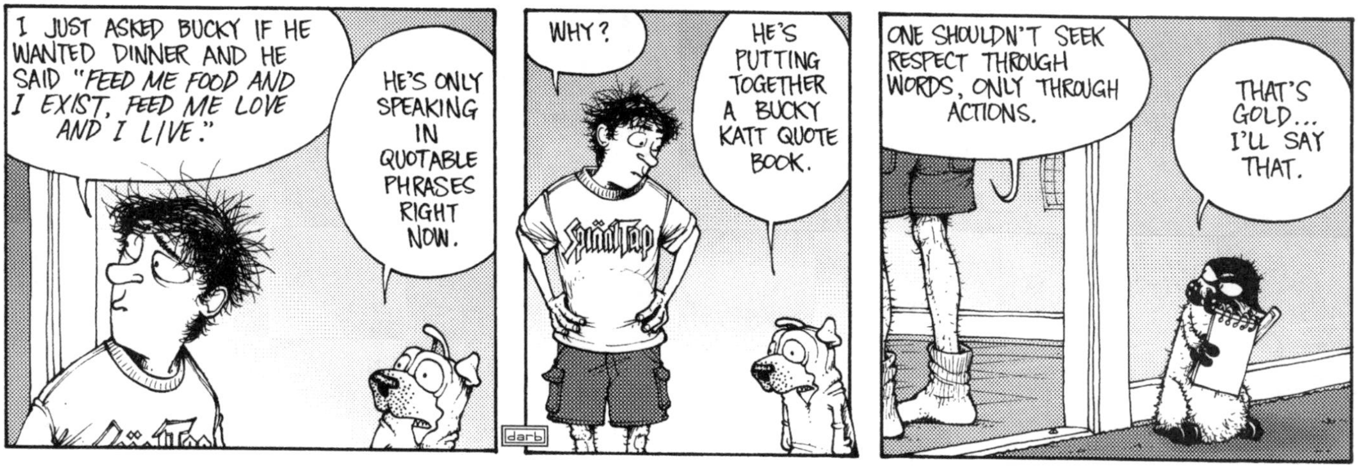
I JUST ASKED BUCKY IF HE WANTED DINNER AND HE SAID "FEED ME FOOD AND I EXIST, FEED ME LOVE AND I LIVE."
HE'S ONLY SPEAKING IN QUOTABLE PHRASES RIGHT NOW.
WHY?
HE'S PUTTING TOGETHER A BUCKY KATT QUOTE BOOK.
darb
ONE SHOULDN'T SEEK RESPECT THROUGH WORDS, ONLY THROUGH ACTIONS.
THAT'S GOLD... I'LL SAY THAT.

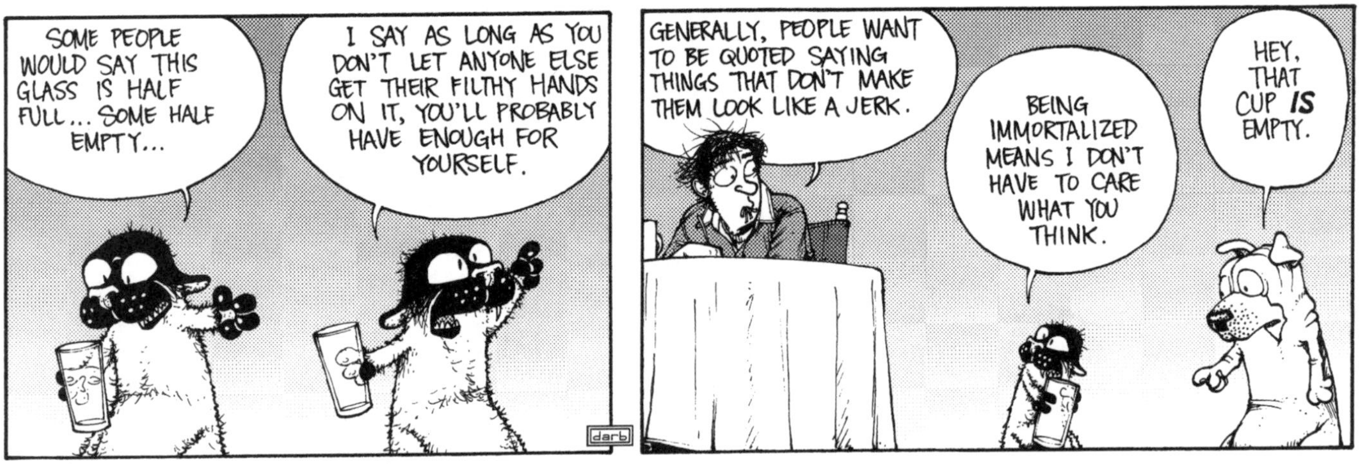
SOME PEOPLE WOULD SAY THIS GLASS IS HALF FULL... SOME HALF EMPTY...
I SAY AS LONG AS YOU DON'T LET ANYONE ELSE GET THEIR FILTHY HANDS ON IT, YOU'LL PROBABLY HAVE ENOUGH FOR YOURSELF.
darb
GENERALLY, PEOPLE WANT TO BE QUOTED SAYING THINGS THAT DON'T MAKE THEM LOOK LIKE A JERK.
BEING IMMORTALIZED MEANS I DON'T HAVE TO CARE WHAT YOU THINK.
HEY, THAT CUP **IS** EMPTY.

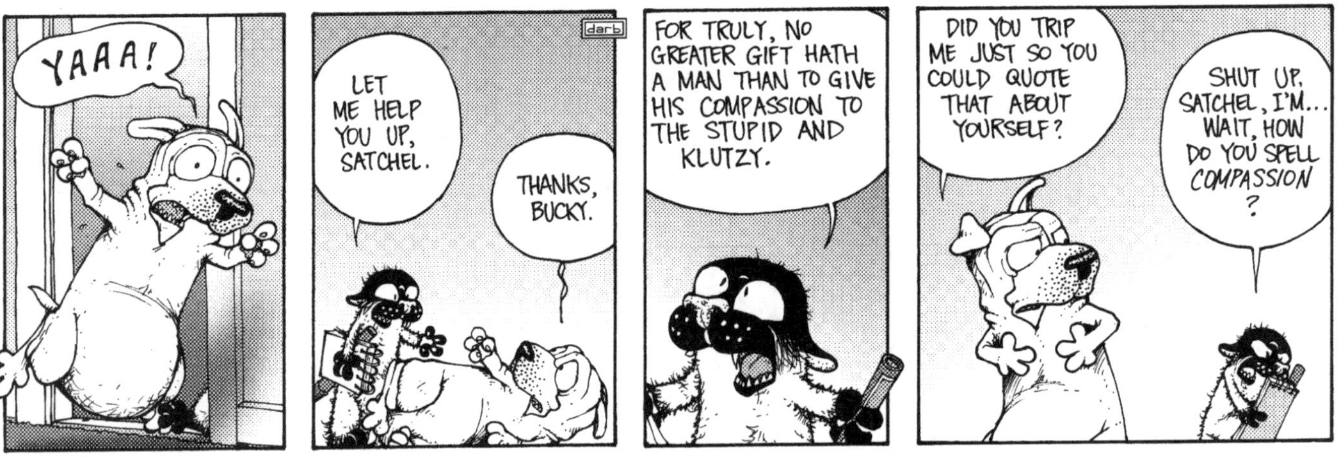
YAAAA!
darb
LET ME HELP YOU UP, SATCHEL.
THANKS, BUCKY.
FOR TRULY, NO GREATER GIFT HATH A MAN THAN TO GIVE HIS COMPASSION TO THE STUPID AND KLUTZY.
DID YOU TRIP ME JUST SO YOU COULD QUOTE THAT ABOUT YOURSELF?
SHUT UP, SATCHEL, I'M... WAIT, HOW DO YOU SPELL *COMPASSION* ?

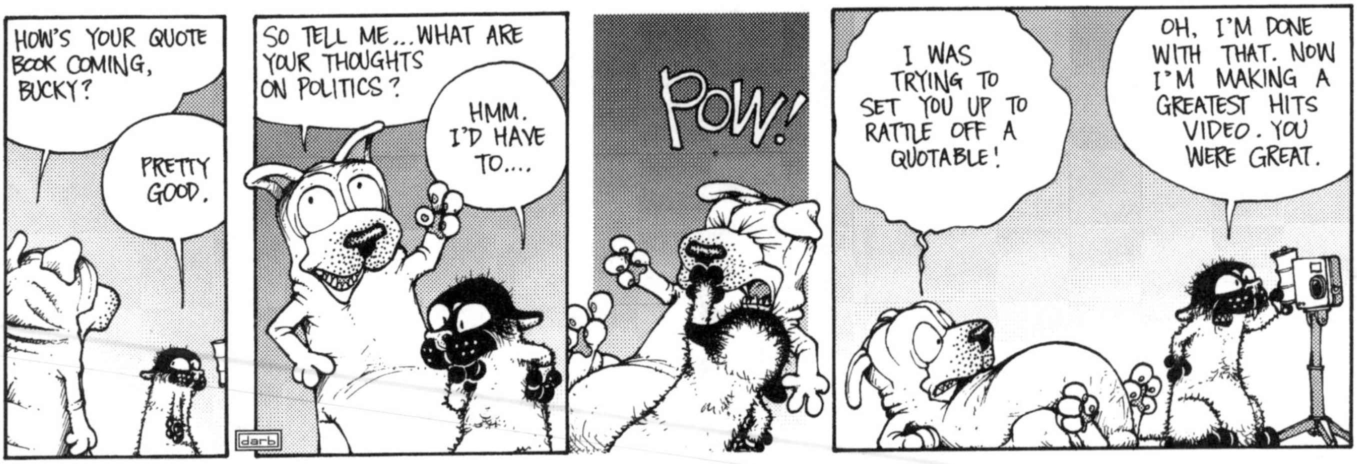
HOW'S YOUR QUOTE BOOK COMING, BUCKY?
PRETTY GOOD.
darb
SO TELL ME... WHAT ARE YOUR THOUGHTS ON POLITICS?
HMM. I'D HAVE TO....
POW!
I WAS TRYING TO SET YOU UP TO RATTLE OFF A QUOTABLE!
OH, I'M DONE WITH THAT. NOW I'M MAKING A GREATEST HITS VIDEO. YOU WERE GREAT.

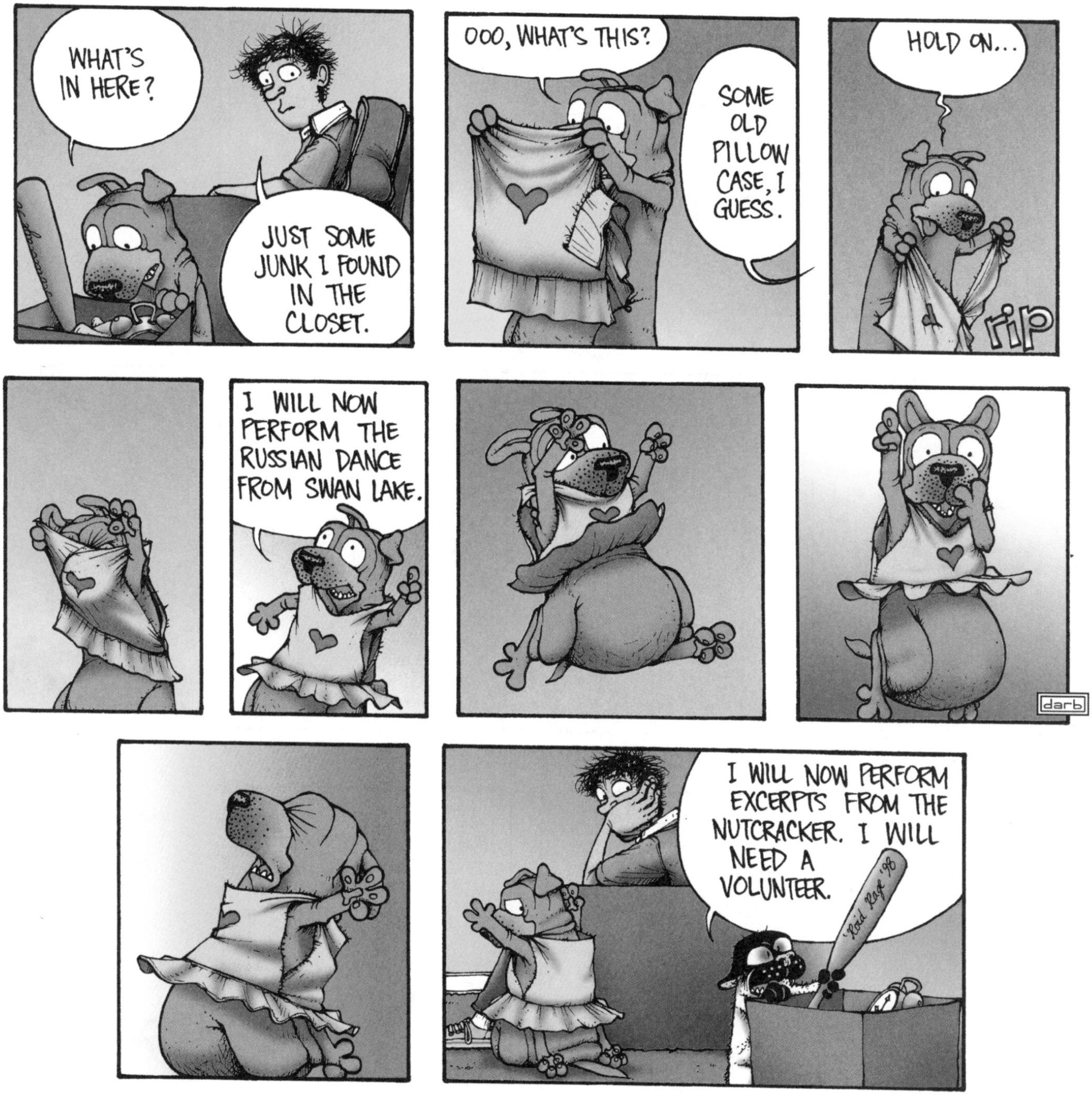
WHAT'S IN HERE?
JUST SOME JUNK I FOUND IN THE CLOSET.
OOO, WHAT'S THIS?
SOME OLD PILLOW CASE, I GUESS.
HOLD ON...
rip
I WILL NOW PERFORM THE RUSSIAN DANCE FROM SWAN LAKE.
darb
I WILL NOW PERFORM EXCERPTS FROM THE NUTCRACKER. I WILL NEED A VOLUNTEER.
'Roid Rage '98

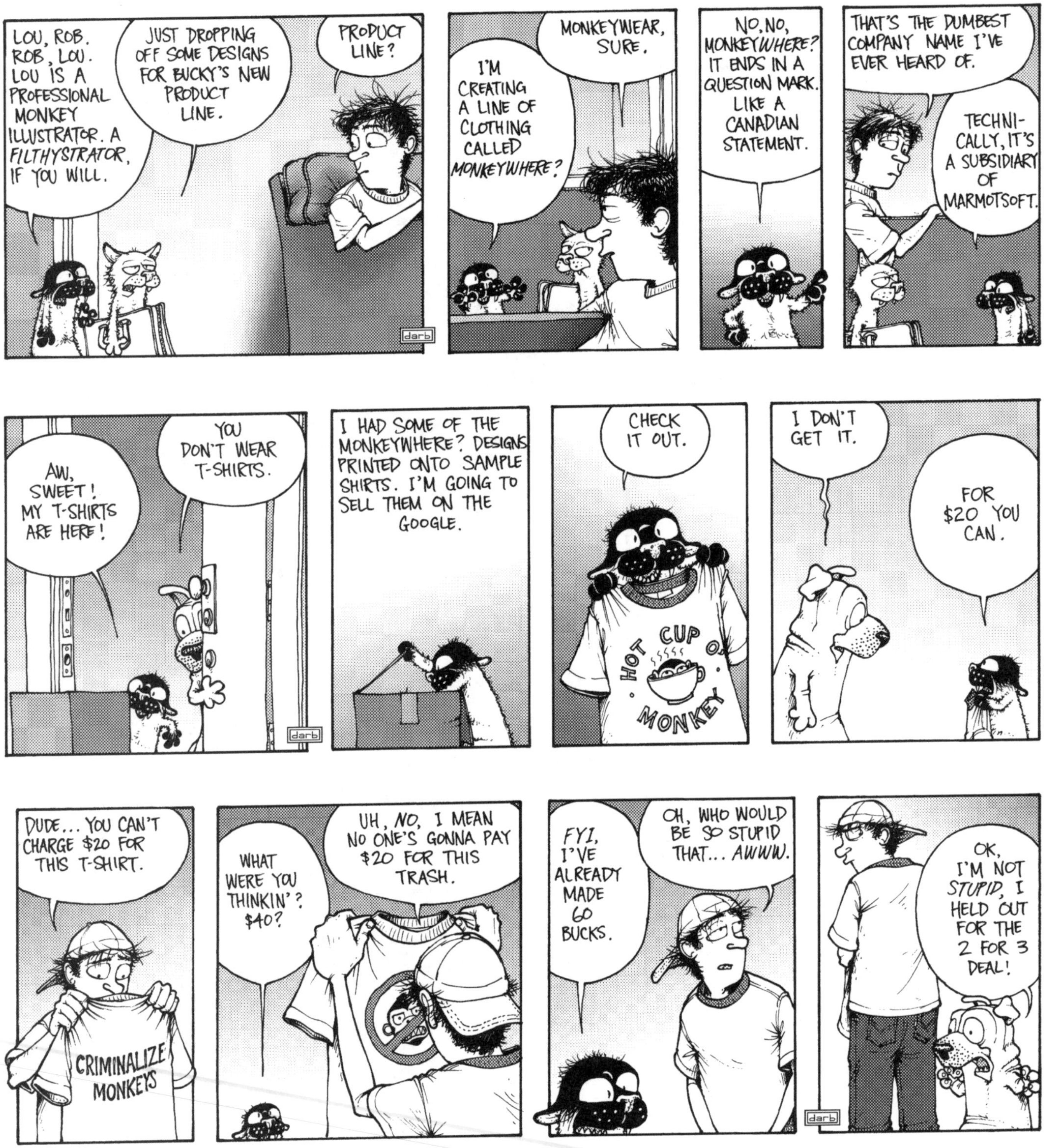
LOU, ROB. ROB, LOU. LOU IS A PROFESSIONAL MONKEY ILLUSTRATOR. A *FILTHYSTRATOR*, IF YOU WILL.
JUST DROPPING OFF SOME DESIGNS FOR BUCKY'S NEW PRODUCT LINE.
PRODUCT LINE?
darb
I'M CREATING A LINE OF CLOTHING CALLED *MONKEYWHERE?*
MONKEYWEAR, SURE.
NO, NO, MONKEY*WHERE?* IT ENDS IN A QUESTION MARK. LIKE A CANADIAN STATEMENT.
THAT'S THE DUMBEST COMPANY NAME I'VE EVER HEARD OF.
TECHNICALLY, IT'S A SUBSIDIARY OF MARMOTSOFT.
AW, SWEET! MY T-SHIRTS ARE HERE!
YOU DON'T WEAR T-SHIRTS.
darb
I HAD SOME OF THE MONKEYWHERE? DESIGNS PRINTED ONTO SAMPLE SHIRTS. I'M GOING TO SELL THEM ON THE GOOGLE.
CHECK IT OUT.
HOT CUP OF MONKEY
I DON'T GET IT.
FOR $20 YOU CAN.
DUDE... YOU CAN'T CHARGE $20 FOR THIS T-SHIRT.
CRIMINALIZE MONKEYS
WHAT WERE YOU THINKIN'? $40?
UH, *NO*, I MEAN NO ONE'S GONNA PAY $20 FOR THIS TRASH.
FYI, I'VE ALREADY MADE 60 BUCKS.
OH, WHO WOULD BE SO STUPID THAT... *AWWW*.
darb
OK, I'M NOT *STUPID*, I HELD OUT FOR THE 2 FOR 3 DEAL!

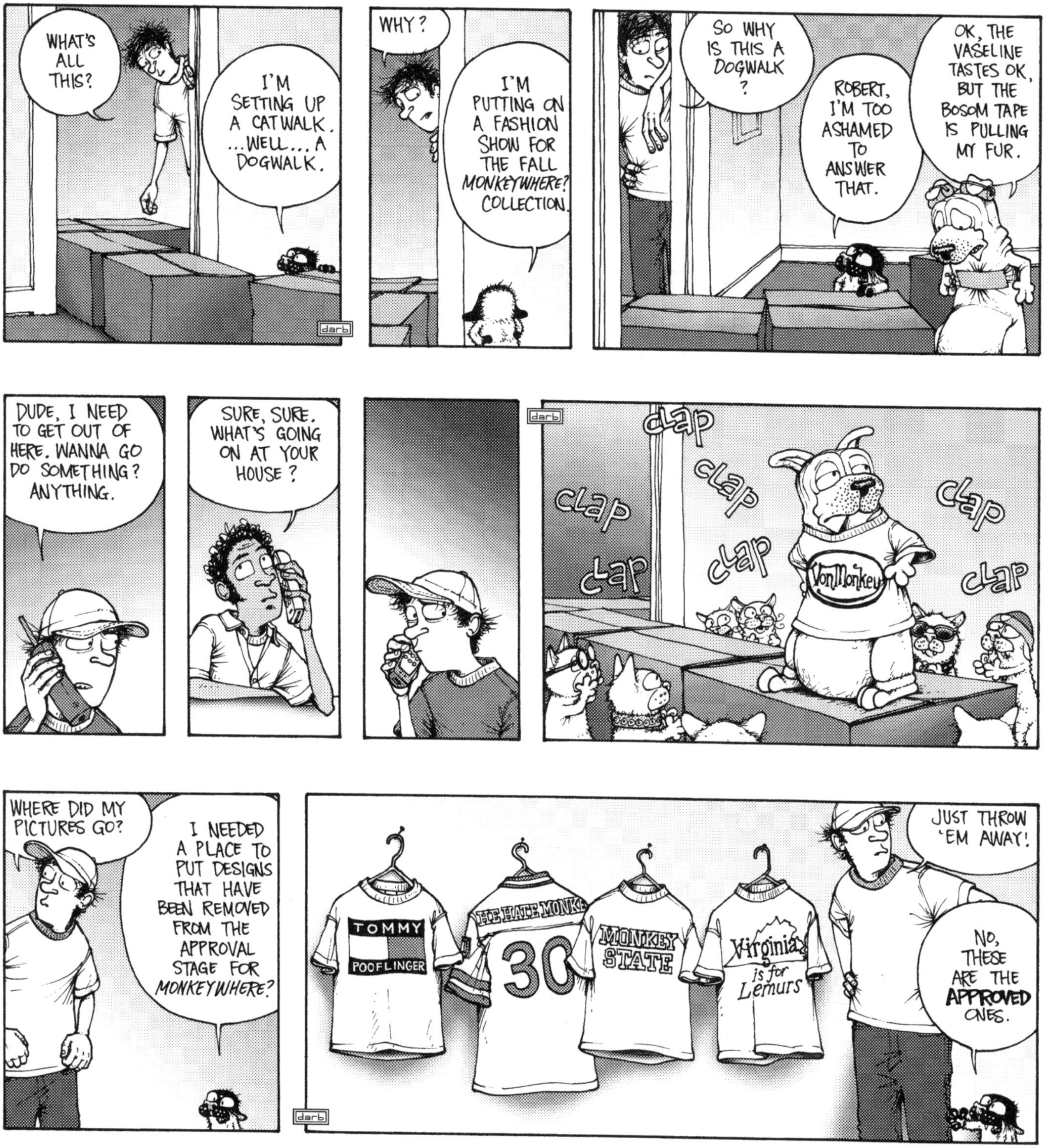
WHAT'S ALL THIS?
I'M SETTING UP A CATWALK. ...WELL... A DOGWALK.
WHY?
I'M PUTTING ON A FASHION SHOW FOR THE FALL MONKEYWHERE? COLLECTION.
SO WHY IS THIS A DOGWALK?
ROBERT, I'M TOO ASHAMED TO ANSWER THAT.
OK, THE VASELINE TASTES OK, BUT THE BOSOM TAPE IS PULLING MY FUR.
darb
DUDE, I NEED TO GET OUT OF HERE. WANNA GO DO SOMETHING? ANYTHING.
SURE, SURE. WHAT'S GOING ON AT YOUR HOUSE?
darb
CLAP CLAP CLAP CLAP CLAP CLAP CLAP
VonMonkey
WHERE DID MY PICTURES GO?
I NEEDED A PLACE TO PUT DESIGNS THAT HAVE BEEN REMOVED FROM THE APPROVAL STAGE FOR MONKEYWHERE?
TOMMY POOFLINGER
HE HATE MONKE 30
MONKEY STATE
Virginia is for Lemurs
JUST THROW 'EM AWAY!
NO, THESE ARE THE APPROVED ONES.
darb

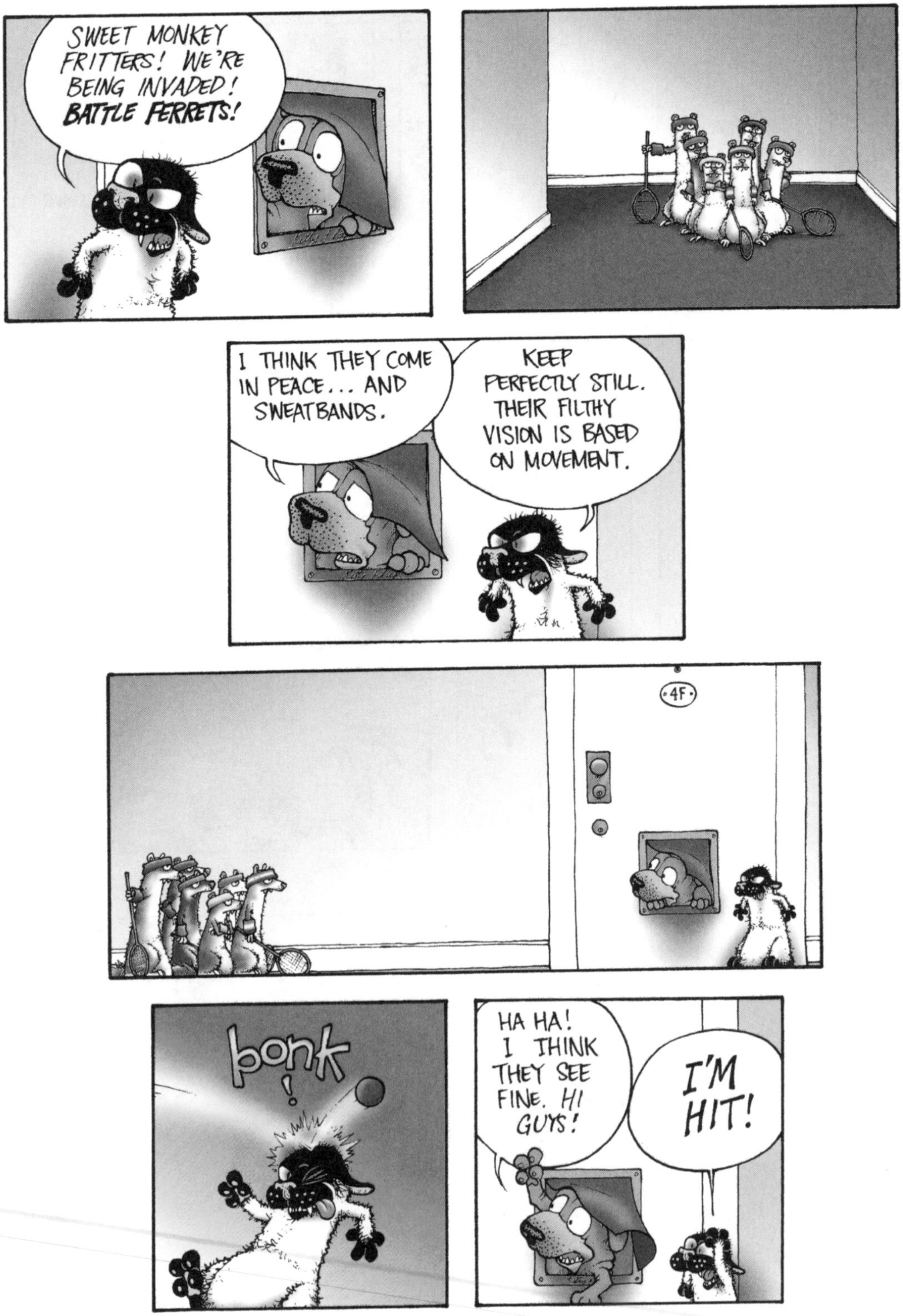
SWEET MONKEY FRITTERS! WE'RE BEING INVADED! BATTLE FERRETS!
I THINK THEY COME IN PEACE... AND SWEATBANDS.
KEEP PERFECTLY STILL. THEIR FILTHY VISION IS BASED ON MOVEMENT.
4F
bonk
!
HA HA! I THINK THEY SEE FINE. HI GUYS!
I'M HIT!

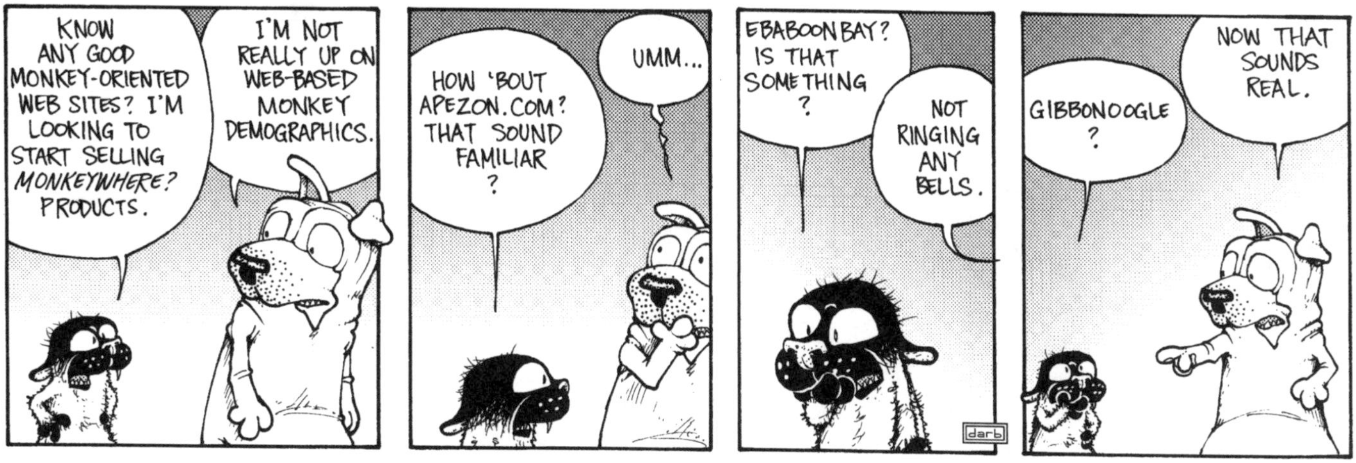
KNOW ANY GOOD MONKEY-ORIENTED WEB SITES? I'M LOOKING TO START SELLING *MONKEYWHERE?* PRODUCTS.
I'M NOT REALLY UP ON WEB-BASED MONKEY DEMOGRAPHICS.
HOW 'BOUT APEZON.COM? THAT SOUND FAMILIAR ?
UMM...
EBABOON BAY? IS THAT SOMETHING ?
NOT RINGING ANY BELLS.
GIBBONOOGLE ?
NOW THAT SOUNDS REAL.
darb

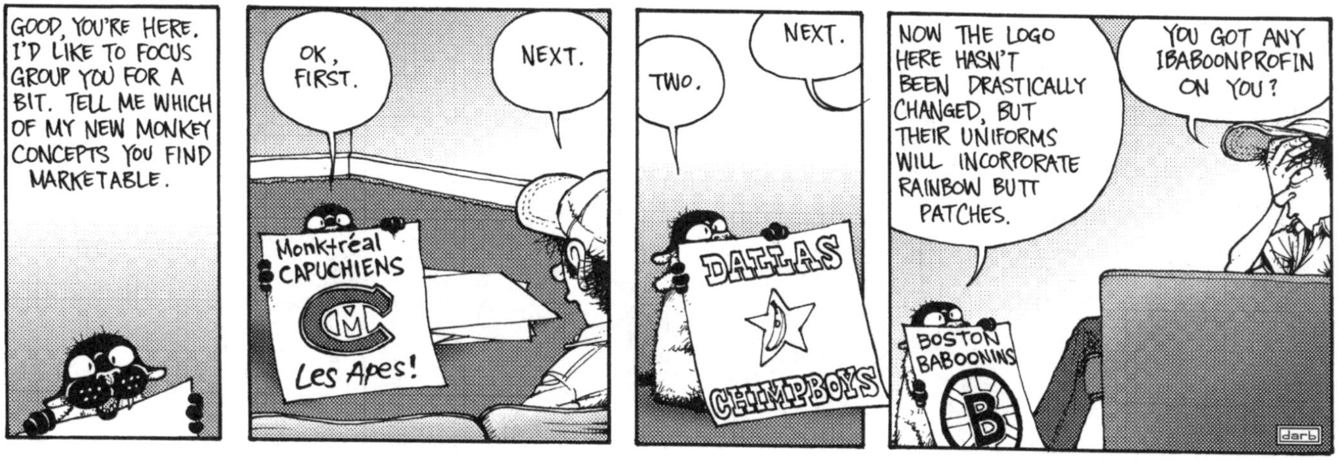
GOOD, YOU'RE HERE. I'D LIKE TO FOCUS GROUP YOU FOR A BIT. TELL ME WHICH OF MY NEW MONKEY CONCEPTS YOU FIND MARKETABLE.
OK, FIRST.
NEXT.
Monktréal CAPUCHIENS
Les Apes!
TWO.
NEXT.
DALLAS
CHIMPBOYS
NOW THE LOGO HERE HASN'T BEEN DRASTICALLY CHANGED, BUT THEIR UNIFORMS WILL INCORPORATE RAINBOW BUTT PATCHES.
YOU GOT ANY IBABOONPROFIN ON YOU?
BOSTON BABOONINS
B
darb

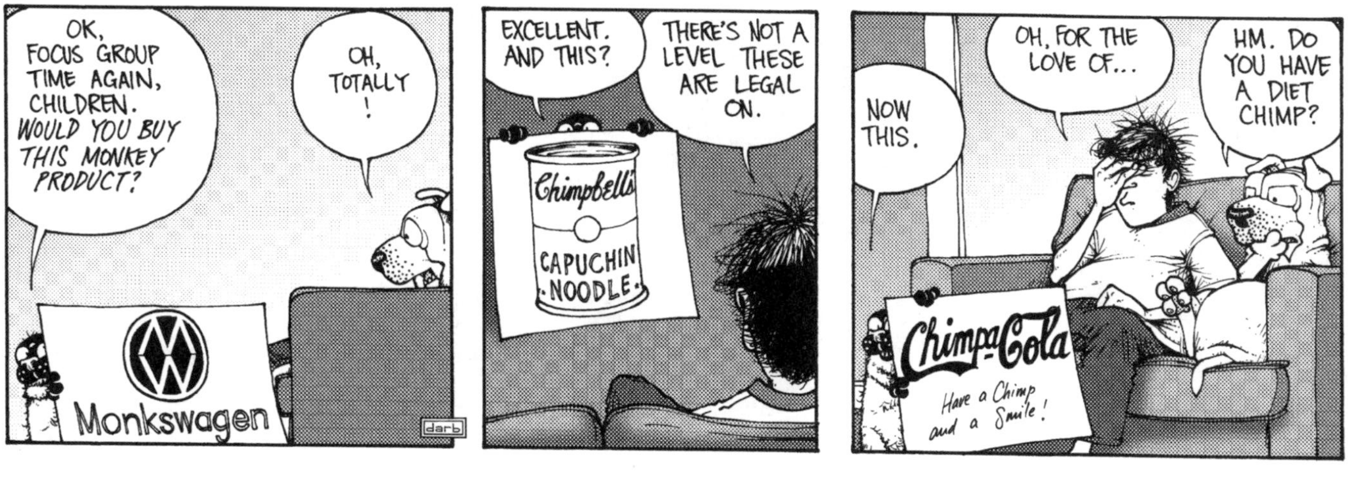
OK, FOCUS GROUP TIME AGAIN, CHILDREN. *WOULD YOU BUY THIS MONKEY PRODUCT?*
OH, TOTALLY !
Monkswagen
darb
EXCELLENT. AND THIS?
THERE'S NOT A LEVEL THESE ARE LEGAL ON.
Chimpbell's
CAPUCHIN NOODLE
NOW THIS.
OH, FOR THE LOVE OF...
HM. DO YOU HAVE A DIET CHIMP?
Chimpa-Cola
Have a Chimp and a Smile!

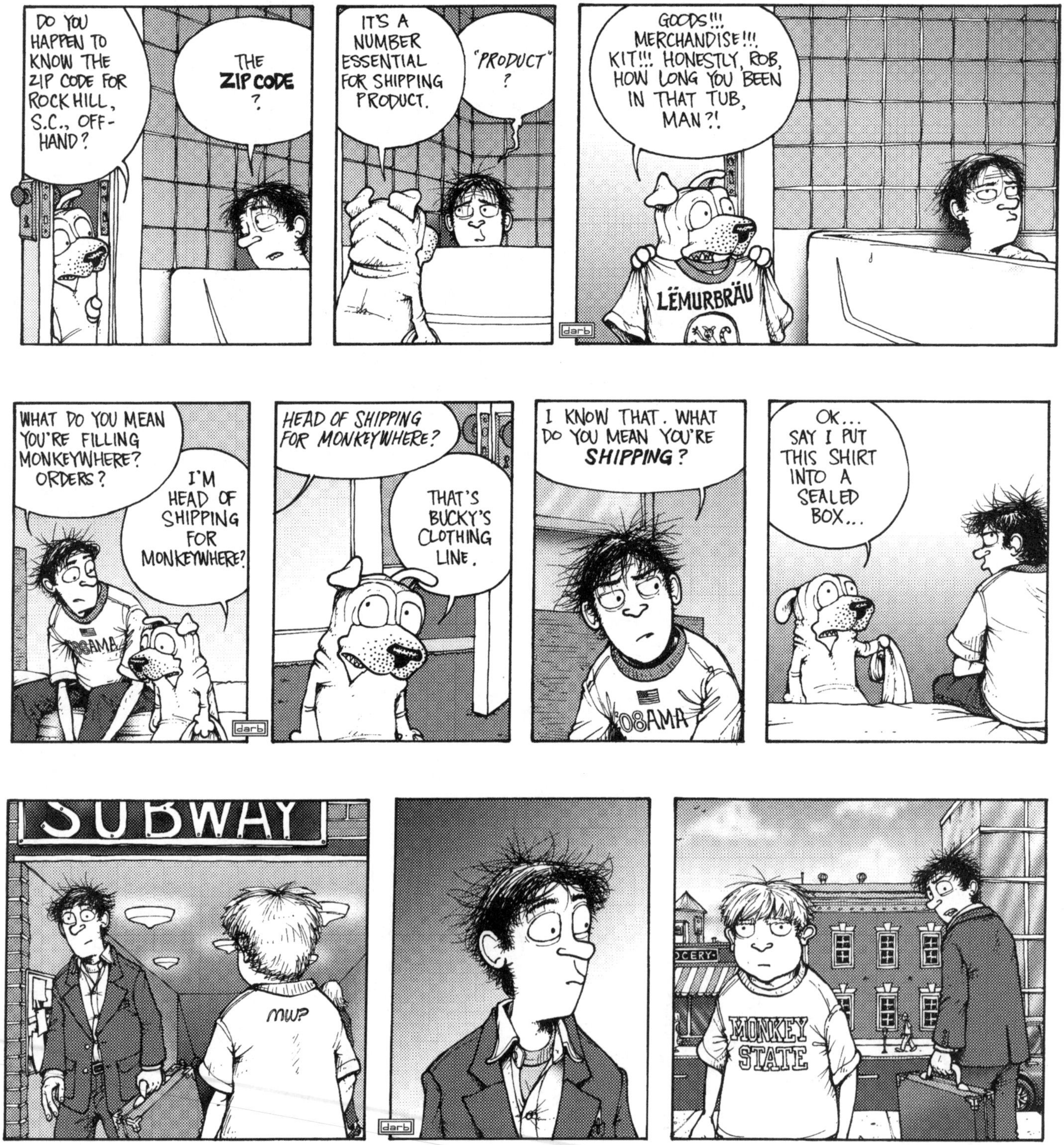
DO YOU HAPPEN TO KNOW THE ZIP CODE FOR ROCK HILL, S.C., OFF-HAND?
THE **ZIP CODE** ?
IT'S A NUMBER ESSENTIAL FOR SHIPPING PRODUCT.
"*PRODUCT*" ?
GOODS!!! MERCHANDISE!!! KIT!!! HONESTLY, ROB, HOW LONG YOU BEEN IN THAT TUB, MAN?!
LËMURBRÄU
darb
WHAT DO YOU MEAN YOU'RE FILLING MONKEYWHERE? ORDERS?
I'M HEAD OF SHIPPING FOR MONKEYWHERE?
'08AMA
darb
HEAD OF SHIPPING FOR MONKEYWHERE?
THAT'S BUCKY'S CLOTHING LINE.
I KNOW THAT. WHAT DO YOU MEAN YOU'RE ***SHIPPING***?
'08AMA
OK... SAY I PUT THIS SHIRT INTO A SEALED BOX...
SUBWAY
MW?
darb
MONKEY STATE

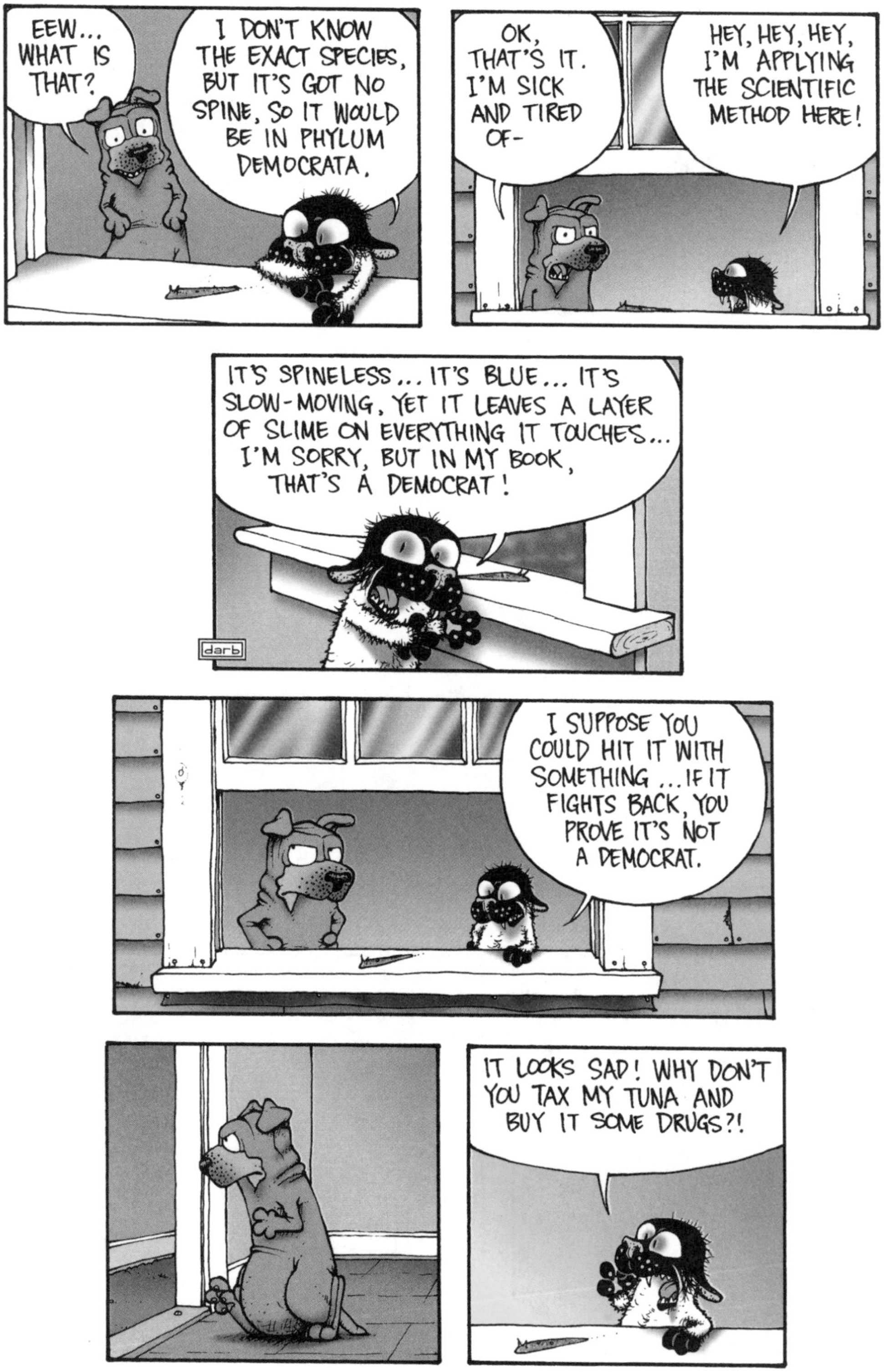
EEW... WHAT IS THAT?
I DON'T KNOW THE EXACT SPECIES, BUT IT'S GOT NO SPINE, SO IT WOULD BE IN PHYLUM DEMOCRATA.
OK, THAT'S IT. I'M SICK AND TIRED OF-
HEY, HEY, HEY, I'M APPLYING THE SCIENTIFIC METHOD HERE!
IT'S SPINELESS... IT'S BLUE... IT'S SLOW-MOVING, YET IT LEAVES A LAYER OF SLIME ON EVERYTHING IT TOUCHES... I'M SORRY, BUT IN MY BOOK, THAT'S A DEMOCRAT!
darb
I SUPPOSE YOU COULD HIT IT WITH SOMETHING ...IF IT FIGHTS BACK, YOU PROVE IT'S NOT A DEMOCRAT.
IT LOOKS SAD! WHY DON'T YOU TAX MY TUNA AND BUY IT SOME DRUGS?!

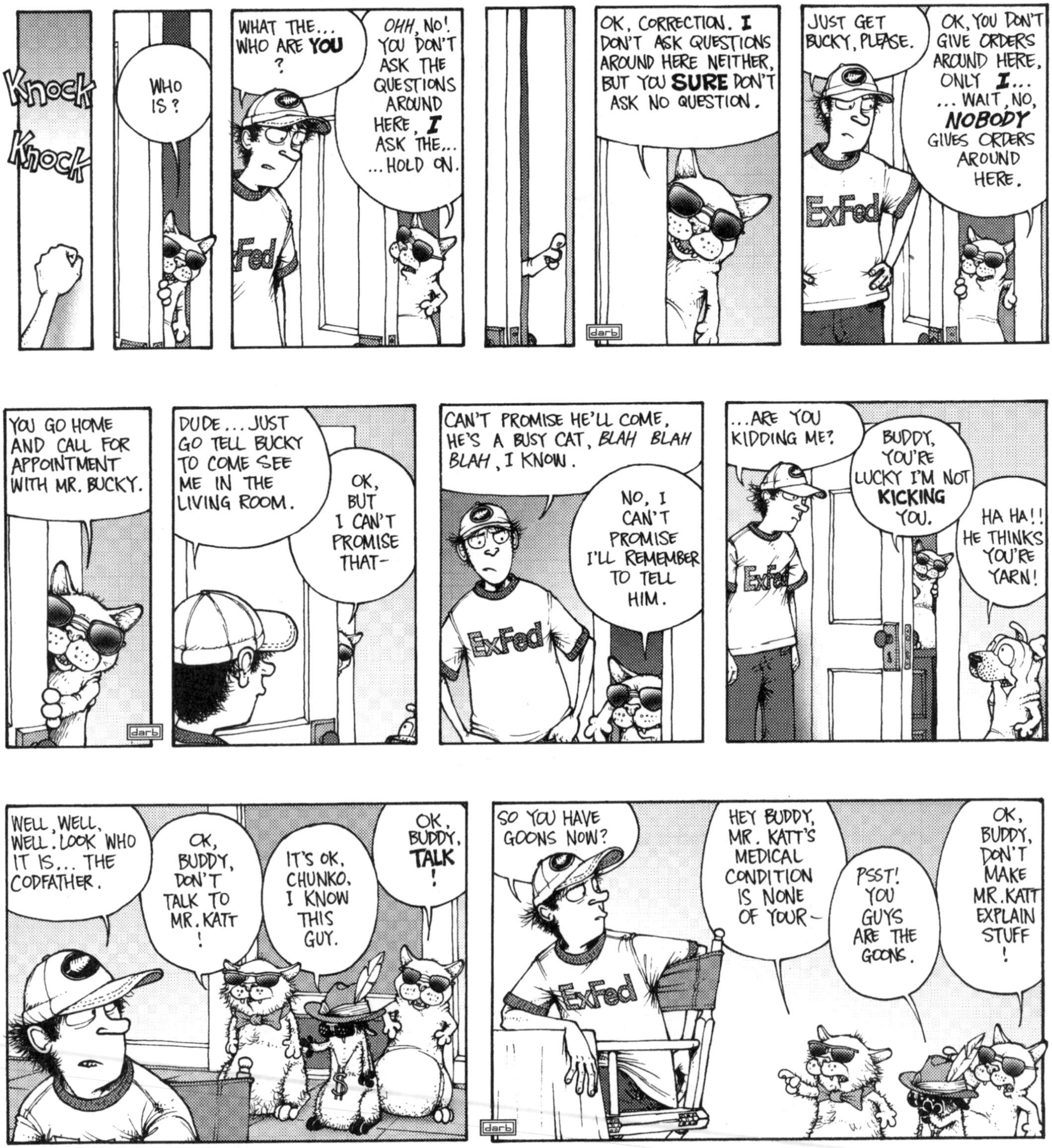
KNOCK KNOCK
WHO IS?
WHAT THE... WHO ARE YOU?
OHH, NO! YOU DON'T ASK THE QUESTIONS AROUND HERE, I ASK THE... ...HOLD ON.
OK, CORRECTION. I DON'T ASK QUESTIONS AROUND HERE NEITHER, BUT YOU SURE DON'T ASK NO QUESTION.
JUST GET BUCKY, PLEASE.
OK, YOU DON'T GIVE ORDERS AROUND HERE, ONLY I... ...WAIT, NO, NOBODY GIVES ORDERS AROUND HERE.
ExFed
darb
YOU GO HOME AND CALL FOR APPOINTMENT WITH MR. BUCKY.
DUDE... JUST GO TELL BUCKY TO COME SEE ME IN THE LIVING ROOM.
OK, BUT I CAN'T PROMISE THAT-
CAN'T PROMISE HE'LL COME, HE'S A BUSY CAT, BLAH BLAH BLAH, I KNOW.
NO, I CAN'T PROMISE I'LL REMEMBER TO TELL HIM.
...ARE YOU KIDDING ME?
BUDDY, YOU'RE LUCKY I'M NOT KICKING YOU.
HA HA!! HE THINKS YOU'RE YARN!
WELL, WELL, WELL. LOOK WHO IT IS... THE CODFATHER.
OK, BUDDY, DON'T TALK TO MR. KATT!
IT'S OK, CHUNKO, I KNOW THIS GUY.
OK, BUDDY, TALK!
SO YOU HAVE GOONS NOW?
HEY BUDDY, MR. KATT'S MEDICAL CONDITION IS NONE OF YOUR-
PSST! YOU GUYS ARE THE GOONS.
OK, BUDDY, DON'T MAKE MR. KATT EXPLAIN STUFF!

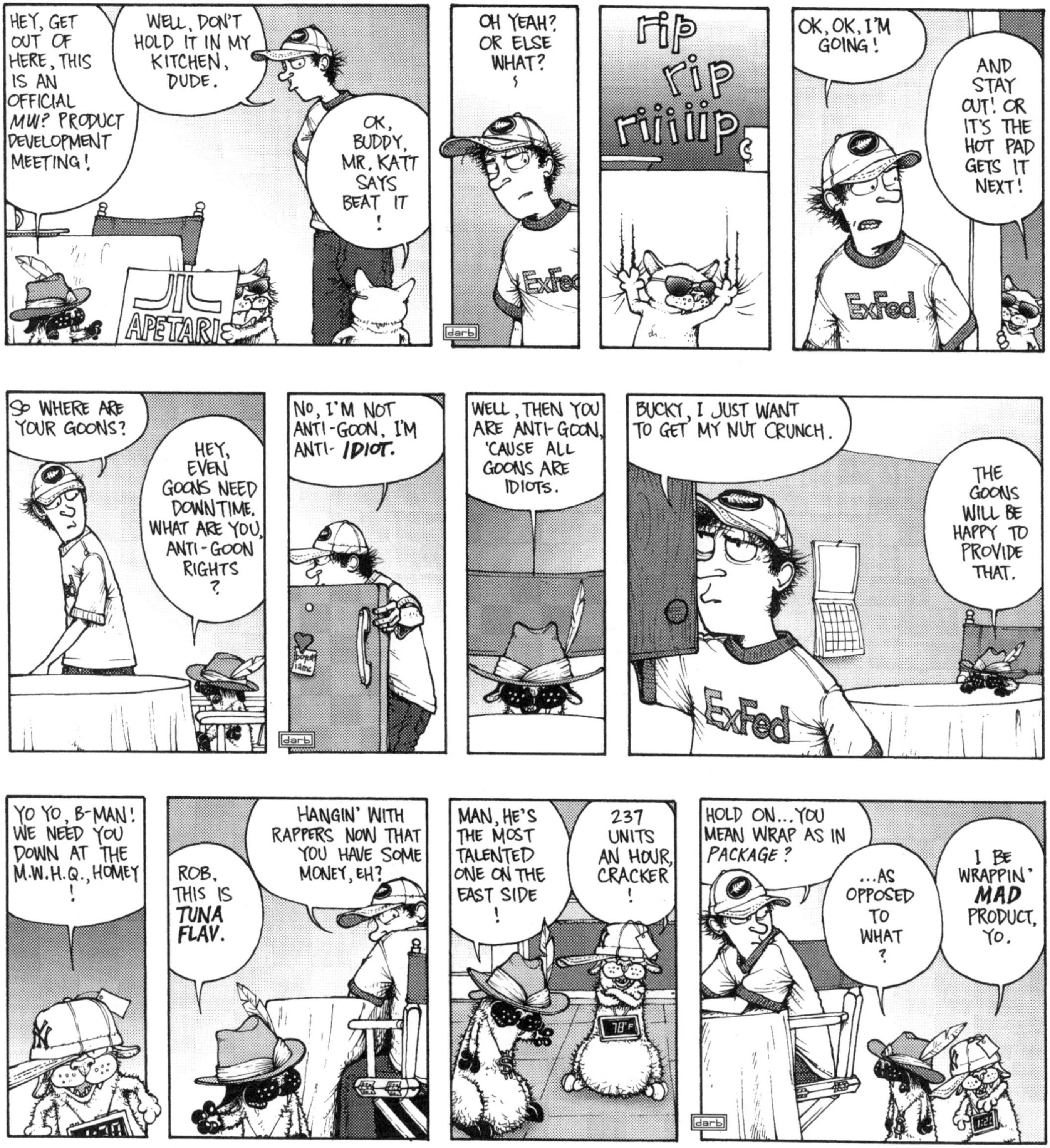
HEY, GET OUT OF HERE, THIS IS AN OFFICIAL *MW?* PRODUCT DEVELOPMENT MEETING!
WELL, DON'T HOLD IT IN MY KITCHEN, DUDE.
OK, BUDDY, MR. KATT SAYS BEAT IT!
APETARI
OH YEAH? OR ELSE WHAT?
ExFed
rip rip riiiip
OK, OK, I'M GOING!
AND STAY OUT! OR IT'S THE HOT PAD GETS IT NEXT!
ExFed
SO WHERE ARE YOUR GOONS?
HEY, EVEN GOONS NEED DOWNTIME. WHAT ARE YOU, ANTI-GOON RIGHTS?
NO, I'M NOT ANTI-GOON, I'M ANTI-**IDIOT.**
WELL, THEN YOU ARE ANTI-GOON, 'CAUSE ALL GOONS ARE IDIOTS.
BUCKY, I JUST WANT TO GET MY NUT CRUNCH.
THE GOONS WILL BE HAPPY TO PROVIDE THAT.
ExFed
YO YO, B-MAN! WE NEED YOU DOWN AT THE M.W.H.Q., HOMEY!
ROB, THIS IS **TUNA FLAV.**
HANGIN' WITH RAPPERS NOW THAT YOU HAVE SOME MONEY, EH?
MAN, HE'S THE MOST TALENTED ONE ON THE EAST SIDE!
237 UNITS AN HOUR, CRACKER!
HOLD ON... YOU MEAN WRAP AS IN *PACKAGE*?
...AS OPPOSED TO WHAT?
I BE WRAPPIN' **MAD** PRODUCT, YO.

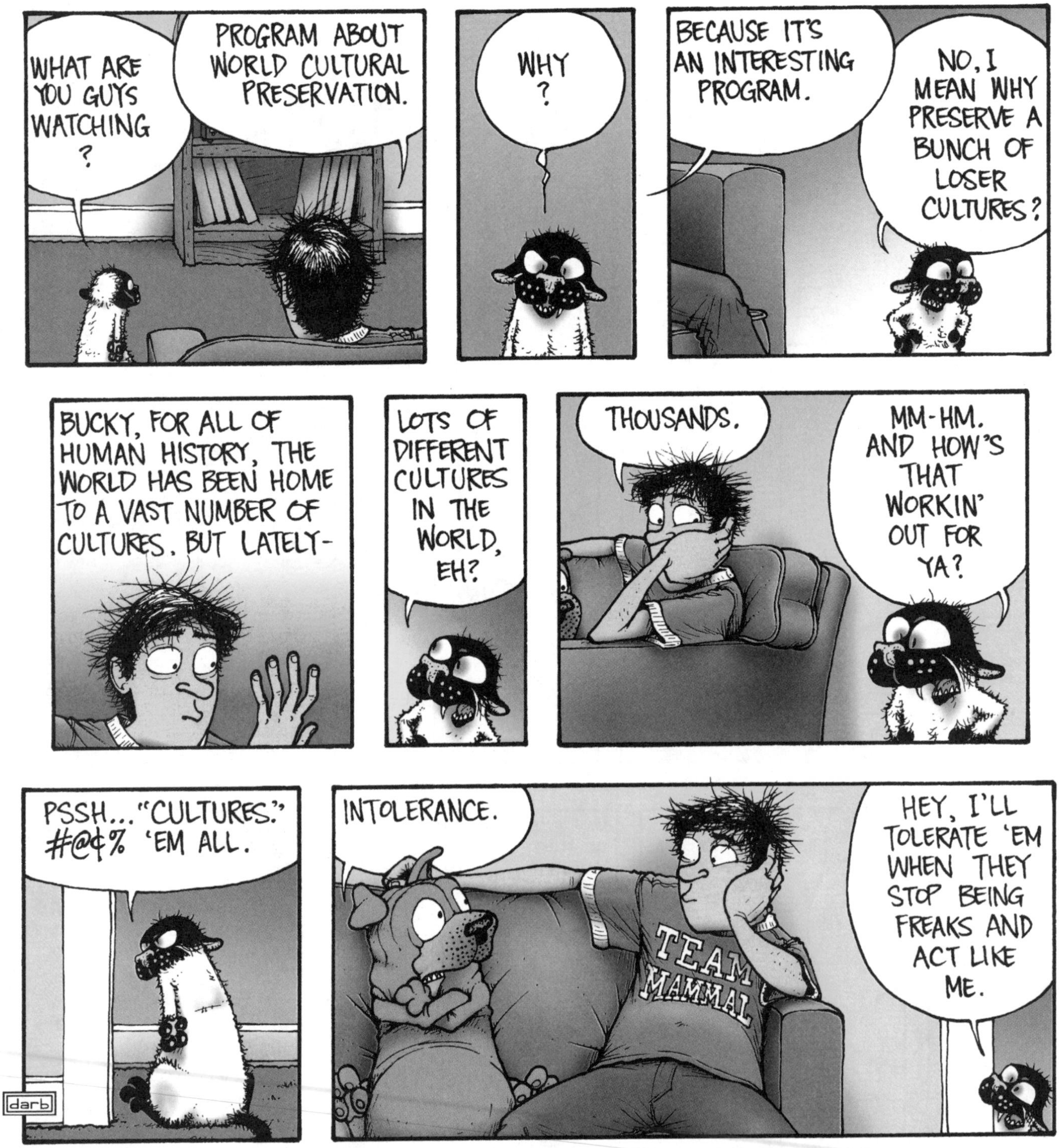
WHAT ARE YOU GUYS WATCHING ?
PROGRAM ABOUT WORLD CULTURAL PRESERVATION.
WHY ?
BECAUSE IT'S AN INTERESTING PROGRAM.
NO, I MEAN WHY PRESERVE A BUNCH OF LOSER CULTURES?
BUCKY, FOR ALL OF HUMAN HISTORY, THE WORLD HAS BEEN HOME TO A VAST NUMBER OF CULTURES. BUT LATELY-
LOTS OF DIFFERENT CULTURES IN THE WORLD, EH?
THOUSANDS.
MM-HM. AND HOW'S THAT WORKIN' OUT FOR YA?
PSSH... "CULTURES." #@¢% 'EM ALL.
INTOLERANCE.
HEY, I'LL TOLERATE 'EM WHEN THEY STOP BEING FREAKS AND ACT LIKE ME.
TEAM MAMMAL
darb

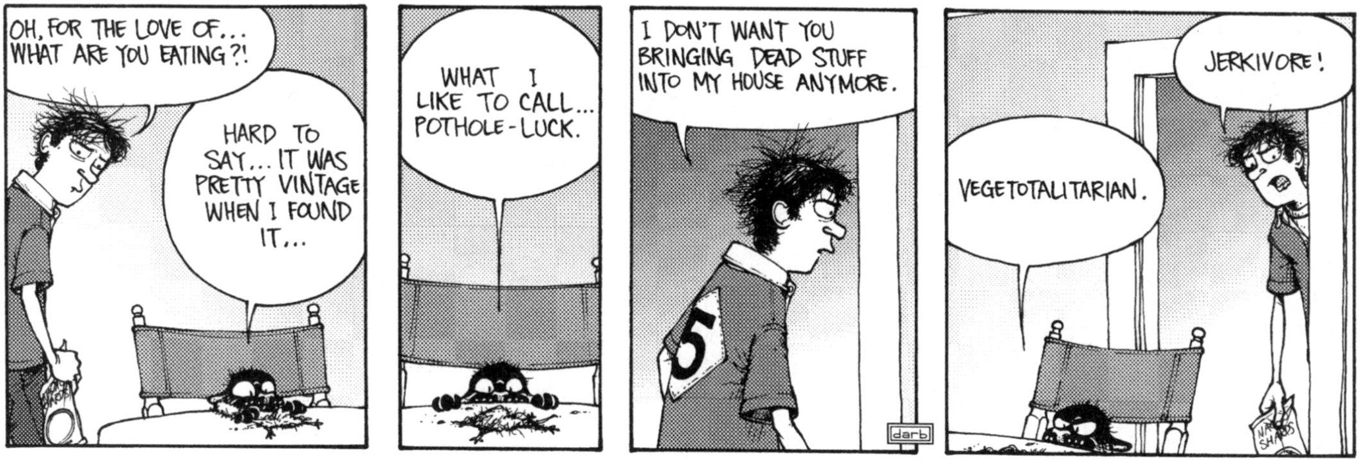
OH, FOR THE LOVE OF... WHAT ARE YOU EATING?!
HARD TO SAY... IT WAS PRETTY VINTAGE WHEN I FOUND IT...
WHAT I LIKE TO CALL... POTHOLE-LUCK.
I DON'T WANT YOU BRINGING DEAD STUFF INTO MY HOUSE ANYMORE.
JERKIVORE!
VEGETOTALITARIAN.

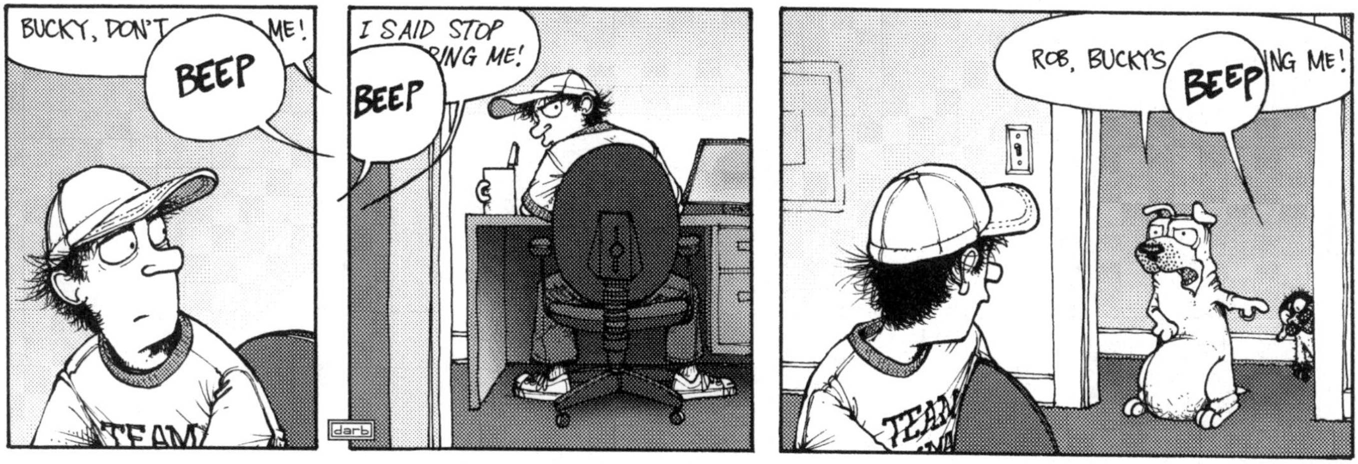
BUCKY, DON'T
ME!
BEEP
I SAID STOP
ING ME!
BEEP
ROB, BUCKY'S
ING ME!
BEEP

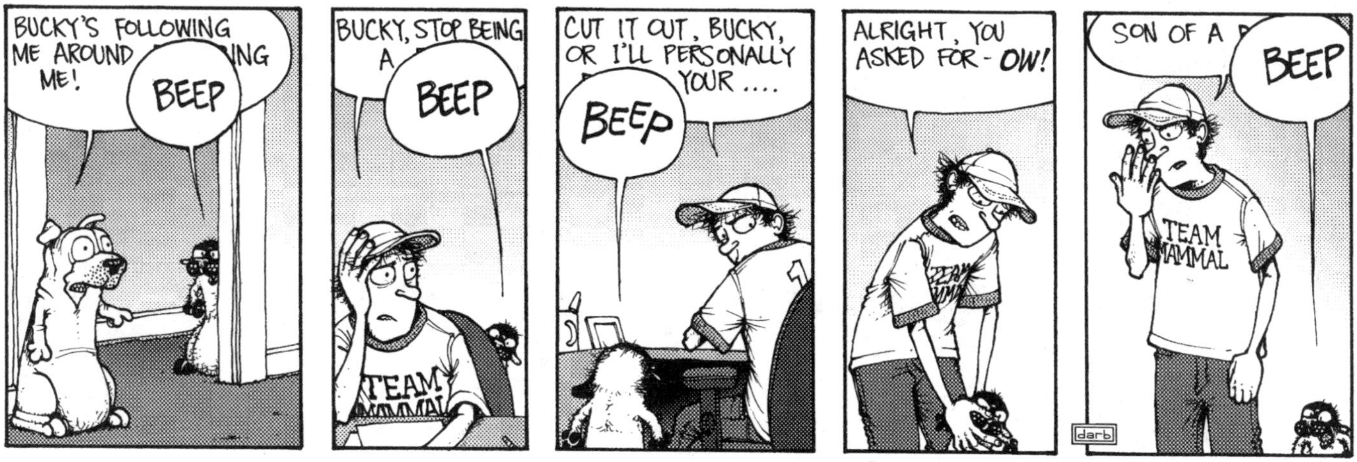
BUCKY'S FOLLOWING ME AROUND
ING ME!
BEEP
BUCKY, STOP BEING A
BEEP
CUT IT OUT, BUCKY, OR I'LL PERSONALLY
YOUR....
BEEP
ALRIGHT, YOU ASKED FOR- OW!
SON OF A
BEEP
TEAM MAMMAL

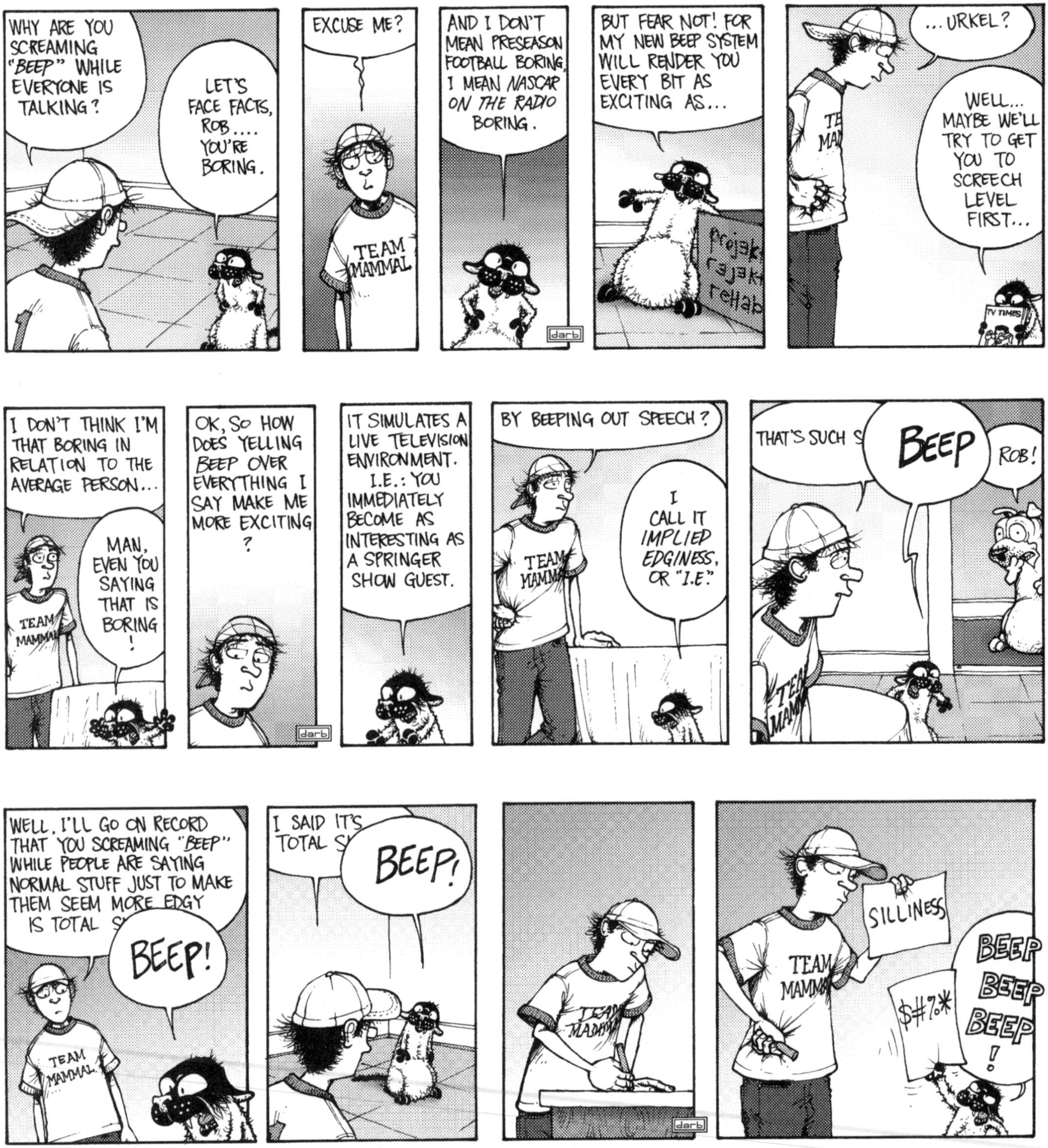
WHY ARE YOU SCREAMING "BEEP" WHILE EVERYONE IS TALKING?
LET'S FACE FACTS, ROB.... YOU'RE BORING.
EXCUSE ME?
AND I DON'T MEAN PRESEASON FOOTBALL BORING, I MEAN NASCAR ON THE RADIO BORING.
BUT FEAR NOT! FOR MY NEW BEEP SYSTEM WILL RENDER YOU EVERY BIT AS EXCITING AS...
...URKEL?
WELL... MAYBE WE'LL TRY TO GET YOU TO SCREECH LEVEL FIRST...
I DON'T THINK I'M THAT BORING IN RELATION TO THE AVERAGE PERSON...
MAN, EVEN YOU SAYING THAT IS BORING!
OK, SO HOW DOES YELLING BEEP OVER EVERYTHING I SAY MAKE ME MORE EXCITING?
IT SIMULATES A LIVE TELEVISION ENVIRONMENT. I.E.: YOU IMMEDIATELY BECOME AS INTERESTING AS A SPRINGER SHOW GUEST.
BY BEEPING OUT SPEECH?
I CALL IT IMPLIED EDGINESS, OR "I.E."
THAT'S SUCH S
BEEP
ROB!
WELL, I'LL GO ON RECORD THAT YOU SCREAMING "BEEP" WHILE PEOPLE ARE SAYING NORMAL STUFF JUST TO MAKE THEM SEEM MORE EDGY IS TOTAL S
BEEP!
I SAID IT'S TOTAL S
BEEP!
SILLINESS
$#%*
BEEP BEEP BEEP!

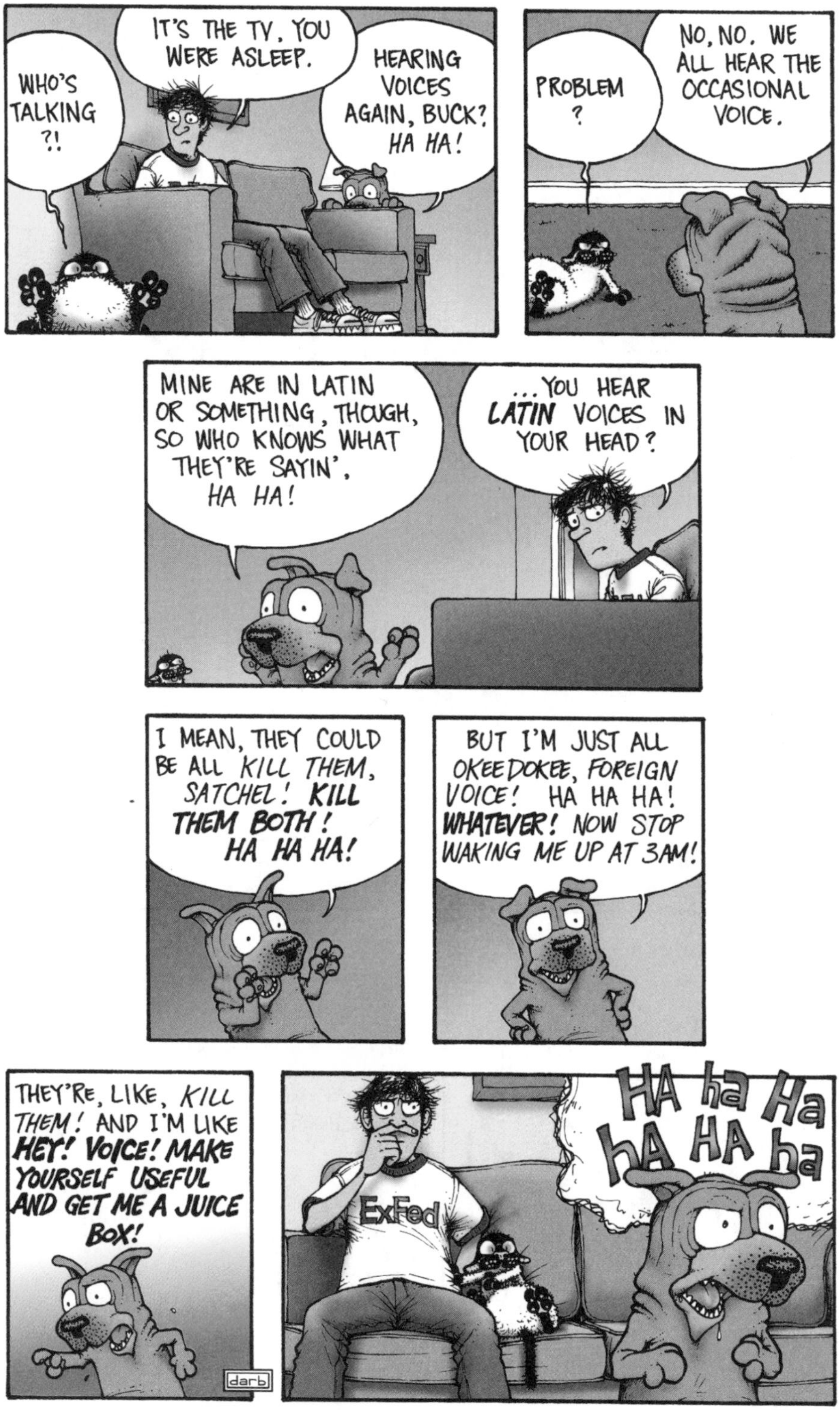
WHO'S TALKING ?!
IT'S THE TV. YOU WERE ASLEEP.
HEARING VOICES AGAIN, BUCK? HA HA!
PROBLEM ?
NO, NO. WE ALL HEAR THE OCCASIONAL VOICE.
MINE ARE IN LATIN OR SOMETHING, THOUGH, SO WHO KNOWS WHAT THEY'RE SAYIN', HA HA!
...YOU HEAR LATIN VOICES IN YOUR HEAD?
I MEAN, THEY COULD BE ALL KILL THEM, SATCHEL! KILL THEM BOTH! HA HA HA!
BUT I'M JUST ALL OKEEDOKEE, FOREIGN VOICE! HA HA HA! WHATEVER! NOW STOP WAKING ME UP AT 3AM!
THEY'RE, LIKE, KILL THEM! AND I'M LIKE HEY! VOICE! MAKE YOURSELF USEFUL AND GET ME A JUICE BOX!
darb
ExFed
HA ha Ha
hA HA ha

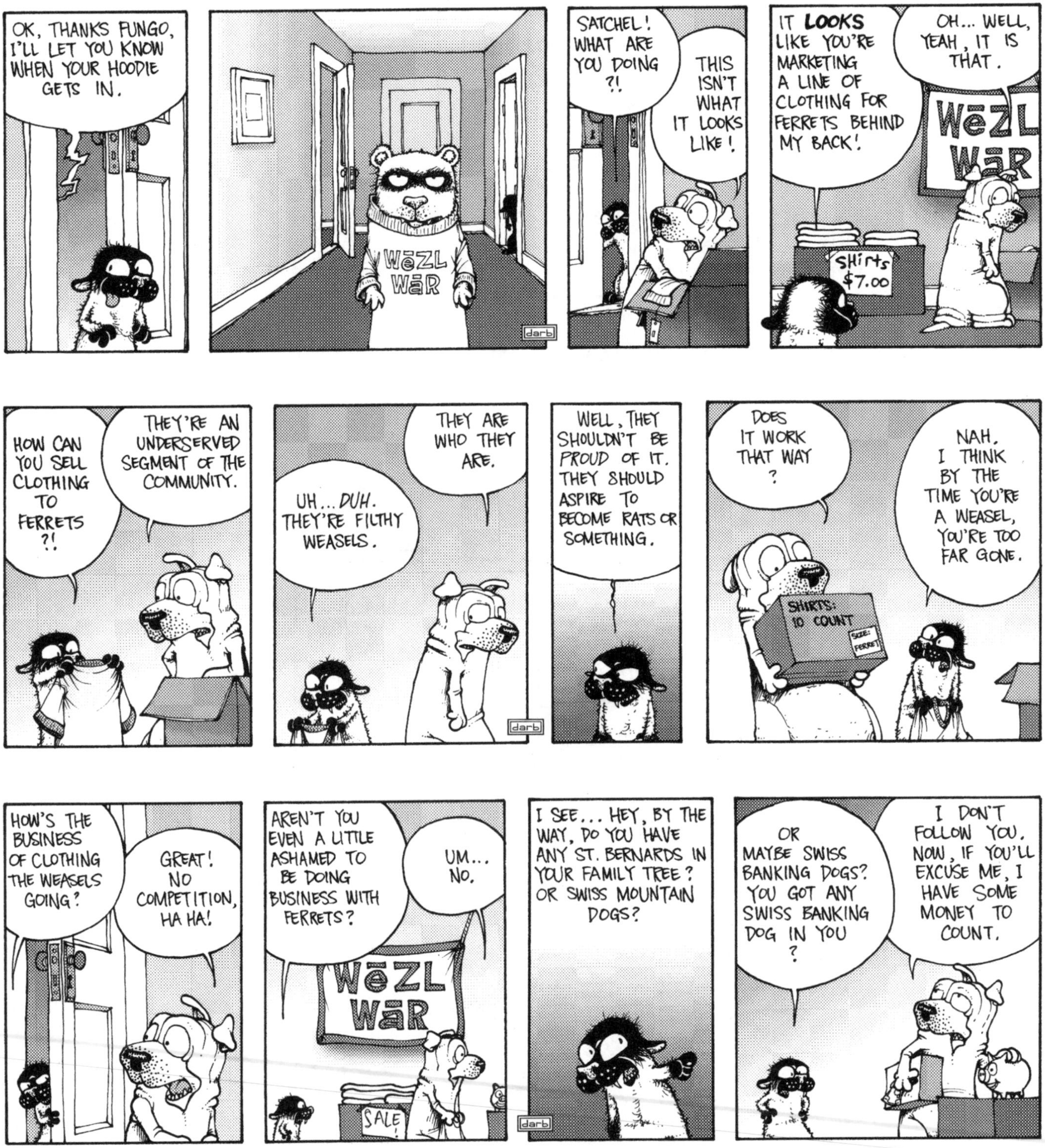
OK, THANKS FUNGO, I'LL LET YOU KNOW WHEN YOUR HOODIE GETS IN.
WēZL WāR
darb
SATCHEL! WHAT ARE YOU DOING ?!
THIS ISN'T WHAT IT LOOKS LIKE!
IT LOOKS LIKE YOU'RE MARKETING A LINE OF CLOTHING FOR FERRETS BEHIND MY BACK!
OH... WELL, YEAH, IT IS THAT.
WēZL WāR
SHirts $7.00
HOW CAN YOU SELL CLOTHING TO FERRETS ?!
THEY'RE AN UNDERSERVED SEGMENT OF THE COMMUNITY.
UH... DUH. THEY'RE FILTHY WEASELS.
THEY ARE WHO THEY ARE.
darb
WELL, THEY SHOULDN'T BE PROUD OF IT. THEY SHOULD ASPIRE TO BECOME RATS OR SOMETHING.
DOES IT WORK THAT WAY ?
NAH. I THINK BY THE TIME YOU'RE A WEASEL, YOU'RE TOO FAR GONE.
SHIRTS: 10 COUNT
SIZE: FERRET
HOW'S THE BUSINESS OF CLOTHING THE WEASELS GOING?
GREAT! NO COMPETITION, HA HA!
AREN'T YOU EVEN A LITTLE ASHAMED TO BE DOING BUSINESS WITH FERRETS?
UM... NO.
WēZL WāR
SALE!
darb
I SEE... HEY, BY THE WAY, DO YOU HAVE ANY ST. BERNARDS IN YOUR FAMILY TREE? OR SWISS MOUNTAIN DOGS?
OR MAYBE SWISS BANKING DOGS? YOU GOT ANY SWISS BANKING DOG IN YOU ?
I DON'T FOLLOW YOU. NOW, IF YOU'LL EXCUSE ME, I HAVE SOME MONEY TO COUNT.

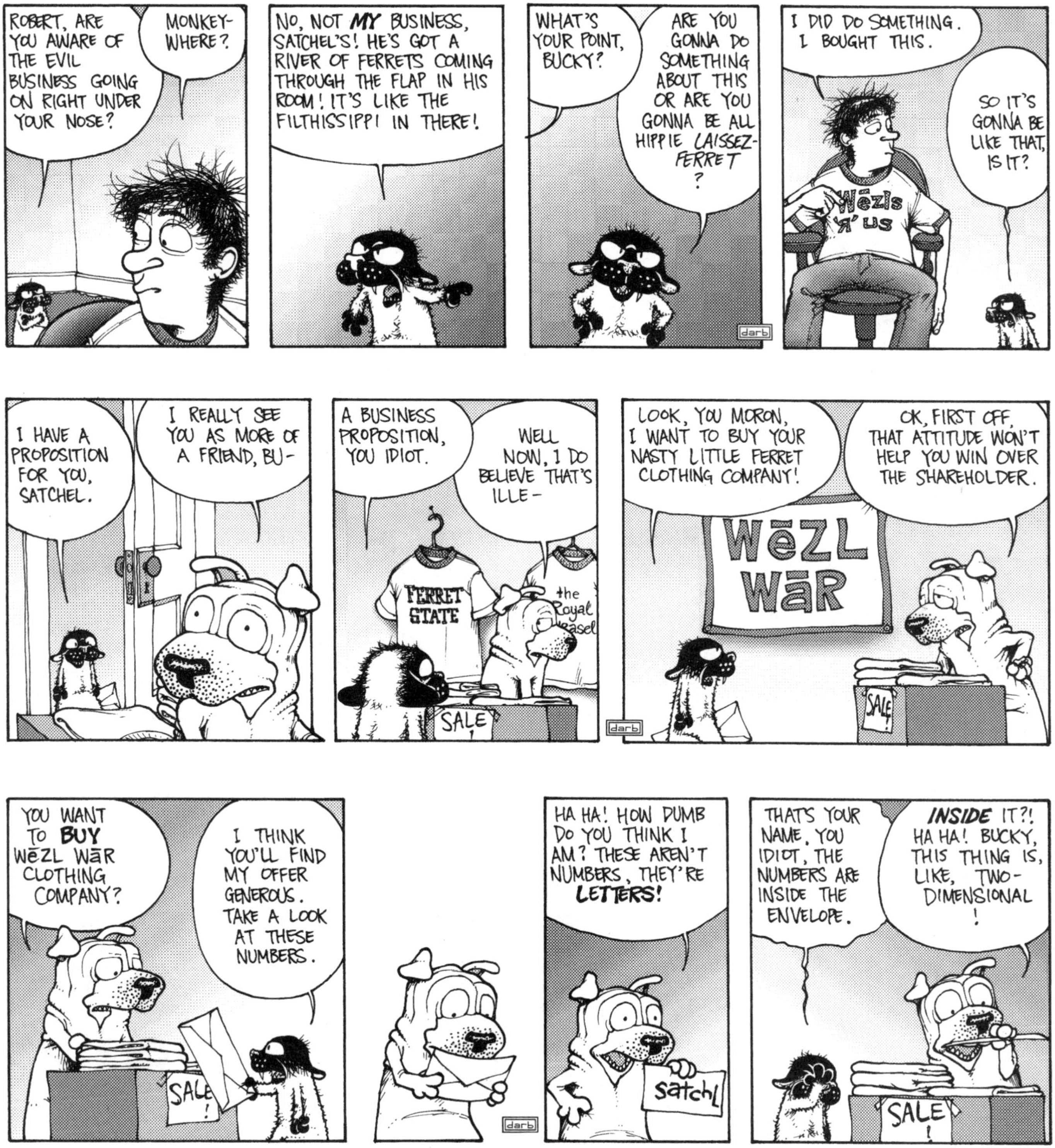
ROBERT, ARE YOU AWARE OF THE EVIL BUSINESS GOING ON RIGHT UNDER YOUR NOSE?
MONKEY-WHERE?
NO, NOT MY BUSINESS, SATCHEL'S! HE'S GOT A RIVER OF FERRETS COMING THROUGH THE FLAP IN HIS ROOM! IT'S LIKE THE FILTHISSIPPI IN THERE!
WHAT'S YOUR POINT, BUCKY?
ARE YOU GONNA DO SOMETHING ABOUT THIS OR ARE YOU GONNA BE ALL HIPPIE LAISSEZ-FERRET?
I DID DO SOMETHING. I BOUGHT THIS.
Wēzls 'R' us
SO IT'S GONNA BE LIKE THAT, IS IT?
darb
I HAVE A PROPOSITION FOR YOU, SATCHEL.
I REALLY SEE YOU AS MORE OF A FRIEND, BU-
A BUSINESS PROPOSITION, YOU IDIOT.
WELL NOW, I DO BELIEVE THAT'S ILLE-
FERRET STATE
the Royal Weasel
SALE!
LOOK, YOU MORON, I WANT TO BUY YOUR NASTY LITTLE FERRET CLOTHING COMPANY!
OK, FIRST OFF, THAT ATTITUDE WON'T HELP YOU WIN OVER THE SHAREHOLDER.
WēZL WāR
SALE!
darb
YOU WANT TO BUY WēZL WāR CLOTHING COMPANY?
I THINK YOU'LL FIND MY OFFER GENEROUS. TAKE A LOOK AT THESE NUMBERS.
SALE!
HA HA! HOW DUMB DO YOU THINK I AM? THESE AREN'T NUMBERS, THEY'RE LETTERS!
satchl
THAT'S YOUR NAME, YOU IDIOT, THE NUMBERS ARE INSIDE THE ENVELOPE.
INSIDE IT?! HA HA! BUCKY, THIS THING IS, LIKE, TWO-DIMENSIONAL!
SALE!
darb

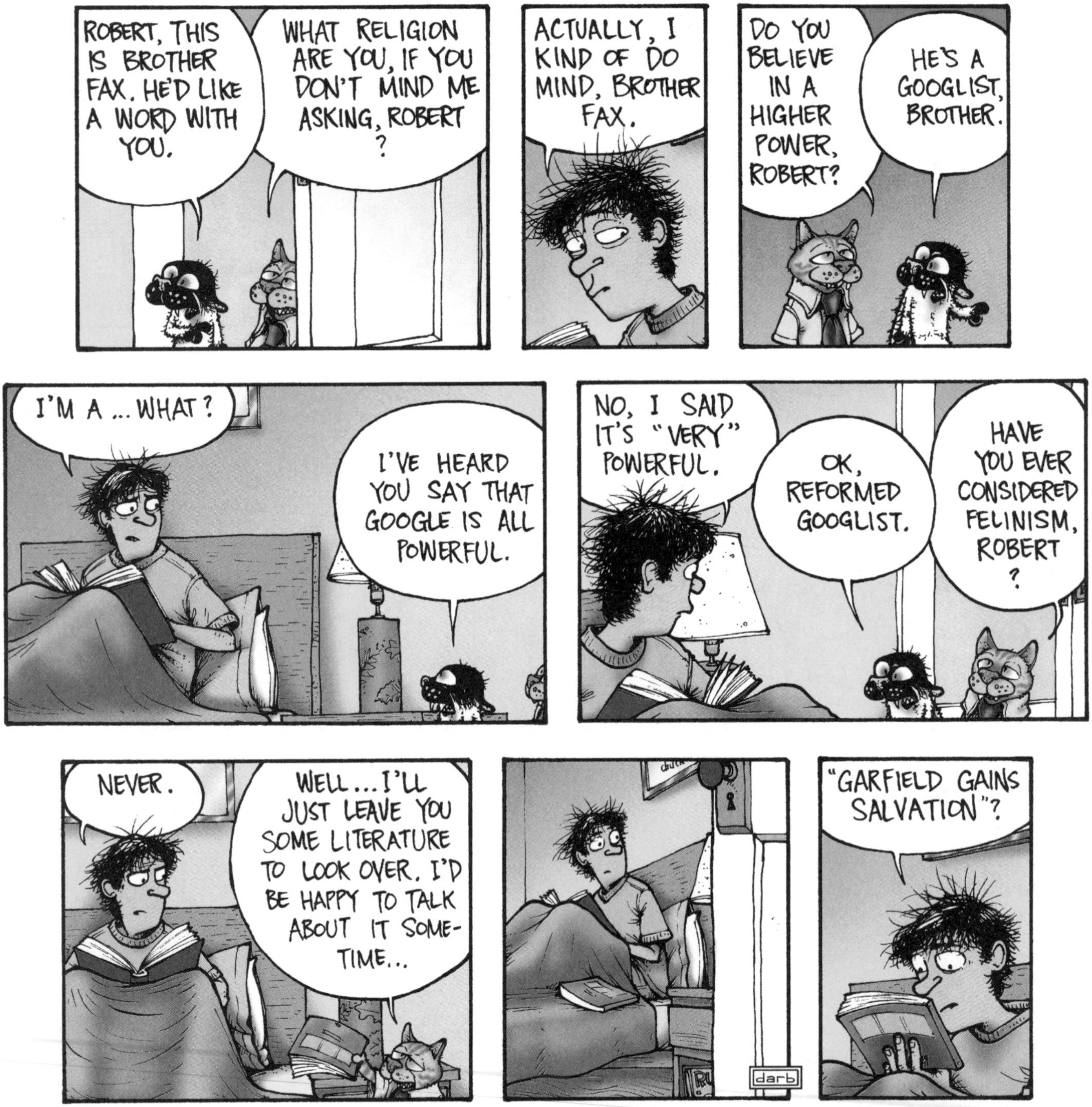

ROBERT, THIS IS BROTHER FAX. HE'D LIKE A WORD WITH YOU.
WHAT RELIGION ARE YOU, IF YOU DON'T MIND ME ASKING, ROBERT ?
ACTUALLY, I KIND OF DO MIND, BROTHER FAX.
DO YOU BELIEVE IN A HIGHER POWER, ROBERT?
HE'S A GOOGLIST, BROTHER.
I'M A ... WHAT?
I'VE HEARD YOU SAY THAT GOOGLE IS ALL POWERFUL.
NO, I SAID IT'S "VERY" POWERFUL.
OK, REFORMED GOOGLIST.
HAVE YOU EVER CONSIDERED FELINISM, ROBERT ?
NEVER.
WELL ... I'LL JUST LEAVE YOU SOME LITERATURE TO LOOK OVER. I'D BE HAPPY TO TALK ABOUT IT SOME-TIME...
darb
"GARFIELD GAINS SALVATION"?

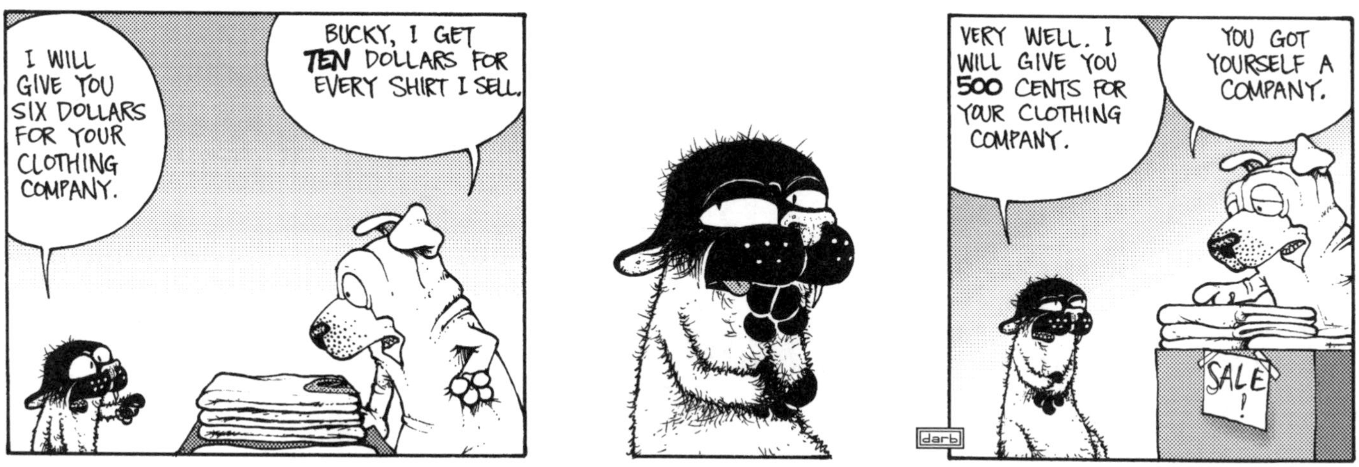
I WILL GIVE YOU SIX DOLLARS FOR YOUR CLOTHING COMPANY.
BUCKY, I GET **TEN** DOLLARS FOR EVERY SHIRT I SELL.
VERY WELL. I WILL GIVE YOU **500** CENTS FOR YOUR CLOTHING COMPANY.
YOU GOT YOURSELF A COMPANY.
SALE!
darb

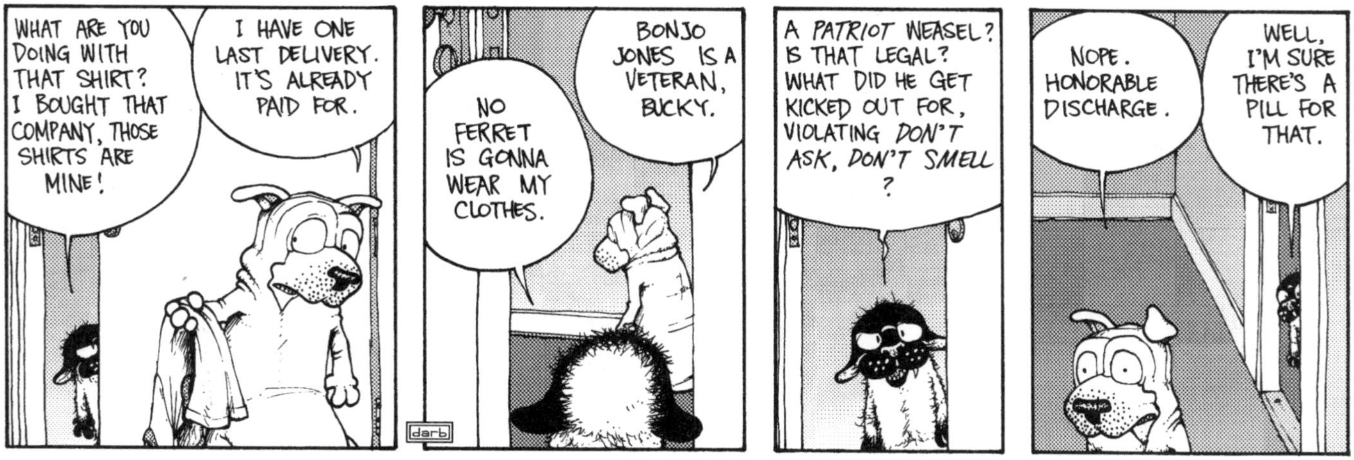
WHAT ARE YOU DOING WITH THAT SHIRT? I BOUGHT THAT COMPANY, THOSE SHIRTS ARE MINE!
I HAVE ONE LAST DELIVERY. IT'S ALREADY PAID FOR.
darb
NO FERRET IS GONNA WEAR MY CLOTHES.
BONJO JONES IS A VETERAN, BUCKY.
A *PATRIOT* WEASEL? IS THAT LEGAL? WHAT DID HE GET KICKED OUT FOR, VIOLATING *DON'T ASK, DON'T SMELL*?
NOPE. HONORABLE DISCHARGE.
WELL, I'M SURE THERE'S A PILL FOR THAT.

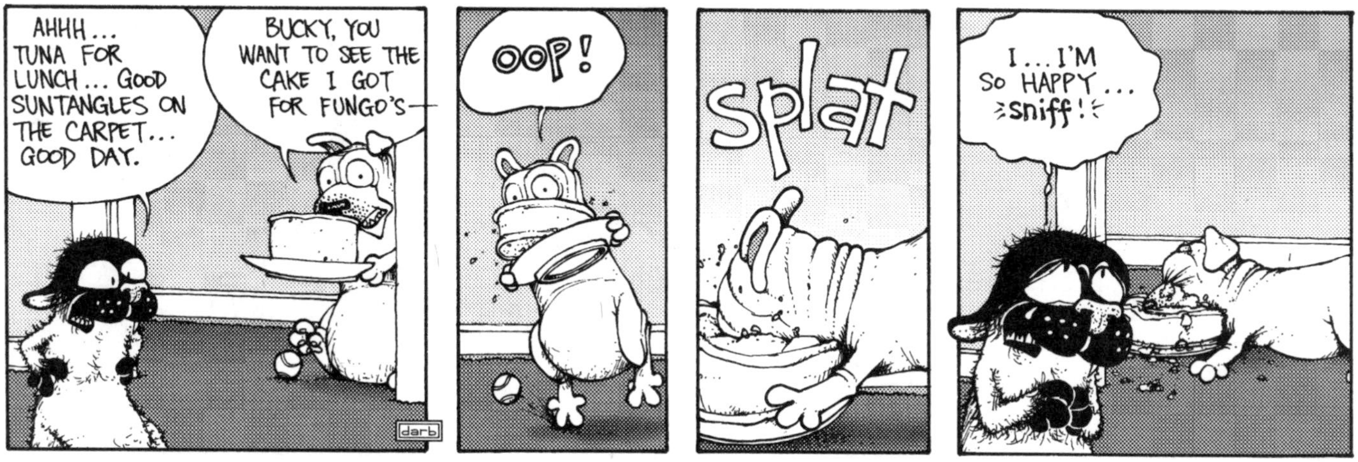
AHHH... TUNA FOR LUNCH... GOOD SUNTANGLES ON THE CARPET... GOOD DAY.
BUCKY, YOU WANT TO SEE THE CAKE I GOT FOR FUNGO'S—
darb
OOP!
SPLAT
I... I'M SO HAPPY... sniff!

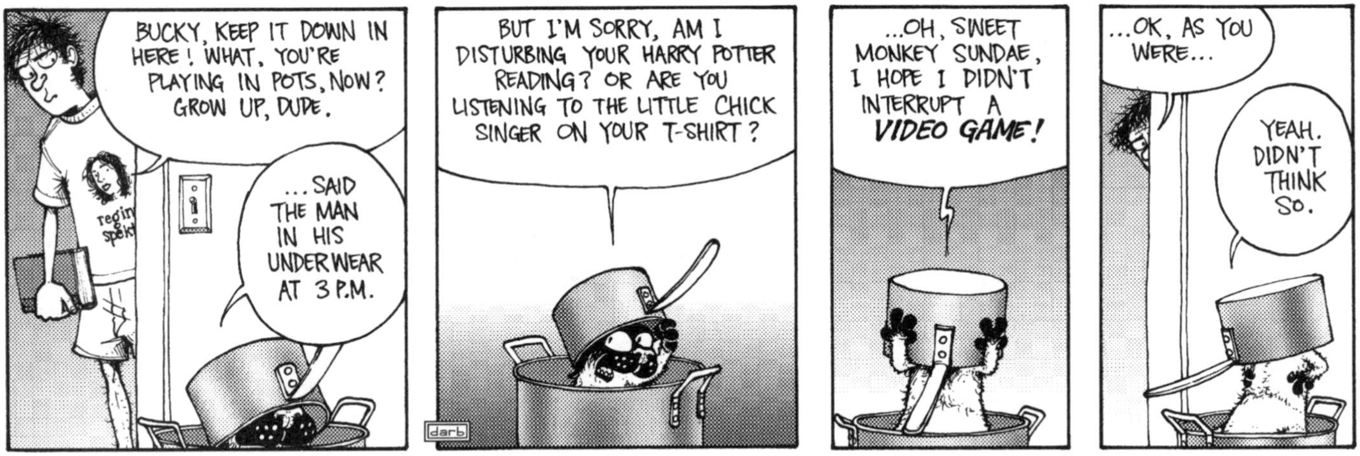
BUCKY, KEEP IT DOWN IN HERE! WHAT, YOU'RE PLAYING IN POTS, NOW? GROW UP, DUDE.
...SAID THE MAN IN HIS UNDERWEAR AT 3 P.M.
BUT I'M SORRY, AM I DISTURBING YOUR HARRY POTTER READING? OR ARE YOU LISTENING TO THE LITTLE CHICK SINGER ON YOUR T-SHIRT?
...OH, SWEET MONKEY SUNDAE, I HOPE I DIDN'T INTERRUPT A VIDEO GAME!
...OK, AS YOU WERE...
YEAH. DIDN'T THINK SO.

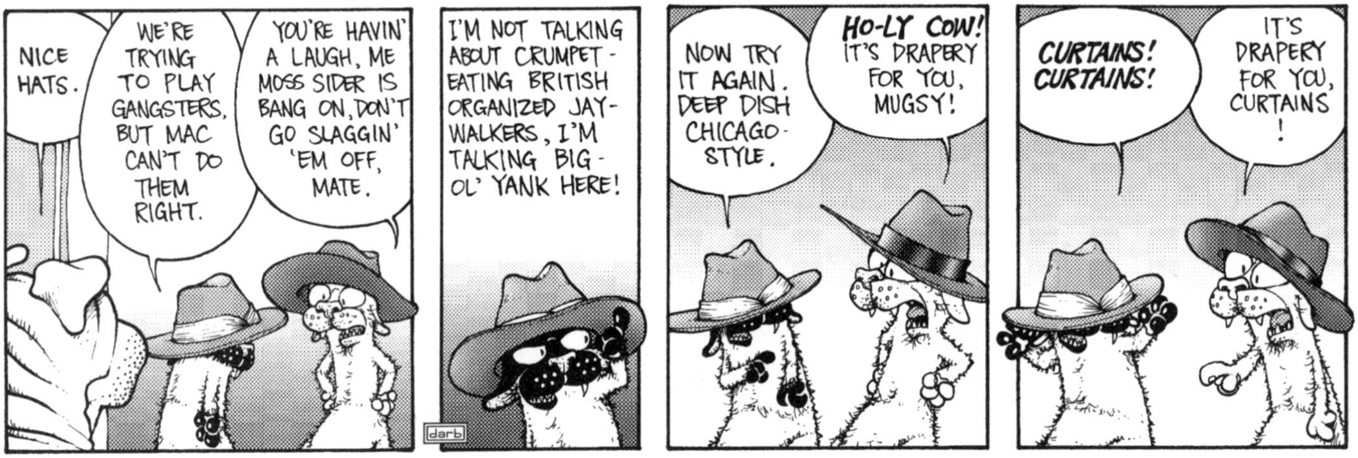
NICE HATS.
WE'RE TRYING TO PLAY GANGSTERS, BUT MAC CAN'T DO THEM RIGHT.
YOU'RE HAVIN' A LAUGH, ME MOSS SIDER IS BANG ON, DON'T GO SLAGGIN' 'EM OFF, MATE.
I'M NOT TALKING ABOUT CRUMPET-EATING BRITISH ORGANIZED JAY-WALKERS, I'M TALKING BIG-OL' YANK HERE!
NOW TRY IT AGAIN. DEEP DISH CHICAGO-STYLE.
HO-LY COW! IT'S DRAPERY FOR YOU, MUGSY!
CURTAINS! CURTAINS!
IT'S DRAPERY FOR YOU, CURTAINS!

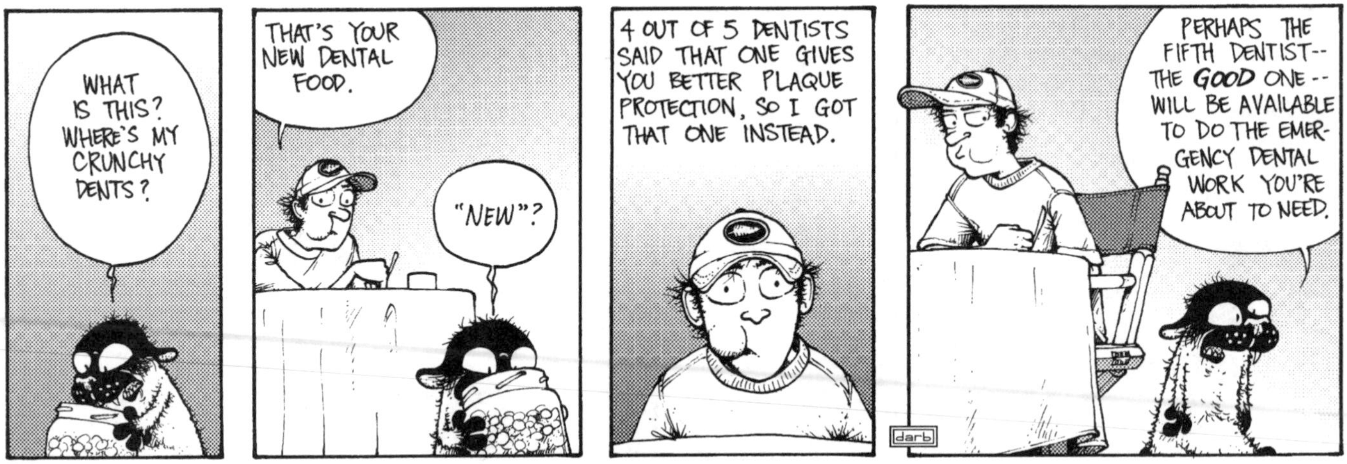
WHAT IS THIS? WHERE'S MY CRUNCHY DENTS?
THAT'S YOUR NEW DENTAL FOOD.
"NEW"?
4 OUT OF 5 DENTISTS SAID THAT ONE GIVES YOU BETTER PLAQUE PROTECTION, SO I GOT THAT ONE INSTEAD.
PERHAPS THE FIFTH DENTIST-- THE GOOD ONE-- WILL BE AVAILABLE TO DO THE EMERGENCY DENTAL WORK YOU'RE ABOUT TO NEED.

WHAT DID YOU DO TO MY RUGBY BALL?
CITIZENS, CAST YOUR EYES ON THE VOTEMASTER 5000. HE IS THE MOST PERFECT POLITICIAN MONEY CAN BUY.
HE'S THE FIRST PROGRAMMABLE POLITICIAN AVAILABLE TO THE GENERAL PUBLIC.
HIS OPERATING SYSTEM USES HAND-PICKED VALUES: REPUBLICAN STUBBORNNESS; GREEN SELF-RIGHTEOUSNESS...
LIBERTARIAN ANTI-TAX; CONSTITUTION PARTY ANTI-*EVERYTHING*; AND A LOUISIANA-DEMOCRAT-APPROVED CASH MONEY RECEPTACLE.
CASH
GO AHEAD. SHAKE HIS HAND-SIMULATION DEVICE.
HA HA!
MY FATHER HAD YOUR JOB AND/OR ETHNICITY!
TYPE A QUESTION IN THERE. ANY QUESTION.
OK...
darb
"DON'T YOU NEED TO RAISE TAXES TO PAY FOR THE WAR?"
NO WAR QUE-
POP
AW! YOU BLEW HIS CONSERVATIVE DENIAL FUSE!
THAT SOUNDS EXPENSIVE.

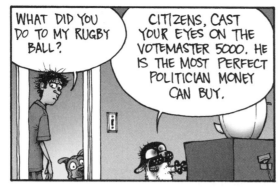

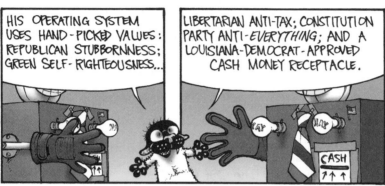

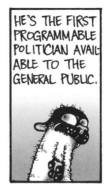

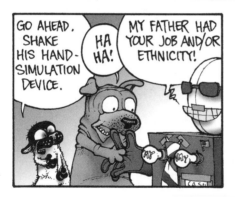

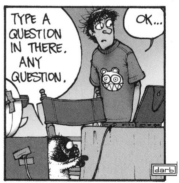

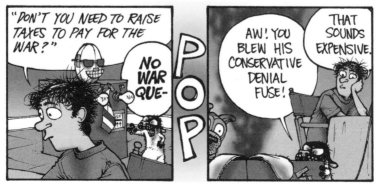

Other *Get Fuzzy* Books

The Dog Is Not a Toy (House Rule #4)

Fuzzy Logic: Get Fuzzy 2

The Get Fuzzy Experience: Are You Bucksperienced

I Would Have Bought You a Cat, But . . .

Blueprint for Disaster

Say Cheesy

Scrum Bums

I'm Ready for My Movie Contract

Take Our Cat, Please!

Ignorance, Thy Name Is Bucky

Treasuries

Groovitude: A Get Fuzzy Treasury

Bucky Katt's Big Book of Fun

Loserpalooza

The Potpourrifc Great Big Grab Bag of Get Fuzzy